Spiritual Despots

SOUTH ASIA ACROSS THE DISCIPLINES

A series edited by Muzaffar Alam, Robert Goldman, and Gauri Viswanathan

DIPESH CHAKRABARTY, SHELDON POLLOCK, AND SANJAY SUBRAHMANYAM, FOUNDING EDITORS

Funded by a grant from the Andrew W. Mellon Foundation and jointly published by the University of California Press, the University of Chicago Press, and Columbia University Press.

South Asia Across the Disciplines is a series devoted to publishing first books across a wide range of South Asian studies, including art, history, philology or textual studies, philosophy, religion, and the interpretive social sciences. Series authors all share the goal of opening up new archives and suggesting new methods and approaches, while demonstrating that South Asian scholarship can be at once deep in expertise and broad in appeal.

Spiritual Despots

*Modern Hinduism and
the Genealogies of Self-Rule*

J. BARTON SCOTT

The University of Chicago Press   Chicago and London

J. BARTON SCOTT is assistant professor of the history of religion at the University of Toronto.

The University of Chicago Press, Chicago 60637
The University of Chicago Press, Ltd., London
© 2016 by The University of Chicago
All rights reserved. Published 2016.
Printed in the United States of America

25 24 23 22 21 20 19 18 17 16   1 2 3 4 5

ISBN-13: 978-0-226-36867-2 (cloth)
ISBN-13: 978-0-226-36870-2 (e-book)
DOI: 10.7208/chicago/9780226368702.001.0001

Library of Congress Cataloging-in-Publication Data

Names: Scott, J. Barton, author.
Title: Spiritual despots : modern Hinduism and the genealogies of self-
   rule / J. Barton Scott.
Other titles: South Asia across the disciplines.
Description: Chicago ; London : The University of Chicago Press, 2016. |
   Series: South Asia across the disciplines.
Identifiers: LCCN 2015042769 | ISBN 9780226368672 (cloth : alk. paper)
   | ISBN 9780226368702 (e-book)
Subjects: LCSH: Hinduism—India—History—19th century. | Hindu
   renewal—History—19th century. | Anti-clericalism—India—
   History—19th century. | Anti-clericalism—England—History—19th
   century. | Anti-clericalism—Comparative studies. | Asceticism—
   Hinduism. | Autonomy—Religious aspects—Hinduism. | Autonomy—
   Religious aspects—Theosophy. | Autonomy—Religious aspects—
   Comparative studies.
Classification: LCC BL1153.5 .S33 2016 | DDC 294.50954/09034—dc23
   LC record available at http://lccn.loc.gov/2015042769

♾ This paper meets the requirements of ANSI/NISO Z39.48-1992
(Permanence of Paper).

A Hindoo prostrating himself at the Feet of his Gooroo, or Spiritual Teacher, (a Brahman.)

Contents

Acknowledgments

This book would not have been possible without the many friends, mentors, and colleagues who supported and sustained me during the years that I took to write it. In the early stages of conceiving the project, I benefited greatly from the interdisciplinary, inter-institutional environment that makes Duke University such a great place for work in the humanities. I am particularly grateful for the warm support and sage advice of Bruce Lawrence, Leela Prasad, Srinivas Aravamudan, David Gilmartin, and Richard Jaffe, who helped me to refine the much earlier version of the project that I submitted as my dissertation. During this time, I also benefited from conversations with other area faculty, particularly Matt Cook, Sandria Freitag, Satti Khanna, Tom Tweed, and Pinki Vaishnava. Just as important are the many graduate school friends who made my years in Durham so intellectually and personally rich, especially Mari Armstrong-Hough, Ali Aslam, Kate Blanchard, Lori Baron, Cristina Corduneanu-Huci, Susanna Drake, Mitch Fraas, Youshaa Patel, Jacob Remes, Kyle Smith, SherAli Tareen, Kristi Upson-Saia, Isaac Weiner, and Brett Wilson.

I could not have asked for a better place to reconceive the dissertation as a book than the Department of History and Philosophy at Montana State University. I want to express my heartfelt thanks to all of my colleagues there for making Bozeman such a happy academic home. Particular thanks are due to my colleagues in Religious Studies, Susan Cohen, Holly Grether, and Lynda Sexson, as well as to Bob Rydell and Brett Walker, both of whom provided key logistical support along the way. Really, however, the entire department deserves thanks for setting such an outstanding model of how to combine first-rate scholarship with unparalleled collegiality: Cassandra Balent, Prasanta Bandyopadhyay, Rob Campbell, David Cherry, Don Demetriades, Catherine Dunlop, Dan Flory, Maggie Greene, Robin Hardy, Kristen Intemann, David Large, Tim LeCain, Jessica Marks, Dale Martin, Michelle Maskiell, Jim Meyer, Mary Murphy, Michael Reidy, LaTrelle Sherffius, Billy Smith, Kellie Stoolman, Molly Todd, Sara Waller, and Katie Yaw. Thanks to David Agruss and Anjali Sundaram for the good company in Bozeman; to Melissa Ragain for making me change the book title; and to Ruth Vanita and Mona Bachmann for welcoming me to Montana. I completed this book after joining the Department of Historical Studies and the Department for the Study of Religion at the University of Toronto. I want to thank my new colleagues here in Canada for their enthusiastic welcome and for their help in putting the finishing touches on the manuscript and seeing it through to press.

Several institutions sponsored the research that went into this book. I am especially grateful for a Scholarship and Creativity Award from Montana State University and a junior fellowship from the American Institute for Indian Studies. I am also indebted to the generous help of staff at several libraries and archives: Montana State University's Renne Library, the British Library, Cambridge University Library, University of Nottingham Library, Nehru Memorial Museum and Library, the Maharashtra State Archives, the Cama Institute, the Forbes Gujarati Sabha, the Theosophical Society's Adyar Library and Research Center, and the Burke Library at Union Theological Seminary. At a crucial moment in the revision process, I benefited from the American Institute for Indian Studies' "Dissertation into Book" workshop in Madison, Wisconsin. I would like to thank all of the workshop participants, especially Luke Whitmore, for their feedback on the project. Finally, I would like to thank the participants in the 2013–2014 SIAS Summer Institute on "Cultural Encounters," who revivified my intellectual energies during two intensive summer meetings in Berlin and Durham.

The editors of the South Asia Across the Disciplines series and the two anonymous readers for the University of Chicago Press provided perceptive feedback on the manuscript at several stages of review. I want to offer particular thanks to Gauri Viswanathan for pushing me to rethink the book's organization in ways that have substantially improved its argument. For shepherding the manuscript through the review and publication process, I would like to thank my editor, Priya Nelson, as well as Ellen Kladky, Randolph Petilos, and Alan Thomas. Portions of chapter 4 previously appeared as "Luther in the Tropics: Karsandas Mulji and the Colonial 'Reformation' of Hinduism" in the *Journal of the American Academy of Religion* 83, no. 1 (2015): 181–209. I thank Oxford University Press for permission to reprint that material here.

Although scholarly writing is mostly a solitary affair, it could not happen without the ongoing support of a broad community of friends and fellow scholars. Of the many people who shaped this project or helped speed it along, I would especially like to thank Cassie Adcock, Jen Callaghan, John Cort, Becca Cain, Thom Dancer, Anndrea Elison, Geraldine Forbes, Leela Gandhi, Dilip Gaonkar, Brian Hatcher, Jack Hawley, Brannon Ingram, Jack Llewelyn, Mitch Numark, Archana Patel, Mitra Sharafi, Dan Sheffield, Amrita Shodhan, Julie Stephens, Jenna Supp-Montgomerie, SherAli Tareen, Usha Thakkar, Susan Visvanathan, Rupa Viswanath, and Yurou Zhong. Conducting research in far-flung places means relying frequently on the hospitality of others. In this regard, I am especially grateful to Raghu and Girish Karnad, Stephen Legg, Archana Patel, Robert Ricks, and Hilary Smith. Several other friends, meanwhile, made the research in London, Mumbai, Delhi, and Ahmedabad more fun: Anuja Ghosalkar, Zahir Janmohamed, Leo Mirani, Dann Naseemullah, Cornelius O'Boyle, Surita Parashar, Rasheed Wadia, and Arastu Zakia. Bruce Lawrence backed this book from beginning to end with unflagging energy and good cheer, without which it would have been much harder to write. Over the course of many conversations, David Gilmartin shaped my interest in the history of liberal selfhood. I owe a similar debt to Srinivas Aravamudan, whose staunch support helped me to write the book, just as surely as his work on "guru English" became one of its key intellectual coordinates. Ann Burlein offered incisive feedback on an earlier draft of the introduction, and I hope to have done justice to her comments here, as well to her own work on Foucault. Finally, I want to extend special thanks to Randall Styers, a friend and mentor whose intellectual generosity and professional wisdom have been among the conditions of possibility for this book.

I want to thank Catherine and John Bishir for giving me a home in Raleigh, and to Jean, Thornton, and Lucile Scott for homes in all the other places—that is, for a lifetime of love and support. Last but certainly not least, Daniel Elam has witnessed and nurtured this project for as long as I've been working on it. So much of what I've been able to think and write during this time, I owe to him. I cannot begin to put words to my gratitude for his patience, his generosity, his intellect, and, above all, his companionship.

Against the Priest

Enlightenment is man's emergence from his self-imposed immaturity. Immaturity is the inability to use one's understanding without guidance from another. IMMANUEL KANT, "WHAT IS ENLIGHTENMENT?" (1784)

The world has slept for many long ages, dreaming dreams and seeing visions. Night is the time when the magician waves his mysterious wand, and fascinates and enthralls the senses with fantastic tricks. Night is the time when interested priests and hierophants hold the human soul in hopeless intellectual bondage and spiritual servitude. But that night of darkness, that dismal and hideous night of superstition and priestcraft has gone, never to return. The world of thought seems to have just awakened to the stern and sacred realities of truth. KESHUB CHUNDER SEN, "GOD-VISION IN THE NINETEENTH CENTURY" (1880)

In his 1880 Calcutta Town Hall lecture on "God-Vision in the Nineteenth Century," Keshub Chunder Sen proclaimed an end to the long night of what he calls *priestcraft*. This word, though it must have seemed old-fashioned even in 1880, was nonetheless central to how Keshub understood his role as a Hindu reformer. His is a religious modernity defined against the priest, and it is emblematic of its era. In the coming dawn, Keshub says, priestly "dreams and visions" will dissolve. Even after "superstition" fades away, however, "religion" will remain, transmuted by the light of truth. The nineteenth century, announces Keshub, will see "with the naked eye, and not through colored glasses." Its denizens will "run straight" to the "Divine Person" to "see Him as He is, without any medium."[1]

Keshub's speech should sound familiar to anyone acquainted with major modern narratives about the history of religion. All the key elements are here—the epic battle of superstition and science, the distinction between magic and religion proper, the progressivist plot arc culminating in nothing less than a glimpse of God himself.[2] Keshub notes the secularizing thrust of this discourse and politely departs from it, insisting, like so many of his contemporaries, that modern religion base itself not on traditional institutions but on unmediated personal experience.

In other words, to borrow a term from Kant, what Keshub seems to be calling for is religious enlightenment. If it is indeed (as Theodor Adorno and Max Horkheimer remark) the "unconditional freedom from tutelage which defines the essence of enlightenment," then enlightenment necessarily entails an end to the night of the priest.[3] Priests, gurus, hierophants, magicians, and other figures of tutelary religious authority are potent symbols of all that enlightenment would disavow: external influence, hierarchical tradition, and coercive power.

But as Keshub was well aware, this promise of total freedom was itself a delusion. Or, put better, it entailed a certain contradiction, as new kinds of tutelage emerged to fill the void that had been left by the priest. Keshub forbade his disciples from labeling him a "teacher": "The very gospel which I have laid before you denies my mission as a teacher. Remember then that by accepting it you are inviolably bound to ignore any authority I may claim as your priest and guide."[4] Keshub's stringent disavowal of his status as charismatic modern-day guru—his command that his followers ignore his commands—makes the point clearly enough. Freedom, as a normative force, remains enmeshed in networks of instruction, which ensure that enlightenment always already contains the traces of tutelage as its ground and condition of being.

My book explores this contradiction by asking how nineteenth-century Hindu reformers theorized the power of priests. Although attacks on priestcraft were ubiquitous in colonial India, the period's rich archive of anticlerical writing has seldom been systematically studied. I argue, however, that the specter of the crafty priest was crucial to how the politics of religion were understood at this time. At least as important as the Orientalist representation of Hinduism and other religious traditions was the effort to reform human subjects by freeing them from external religious influence. By analyzing anticlerical texts, the book shows how the critique of spiritual despotism in colonial India gave rise to the ideal of the self-ruling subject. Even as reformers decried the spiritual power of priests, they promoted new types of religious discipline by mobilizing Hindu and Protestant ascetic practices and extending them to worldly householders.

The result was a problematic of self-governance that was as important to later nationalist thought as it was to nineteenth-century reform culture.

Spiritual Despots has two broad aims. First, it seeks to provide an expanded genealogy for the liberal ideal of the self-governing individual. By pointing to apparent affinities between secular and Protestant technologies of the self and their nineteenth-century Hindu counterparts, I hope to suggest that any adequate account of a globalized liberal governmentality has to consider a longer and far messier history of religious subjectivity—a history that, not incidentally, was a significant point of reference for metropolitan theorists of liberal selfhood. As is now well known, the modern ideal of political freedom arose concurrently with empire and took the chains of the colonized as a principle foil.[5] Something similar, I suggest, holds in the case of colonial priests. British liberty defined itself against "Hindu priestcraft," and, in doing so, became entangled with Hindu discourses on spiritual self-governance. Consequently, a proper genealogy of liberalism should place the liberal subject within this expanded field of inquiry by considering the multiple techniques of self-formation that were mobilized by empire. In this book, I triangulate three such technologies of the self as they circulated in the nineteenth century: liberalism, Protestantism, and Hinduism.

Second, and complementarily, *Spiritual Despots* seeks to demonstrate that nineteenth-century Hindu reform movements should be studied alongside other reform movements of their period so that we can better see how colonial Hinduism shaped major modern discourses about the nature of the self. Modern Hinduism, in other words, should be situated synchronically, in relation to empire, and not just diachronically, in relation to precolonial tradition. Reading modern Hinduism contrapuntally in relation to Britain, I suggest, allows modern Hindu thinkers to emerge as theorists in their own right, who were in conversation with their contemporaries outside India. Indeed, by studying the history of liberal subjectivity contrapuntally, we can see how twentieth-century theorists like Max Weber and Michel Foucault inherited a problematic of spiritual self-rule that took shape partly in colonial India.

This introduction lays the groundwork for this project by developing a theoretical account of the relationship between priestcraft, or spiritual heteronomy, and asceticism, or spiritual self-rule. As a whole, it asks whether the genealogy of secularism in South Asia would look different if it were centered on the priest rather than the sovereign state. Exploring one possible affirmative answer to this question, I define secularization as the exit from priestcraft: asceticism corresponds to secularism insofar as both connote the critical autonomy of the untutored individual. Both, in other words, become figures for self-rule. As Peter Berger once observed, secularization can "stand for the liberation of modern man from religious tutelage."[6] This clearly Kantian formulation, I argue, distills a dominant narrative about the emergence of secular selfhood. Secularism and self-rule may not be equivalent terms; but from Kant forward, they have been imagined in close relation to one another.

In what follows, I blur the line between theory and history in the style of postcolonial studies and other fields within what are sometimes called the "new humanities." By approaching Max Weber's notion of "worldly asceticism" through the emergent methodologies of what can be described as connective (rather than comparative) religion, I try to rethink that notion. Over the course of the discussion, I interleave Weber's writings on asceticism with those of other theorists (Gandhi, Foucault, Taylor). I then turn to an extended close reading of the story of Ekalavya from the *Mahabharata*, which I use to develop a model of the worldly ascetic as situated within an open-ended network of tutelary relations. This refigured worldly ascetic structures much of the rest of *Spiritual Despots*. The remainder of the introduction returns to the terrain marked by Keshub Chunder Sen's comments on priestcraft. How, I ask, did anticlerical critique shape subjectivity in colonial India? What did it mean to define Indian modernity against the priest? The introduction concludes with an outline of how the following chapters explore these questions.

Empire and Asceticism

The key concept that I take up and revise in *Spiritual Despots* is Max Weber's notion of "worldly asceticism"—a notion that was central to his critique of modern capitalism as well as his comparative research on world religions. Talcott Parsons (Weber's translator and major American interpreter) chose this "seemingly paradoxical term" as a rendering of Weber's *innerweltliche Askese*, "which means asceticism practiced within the world as contrasted with *ausserweltliche Askese*, which withdraws from the world (for instance into a monastery). . . . It is one of the prime points of his [Weber's] essay that asceticism does not need to flee from the world to be ascetic."[7] If otherworldly asceticism entails a negation of the world, its worldly counterpart restores religion to the world, but without thereby resolving the implied tension between religion and worldliness. Indeed, as a "seemingly paradoxical" term structured around an internal contradiction, worldly asceticism arguably heightens the tension between these two poles.

This tension structures the genealogical narrative about the emergence of modern subjectivity that Weber influentially outlined in his *The Protestant Ethic and the Spirit of Capitalism* (1920). The book's narrative unfolds in two principle movements. First, Weber suggests, Protestantism generalized monastic discipline to the lay population, reimagining asceticism so that it could be practiced within the world. It did this partly via the Lutheran notion of "the calling" (*Beruf*), which celebrated "the fulfillment of duty in worldly affairs as the highest form which the moral activity of the individual could assume."[8] In the world but not of it, Weber's Protestants work hard, not because it brings them pleasure, but because it is their divinely ordained duty. Second, this worldly asceticism later dispensed with the Protestant doctrine that had given rise to it in the first place. The work ethic that (in Parsons's much-quoted translation of Weber) the Puritans wore like a "light cloak" has since become an "iron cage": "The Puritan wanted to work in a calling; we are forced to do so. For when asceticism was carried out of monastic cells into everyday life, and began to dominate worldly morality, it did its part in building the tremendous cosmos of the modern economic order."[9] Once built, this cosmos became self-sustaining. Of crucial importance for this narrative is the analytic distinction that Weber draws between ethics and doctrine: the history of the Protestant ethic is semi-independent of the history of Protestantism. A person can thus inherit the Protestant work ethic without being Protestant or even Christian. Indeed, one could say that the Protestant ethic assumes its most characteristic or ideal form only after it has left the "Protestant" behind so that, by force of ethic alone, even an atheist will work as though her soul depends on it.

The Protestant Ethic (initially published in 1904–5 and later revised for republication in 1920) brought a prominent nineteenth-century narrative about the origins of Western modernity into the twentieth century, while also substantially rethinking that narrative. Compare, for example, James Mill's 1820 claim that the Protestant Reformation "totally altered the condition of human nature, and exalted man to what may be called a different stage of existence" or Thomas Carlyle's 1841 claim that "Protestantism is the grand root from which our whole subsequent European History branches out."[10] For Mill and Carlyle, Protestantism is what marks Britain as different from and superior to its cultural others—others that, not incidentally, it was in the process of colonizing during the very period in which Mill and Carlyle were making these claims. If Ireland's Catholicism revealed it to be at an earlier "stage of existence" than England and Scotland, so too did India's Hinduism.

Like his predecessors, Weber places Protestantism at the root of Western modernity, but he does this in a way that puts him at a considerable remove from the likes of Mill and Carlyle. *The Protestant Ethic* offers a critique, not a celebration, of modern society, and it goes out of its way to avoid the simple causal claim (sometimes attributed to Weber) that the Reformation created capitalism.[11] Even so, the book's passing quotation from Carlyle is indicative. Nineteenth-century discourses necessarily provide the backdrop to Weber's argument that Puritanism "stood at the cradle of modern economic man."[12]

Weber's debt to earlier civilizational discourses arguably became more pronounced between 1905 and 1920, as he broadened his research on the Protestant ethic into a comparative inquiry on the economic ethics of the world religions. In doing so, he increasingly came to suggest that the rise of Protestant worldly asceticism explains why modern capitalism developed in Europe and not elsewhere. Weber's comparative method differed from that of many of his contemporaries, for whom comparative religion was often a just means of "proving" Protestant Christianity's superiority to its religious others.[13] Even so, his work remains of a piece with its times.

Consequently, Peter van der Veer has called for the development of a "post-Weberian project" that sets aside the search for civilizational essences in favor of analysis of "networks of historical interaction."[14] As he remarks, Weber's *Protestant Ethic* is a text that fails to account for Protestantism's hold on capitalist modernity because, in its rush to Protestant origins (and thus, presumably, the "essence" of Protestantism), it neglects the more recent moorings of its own historical conjuncture in the colonial nineteenth century. To theorize the Protestant ethic, much less to pose a comparative question about it, one first has to parse its relationship to empire.[15] In other words, instead of asking how Protestant worldly asceticism *compares* to other forms of religious subjectivity, we should be asking how it *connects* to them in particular historical contexts. In place of comparative religion, then, we find the emergent methodologies of what could be described as "connective religion," a discipline that would take the cultural crosscurrents of empire as its critical starting point.

This book is meant as a contribution to that larger project. By rerouting worldly asceticism through empire, I attempt to alter the archive of *The Protestant Ethic* so that we can reimagine it as an exercise in connective rather than comparative religion. Such an endeavor necessarily entails denaturing certain of Weber's key terms—starting with "worldly asceticism" itself. Throughout *Spiritual Despots*, I link this term to several other terms that I use to expand its scope and rethink its stakes. In the chapters that follow, most of these terms are taken from nineteenth-century texts. In this introduction, by contrast, I work to situate Weber within a theoretical conversation that postdates the nineteenth century, even while remaining indebted to it.

The major term that I align with worldly asceticism is M. K. Gandhi's notion of swaraj or "self-rule." With good reason, Gandhi has been described as a "worldly ascetic." During his lifetime, popular songs described him as *na sannyasi na sansari*, neither a renunciant nor a worldly householder.[16] A few decades later, Lloyd and Susanne Rudolph influentially analyzed Gandhi's worldly asceticism in explicitly Weberian terms by comparing him to Benjamin Franklin, Weber's paradigm for the Protestant ethic.[17] A better comparison, I suggest, would be to Weber himself. After all, Weber (b. 1864) and Gandhi (b. 1869) were close contemporaries, whose major works—*The Protestant Ethic* (1904–5) and *Hind Swaraj* (1909–10)—appeared within five years of one other. The two texts, moreover, take up a closely related set of themes, asking how ethics, or the practice of the self, can shape larger economic and political forms. As recent scholarship has stressed, Gandhi was as much a political theorist as he was a politician. It is thus high time that we took him as Weber's counterpart—a theorist of worldly asceticism in his own right, rather than an object to which theory is applied.

By taking Gandhi as a theorist, I suggest, we come to a revised understanding of Weber's genealogy of worldly asceticism. Gandhi indicates that we should append a third movement to Weber's narrative: after it was released from the monastery into the world, there is no reason to assume that asceticism had a single-stop itinerary, ending its travels with the ascetic capitalist. Rather, it seems more reasonable to assume that, once mobilized, "Protestant" self-discipline remained on the move.

When it arrived in India, for example, the Protestant ethic discovered an affinity for various practices of the self associated with Hindu tradition. It is this conjuncture of Protestant and Hindu asceticisms that interests me in this book. One could, of course, study this conjuncture by several means. Some scholars have traced how Protestant norms reshaped the religious practice of South Asian elites during the nineteenth century, resulting in hybrid cultural forms like "Protestant Buddhism."[18] Others have asked whether a shared economic base may have shaped North Atlantic and South Asian religions alike. Thus, as Brian Hatcher implies, if the "bourgeois Hinduism" of Calcutta's elite strongly recalls Weber's bourgeois Protestants, this may attest to an elective affinity between neo-Vedanta and the bourgeoisie rather than to Protestant influence per se.[19]

In *Spiritual Despots*, I come at the same set of problems from a slightly different angle—and one informed by a rereading of Weber's methodological notion of "elective affinity." It is sometimes said that Weber used the phrase to bypass questions of causation in his description of the relationship between Puritanism and capitalism: certain economic and cultural forms are reliably drawn to each other, but this does not necessarily imply that the economic base determines its superstructure (i.e., vulgar Marxism) or vice versa (i.e., idealism). It is perhaps more correct, as Andrew McKinnon points out, to say that Weber used the term to indicate the relationship between ethics and doctrine (i.e., Protestant industriousness has an affinity for Protestant belief).[20] Either way, it is clear why Parsons decided to translate the term into English as *correlation*, thus aligning it with American social science: like correlation, electivity affinity interlinks empirical phenomena while resisting oversimplified causal claims about them.

As McKinnon argues, however, this translation significantly flattens the texture of Weber's German. "Elective affinities" (*die Wahlverwandtschaften*) is an allusion to an 1807 Goethe novel of the same title—a reference that would have been obvious to Weber's educated German contemporaries. In the novel, the major characters encounter the title phrase in a science book, where it denotes a principle of chemical attraction. They then adopt it as a metaphor for describing human relationships. As Goethe's heroine Charlotte observes, entities joined by means of affinity "seem to me not so much blood relations [*Blutverwandte*] as related in spirit and soul [*Geistes- und Seelenverwandte*]."[21] Over the course of the novel, such affinities (rendered by Goethe as romantic attractions) threaten to unravel established marriages and disrupt the inheritance of aristocratic family property. The novel concludes with an apparent miracle: two married characters produce a baby who physically resembles neither of its biological parents, but rather the people whom they felt spiritually drawn to while they were conceiving it. Here, spiritual relations eclipse blood relations, writing themselves (however impossibly) into the body and its genetic inheritance.

In *Spiritual Despots*, my usage of the term *affinity* veers closer to Charlotte than to Weber. I am interested in affinity as a principle of connection that disrupts linear family relations in favor of a different kind of kinship—one that, during the nineteenth century, was often associated with spirit or soul. Comparative religion, I suggest, operates by a blood principle: it primarily conceives of civilizations as lines of family descent. Connective religion operates by something like a spiritual principle: it looks for elective affinities that cut across blood relations of this type. I return to the term *affinity* in chapter 3. Here, suffice it to say that the possibility of reading Gandhi's *Hind Swaraj* and Weber's *The Protestant Ethic* as affine texts underlies much of my analysis in this book.[22]

Secularism and Self-Rule

Famously, Gandhi wrote *Hind Swaraj* at sea, while en route from London to South Africa aboard the H. M. S. *Kildonan Castle*. One of my aims in *Spiritual Despots* is to keep the notion of swaraj or self-rule similarly afloat, circulating with the cultural crosscurrents of empire. Now generally considered the centerpiece of Gandhi's political thought, *Hind Swaraj* cues its argument in the doubled sense of its Gujarati title. In the title of the English edition, Gandhi translated *swaraj* as *home rule*. This translation, however, is misleading. Swaraj, for Gandhi, entails something more than the simple transfer of state sovereignty from Britain to India; instead, it requires a radical dissemination of sovereignty as a principle of ascetic "self-rule." As Gandhi argues, "it is Swaraj when we learn to rule ourselves" by adhering to an ethic of ascetic self-discipline. If Gandhi's own highly publicized flesh eventually came to serve as the chief symbol of this ethic, it did not thereby eliminate the unresolved question that hangs over *Hind Swaraj*: "how can the millions obtain self-rule?"[23] It is one thing for ascetic swaraj to be developed as an elite practice. It is another thing for it to be generalized to the nation.

In a sense, *Hind Swaraj* explores the same questions that Weber had posed in his essay on the Protestant ethic: How, historically, has religion shaped human subjectivity? How can religion's power to shape subjectivity be used to intervene in the economic and political order of the modern world? Gandhi and Weber were both sharp critics of what they referred to respectively as "modern civilization" and "the modern economic order." In particular, both resisted the idea that this order resulted in greater human freedom. They parted ways, however, on the question of asceticism. Where Weber saw asceticism as the scaffolding of capitalism's iron cage, Gandhi saw it as a tool that could undermine capitalism: by exercising greater control over their consumer desires, he suggested, Indians could staunch the flow of mass-produced British goods into India. Thus, where the Weberian subject appears as entrapped by ascetic self-discipline, the Gandhian subject appears—at least at first glance—as deriving greater autonomy from his ascetic self-rule.

It bears asking, then, whether the self-ruling Gandhian subject reproduces the ideal of individual autonomy that had been an important part of British rhetoric in South Asia since the nineteenth century. During this period, the ideal of autonomy was widespread; moreover, it brought religious and secular groups together within a shared cultural framework. Thus, as Eric Stokes suggests, utilitarianism and Evangelicalism were both "movements of individualism" that sought "to liberate the individual from the slavery of custom and from the tyranny of the noble and the priest. Their end was to make the individual in every society a free, autonomous agent, leading a life of conscious deliberation and choice."[24] This project of subjective reform was central to the civilizing mission of empire.

Speaking in very broad terms, I would describe this project as liberal. Liberalism was, of course, a complex and ever-shifting constellation of ideas and practices that changed substantially over the course of the nineteenth century in both colony and metropole. As scholars, we should remain attuned to the differences among discrete moments in its history.[25] At the same time, however, we should not lose sight of major continuities. That the ideal of the autonomous individual is among the latter is suggested by Shruti Kapila's recent work on the "culture of the self" in early twentieth-century India. By 1900, as she shows, the critique of the autonomous individual had become an important means of critiquing liberalism more generally.[26] In India, as elsewhere, the history of liberalism was inseparable from the history of subjectivity. Liberal subjectivity could thus serve as a metonym for liberalism per se. Gandhi was integral to this early twentieth-century scene. As Ajay Skaria has shown, Gandhi's experiments with religion were one means by which, as an anticolonial thinker, he set out to reimagine liberalism.[27] His notion of swaraj, moreover, was essential in this regard.

Liberalism, we might say, sanctifies the abstract individual. The abstract citizen-subject is to democratic states what the divine sovereign had been to monarchical states: as constituting power, both are exterior to the field of power that they anchor and define. It is thus only insofar as the liberal subject can lay claim to a position of abstract generality that it can serve as the conceptual basis for the modern state. This claim, however, results in an irresolvable contradiction. In assuming a position of generality, any given subject necessarily renounces a portion of its lived particularity: in my formal capacity as citizen (the sovereign ground of the state), the mundane details of my human life simply do not matter. The self-alienated liberal subject lives simultaneously in heaven and on earth, split between his political existence as mediated by the sovereign state and the mundane immanence of his daily life.[28] I would describe this condition as a type of worldly asceticism.

Gandhi thus heightens a latent contradiction that is constitutive for liberal asceticism, and he uses it to erode the sanctity of the liberal individual. Where liberal political thought is predicated on the positive value of the self-interested citizen-subject, Gandhi set out to reduce the self to "zero," in the belief that such a renunciation of self would establish nonviolence as the basis of politics.[29] In place of the sovereign citizen, he presents us with the ascetic cipher, the self-negating man without qualities.[30]

Because the priestcraft narrative was paradigmatic for the liberal ideal of individual autonomy, it can also provide a means of rethinking that ideal. I turn to Gandhi's direct engagement with the figure of the crafty priest in the conclusion; in *Hind Swaraj*, I argue, Gandhi implicitly contrasts the priestly charlatan and the self-negating ascetic as competing figures for worldly religion. Here, in order to begin to situate both Gandhi and Weber at the latter cusp of the nineteenth century, I use a slightly different tactic. Turning away from *Hind Swaraj*, I suggest that its meditation on political religion can be productively read alongside nineteenth-century British accounts of the Protestant Reformation—accounts that worked to valorize and naturalize the ideal of the autonomous individual that Gandhi later undermined (I return to this material in chapter 1's discussion of the "Victorian Luther").

Let us return, then, to Thomas Carlyle's claim that Protestantism was the "grand root" of European modernity. The Reformation, by Carlyle's account, was a "revolt against the Pope"; through it "every man became his own Pope; and learnt among other things that he must never trust any Pope, or spiritual Hero-captain, any more!" This liberatory process is significant because of how rapidly it spread: the Protestant "revolt against spiritual sovereignties" gave rise to the French revolution and other revolts against temporal sovereignties. As Carlyle opines, "the spiritual will always body itself forth in the temporal history of men."[31] Here, the political theology of the sovereign gives way to the political theology of the rights-bearing individual. The truly radical rupture that marks the dawn of the modern age is not the political revolution that unseated the king, but rather the revolution in subjectivity that unseated the priest.

Structurally, this narrative is what Charles Taylor would describe as a "subtraction story" about the coming of secular modernity: subtract the priest, it implies, and you find "modern man" just waiting to be free. Such stories, as Taylor argues (in a surprisingly Foucauldian vein), are inadequate because they occlude the historically contingent techniques of self-discipline that arose alongside of and gave rise to modern subjectivity. Subtraction stories serve an ideological function: they reify and naturalize a mode of subjectivity that is the contingent product of the modern social imaginary rather than its antecedent source.[32] Critiquing priestcraft, in other words, does not liberate subjects; it produces them.

Carlyle's paean to the Reformation thus runs aground on a constitutive contradiction. Defining priests as "spiritual Captains," Carlyle positions them as that which modernity necessarily excludes. He then calls our attention to the consequent paradox. If a priest is defined broadly as a "spiritual Captain" (i.e., someone who conducts the souls of others), then even Protestant reformers qualify as priests: "Is not every true Reformer, by the nature of him, a *Priest* first of all?"[33] Subtracting the priest, it seems, is not so simple. As Michel Foucault insists, the Reformation was not an "anti-pastoral revolt" (i.e., Carlyle's "revolt against the Pope"), but rather a "revolt *around* the pastorate" or priesthood. As a struggle over who "would actually have the right to govern men, and to govern them in their daily life and in the details and materiality of their existence," it prompted a reorganization of the pastorate, but never "definitively expelled it from history."[34] On the contrary, it generated new, more intensive forms of pastoral control. Carlyle seems to gesture to this reorganized pastorate with his claim that, during the Reformation, "every man became his own Pope." Instead of outright freedom from religious tutelage, we have what could be termed *auto-popery*. Repositioned as a principle of internal rather than external control, the Pope has not only not been eliminated; he is even closer to the subject than he was before.

To read Carlyle in this way is, of course, to push his triumphalist nineteenth-century narrative closer to Weber's pessimistic early-twentieth-century revision of it. It is also to push both Carlyle and Weber closer to Foucault—a thinker whose affinity for Weber has been frequently noted.[35] Just as importantly, however, Carlyle's account of the Reformation helps us to see how the standard narrative of the exit of priestcraft entails a sanctification of the self-guided subject. For a man to become his own Pope is for him to split himself into two. One part of the subject remains in the world, as the object of spiritual government. The other part identifies with the Pope: setting itself apart as sacred, it stands over the immanent domain as its sovereign governor.

This sanctification produces a difficulty for the definition of secularization that I proposed at the beginning of this introduction. To define secularization as the exit from priestcraft is misleading. Liberation from priestly rule preserves the sacred enclosure once occupied by the priest; it simply installs a new sacred subject in his place. Instead of the sovereign priest who stands above the world that he governs, we find the sovereign subject of liberalism.

Gandhian asceticism, I suggest, indicates one means of rethinking this model of subjectivity. Gandhi refuses the self its sacred enclosure. By transferring the principle of self-rule from the sovereign state to the ascetic "millions," he renders this principle immanent to society—and thus not sovereign, if sovereign is taken in its etymological sense, as that which stands above. Where the priest stands over his flock in sovereign fashion, the ascetic facilitates a politics of horizontal connection, his body a dense transfer point for the lateral transmission of technologies of self-rule.

Gandhian self-rule thus implies a revised definition of secularism. Early uses of the English verb *secularize* indicated the civil appropriation of ecclesiastical properties, as when Henry VIII seized church lands for the crown. Secularization was the process by which something set apart as sacred is returned to the flow of mundane time (the *saeculum*). Later usage tends to retain this basic meaning, although in more abstract form (e.g., capitalism secularizes the Protestant ethic). Such narratives typically imply a one-way transfer of goods: the secular sphere lays claim to religious objects and does not return them. In actuality, however, movement occurs both ways, with the religious borrowing from the secular at least as often as the secular borrows from the religious. This movement produces a field of signatures in which apparently discrete cultural practices come to refer to each other in an increasingly dense citational network.[36] Secularism may insist in theory on the separation of spheres; but in practice it routinely produces the very hybrids that it so strenuously disavows, passing cultural properties back and forth across the secular-religious divide. To capture this scene, one might suggest that "to secularize" something is simply to move it from one domain to another. Secularization implies circulation. The sacred is immobile; the secular moves.

To secularize the self, then, is to refuse it its zone of enclosure as the sovereign ground of liberal politics. This refusal becomes the basis for my revised definition of secularization. Secularization entails not just a single transfer of spiritual governance, from the sacred priest to the sacred self. It involves continual movement. Techniques of self-rule circulate relentlessly across subjects, cultures, and continents. The "self," moreover, does not exist independently of this scene of circulation; it is its contingent effect.

In the nineteenth century, experiments in ascetic self-discipline drew promiscuously on a number of archives of possible selfhoods. In *Spiritual Despots*, I am interested primarily in three of these: liberalism, Protestantism, and Hinduism. Over the course of the century, I argue, the circulation of technologies of self-rule led to the increased entanglement of these three cultural fields.

The Obedient Ascetic

To make sense of this broadened scene, the Weberian problematic of worldly asceticism needs to be recast. By my account, worldly asceticism is a technology of the self that uses the division between the transcendent and the immanent to split the subject so that it assumes the internally doubled posture of self-rule.

Foucault's writings on classical *askesis* are one key reference for this reformulated worldly ascetic. As Foucault explains, the ancient Greeks saw ethical practice as establishing "a sort of permanent political relationship between self and self."[37] Ethics, as the practice of the self, entailed a power relation that split the self in two. One of the many metaphors used to describe this relationship was that of the wrestler's match: *askesis* transposes the agonistic conflict between two subjects into the psyche of a single subject, who is thus rendered double, a stranger to himself.[38]

My other key reference for retheorizing worldly asceticism is Charles Taylor's neo-Weberian account of modern "buffered" subjectivity. Taylor's story begins in the misty reaches of the Axial Age, when the desire for the transcendent allegedly first disrupted the human focus on immanent or worldly flourishing. What follows is a two-millennium effort to resolve the resulting contradiction between the immanent and its transcendent negation. Two provisional resolutions of this dialectic eventually emerge: a system of "two-speed" religion, in which monks (devoted to salvation) and laity (enmeshed in the world) were seen as complementary; and a "Reform impulse" that denies this complementarity in order to synthesize these two orientations within a single person. Disembedded from and buffered against the world by her desire for salvation, the Reform subject remains oriented toward the world, but nevertheless subordinates the world to transcendent ends. In this, Taylor's Reform subject is parallel to Weber's worldly ascetic. Like Weber's Puritans and their capitalist descendents, Taylor's disembedded secular subjects could be said to suffer a "feeling of unprecedented loneliness of the single individual."[39] Both Taylor and Foucault present us with an ascetic subject defined by self-estrangement. Where Foucault helps to restore a sense of social antagonism to Taylor (the relation between the transcendent and the immanent is necessarily a power relation), Taylor lends some needed texture to Foucault's analysis of religion. Taken together, they present worldly asceticism as (to return to Carlyle) a form of auto-popery.

Building on both these accounts, I define asceticism in the broadest possible terms as disciplined self-government or self-rule. It is the process by which the subject steps back from a field of objects that also includes an objectified version of the self. Asceticism thus enables what Weber describes, in strikingly Foucauldian terms, as a rationalized "conduct of life" (*Lebensführung*).[40] In learning to direct the self, the subject also learns to instrumentalize a world now seen as discontinuous with the self.

This retreat from immanent things would, arguably, have been impossible without the otherworldly orientation of religion. Taylor makes this case for the North Atlantic world; but much the same can and has been said about South Asia. Thus, in a neo-Weberian narrative that parallels Taylor's, Louis Dumont presents the history of Hinduism as propelled by a dialectic between the ideal types of the renouncer and the man-in-the-world. For Dumont, as for Taylor, the renunciant invents individuality: the man-in-the-world, being defined by his network of social relations, has no substantial existence of his own. It is only when the renunciant buffers himself against social bonds, retreating introspectively into the forest, that individuality proper can emerge.[41] For both Taylor and Dumont, then, the individual is necessarily a worldly ascetic: he buffers himself against the world, as though seeking salvational release from it; but, unlike the otherworldly ascetic, he orients himself toward action in the world. It is certainly not my intention to defend Dumont against the just criticisms of his work.[42] Rather, by pairing Taylor and Dumont, I mean to recast Weber's comparative question about worldly asceticism by suggesting the potential for movement between the North Atlantic and South Asia. For Weber, the Protestant ethic gives way to the capitalist ethic once asceticism sheds its transcendent referent: for the dour Weberian, the disenchanted immanent domain is all there is. Buffer has become "iron cage"—or, departing from Parsons's translation, a "shell as hard as steel" (*stahlhartes Gehäuse*). Without necessarily contradicting this narrative, I mean to alter its terms.

By mobilizing the self-enclosed or encaged subject, we can better see how ascetic technologies circulate across domains normally thought separate. In place of the steel-hard shell, we have something more like a shell game in which different ascetic encasements switch places as habitations for the subject. Such ascetic encasements circulate across the presumed division between "the secular" and "the religious." Thus, where possible, I try to avoid using these terms (at least in their conventional sense), preferring instead to speak of liberal, Protestant, and Hindu technologies of ascetic self-rule. Technologies of the self also circulate across what I would describe as different registers of governance: a technique developed by a priest to manage his flock can be readapted to the management of a household, a family, a national territory, or an individual psyche in manner akin to how a disciplinary technique can, by Foucault's account, migrate from monastery to prison to factory to school. To study the circulation of ascetic technologies, we need to track their movement across these different registers, as well as across cultures and religions.

Circulation of this type poses a challenge to theorists who see the ascetic subject as constitutively disembedded from or buffered against her surroudings. This group of theorists includes not only Taylor and Dumont, but also many Indian thinkers. Consider, for example, Debendranath Tagore's paraphrase of the *Katha Upanishad*: "As the charioteer restrains his steeds, so shall ye restrain the senses engaged with objects."[43] Here, in the classic metaphor, the essential self is merely a passenger in the chariot of the body; it should stand back from objects so as to better steer a course through them. We find a slightly different version of the same sentiment in an early essay by Keshub Chunder Sen. A "soul entirely dependent on external influences," he remarks, is no different from a piece of wood at sea or a feather in the air. "In this condition, man is not a *person* but a *thing*." To be a person, according to Keshub, is to orient oneself toward the transcendent: "We must move heavenward, come what may."[44] It is only by cultivating an ascetic sense of distance from the world, it seems, that the subject can emerge as such. For both of these bourgeois Bengalis, asceticism appears as a "practice of freedom": it is what allows the human organism to separate itself from mere things, buffering itself against the world so that it can achieve independence from external influence.[45] This form of worldly asceticism bears a clear affinity for the liberal ideal of the autonomous individual.

In *Spiritual Despots*, I propose a different model of ascetic self-rule. Asceticism, I argue, entails obedience, asking that the subject inhabit a norm or rule that by definition precedes him. In learning to inhabit this rule, the subject steps outside himself, rendering subjectivity as an agonistic space wherein self-government becomes (in Foucault's terms) a sort of permanent political relation. By doubling the subject, self-rule thus also opens the subject to identification with, and thus potentially domination, by others. Asceticism entails relationality, not buffer.

To clarify what I mean by this, I turn to two contrasting depictions of the figure of the guru: the frontispiece to this book and the story of Ekalavya from the *Mahabharata*. First, the frontispiece. This image, published in 1822 in the quarterly papers of the Baptist Missionary Society, offers an especially vivid illustration of how early-nineteenth-century British writers represented Hinduism. By the standard account, it was a ruse concocted by sacerdotal elites to dupe and debase the gullible masses. The rhetoric of "Hindu priestcraft," of course, said more about Britain than it did about India: Protestant missionaries transposed well-worn anti-Catholic polemics onto the subcontinent's unfamiliar religious terrain. Christianity was no stranger to the ideal of absolute obedience to religious authority. Indeed, if we follow Foucault, it was precisely this ideal, as cultivated in monasteries, that marked Christian pastoral power as different in kind from its Greek predecessors.[46]

But if the trope of spiritual despotism was an Orientalist projection onto India, it also, even if inadvertently, resonated with a significant strand of Hindu tradition. The *Guru Gita* may be the most famous text to advocate absolute obedience to teachers, but it is hardly alone. Absolute obedience has been extensively thematized in India from the classical period to the present day, whether prescriptively (one should submit to a guru) or satirically (people who blindly follow gurus are fools). *Contra* the missionaries, then, a concern with the proprieties of pastoral power is something that South Asia and the North Atlantic have had in common for a very long time. It even makes sense, I think, to take the missionaries as acting in sympathy with certain strands of South Asian tradition when they criticized radical submission to religious authority, just as they were writing in opposition to certain strands of Christian tradition. Our 1822 image distills the core problematic. But the question remains: What kind of relationship is this? More importantly, how might we complicate the picture of absolute heteronomy that this image conveys?

To suggest one answer to this latter question, I turn to a story from the *Mahabharata*. It concerns a youth named Ekalavya, the son of the chief of the Nishadas—literally a hunter, but in this case apparently either a tribal or a mixed-caste group. When Ekalavya asked to apprentice himself to the renowned archery teacher Drona, Drona declined to accept him, worried that the boy might outperform his other pupils: the five princely Pandava brothers, of whom Arjuna was the most adept. Undeterred, Ekalavya bent his head to Drona's feet and returned to the forest, where he made "a clay image of Drona [and] began to worship it respectfully as his real preceptor and practice weapons before it with the most rigid regularity." In the process, he mastered the art of archery.

One day, the Pandavas decided to take a hunting trip in the forest. Their dog came upon Ekalavya, "the Nishada of dark hue," and began to bark; to silence him, Ekalavya shot seven arrows into his mouth. When the dog ran back to the Pandavas, they were filled with wonder and realized that whoever had shot these arrows was a better archer than they were. Searching in the woods, they found Ekalavya, who identified himself as a Nishada prince—and as Drona's pupil. Arjuna was distraught. How could his preceptor, who had promised him that none of his other pupils would even equal him, have allowed this Nishada to surpass him? When Arjuna confronted him, Drona resolved on a course of action: he would visit Ekalavya in the woods. Upon his teacher's arrival, Ekalayva "touched his feet and prostrated himself on the ground" before him. Drona then demanded the traditional fee given by a disciple to his guru. Ekalavya readily consented: "Command me, for there is nothing . . . I may not give unto my preceptor." For his fee, Drona demanded Ekalavya's right thumb. The pupil, "with a cheerful face and an unafflicted heart, cut off without ado his thumb and gave it unto Drona." After this, as the *Mahabharata* laconically puts it, "he was no longer as fast as he had been before." Henceforth, Arjuna would be the best of archers.[47]

The tale of Ekalavya is first and foremost the tale of an enduring social injustice. With all of the moral ambivalence that one would expect from the *Mahabharata*, it dramatizes the violence by which high caste institutions maintain their dominance over marginalized groups. The story invites the subaltern Ekalavya to emulate high caste norms, even as it denies him the ability close the gap that separates him from his princely counterpart. At the same time, the story also positions Ekalavya as its implicit hero. Indeed, subsequent retellings have celebrated him as an exemplary pupil and a model of proper devotion to a guru. To underscore this point, a recent mass-market Hindi retelling gives Drona the final word: "My son, in this world there have been and will remain countless people with great knowledge of archery, but I give you my blessing that the glory of your great renunciation [*tyāg*] will endure forever."[48] It seems Ekalavya bested Arjuna after all, precisely through his selfless devotion to their shared guru.

My reading of the story centers on this renunciation. Among Ekalavya's transgressions was his doubling of the guru—a doubling that reveals the internally doubled structure of pedagogic relations as such. It is a different doubling that propels the plot, of course: Ekalavya doubles and threatens to displace Arjuna, and the story punishes him for this potential violation of the social order. But behind these two princes lurks a second duo. The story's central puzzle, surely, is that Ekalavya can learn archery from a clay image of Drona as though copy and original were equivalent. Alone in the woods, training himself in archery, Ekalavya externalizes the scene of ascetic self-control, literalizing the political relationship of self to self that characterizes Foucault's heautocratic subject. His guru is simply his higher self, projected onto the clay image.

One might mistake this idyllic scene of ascetic self-rule as suggesting a practice of freedom in the face of an unjust society. But the *Mahabharata* quickly disabuses us of this error. The clay image is Ekalavya. But it also always has the potential to become Drona, opening the self to the unreasonable demand of the other. The prior sacrifice, the sacrifice that makes the renunciation of the thumb all but inevitable within the diegetic economy of this tale, is the renunciation of self implied by the scene of self-rule. To discipline himself, Ekalavya first has to quarrel with the immanent domain, renouncing his actuality to become other than what he is. The clay guru is the figure of that which he hopes to become: an archery master. It is the mediating term through which the self-identical subject splits into two so that it can become self-ruling. But this image does not belong to the ascetic. Rather, it articulates a zone of indistinction that blurs the line between self and other in a way that is potentially dangerous to both. Where the clay guru had disrupted the embodied disciplinary relations of classical caste society, Drona proposes an exchange of flesh to restore them, asserting his functional identity with his doppelganger. But this narrative resolution cannot close the problem space that Ekalavya has opened. The pedagogic encounter, we discover, is as much about an exchange of identities as it is about an exchange of knowledge. In asking to be recognized by Drona as his pupil, Ekalavya also insists on his ability to become Drona or to show that, as a teacher, Drona is never quite equivalent to himself.

What emerges here is something like a guru-disciple dialectic, which brings Foucault and Taylor (with his recurrent Hegelianisms) into closer conversation. This struggle for recognition entails a confusion of identities. If the transcendent is that which negates the immanent, calling it into question by submitting it to the control of that which exceeds it, then it also establishes a chain of mediations that, by refusing the immanent its unmediated particularity, also situates it within a set of hierarchically structured social relations. This is the situation of what I describe as "spiritual despotism." Here, I substitute *spiritual* for Taylor's *transcendent*, in keeping with nineteenth-century convention, both Hegelian and otherwise. The spiritual is that which negates the particularity of the self or the givenness of society, thus entering the immanent into a potentially transformative network of mediations.

The frontispiece suggests a first definition of spiritual despotism: a spiritual despot is a crafty priest who exercises absolute control over another person. The tale of Ekalavya suggests a revised definition: spiritual despotism becomes a way of describing the function of the clay guru. The spiritual despot is never entirely equivalent to himself. A cipher for the projection of his pupils, he articulates a zone of indistinction in which the tutelary encounter becomes the occasion for a critical cross-wiring of identities, for the blurring of the line between self and other. *Spiritual Des-*

pots will move between these two definitions, using the second to reframe the first.

As should be clear, I think that Eklavya provides one means of re-thinking the Kantian maxim that enlightenment or political "maturity" requires an exit from tutelage. As Leela Gandhi suggests, Kant presents us with a "fantasy of autonomous subjectivity" and an "antirelational" politics that "severs the ethical subject's access to all external influences, be they divine, human, or animal." To bypass this "crisis of nonrelation," Gandhi proposes an "immature" politics of radical connectivity that, for her, goes by the name of friendship.[49] In sympathy with this project, my aim here is to show how self-rule likewise implies relationality. If it is the desire for self-transcendence that disrupts the subject's relationship to worldly things and that would seem to buffer him against them, it is this same desire that entwines the subject with others. By allowing Ekalavya to displace Kant, we see how worldly asceticism as a technology of self-rule sits uneasily at the margins of freedom and domination. In this, it is akin to governmentality, which entails a similar admixture of internal and external control. Managed into managing herself, the internally differentiated subject of self-rule is always necessarily open to incorporation into networks of guidance that exceed and constrain her.

These theoretical reflections provide a general framework for *Spiritual Despots* as a whole, which explores how spiritual despotism and spiritual self-rule converged during the nineteenth century around the figure of the worldly ascetic. In my account, this figure is shadowed by the various terms outlined above: ethic, discipline, Reform, swaraj. It is also shadowed by the figure that remained its standard foil throughout this period: the despotic priest. The rhetoric of "priestcraft," I suggest, was closely linked to the problematic of self-rule that rose to prominence by the late nineteenth century. To understand the genealogy of self-rule, then, we need to know something more about the history of anticlerical polemics.

Anticlerical Modernity

First appearing in English in the fifteenth century to denote the skilled work performed by professional clerics, *priestcraft* rapidly degenerated into an insult. During both the Reformation and the Enlightenment, the term represented all that was wrong with religion. Some charged priests with having usurped and perverted the true Church. Others claimed that they had invented religion outright, fabricating the supernatural to dupe and control the gullible crowd. Either way, the meaning of *priestcraft* was clear: it denoted clerical fraud and religious imposture.

Early modern England produced what in retrospect seems an unlikely alliance of anticlerical critics: Protestants and atheists banded together against the notion of *sacerdos* or priestly authority. To describe the modernity that they gave rise as secular is thus, as Justin Champion suggests, a misnomer. It is more properly described as anticlerical.[50]

Among its many mutations and migrations, the stock narrative of religious imposture eventually found its way to colonial India. In the nineteenth century, it was arguably *the* dominant idiom for describing India's religious traditions, particularly Hinduism—routinely decried by Protestant missionaries and colonial administrators as a vast Brahmanical conspiracy, comparable only to the Catholic Church in its ability to oppress the masses. But missionaries and colonizers were not the only people to make use of the discourse of priestcraft. The English word soon entered the lexicon of Hindu reformers, taking on new life in vernacular languages like Gujarati and Hindi.[51] It likewise structured the "Guru English" taking shape at this time, in the writings of Keshub Chunder Sen and others.[52]

In good Orientalist style, the rhetoric of priestcraft tells us more about the reformers who used it than it does about the priests it ostensibly describes. To learn about how temple priests, Sanskrit pandits, and other traditional religious authorities understood the institutions of which they were a part and restructured those institutions in response to colonialism, we need to look elsewhere.[53] The story of priestcraft is the story of reformers who defined themselves in opposition to priestly power, not the story of the Hindu "priesthood."

Polemical attacks on priestcraft would seem to be coextensive with modern Hinduism as such—if by "modern Hinduism" we mean the series of religious reform movements that commenced with Rammohun Roy in the 1810s and 1820s and remained a dominant feature of South Asian public culture until the rise of nationalism after the 1880s.[54] Modern Hinduism is a fraught category for any number of reasons. It can tend, for instance, to overstate the difference between a "modern" reformer like Rammohun Roy (1772–1833) and a "premodern" reformer like Sahajanand Swami (1781–1830).[55] Indeed, to suggest that Rammohun's English education makes him different in kind from his vernacular-medium contemporaries is to replicate a rhetorical position already well articulated *within* the nineteenth century. English-educated, urban elites were keen to carve out their own sphere of influence by dispensing with precolonial tradition and its institutional authorities. They thus staged a narrative of colonial rupture that was as much performative as it was descriptive. To designate Hindu reform movements as modern is, by this view, similarly performative: it enacts the historic break that it purports to explain. If the category "modern Hinduism" simply replicates the rhetorical position of these nineteenth-century urban elites, then one might think that as scholars we should dispense with this term: to analyze a historical period one must describe it in terms different from those in which it narrated itself. Surely, however, this is easier said than done. Rammohun Roy's world is continuous with our own. In significant ways, his categories remain our categories, and we cannot just step outside of them.

Precisely because of this continuity, however, the scene of nineteenth-century Hindu reformism, far from a mere historical curiosity, remains a dynamic site through which we can interrogate how we understand our own modernity. If modernity is an orientation toward the past, a self-conscious declaration of temporal rupture rather than a specific social or economic form (capitalism, democracy, science), then the modernity of these Hindu reformers revolves very much on their rejection of the priest.[56] When Hindu reformers used the English word *priestcraft* (as Keshbhub Chunder Sen does in the above epigraph), they implicitly aligned themselves and their anticlerical modernity with imperial Britain. At the same time, however, by generalizing the English "priest" to India, they also suggest that this anticlerical modernity might be redefined through reference to South Asia's own rich tradition of anticlerical critique.

But this poses a problem. Continuity with the past is precisely what a modernity predicated on rupture must preclude. Strong ambivalence toward tradition was common in colonial India. Colonial intellectuals disavowed the Indian past in laying claim to a universal modernity, while also proclaiming allegiance to Indian tradition in order to assert the distinctiveness of India as a nation, different from but formally equivalent to other such nations.[57] Perhaps something of this ambivalence is implicit in the very word *reform*, which simultaneously promises rupture and continuity, but without indicating how the two are to be reconciled.

Aurobindo Ghosh once remarked that "to seize on a vital thing out of the past and throw it into the stream of modern life is really the most powerful means of renovation and new-creation."[58] This formulation, taken from Aurobindo's short essay on the career of Swami Dayananda Saraswati, seems a useful gloss on nineteenth-century Hindu reform more generally. Time here is uneven. Aurobindo's modernity, self-consciously located in the living "stream" of the present, thrives on uncanny eruptions of a past that is still, apparently, eerily alive. At the same time, his present drives relentlessly forward into a fully "renovated" future. By seizing on

Hindu tradition as the uncannily "vital thing" that can be wrested from the past and reanimated in the present, Aurobindo uses history (however counterintuitively) to secure the present against the past, tipping it toward a "new creation." The result is the jagged temporality characteristic of modern Hinduism.

To study this Hinduism's modernity, then, is to ask how nineteenth-century reform texts reorganize the past's relationship to the present. To remain true to these texts, we need to preserve something of their own sense of time. Accordingly, instead of trying to construct a linear narrative about how Hindu reformers altered the structure of priestly power in the subcontinent, *Spiritual Despots* asks how the scattered pieces of the precolonial past, strewn across the nineteenth century, could be seized upon as vital things. Its method is to hover close to period texts, asking how they present the forms of power and the lines of cultural difference that they were in the process of remaking.

These texts offer a glimpse, however fragmented, into the world of what Indrani Chatterjee has termed "monastic governmentality."[59] In early modern South Asian polities, Chatterjee explains, power did not emanate from the state alone. It was produced at a range of different institutional sites, many of which were, broadly speaking, "monastic" in that they centered on ascetics of various stripes (Sufis, Shaivas, Buddhists, Jains, Yogis, Tantrikas, etc.). Prior to the nineteenth century, the political, the religious, and the domestic intertwined in a dense ritual economy that interlinked kings, ascetics, temple priests, and ordinary householders. Power was both a circulatory force and a transferrable commodity. It was produced partly via the usual political means (large palaces, fearsome battles). Just as frequently, however, it emerged from the disciplined body of the ascetic-sage, or from the lines of power that linked that sage to his followers. Ascetics could bequeath their ritual power on kings and other political authorities; they could also use it regulate the gendered world of everyday life. Two intersecting axes structured the field of monastic governmentality: *asceticism* (or the technologies by which a person inscribes power onto her own body) and *pastoralism* (or the technologies by which a religious professional governs the conduct of his flock). The body of the professional ascetic, as both the object and the instrument of religious discipline, was situated at the intersection of these two axes; consequently, it was an especially dense transfer point for the communication of ritual power.

The king's body was another such transfer point. When his crown was hollowed out by colonial rule, the ritual economy of the earlier era necessarily changed.[60] But precisely because power in precolonial India was so widely distributed, exercised by sadhus and monks and inscribed in the sometimes-eroticized bodies of their followers, any adequate account of the changes occasioned by colonialism must attend to how monastic governmentality lived on into the nineteenth century. As Chatterjee argues, several major institutions of the era (including the bourgeois family, romantic love, the popular novel, and colonial law) need to be understood as having reconfigured terrain that was once regulated by this earlier ritual economy, especially by replacing its political erotics with the globalizing discourse of "sexuality."

Modern Hinduism seems to have split the field of monastic governmentality into two, reorganizing it around the twin figures that were reform's most urgent objects: "priest" and "woman." A good deal of energy was expended in keeping these two objects separated, and it is surely not coincidental that several of the nineteenth century's most celebrated scandals centered on sexual liaisons between priests and bourgeois housewives. In *Spiritual Despots*, however, my focus is squarely on the priest. I ask how we can read nineteenth-century writings about priestcraft as efforts to theorize governmentality or pastoral power, making this mode of power more available to colonial and anticolonial politics by fixing it within a form of knowledge.

The key terms of art here are, of course, borrowed from Foucault. In adopting them, I do not, however, mean to simply "apply" Foucault to South Asian materials. Rather, to relocate Foucault to South Asia is necessarily to rethink Foucault by returning him to the history that gave rise to his thought in the first place. As a number of scholars have recently pointed out, Foucault's work on governmentality in the 1970s coincided with the rise of neoliberal economic policies in France; the idea of governmentality was Foucault's way of strategically endorsing neoliberalism as a form of power that appeared to bypass certain problems attendant on the mid-century social welfare state.[61] 1970s Paris is, of course, a long way from nineteenth-century India. But if we situate both within the long transnational history of liberalism—which, as C. A. Bayly and others have shown, took shape at least partly in the colonies—then Foucault and India begin to appear as part of the same story.[62]

To stress this continuity, I argue that we should take *priestcraft* as a period-specific term for what Foucault called "pastoral power." According to Foucault, governmentality (a mode of power concerned with the management of conduct) secularized technologies of spiritual direction that had been developing within Christian institutions since late antiquity. By his account, what distinguishes the modern state as modern is its ability to simulate the powers of the priest—managing all and each, the population and the individual, much as priests had been managing their flocks for centuries. I suggest that when nineteenth-century writers debated whether priests exercised a "singular species of despotism" over the deluded masses (chapter 1), they anticipated Foucault's identification of the pastorate as constituting a distinct species of power. Indeed, doing a Foucauldian interpretation of such texts starts to seem a rather circular endeavor: reading Foucault via colonial India seems at least as plausible as reading colonial India via Foucault.

If to read Foucault as a theorist of priestcraft is to stress the continuity between nineteenth- and twentieth-century social theory, it is also to stress the continuity between high theory (i.e., the work of a Foucault or a James Mill) and what I would term "vernacular theory"—texts like the lectures of Keshub Chunder Sen, which, although not overtly theoretical, can and should be read as venturing theoretical claims (see chapter 3). Much the same can be said for reformist Gujarati journalism, Arya Samaji polemicism, and theosophical occultism (see chapters 4, 5, and 6 respectively). Indeed, certain texts, such as James Mill's *History of British India*, so thoroughly blur the line between high and vernacular theory as to confound the distinction between the two. In short, to think empire through Foucault is not to impose a body of extraneous theory onto historical materials. Rather, it is to show how these materials, which are always already theoretical, anticipate and give rise to late twentieth-century social thought.[63]

Foucault's writings on priestcraft provide a novel point of entry onto the history of secularism in South Asia. "Religious power," as Foucault argues, "is pastoral power." In other words, if there is a form of power that is specific to religion, it is the granular power wielded by priests and not the sovereign power of the state (even a theocratic state). Consequently, the "essential aspect" of the history of secularism is not the "interplay between Church and state, but rather between the pastorate and governmentality."[64] We should, of course, continue to study the political theology of the sovereign in different historical contexts. As Mithi Mukherjee and A. Azfar Moin have in their different ways shown, such research can be enormously fruitful for the study of South Asian secularisms.[65] We should not, however, stop with the sovereign. Instead, with Indrani Chatterjee, we should also look to the history of monastic governmentality—or what, in more strictly Foucauldian terms, could be described as the precolonial pastorate.

This approach to secularism is perhaps uniquely well suited to the nineteenth-century materials that I consider in this book. The problematic of "Indian secularism" did not emerge as such until the twentieth century, and, when it did emerge, it did so in relation to the state: by re-framing an earlier set of colonial policies about "non-interference" in religion, the problematic of secularism became a site for discussing the state's relationship to majority and minority communities defined in terms of both religion and caste.[66] Nineteenth-century religious reform, I suggest, implies a different approach to the question of political religion. In experimenting with a mode of politics that centered on the reform of subjectivity, reformers did often understand themselves as intervening against the state's efforts at subjectivation. Just as often, however, they presented religion as a utopian principle of intersubjective connection that operated below the purview of the state. In studying reform, then, we need to remain aware of the difference between these two political registers.

Structure of This Book

Spiritual Despots asks how nineteenth-century religious reformers proclaimed a modernity defined against the priest (which is to say, against the pastorate or spiritual heteronomy). Eliminating heteronomy entirely was, of course, impossible. But precisely by enacting a break with the priestly past, these reformers articulated a problematic of self-rule that became central to one influential vision of Indian modernity.

As a study of the mobility of cultural forms, or of "words in motion," *Spiritual Despots* is, in the first instance, an effort to track the discursive object *priestcraft* as it circulated between Britain and India in the nineteenth century.[67] But this begs a methodological question: How does one study the travels of a term like this? One could, taking Edward Said's prescription, identify its point of origin; measure the distance traversed; chart its conditions of acceptance or resistance; and then, finally, detail the idea's inevitable transformation in its new home.[68] This study will do some of that. But priestcraft's precise routes are hard to identify. It was, most centrally, an insult hurled in interreligious polemics, and, like many such polemic terms, its electric mobility is difficult to track. Although it appears in the written record in pamphlets, books, newspapers, letters, and other textual artifacts, it did much of its most important work elsewhere.

To complicate matters still more, when priestcraft entered India, its semantic range swelled substantially via the vagaries of translation, with sundry Brahmans, gurus, *purohits*, pirs, swamis, fakirs, and other figures of religious authority, both institutional and charismatic, swept up more or less indiscriminately by the omnivorous Anglophone "priest." To map *priestcraft*'s nineteenth-century itinerary thoroughly would thus be difficult, if not outright impossible. Consequently, I have limited myself to examining particular conjunctures in its travels. I try to remain attentive, as Said recommends, both to the "internal coherence" of any single conjuncture as well as to its "system of external relationships" with other conjunctures.

The circulation of *priestcraft* is this book's organizing trope; but the book's questions do not end there. Rather, I use priestcraft to frame an inquiry into the colonial circulation of pastoral technologies of spiritual guidance and ascetic technologies of self-rule. Along with priests, then, we find many types of ascetics in the following pages—Calvinists, *karmayogis*, *brahmacharis*, *sadhus*, and fakirs, to name just a few. In analyzing the relationship between priests and ascetics in colonial India, the book circles around the question that has been the topic of this introduction: how do tales about the end of priestcraft and the exit from religious tutelage work to structure a particular form of modern subjectivity?

This book's six chapters pursue this question across various sites, the very dispersion of which demonstrates the mobility of Anglophone anticlericalism during this period. I do not mean for the chapters to add up into a single continuous narrative, nor do I mean them as "case studies" that render up general laws or represent broader populations. I use the figures in the following chapters as metonyms for what I describe in chapter 3 as the nineteenth-century reform assemblage, but without positioning them as representative of it. This is for methodological reasons. The representative steps outside the group that he represents in the very moment that he represents it; he becomes the norm or paradigm that defines the group as group.[69] The metonym, by contrast, makes no pretense to be anything other than a part or fragment; rather than standing *for* the whole, on the logic of representation, it stands *in* for a whole that cannot be represented as such. The study of circulation, as my structuring method, highlights the jagged non-continuity of globally mobile cultural forms. It gives us networked particularities, not homogenized wholes. Accordingly, the discussion below notes some of the concrete connections that link the book's reformers to one another to suggest the close-knit texture of the nineteenth-century reform assemblage.

Throughout *Spiritual Despots*, my preferred method is the theoretically informed close reading of non-literary texts, in the mode of historicist cultural studies. The book's first three chapters move between Britain and India over a relatively broad period of time, from the 1810s through the 1870s. The latter three chapters, which constitute the core of the book, trace the development of the ideal of self-rule from the 1860s to the 1880s through close analysis of the writings of three different religious reformers: Karsandas Mulji, Dayananda Saraswati, and Helena Blavatsky. The book unfolds chronologically, but the chapters should be read less as offering a history of ideas than as circling around a set of themes or questions that emerge during the latter half of the nineteenth century.

Chapter 1, "A Singular Species of Despotism," continues the theoretical discussion begun by this introduction. It asks how colonial thinkers used the figure of the Hindu priest to theorize a mode of power that could push past the relatively limited apparatus of the colonial state to govern the very soul of society. In particular, it argues that James Mill's *History of British India* (1818) frames a theory of pastoral power that is likewise implicit in contemporary works by Jeremy Bentham and Charles Grant. At the same time, I suggest, Mill's *History* also offers a theory of the Protestant Reformation, working to disarticulate the "spirit" of the Reformation from the historical event in much the same way that the phrase "the Luther of India" would come to do later in the century.

As we see in chapter 2 ("A Popular History of Priestcraft in All Ages and Nations"), debates over the spirit of Protestantism extended well beyond Mill. Here, I use the career of English Quaker William Howitt to trace how the category of the Protestant came under pressure from *within* Britain, being rethought, abstracted, and generalized in the metropole at roughly the same time that it was being similarly reworked in the colony. Upon publishing *The Popular History of Priestcraft in All Ages and Nations* (1833), Howitt quickly found himself at odds with Britain's staid Quaker establishment. Aligning himself with a range of radical causes, he sought to recuperate what he saw as the lost dissenting spirit of George Fox. Over the course of a varied career, Howitt claimed to rediscover Fox's radicalism in anticolonial critique, Romantic poetry, spiritualist séances, and Catholic tradition.

Where chapter 2 foregrounds how one nineteenth-century Briton reimagined the Reformation, chapter 3 ("Reform Affinities") pushes reform onto the transnational terrain of what I call the period's "reform assemblage." Opening onto the 1833 Bristol deathbed of Rammohun Roy, the chapter offers a broad overview of the mid-nineteenth-century reform networks that intersected around this scene. Its principal topic is the lectures and essays of the later Brahmo Samaji thinker, Keshub Chunder Sen. Taking Keshub as a theorist of cross-cultural affinity, I ask how his essays lay the groundwork for a mode of egalitarian spiritual fellowship that develops out of, without ever quite displacing, the hierarchies of priestly religion.

The second part of the book moves away from this broad transnational scene to focus instead on particular reformers who were active in India between the 1860s and the 1880s. Where the first three chapters trace how terms like *Luther* and *reform* were divested of their historically specific referents, these chapters trace how a distinctively South Asian discourse on self-rule emerged from within the conceptual space that they vacated.

Chapter 4, "Guru Is God," reconsiders one alleged Indian Luther's attack on Hindu priestcraft by arguing that the Luther in question—Gujarati journalist Karsandas Mulji—did not seek to liberate Bombay's Hindus so much as to reform them by disseminating ascetic technologies of self-rule. Mulji may have modeled his asceticism on the Protestant sermons that he translated into Gujarati. Once we place his essays in their historical context, however, we begin to see that Mulji's nemesis, Jadunathji Maharaj, had been engaged in a parallel project, retailoring bhakti devotionalism as a print-mediated practice of self-rule.

Chapter 5, "Pope-lila," turns from Mulji to Swami Dayananda Saraswati, the quintessential Indian Luther, who founded his Arya Samaj in 1875 among the same Bombay elites who had avidly followed the contest between Mulji and the Maharaj. The chapter offers an extended close reading of Dayanand's magnum opus, *The Light of Truth* (1883). Dissecting Dayananda's translation of *priestcraft* into Hindi as *pope-lila*, I trace the relationship between his anticlericalism and his effort to generalize asceticism (brahmacharya) to all Hindus.

Finally, chapter 6, "Astral Ethics," leaves Dayanand behind to consider the career of one of his least favorite friends: theosophist Helena Petrovna Blavatsky, whom he denounced as a "humbug" in an 1882 Bombay lecture. To him, theosophy's marvelous "Mahatmas" seemed like pure hokum. To others, they seemed to represent a principle of absolute spiritual heteronomy; they were, after all, called the "Masters." But because of their "astral" form, I argue, these cryptic beings served instead to promulgate a type of asceticism. Theosophical interest in ascetic self-rule became more overt after the Coulomb Affair of 1884–85, during which Blavatsky and her apparent miracles were pilloried in the press. After this time, theosophists placed relatively greater emphasis on the ethical regulation of the self. This was evident in the rise of theosophical conduct manuals during this period, as well as in theosophical commentaries on the worldly asceticism of the *Bhagavad Gita*.

One could, of course, follow the history of *priestcraft* well into the twentieth century—to the foundation of India's "Anti-Priestcraft Association" in 1930 or, decades later, to the global guru Osho's fulminations against corrupt priestly power.[70] This book's story, however, ends in 1910 with the publication of Gandhi's *Hind Swaraj*. Via Gandhi, my conclusion asks how the nineteenth-century problematic of self-rule entered the early twentieth century—a time when what Kapila calls the "culture of the self" was at a peak.[71]

Secularism, says Talal Asad, is best studied by its "shadows"—those sites where the secular, as a pervasive and thus mostly invisible feature of modern life, comes obliquely into view.[72] Recent scholarship has enumerated several such shadows: tolerance, progress, the public sphere, and even the concept of religion itself. *Spiritual Despots* inserts "the priest" onto this list. Arguing that priestcraft is one of the fundamental concepts around which secular modernity has been defined, it uses the unresolvable contradiction implicit in the normative desire for an unconditional freedom from tutelage to help move the secular—metonymically, and only ever in part—from the background to the foreground of modern thought.

Tracing the contours of a modern God-Vision that defines itself against the priest (to recall Keshub Chunder Sen), I ask how the circulation of the discursive object *priestcraft* interleaved the Protestant and the secular and, as it entered India, put both into relationship with the Hindu. Nineteenth-century reformers, I suggest, sought to articulate a politics that did not take the state as its primary point of reference but instead unfurled from below through micrological networks of human relationships that were, to varying degrees, tutelary. If modernity aims for the absolute freedom from tutelage, it ensures that its work will never end. Anticlerical modernity, in India as elsewhere, does not eliminate pastoral technologies; it proliferates them and intensifies their circulation.

ONE

A Singular Species of Despotism

No sooner are you born than priestcraft lays hold of you, and till you have paid toll to it, keeps shut against you the gate of the road which conducts you to your rights. JEREMY BENTHAM (1832)

Gautama did for India what Luther and the Reformers did for Christendom; like Luther, he found religion in the hands of a class of men who claimed a monopoly of it and doled it out in what manner and in what measure they chose; like Luther, he protested that religion is not the affair of the priest alone, but is the care and concern of every man who has a reasonable soul. *JOURNAL OF SACRED LITERATURE* (1865)

James Mill's *History of British India* (1817) looms large in the archive of empire, both literally and figuratively. The massive multivolume tome, which took almost a decade to write, established Mill as a major authority on India despite his never having been there. It also earned him—and, by extension, his son John Stuart—a position at the East India Company. Adopted as an official textbook for the training of Company employees, Mill's *History* eventually became, as Thomas Trautmann argues, "the single most important source of British Indophobia."[1] Where earlier Orientalists like William Jones had celebrated precolonial Indian culture, Mill roundly dismissed it as savagely barbaric, thereby pointing the way to the Anglicizing educational policies of the 1830s.

Mill's *History*, however, is more than just a racist diatribe. Its fulminations against Hindu "priestcraft" can and should be read as an attempt to develop a political theory of the priest as spiritual despot. Like many of his contemporaries, Mill held that, "despotism and priestcraft taken together, the Hindus, in mind and body, were the most enslaved portion of the human race."[2] Such claims served a significant ideological function for empire by broadcasting images of abject Indians, crushed beneath the weight of iniquitous tradition and in desperate need of redemption at British hands; but they also did more than this. Far from just an ideological smokescreen, decrials of Hindu "priestcraft" were a means of delineating a type of power that extends beyond the state into the very fabric of society.

The missionary apologist Charles Grant once described Brahman priests as exercising a "singular species of despotism" over the subcontinent.[3] Taking my cue from Grant, I ask how priestly despotism was identified as a distinct "species" of power in the early nineteenth century. In the above quotation, Mill presents priestcraft as complementary to "Oriental despotism," the preeminent model by which eighteenth-century European intellectuals had interpreted Asian politics. Priest and despot, he suggests, collude to oppress the Indian masses. Upon closer examination of the *History*, however, a different picture begins to emerge: rather than complementing the sovereign, the priest displaces him as the ultimate source of despotism as political principle.

This shift in the theory of Oriental despotism had significant implications for the East India Company. To truly rule India, it seems, the Company would not only have to claim the powers once held by kings and princes; it would also need to arrogate the powers of the priest. Grant seems to have recognized this need. His proposed solution was for the Company to allow Protestant missionaries into its territories. The Company would, in effect, rule India by spiritual proxy, relying on missionaries to refashion colonial subjectivity on its behalf. In practice, of course, the missionaries who flocked to the subcontinent after Grant's proposal was officially adopted as part of the 1813 Company charter did so with highly variable aims and intentions; moreover, they often found themselves in direct or indirect conflict with the Company-state.[4] But for Grant, arguably, this difference was precisely the point. The sovereign Company, by definition, could not stoop to the level of the priest. To combat the singular species of despotism that prevailed in India, it had to experiment with other, more indirect modes of rule. Thus, the relationship between sovereign and priest appears less as a conflict between church and state than as a set of technical problems about whether and how the state can organize society from below—or, in more conventionally liberal terms, to govern by not governing too much.

Where Foucault's turn to priestcraft in the 1970s was his way of thinking through the political implications of neoliberalism, early nineteenth-century writings on priestcraft were imbricated with classical liberalism.[5] As a rich scholarship now attests, British liberalism took shape between colony and metropole and thus needs to be studied contrapuntally, with attention to the movements between these two fields.[6] Mill's *History of British India* is a case in point. India may be its nominal topic. But, as Javed Majeed has argued, it is primarily addressed to metropolitan concerns—not least the status of British tradition after the French Revolution felled the ancien régime. The real object of Mill's ire is Burkean conservatism. Even so, Mill's *History* was also necessarily a colonial document, shaped by British missionary literature sent home from the subcontinent, among other types of colonial writing. As Majeed summarizes, "colonial and domestic issues could not be separated in this period."[7] Mill's *History* thus needs to be read as a text that binds colony and metropole together.

Toward this end, this chapter traces several circles around Mill's *History*. My discussion consists of theoretically informed close readings of texts, often against the grain of those texts. It is primarily in conversation with postcolonial studies scholarship on Mill, although I use this "postcolonial Mill" to raise broad questions about the genealogy of liberalism. My first pass at Mill interprets the *History of British India* via the missionary literature that Mill read while writing his book. Missionary polemics against Hindu priestcraft, I suggest, should be taken as articulating a vernacular theory of capillary power relations. By painting a nightmarish picture of absolute spiritual despotism, they not only implied that pastoral power is prior to sovereign power. They also indicated a key difficulty in theorizing a non-sovereign form of power that emerges from within rather than from above society. For the missionaries, priestcraft fuses the immanent and the transcendent in impossible fashion: it is absolutely independent of society and yet absolutely everywhere. Priests, in Mill's words, are the "uncontrollable masters of human life." This paranoid vision (which Mill shares with Charles Grant) makes for good reading. But, as a theory of power, it requires significant revision.

In my second pass at Mill, I suggest that we find such a revision in the writings of Mill's friend Jeremy Bentham. In turning to Bentham, I mean to do two things. First, I use the Bentham-Mill pairing to revisit certain questions in Foucault. Bentham's Panopticon has often been taken as a figure for precisely the sort of power that I discuss here under the rubric of "priestcraft": as its name implies, the Panopticon allows the prison inspector to see everywhere, thus apparently standing outside of a system of power that he controls in capillary detail. By rereading the Panopticon through Bentham's later book, the *Analysis of the Influence of Natural Re-*

ligion on the Temporal Happiness of Mankind (1822), I suggest that the Panopticon departs from priestcraft in a significant way. As an experimental theory of purely immanent power relations, the Panopticon provides no position exterior to the system itself. All parties, including the inspector, are subject to checks and controls. Thus all parties, no matter how self-interested, are forced to become ascetic subjects, immolating a portion of their happiness on the altar of the collective good. Second, and more incidentally, I use Bentham to situate Mill's *History* as heir to the radical side of the English Enlightenment.[8] Since the seventeenth century, *priest-craft* had had two overlapping histories. On one hand, it was central to Protestant anticlericalism (whether anti-Catholic or anti-Anglican). On the other, it was central to Deist and (to a lesser extent atheist) accounts of the history of revealed religions, which were presented as the fabrications of priestly charlatans. Mill's book on British India stands uneasily at the intersection of these two histories. Read via Grant and the missionaries, he appears as crypto-Evangelical; read via Bentham, he appears as an Enlightenment philosopher.

In my third pass at Mill, I suggest one means by which he sought to resolve this contradiction: the Protestant Reformation. Before writing the *History of British India*, Mill translated Charles Villers's *Essay on the Spirit and Influence of the Reformation of Luther* (1804) from French into English. This book, I argue, shaped Mill's account of Indian civilization in a crucial way. Much like Thomas Carlyle would do almost forty years later, Villers positioned the Reformation as the grand root of European modernity: it was a necessary stage on the road to the French revolution and political democracy. Mill's theory of civilizational stages, I suggest, follows Villers on this point. This argument, moreover, required both thinkers to make a key conceptual move. Villers had tried to separate what he called the "Particular" from the "General" Luther; that is, he sought to distinguish between the sixteenth-century German and the general spirit of reform that he thought had continued to animate world events into the nineteenth century. The Particular Luther was, by definition, provincial (in Dipesh Chakrabarty's sense). The General Luther purported to be of universal significance. So long as he remained tethered to his particular counterpart, however, he served to render this universal crypto-European. In other words, this is a classic instance of a major technique of imperial ideology: "the universal" is a means by which particular social groups assert global dominance; by revealing the provinciality of the universal, we thus neutralize such groups' claim to power.

It is possible, however, to read this procedure against the grain—or so

I suggest in a detour that moves away from Mill to trace a thumbnail ge-nealogy of the phrase "The Luther of India." This phrase had two distinct meanings during the nineteenth century: it could denote someone who converts Indians to Protestant Christianity, as well as someone who ef-fects a Reformation from within a non-Christian Indian religion. This lat-ter meaning, I suggest, corresponds to Villers's General Luther. I suspect that the generalized process of reformation denoted by this "Luther" rep-resented a significant conceptual innovation—one that took shape un-derground over the course of a very long period of time. In fact, I would speculatively suggest that this generalized reformation was part of the conceptual background that enabled Max Weber's comparative inquiry into world religions. In the nineteenth century, I argue, the General Lu-ther came to denote a form of spiritual self-government defined in oppo-sition to the priest. This highly generalized problematic, largely divested of specifically Protestant content, could then be appropriated by colonial actors. I pursue the latter part of this story in subsequent chapters of *Spiri-tual Despots*.

Here, in my fourth and final pass at Mill, I explore how the General Luther intersected within the liberal ideal of self-government. This ideal, I suggest, is implicit in the *History of British India*'s turn to Luther. Analyz-ing the contradictions implicit in the liberal norm of the sovereign indi-vidual, I argue for liberal self-government as a form of worldly asceticism that blurs the line between autonomy and heteronomy. Liberalism had typically presented empire as a pedagogic space, in which Britain would tutor India toward self-rule. Consequently, to suggest that liberal subjec-tivity is itself always "tutored" (in the Kantian sense that I develop in the Introduction) is to undermine the rule of colonial difference.

The "Spiritual Invasion" of India

The rhetoric of priestcraft was central to how Indian religions, particularly Hinduism, were represented in English in the early nineteenth century. Missionary writers in particular helped to naturalize the idea that India's overlapping devotional cultures formed a single, subcontinental system devised and managed by a priestly elite. As Geoffrey Oddie argues, this "brahmanical pan-Indian model," which presumed the omnipotence of Sanskrit texts and their Brahman interpreters, was of crucial importance to the consolidation of Hinduism during this period.[9] It also, relatedly, seems to have helped to confirm the equation of India with Hinduism.

Indian Muslims, although allegedly tyrannized by their "Moulahs, Imans [sic], and Moonshees," were not thought to be "quite so much tyrannized" as the Hindus.[10]

Anticlerical discourse circulated at the level of metropolitan theory, as well as in the more ad hoc accounts of Indian religions composed in the missionary field. Indeed, it seems fair to say that what Alexander Duff dubbed the missionaries' "spiritual invasion" of India took *priestcraft* as its trademark battle cry.[11] This cry resounded across varied sites of polemical encounter and controversialist practice, including formal public debates, street-side sermons, princely soirees, spectacular baptisms and public conversions, and in the many modes of print media that crisscrossed the subcontinent, such as newspapers, pamphlets, scriptural translations, scholarly monographs, diaries, and works of fiction.

Baptist missionary William Ward's *View of the History, Literature, and Mythology of the Hindoos* (1811–22), one of the period's most widely circulated texts, was particularly influential in this regard. As Ward remarked in an 1805 letter, his aim in writing the book was to expose "the greatest piece of priestcraft and the most formidable system of idolatry that has ever existed in the world."[12] His *View* surveys a litany of horrors that would become cliché by mid-century. Hook-swinging, erotic sculptures, widow immolation, and the unstoppable "Juggernaut" (i.e., the *rath yatra* of Lord Jagganath at Puri) all appear in these pages to scandalize the Baptist reader back home—and perhaps stir him or her to make a donation to the missionary cause. Behind most if not all of these horrors lurks the figure of the priest. The "Hindoo," claims Ward, is from a very early age "led to adore the priests of his native land." Sometimes Ward's priests exercise their power indirectly, through the various "enchantments" that they have available to them. At other times, the "degradation" of religious hierarchy is on bolder display, as when a disciple prostrates himself "and the priest places his foot on his head."[13] The *Missionary Register* summarized Ward's book succinctly in 1822: "And thus it is that a sixth part of the Human Race are mocked and deluded, for the benefit of crafty men!"[14]

Such sentiments were clearly anti-Catholic in tenor. As one commentator put it, Hinduism was "admirably adapted to illustrate the Roman Catholic motto, viz. 'Ignorance is the mother of devotion.'"[15] At the same time, however, the rhetoric of priestcraft also helped delineate a species of power that extended beyond any given religious group. India may have been especially useful in this regard: Orientalist fantasy lent itself to nightmare visions of impossibly penetrative absolute power. As one writer opined, the "Brahmins have seized on everything that is agreeable or wonderful, and made it subservient to their priestcraft. The rivers, the springs, the mountains, the plains, the trees, the stones, all that is animate, and all that is inanimate, are fashioned and moulded into their system, and made to uphold their hydra-headed superstition."[16] This is a system of power that is as remarkable for its breadth (it seizes everything, disposing of objects and people alike) as it is for its durability (decapitate one of its extrusions, and two more arise to replace it). It is also remarkable for its depth—its ability to reach into the human soul. Hinduism, as Thomas Maurice wrote in his *Indian Antiquities* (1800) was a "most dreadful species of despotism; a despotism, which, not content with subjugating the body, tyrannized over the prostrate faculties of the enslaved mind."[17]

The theory of Oriental despotism, of course, had long provided an important foil for political philosophers. With a history stretching from Aristotle to Marx, the Oriental despot had by the nineteenth century come to be identified with the sort of feudal tyrant who, through his sadistic deputies, extracts excessive wealth from slaves and peasants so as to build lavish monuments to his own glory.[18] What we see in this missionary literature is an effort to distinguish between the physical force wielded by these temporal despots and the more "dreadful" force wielded by the priest. Where the earthly tyrant binds only the body, the priest also subjugates the mind.

Enter James Mill. As a young man in Scotland, Mill had studied to become a Presbyterian minister—a career he never pursued. In London, he instead became a "philosophic radical," much more closely associated with the atheist currents of the Enlightenment than with the early nineteenth-century evangelical revival. Even so, his Calvinist proclivities stayed with him.[19] It is not surprising then that, in researching his *History of British India*, Mill drew extensively on Protestant missionary writings. As a result, the book has an almost evangelical flavor.[20]

In fact, as Trautmann observes, Mill's *History* can be read as "secularized version" of Grant's "Observations on the State of Society among the Asiatic Subjects of Great Britain"—the 1792 treatise that circulated widely in the early 1810s in advance of the 1813 renewal of the East India Company charter.[21] As we have seen, Grant claims that India was afflicted by a "singular species of despotism."[22] Long ago, he alleges, a cadre of crafty priests appointed princes to govern on their behalf, even while retaining all real power for themselves. Thus, from a very early date, the Indian state was superfluous to the actual business of rule. Even when "the Hindoos lost the dominion of their own country, the influence of their religion, and their priests, remained."[23] Here Grant reworks a familiar Enlightenment tale about the early corruption of natural religion at hands of crafty priests.[24] If India is "singular," it is in the extent and not the mere fact of priestly power.

"Despotism," as Grant opines, "is not only the principle of the government of Hindostan, but an original, fundamental, and irreversible principle in the very frame of society."[25] Where the figure of the Oriental despot had implied an absolute centralization of power, Grant disperses the despotic "principle" throughout the "whole fabric" of the social body.

Grant uses the priestcraft narrative to resolve an analytic problem that arose from the British tendency to read Indian political history as comprised of a sequence of rotating sovereigns, standing at a great remove from society: if the Indian state was perennially unstable, how could Indian society remain as unchanging and utterly without history as it was alleged to be? The proposed solution is that priests, not kings, are India's real rulers. But this creates another, even more substantial difficulty. If the British are to rule India, it seems, they need to find a way to displace the priests. The resulting conundrum propels the moral mission of empire. A "decisive question," avers Grant, confronts the East India Company. It can either "wink at the stupidity which we deem profitable to us; and as governors, be in effect the conservators of that system which deceives the people." Or, it can instruct India in "the divine principles of moral and religious truth, which have raised us in the scale of being."[26] In effect, Grant argues that once priestcraft has been explicitly identified as a form of power, the state can no longer exist independently from it. Either it conserves the old system of priestcraft, or it installs a new system. The old system aligns the imperial profiteer and the crafty priest—two figures who stand over society, exploiting it for their benefit. The second system insists that the immanent good be the state's ultimate end: the ethical imperialist will instruct society for *its* benefit, not his own. Grant claims that, in India, a "crafty and imperious priesthood" has invested itself "in perpetuity, with the most absolute empire over the civil state of the Hindoos, as well as over their minds."[27] Surely this "absolute empire" has a double edge: it indicates Grant's own imperial aspirations, only partly disavowed.

James Mill's *History of British India* adopts Grant's basic narrative. Like the rest of Asia, Mill argues, India is accustomed to rule by "the will of a single person," whose power is, "with the usual exception of religion and its ministers, absolute."[28] This aside, however casual, introduces a notable gap in the otherwise "unlimited authority" of the Oriental despot. At first glance, it simply seems to reflect the "natural" division of the secular and the sacred, of priests and kings. But, as Mill explains, such a division does not prevail in theocratic India, where the priests actually control the kings, having cleverly delegated the tedious business of rule to their royal subordinates in order to save themselves from onerous and needlessly dangerous drudgery.[29] Religion, then, is not an exception to the despot's authority, protectively sealed off from politics; it is the hidden source of his temporal power.

I turn to Mill's proposed solution to the problem of priestly power below. Here, I want to linger on the question of what it means to say that Mill secularized Grant. Grant's "Observations," I suggest, implies a distinctive way of conceiving the the relationship between politics and religion; indeed, to see Grant clearly, we may need to put the term *secular*, with all its implied baggage, aside. For Grant, priestly misrule is not just a problem of the soul or of salvation. It is also very much a political problem. What is more, it reveals how politics is itself structured around a problem of immanence/ transcendence. It is this binary, I think, rather than the division between the religious and the secular per se, that structures Grant's discussion of priestcraft. The sovereign state (at least etymologically) is an entity that stands above society in a manner transcendent to it. The same holds for the priest insofar he speaks for a transcendent divinity or truth. The priest, however, poses a problem for political transcendence in a way that the sovereign does not. For Grant and other missionary writers, priestly power is singular precisely insofar as it is immanent to society. Priestcraft, as a capillary form of power, is everywhere. Unlike the sovereign, then, the priest cannot relinquish his hold on the minute details of human life without thereby ceasing to exercise the mode of power specific to him.

If we read this insight back into the missionary literature, we start to see how that literature comes into its paranoid fantasy of totalitarian power. Priests are singularly despotic because they fuse immanence and transcendence in an absolute fashion probably only possible in nightmares. The crafty priest sits outside the system of power that he controls—he is the "unduped" master subject who pulls all strings.[30] At the same time, he is omnipresent, reaching into every corner of daily life. As we saw above, the *Missionary Register* describes how the "Brahmins have seized on everything" by appealing to the metaphor of the hydra (a metaphor that William Howitt used for the same purpose one year later, in 1833). This is a revealing figure of thought. The hydra's body is external to the field of power that its heads terrorize, extracting nourishment to feed the transcendent beast. As Foucault once quipped, modern politics has beheaded the king in practice but not in theory; we still structure political thought around the transcendent sovereign, even as modern power comes to rely less and less on sovereign law. Here, we see the same problem figured in reverse. It is the body of the hydra, and not its heads, which is extraneous to the immanent domain of power relations. It is thus the body that has to be eliminated if we are to think past the missionary problematic of priestly despotism—in which, impossibly, priestcraft is both absolutely diffuse and absolutely centralized, a form of power that rules every micro-scopic detail of life from a position of transcendent control.

"The Uncontrollable Masters of Human Life"

This problematic is central to James Mill's *History of British India*. As Mill rather melodramatically puts it, Brahmans are "the uncontrollable mas-ters of human life," and India is a land where everything is done "by di-vine prescription."[31] Priests impose the "performance of an infinite and burdensome ritual" on their followers and thus gain control over "almost every hour of the day, and every function of nature and society," ruling the Hindu masses "from the cradle to the grave."[32] Priestcraft thus becomes a useful site for reconsidering the genealogy of panopticism: priestcraft and panopticism traverse similar conceptual territory, and both open them-selves to similar fantasies about absolutely integrative forms of power.

Jeremy Bentham had devised his model for the Panopticon prison-house in the late 1780s. He remained frustrated that the project was never officially adopted and continued to advocate for it for the rest of his career—in the late 1820s, he even mailed a copy of his Panopticon writings to Rammohun Roy in Calcutta, in hopes that Rammohun might implement the project in Bengal.[33] It seems likely that these frustrations are part of what prompted a shift in Bentham's work in the 1810s, espe-cially with regard to religion. Since the 1770s, he had written a number of tracts decrying priestcraft in a manner more or less consonant with other texts of the radical Enlightenment. But, as James Crimmins explains, his approach to religion changed sometime around 1809: he decided that reform would remain ineffectual without a fundamental transformation in social structures of a kind that only direct engagement with religion could achieve.[34] The result was his *Analysis of the Influence of Natural Reli-gion on the Temporal Happiness of Mankind*. Although not published until 1822 (under the pseudonym Philip Beauchamp), the book was the prod-uct of the previous decade. Bentham first outlined it in 1811, three years after he met James Mill, and he continued to work on it during the very years in which Mill was writing the *History of British India*. At this time, the two men were also involved in one of modern history's most famous pedagogic experiments, carried out on Mill's son John Stuart. Bentham showed a draft of his *Natural Religion* to James, who in turn shared it with John Stuart, on whom it made a "great impression."[35]

If the comparison to Grant's "Observations" suggests the *History of British India*'s affinity for missionary writings about Hindu priestcraft, a comparison with Bentham's *Natural Religion* suggests its affinity for Enlightenment anticlericalism. The very title of Bentham's book, after all, recalls such eighteenth-century classics as David Hume's *Natural History of Religion* (1757), as does the careful distinction that it draws between "natural" and "revealed" faiths. But where English Enlightenment thinkers valorized natural religion, using the notion to argue that rationalist Deism was the first religion of humanity, Bentham decries it. For Bentham, all religion is bad religion.

Bentham's critique centers less on the truth-value of religion than on the type of power relation that it establishes. Like his seventeenth- and eighteenth-century counterparts, he was at war with priestcraft, or the principle of sacerdotal authority.[36] The problem with God, for Bentham, is that he is a priest in another form, requiring absolute and uncontrolled obedience from his followers. Bentham's *Natural Religion* can be read as working through a theory of purely immanent power relations that would eliminate the possibility of a God of this type, as well as his priestly counterparts.

Bentham defines the Deity as a "despot—that is, the possessor of unrestricted sway." He then contrasts this Deity-despot with a diametrically opposed figure: the "beneficent judge," who remains beneficent only because his "power is derivative." Its "force" is "borrowed from the society" that the judge regulates, and so it cannot be "used for other purposes" than the "well-being" of that society. Beneficence, in short, is produced by structures not persons: if the judge were "unshackled" from society, he would become just like the Deity-despot, an "independent unresponsible power" exercising "extraneous directive rule" over the social body.[37] Having distinguished between these two types of power (the extraneous and the derivative), Bentham goes on to identify priests with the first of them. As a member of a "class of persons incurably opposed to the interests of humanity," a priest will always try "to subjugate the minds of the community, in the highest practicable degree, to himself and to his brethren, and to appropriate for the benefit of the class as much wealth and power as circumstances will permit."[38] Here, the priest becomes paradigmatic of possessive individualism per se: separated off from the community, the priest promotes his self-interest at the expense of the common good. Insofar as his power is extraneous, it is also—to recall Mill's term—uncontrollable. It follows that to control it one would need to render it derivative.

Bentham goes on to describe the position of the governed. If the priest is defined by unalloyed self-interest, the devotee is defined by self-denial. The "essence of power," says Bentham, is "to exact obedience," and obedience necessarily entails "privation and suffering on the part of the inferior." For humans to obey the Deity, then, is for them to "immolate to his supremacy a certain portion of their happiness."[39] A more succinct definition of religion would be hard to come by. As that which sacrifices the immanent good on the altar of the transcendent, religion is, for the utilitarian philosopher, necessarily a moral evil. It can only deplete the total stock of pleasure or happiness in the world because it turns the pleasures into "objects of renunciation and abhorrence," of "self-denial and asceticism."[40] For Bentham, we might say, asceticism (or the immolation of happiness, in the technical utilitarian sense of that term) is the essence of religion. The ascetic subject, moreover, not only poisons his own life. He also reduces the pleasure of his neighbors, for "whatever curtails the personal comfort and happiness of any individual disqualifies him to an equal extent from imparting happiness to his fellow creatures."[41] Religion, in short, is unhappiness writ large.

This regime of unhappiness quickly gives rise to a network of religiously inspired surveillance. People are rightly disinclined to immolate pleasure to the Deity, and so, to curry divine favor, they try to exact privations on those around them. "Each man is thus placed under the surveillance of the rest."[42] Here, religion comes to serve what can only be called a panoptic function: whether by priest or by public, it sees everywhere, turning society into a surveillance machine.

This society of mutual surveillance and ascetic obedience would appear to be a means of revisiting and even rethinking the scene of pervasive control described in Bentham's earlier writings on the Panopticon. As Mirin Božovič suggests, the Panopticon's conceptual force becomes clearer if we read this "simple idea in Architecture" as a "fiction of God." In the terminology developed by Bentham's "Fragment on Ontology," the Panopticon brings the non-entity God into being as an inferential fiction, immanent to the inspective force of the building itself.[43] Departing somewhat from this formulation, we might say that as a "mode of obtaining power of mind over mind," the Panopticon lays claim to techniques of management more often associated with priests.[44] As a manager of souls, the Panopticon makes a key intervention into the field of priestly power: it eliminates the priest and his extraneous directive rule. The Inspector, concealed in his Inspection House, might seem similar to the priest, but he is regulated by the design of the building; his "inspective force" derives from the structure of the Panopticon itself.[45] Inside the Panopticon, no party can become an "uncontrollable" master of the lives within. Control, famously, is everywhere.

As Crimmins explains, "continual inspection" was Bentham's solution to the problem of self-interest. The legislator develops structures to ensure that rulers advance the interests of society rather than their own interests.[46] To this extent, panopticism is akin to the more conventionally liberal notion of "checks and balances," which also posits mutual surveillance as essential to good government. Indeed, James Mill's *Essay on Government* (1820) takes up a similar set of concerns in proposing a "doctrine of checks" that will ensure an "identity of interests" between the people and their representatives; regular reelection ensures that the ruler's power is derivative from society.[47] Where the Panopticon departs from this liberal tradition is in its insistence that power derives not from the inmates (i.e., society), but from the apparatus of the prison—a structure that is immanent to society, without ever quite coinciding with it. This structure, then, becomes the immanent God: it is what renders all subjects obediently ascetic, inducing them to immolate a portion of their happiness for the general good. Here, the act of obedience and the structure that induces obedience enter a zone of indistinction, such that it becomes unclear where one ends and the other begins.[48]

Both the Panopticon writings and the *Analysis of the Influence of Natural Religion*, then, ask how pastoral power can be reengineered so that it functions even in the absence of the priest. Bentham may criticize religious asceticism for reducing human happiness; but he also implies that some form of asceticism is necessary for society to function. To exist in society, the person must sacrifice some portion of her happiness on the altar of the greater good. The order of mutual benefit, in other words, is predicated on an interlocking network of mutually derived force relations that inscribe themselves on the self-abnegating body of the utilitarian ascetic.[49]

If priestcraft was one key coordinate around which Bentham built his revised theory of power, empire was another. Indeed, priestcraft and empire were in many respects inseparable. The tradition of Enlightenment anticlericalism that Bentham inherited was not reducible to the history of colonialism; even so, it cannot be readily extricated from it. In the 1680s and 90s, as Peter Harrison explains, Deists and other elites transformed ordinary anticlericalism into a "full-blown theory of religion"—turning the "priestly imposter" into a "universal religious type."[50] "Priestcraft," as Mark Goldie puts it, "was popery universalized."[51] This universalization of the priest took place in the wake of early imperial expansion. Priestcraft became a theory of the origins of "religion" (rather than a critique of Christian institutions) only by drawing on the deluge of travelogues that poured in from Asia, Africa, and the Americas—travelogues that had been crucial to the seventeenth-century reinvention of the category "religion" in the first place. Fully enmeshed in the emergence of religion as a comparative category, the crafty priest only came into his own when placed within this broadened cultural field. Already in the 1690s, then, the figure of the crafty priest was a contrapuntal property, who was most himself when spanning colony and metropole.

This seems to have been true in Bentham's day as well, although with perhaps a slightly greater emphasis on India than had been the case a hundred years previously when the Americas had been more central to England's imperial imaginary. Bentham liked to use the term "Jug" (adjective, "Juggical") to denote religion, as by contrasting "natural Jug" with "alledged revealed Jug."[52] This word is a shortened form of "Juggernaut" (i.e., Lord Jagganath at Puri, beneath the crushing wheels of whose chariot frenzied devotees were said to fling themselves), a standard missionary illustration of the despotic power of Hindu priests. Even for Bentham, it seems, Hindu priestcraft was the paradigm for religious oppression per se.

It is tempting to speculate about the conversations that Bentham and Mill must have had about priestcraft in the 1810s, while Bentham was hard at work on his *Natural Religion* and Mill on his *History of British India*. Each of these two texts, in their different ways, puts the priest at the heart of its theory of power. Where Bentham's anticlericalism leads him to reject all religion, Mill celebrates certain priest-free forms of it. His *History* bridges Bentham and Grant, straddling the anticlerical sentiments of Protestant evangelicalism and atheist radicalism.[53] These two strands of Britain's anticlerical modernity may have been difficult to reconcile; even so, Mill tried.

He did this partly via what I will describe, borrowing a term from Charles Villers, as the "General Luther." Luther, Villers suggests, was at the root of both Protestantism and Enlightenment—and thus, presumably, of Mill himself, the lapsed Presbyterian philosophic radical. Where Bentham proposed a system of controls that would induce all subjects to internalize the rule of government, Mill's *History* implies that such self-government emerges spontaneously as part of the natural progress of civilization. Like his missionary counterparts, he implies that a "Luther of India" could eliminate priestcraft by catalyzing an ephocal shift in subjectivity.

The Spirit of Reformation

The *History of British India* is a text bracketed on both sides by the Reformation. In 1805, one year before he commenced work on the *History*, Mill published an English translation of Charles Villers's *Essai sur l'esprit et l'influence de la reformation de Luther* (1804).[54] A few years after the 1817 publication of the *History of British India*, meanwhile, Mill opined in his

Essay on Government (1820) that the Reformation "totally altered the condition of human nature, and exalted man to what may be called a different stage of existence."[55] Given the confidence with which both these texts herald the Reformation as the dawn of European modernity, it seems reasonable to ask whether the *History of British India* also refers to this allegedly transformational event. I argue that it does, but only indirectly. The *History*'s diatribe against Hindu priestcraft implicitly frames India as in need of a "Reformation" that would end the night of the priest. It also (although only in passing) uses "reformation" as a general term for the transition points between civilizational "stages."

Jennifer Pitts has clarified the extent to which Mill departed from the Scottish Enlightenment tradition of "conjectural" history. Where Scottish thinkers had elaborated multiple civilizational stages in a relatively non-judgmental manner, Mill plies a "crude dichotomy" that classes all societies as either civilized or "backwards."[56] Without disputing that Mill's theory of civilizational progress is incompletely developed, or that its overall rhetorical effect is to dichotomize the world, I nonetheless want to suggest that it is more complicated than Pitts's account would seem to indicate. Moreover, by schematizing the civilizational stages mentioned in Mill's *History*, we get a clearer sense of how religion shaped his understanding of "civilization."

Religion, for Mill, is what binds the social. As it changes, so does the shape of society. In his discussion of Hinduism, Mill describes three distinct phases of social development: the familial, the tribal, and the priestly. India, he argues, has become stuck in the third of these. In stage one, the world remained sparsely populated such that its "barbarian" inhabitants had no need for law or government; wandering "immense plains and valleys" with their "flocks and herds," they were organized only into family units.[57] Once their numbers increased, a new social form—the tribe— had to emerge. Young men separated their herds from those of their fathers, forging tribal networks that marked a "new stage in the progress of civil society" and the "first rude form of a national polity."[58] As population increased again, the "inconveniences" of this stage two organization became apparent. Stage three, however, was slow to emerge: "No little time is spent; first, in maturing the conviction that a *great reformation* is necessary; and next, in conceiving the plan which the exigency requires."[59] In this passage, Mill uses "reformation" as a general term for the transition between civilizational stages. Here, the usage may seem incidental. But, as I will argue, when put in the context of Mill's broader body of work, its significance becomes clear.

When the third or priestly stage of civilization did finally emerge, India entered a state of arrested development. "In every society," writes Mill, "there are superior spirits, capable of seizing the best ideas of their times, and, if they are not opposed by circumstances, of accelerating the progress of the community to which they belong." It was "some individual of this description" who first established "a system of government and laws," thus ending the earlier era of tribal organization.[60] That this "primary institution of government" was "founded upon divine authority" was a necessary evil. Because savages are "perpetually haunted with the apprehension of invisible powers," the "assumption of a divine character" is "evidently the most effectual means which a great man, full of the spirit of improvement, can employ to induce a people, jealous and impatient of all restraint, to forgo their boundless liberty and submit to the curb of authority."[61] Only a priestly imposter, in other words, can found civilization. By manipulating humanity's barbarian fears, he tricks them into accepting "restraint" and "the curb of authority" necessary for further development. This version of the priestcraft narrative departs from its Deist predecessors, which tended to present priestcraft as an unmitigated evil responsible for the eclipse of humanity's original monotheism. Beginning from utilitarian premises (which are likewise evident in Bentham's *Natural Religion*), Mill suggests that only fraud can initially induce people to sacrifice a certain portion of their individual happiness on the altar of the collective good. Founded on discontent, civilization requires a certain measure of illusion—at least during the period of humanity's childhood.

According to Mill, India underwent the transition to stage three just like other societies. A great man perceived that a division of labor would help his country to advance and so, "clothing himself with a Divine character," he "established as a positive law, under the sanction of Heaven, the classification of the people, and the distribution of occupations." That is, he established caste. Mill holds that, at this stage, caste was an innovative form of economic organization. The problem was that the "first legislator of the Hindus," by making occupation hereditary, ensured that the system would never change. This was a major "barrier against further progress," and it reduced India to a perpetual state of political and spiritual immaturity.[62]

As H. H. Wilson objects in a footnote to his edition of Mill's *History*, this is an entirely "imaginary" scenario. How then is one to read it? Like many other theorists of priestcraft, Mill blurs the line between "theory" (a means of articulating a form of thought) and "history" (an account of empirical objects). Indeed, in later essays, Mill redraws this quasi-historical narrative in more expressly theoretical terms. Thus, in an essay on "The Ballot," he distinguishes among three distinct forms of the "art of government":

force, fraud, and rational conviction. In the past, he suggests, government consisted of "a mixture of fraud and force; in which commonly, the fraud predominated." In modern Britain, however, thanks to the printing press, profuse information has made pervasive fraud all but impossible. As a consequence, the art of "government will be left either to rational conviction or to naked force. This is the grand revolution of modern times. This is the new era." What is more, rational conviction will eventually become "the sole [governing] power."[63] It is not accidental that Mill formulates these distinctions in a discussion of the secret ballot—which, as Elaine Hadley suggests, distills the mode of detached subjectivity that characterized mid-Victorian "lived liberalism." By buffering the voter against coercive external influence, ballots and polling booths performatively enact the isolate autonomy of the rational citizen.[64] This was true both in Britain and British India, where, as David Gilmartin shows, religious leaders' potentially coercive influence on voters was a source of particular concern for colonial authorities.[65] Mill's *History of British India*, although distinct from these later debates, nonetheless anticipates some of their core concerns. Priests, Mill implies, have to fool humanity into accepting the yoke of civilization; but after this, they must be dispensed with so that the modern citizen can claim critical autonomy. Before a given country can become modern, it first has to exit from priestly tutelage.

Mill's *History* strongly implies that the transition to stage four, the reformation that ushers humanity into this political modernity, is a Protestant reformation, or a reformation that abolishes the power of priests. This equation is never explicitly stated. Even so, it is fairly evident—and not just because of Mill's clear reliance on a wider body of anticlerical writing that routinely made just this point. Mill understands India's contemporary state, as he indicates in a footnote, as analogous to the period in Europe's history when "the Romish priesthood usurped so many privileges."[66] While "rude and ignorant" men may "pay unbounded veneration and obedience to those who artfully clothe themselves with the terrors of religion," educated men with more "refined conceptions of the Divine nature" reject the idea that "the Deity makes favourites of a particular class of mankind." They realize that he is equally, or perhaps even more, "pleased . . . with those who discharge with fidelity the various and difficult duties of life."[67] True sanctity, in other words, cannot be claimed by the sacerdotal class; it resides in ordinary people fulfilling their everyday duties. If the priestly legistalor is the "great man" who inducts humanity into stage-three civilization, the quasi-Protestant reformer is the great man who inducts it into stage four.

In the 1820 *Essay on Government* Mill makes the analogy even more explicit by drawing a "parallel" with contemporary debates over political representation. Mill argues that when "the powers of Government are placed in the hands of persons whose interests are not identified with those of the community, the interests of the community are wholly sacrificed to those of the rulers." Thus, during the Reformation, the priesthood tried to deny lay Christians access to the Bible by insisting that "the people did not understand their own interest." Something similar obtains in the case of aristocrats who claim to speak for the people as a whole.[68] Bentham's *Natural Religion* decried the "extraneous directive rule" that priests exercise over society and proposed to solve it by making sure that all power was "derivative" from, rather than, transcendent to, the social body. Here we see a variant on this basic formula. The problem with priests is their pretended transcendence, their claim to be the uncontrollable masters of human life. To advance, humanity must pull them back into the immanent political order. In place of faith in priests, then, Mill promotes "fidelity" to the "duties" of mundane life: stage four marks the dawn of the worldly ascetic who, as a figure for self-government, replaces the priest, as a figure for external religious guidance.

Mill's reformation is thus a doubled affair. It is both a discrete historical event and a generalizable phenomenon. At one level, this was nothing new. Since the Enlightenment, histories of the Reformation had proved an important means of intervening in contemporary politics. Some histories set out to defend the Church of England against its Catholic and Dissenting detractors. Others sought to curb the power of Anglican clerics by decrying the ills of priestcraft. Still others used stories of the Reformation to inculcate virtue in their readers. In short, these histories aimed at something quite different from the empiricism of history as a modern academic discipline, as Justin Champion emphasizes.[69] Normative rather than descriptive, their Reformation is never quite reducible to the events of the sixteenth and seventeenth centuries.

Mill builds on this tradition. But he also takes it in a different direction by using it to frame a comparative analysis of civilizations. In both the *History of British India* and the *Essay on Government*, we can see Mill trying to identify a spirit of the Reformation that is analytically separable from its historical facts. In doing so, he carries forward the project of the book that he had translated from French in 1805: Charles Villers's *Essay on the Spirit and Influence of the Reformation of Luther*. The book, as Mill wrote in his preface, details "the consequences of the Reformation of Luther upon the political condition of man, and upon his intellectual improvement in Europe."[70] This formulation, so closely parallel to the paean to the Reformation in the *Essay on Government*, suggests the extent of Villers's influence on Mill's thought. It also indicates the doubled valence of the rhetoric of reformation: claiming to be about the "political condition of man" in general, it takes Europe a paradigm for "intellectual improvement." As a paradigm (literally, that which is "shown beside"), Europe thus stands outside itself, doubled in unstable fashion.[71]

Villers sets out, as his chapter titles indicate, to analyze "The Essence of Reformations *in General*" and that of "Luther *in Particular*." But this produces a difficulty: how is it possible to disarticulate the "general" from the "particular" Reformation? In the general sense, says Villers, reformations are the "milestones" of human history. Humanity's "gradual improvement" is structured by "an uninterrupted series of reformations; partly silent and gentle . . . and partly tumultuous and violent." This formulation reappears in Mill's *History of British India*, which uses *reformation* in precisely this sense. Like Mill, Villers holds that religious developments can forge a "new political order." Under Luther's influence, for example, people "dared to think, to reason, and to examine what before only challenged a blind submission. Thus a simple stroke aimed at the discipline of the church was the cause of a considerable change in the political situation of the states of Europe."[72] As the phrasing here suggests (i.e., *sapere aude*), Villers understands the Reformation as having produced the critical attitude of the Enlightenment. "Protestantism," he writes (quoting M. Greiling), is the "repulsive power with which reason is endowed to remove and throw off whatever would occupy its place."[73] Through the Reformation, the "human mind was delivered both from the external constraint imposed upon it by the hierarchical despotism, and from the internal constraint which it endured from the apathy of a blind superstition. It escaped suddenly from a state of tutelage."[74] It was because of the Reformation that the "European nations" began to "throw off the swaddling clothes which embarrassed them and [to] enter upon a new epoch."[75] Realizing the dangers of historical oversimplification, Villers tempers this causal claim throughout the book by pointing to other factors (the invention of artillery, the discovery of America) that helped to produce the modern world. His real argument, he insists, is merely that the Reformation "ought to be ranked among those important events which have most powerfully contributed to the progress of civilization and knowledge."[76] Even so, the book's underlying hyperbole remains clear. As one of his critics summarized, Villers holds that "most of the improvements that followed [the sixteenth century], whether in the political condition of nations, or in the arts and sciences, are due to the reformation of Luther."[77]

The very expansiveness of this claim creates a productive tension in Villers's text. As he seems to know, by equating the Reformation to "liberty of thought" per se, his *Essay* inevitably departs from the rigors of academic history, even as he remains determined to pass his book off as historical.[78] The text cannot quite decide, in other words, whether it is about the "general" or the "particular" Luther. Here, the "spirit" of Villers's title becomes a marker of dehistoricization: reformations are mechanisms for human progress in the most general sense. In this world, writes Villers, there is a clear "tendency towards the better, towards an order of things more just, more beneficent." Although "absolute perfection will never be the lot of mortals . . . it is certain they will aspire to it." The arc of history can thus be described in mathematical terms: "The phenomenon of the geometrical asymptote is destined to be repeated in the moral world"; humanity "shall forever approximate to the ellipse without being able to touch it."[79] As a meditation on the attainability of godly virtue, this passage seems to echo Christian theology's longstanding concern with moral reform as the means by which humanity can recoup its lost "image-likeness" with God.[80] In Villers's spare geometry, however, this tradition is stripped of theological specificity. "Reform" becomes simply a principle of curvature that orients the immanent domain toward the axis of the transcendent.

One approach to Villers would be to force his Reformation back into its proper place in historical time, trading the general for the particular Reformation. Instead, one might just as well ask what it would mean to catapult "Protestantism" out of history entirely so that it becomes (to take one of Villers's terms, translated by Mill) fully "cosmopolite."[81] This, I will suggest, is what the notion of the "Indian Luther" had accomplished by the latter part of the nineteenth century. It helped to articulate a problematic of self-rule that was analytically separable from Protestantism, even though it remained linked to it. This link was important in that it allowed Hindu reformers to lay claim to the "civilized" status Mill would have reserved for the West alone, even while critiquing and rethinking "modern civilization" (to use Gandhi's term).

The Luther of India

For thinkers like Mill and Villers, Luther was a figure of thought rather than a historical personage. Just as the Pope became a symbol for spiritual despotism per se, Luther became a symbol for spiritual self-rule, an icon of reformation in the generalized sense. This is the figure that I will refer to as the "Victorian Luther."

In nineteenth-century Britain, Luther's patent un-Englishness was rhetorically useful: he could represent the entirety of British Protestantism, whereas other more proximate reformers (a Knox or a Fox) would only remind Protestants of their differences. Caught up with popular anti-Catholicism at home, the Victorian Luther also shaped perceptions of the colonies: if Ireland's Catholicism disqualified it from self-rule, India's quasi-Catholic Hinduism did much the same.[82] As we have seen, the Victorian Luther was caught between two different types of Reformation: Is "Reformation" a sixteenth-century historical event, which is by definition entirely particular and impossible to replicate? Or, is it a generalizable process?

By tracing shifts in how the phrase "the Luther of India" was used between the 1820s and the 1880s, I suggest, we can see how the latter sense gradually became dominant. Throughout the nineteenth century, British and Indian Anglophone writers liberally bestowed the moniker "the Luther of India" on South Asian religious leaders, both ancient and modern. By the 1880s, the list of alleged Indian Luthers included the Buddha, Shankaracharya, Kabir, Guru Nanak, Chaitanya, Rammohun Roy, and Swami Dayananda Saraswati.[83]

At first glance, this honorific title seems to perform one of colonial discourse's standard ideological functions: it forces Indian culture into British categories, inviting the colonized to identify with the culture of the colonizer, even while refusing the complete elimination of difference. An Indian can be *like* Luther, but he can never *be* Luther.[84] Sensitive to such concerns, more recent scholarship on religious dissent in South Asia has tried to sidestep Luther as a paradigm for reform. Some works map the different "traditions of protest" that converged on colonial India; others identify premodern Indian analogues to the tolerant values of secular liberalism.[85] I worry, however, that in trying to chart a history of religious criticism that bypasses or decenters the West, such efforts inevitably retain Europe as their "silent referent."[86] If we want to rethink secularism through the framework of heterodoxy by excavating the critical functions of religious dissent, we need first to exorcise the specter of Luther.[87] Otherwise, the purely formal category of "protest" (designating dissent without determining its contents) slips irresistibly into the "Protestant," dragging "reform" with it back to the "Reformation." As Dipesh Chakrabarty has it, the experience of European modernity is "both indispensible and inadequate" in theorizing non-Western modernity.[88] Surely the same holds for the cultural sign "Luther."

I would argue that by rendering "Luther" as a comparative category, the phrase "Luther of India" generalized its referent in a curious and provocative manner: the particular Luther may be Christian, but the general Luther is not. Instead, he implies an anticlerical commitment to producing self-governing religious subjects immune to the seductions of spiritual guidance. Here, the tension between the general and the particular Luthers works to destabilize imperial ideology. To put the point in the bluntest terms: no British person could be Luther either. Indeed, not even Martin Luther himself was entirely equivalent to his Victorian counterpart. The more the Victorian Luther pulled away from historical particulars, the more it assumed a mediating function—linking various reformers together within a shared problematic of spiritual self-rule.

The phrase "the Luther of India" had two distinct meanings that jostled for dominance during the nineteenth century. The first, which implicitly defined an "Indian Luther" as a person who successfully converts Indians to Protestant Christianity, appears to have been more common earlier in the century, when it was applied (in the 1830s) to East India Company chaplain Claudius Buchanan (1766–1815).[89] This was also clearly the sense meant by Alexander Duff, when he stated his hope that "some Indian Luther may be roused to give expression to the sentiments that have long been secretly . . . cherished in the bosoms of thousands" of Indians—whom, despite their best efforts, Duff and the missionaries had yet to convert. The eventual coming of the Indian Luther would demonstrate India's "latent progress" toward Christianity.[90]

In its second meaning, an "Indian Luther" was implicitly defined as a person who effects a Reformation from within *any* religious tradition. If Buchanan was paradigmatic for the first meaning, Dayanand was paradigmatic for the second. Notably, this second type of Luther thwarts the hopes of the first type: Dayanand's "Reformation" was said to have protected Hinduism against Christianity. By the end of the century, the second meaning seems to have largely displaced the first. How and why this happened remains obscure; like other such discourses, the notion of the Indian Luther seems largely to have "taken shape underground."[91] Even so, it does surface occasionally. To give a sense of how the shift unfolded, I turn to two different sites where it becomes visible. Both center on a figure whose status as "a Luther" was contested: the Buddha and Rammohun Roy.

In the 1830s, Buddhism remained something of a puzzle to Western scholars, who were unsure about its relationship to Hinduism. Was Buddhism a Hindu reform movement, analogous to Protestantism? Or was it a heterodoxy that launched a new religion? In the former case, the Buddha qualified as a Luther; in the latter, he did not. Thus, in 1831, Charles Neumann equated Buddhism to "Lutheranism" in describing it as "a reform of the old Hindoo orthodox church"; it was "a new building on the same ground, and with the same materials."[92] This claim was immediately disputed and before long would be rejected entirely by scholarly specialists (whose understanding of Buddhism was transformed once Brian Hodgson shipped a cache of Sanskrit texts from Kathmandu to Europe in 1837).[93] Nonetheless, the idea that Buddhism was Protestant persisted in popular literature and seems to have become more prominent in the 1850s (possibly influenced by the rise of British anti-Catholic sentiment during the same period). By the time the *Atlantic Monthly* published an article describing Buddhism as "The Protestantism of Asia" (1868), the comparison was commonplace.[94] The case of the Protestant Buddha indicates how the Victorian Luther (as icon for a generalized reformation) was used to map the boundaries between religions, confirming the distinction between a mere heterodoxy or schism and a "world religion" proper. It also suggests the extent to which, even after a given religious boundary became self-evident to scholars, popular literature could continue to unsettle it. The notion of reform, like the notion of heterodoxy, destabilizes the borderlines separating world religions.

The case of Rammohun Roy suggests a slightly different trajectory. Strikingly, Rammohun's 1833 English obituaries do not refer to him by what would later become his standard epithet: the "Bengalee Luther." He had been compared to Luther in the late 1810s, (including by Samuel Taylor Coleridge, who dubbed him the "Luther of Brahmanism").[95] But, as far as I can tell, the comparison did not become routine until long after his death. In the 1820s and 1830s, it was more common to refer to him as "the Hindoo Reformer."[96] During this period, I suspect that there were good reasons *not* to identify Rammohun too closely with Luther. To do so would have risked depicting him as a Christian convert, a public image that Rammohun was careful to avoid, partly out of concern that his conversion would disinherit his sons. Rammohun thus positioned himself as in solidarity with Luther, while also marking Luther as specifically Christian; in one letter, for example, he expresses his hope that his English and American Christian colleagues will be as successful as Luther in freeing their religion from "Roman power."[97] Luther is for Rammohun's friends, apparently, but not for him. Tellingly, as late as 1879, a biographer of Alexander Duff described Rammohun as a failed Luther, using that term to denote a person who converts India to Christianity. He laments that Rammohun did not meet Duff sooner so that "Eastern and Northern India might have been brought to Christ by a Bengalee Luther greater than their own Chaitunya."[98] Here, the author unquestioningly presumes that Luther and Chaitanya (the sixteenth-century Bengali Vaishnava saint, also occasionally compared to Luther in the 1860s and 1870s) are in opposite camps.

By 1879, however, this seems to have been a minority view. One reason for the shift was probably the changing status of the Brahmo Samaj, the society that Rammohun had founded in the 1820s, but which became far more prominent during the 1840s and 1850s thanks to the work of Debendranath Tagore. By 1870, it was plausible to claim that Rammohun had launched a "Reformation" that promised "the deliverance [of India] from Brahminism . . . through the spontaneous efforts of her own people."[99] The Brahmos, it seemed, had stepped into the conceptual space vacated by the Buddha: they were reforming Hinduism from within.

Rammohun's status as modern India's preeminent Luther was, however, apparently short-lived. Courting the image of a Christian convert, while identifying as a Hindu and criticizing Brahman priests, he brought the two senses of the "Indian Luther" together with remarkable ease—thus making him especially useful for those who would pry these two meanings apart. As theosophist Henry Steel Olcott remarked in 1879, the title of "the Luther of Modern India" had been "chiefly" bestowed on Rammohun, despite his having been "thoroughly a Christian convert"; "delicate and feminine," he was utterly unlike the "intensely masculine and combative" German. Sitting in Olcott's audience was the man whom he proposed as Rammohun's replacement: Swami Dayanand Saraswati. Like Luther, Dayanand sought to "re-establish the authority of the national sacred books, by stripping away the rubbish that selfish priests have adulterated and covered them with."[100] Olcott's direct transfer of the title of "Luther" from Rammohun to Dayanand indicates the semantic shift that was occurring more broadly: poised between conversion and reform during the first part of the century, by 1900 "Luther" had come to primarily denote the latter. Rammohun was a convenient pivot for this semantic turn.

This thumbnail genealogy is necessarily tentative, and I do not mean to suggest that there was ever a clean break from one Luther to the other: the convolutions in the above narrative demonstrate otherwise. Nonetheless, what I have been calling the "general" Luther does seem to have become the more common denotation of the phrase "the Luther of India" by around the 1880s or 90s. This general Luther was the icon for an equally generalized reformation that was, in principle, analytically separable from Christianity. In actuality, of course, this generalized reformation was shaped profoundly by Christianity as a normative model for what a religion should be. As Tomoko Masuzawa has shown, the now-standard roster of reified "world religions" was assuming its current form during the very decades that the second meaning of the "Luther of India" became dominant. As she suggests, all world religions had to pattern themselves on Christianity in order to become legible as religions.[101] This process established the crucial background condition for the generalization of reform: if all religions are fitted to the same Christian model, then any religion can play host to a Luther.

In separating the "general" from the "particular" Reformation, I suspect that nineteenth-century writers opened up a conceptual space that was later consolidated by twentieth-century social theorists like Max Weber (whose comparative project could be construed as a prolonged search for the "Indian Calvin" and his counterparts in China, the Islamic world, etc.). Still later in the twentieth century, this Weberian problematic was reframed by the social scientific scholarship on the "Protestantization" of Asian religions.[102] (In this later literature, arguably, the question of conversion recurs in an interesting way. By simulating Protestantism, religious reformers risk seeming like they have converted to Protestantism; or, perhaps more troublingly, they risk blurring religious boundaries by, in effect, converting an entire religion (Hinduism or Buddhism) to Protestant norms. It is indicative in this regard that the verb *to protestantize* initially denoted conversion to Christianity.[103])

I want to resist the implied teleology of this Protestantization narrative. At times, the narrative of Protestantization can seem almost mechanical: when we use it, we tend to assume not only that we know what "Protestantism" means, but also that Hindus and Buddhists who set about becoming Protestant are likely to succeed in doing so. In the late nineteenth century, however, the Protestant Reformation remained a highly contested cultural category, the boundaries of which were far from clear. Thus, it seems worth asking whether nineteenth-century efforts to generalize Luther and strip him of his historical particularity worked to undermine rather than reinforce the rhetoric of Protestant supremacy. Instead of assuming that Protestantism overdetermines all that it touches, constantly returning contemporary culture to Luther as master sign, it makes at least as much sense to assume that every citation of Luther is also a diversion of Luther—a performative perversion of a referent that it necessarily works to reimagine and reterritorialize.

By taking a detour away from Mill's *History of British India* to search for the Indian Luther, we have in fact followed through on one of the key questions posed by Mill's text. If India has not entered the fourth stage of civilization, it is because it has not yet found its Luther. If it had, it would already be populated by worldly ascetics—subjects who transpose their faith in sacerdotal authority to faith in the duties of daily life. Here again we find echoes of Charles Grant, who likewise insisted that only an "Indian counterpart of the European Reformation, capable of liberating the individual conscience from the tyranny of the priest" could change the "inner workings of the individual soul" such that India would be capable of self-government.[104] To liberate the subject from priestcraft is to submit the subject to self-government, putting the individual in charge of his own soul. Self-government becomes a form of religious asceticism. This approach to the topic of self-government has an obvious relevance to the history of modern Hinduism, at least as interpreted by M. K. Gandhi. It also, however, resonates with the history of liberalism in Britain, which was similarly preoccupied with questions of tutelage and ascetic detachment from the material world.

On Self-Government: Liberalism as Asceticism

For postcolonial critics, the most infamous passage in John Stuart Mill's *On Liberty* (1859) comes toward the beginning, when Mill clarifies that his treatise is "meant to apply only to human beings in the maturity of their faculties." Among adults, "the individual is sovereign." Among "children" and people in "those backward states of societies in which the race itself may be considered as in its nonage," however, "despotism is a legitimate mode of government" if its "end" is the "improvement" of the governed.[105] There can be little doubt of which "backward" society the younger Mill had most on his mind. For decades, he had been a clerk at the East India Company, resigning the post of Examiner only in 1858 when the Crown assumed direct rule of its colony. One year later, he published *On Liberty*.

Liberals like Mill were able to sustain their doubled commitment to political liberty and imperial domination through a rhetoric of deferral (liberty for all, but not yet). They thus structured empire as a pedagogic space, with racial difference reread as the difference between teacher and pupil.[106] Although a different logic prevailed earlier in the century, when liberal thinkers were some of the most vocal critics of empire, Mill's colonial pedagogy does foreground a key contradiction within liberal thought.[107] In her reading of this passage, political theorist Susan Mendus argues that it demonstrates how "liberalism must rely upon, yet cannot sustain, a distinction between the condition of autonomy and the development of autonomy."[108] Mill insists that the restrictions he places on liberty are temporal and local (once a child becomes an adult, she no longer requires tutelage); but, as Mendus suggests, this narrative implies an unsustainable notion of adulthood. Although liberalism celebrates a "heroic" subject, who stands confidently over his world to assert absolute independence from it, even Mill recognizes (as he puts it in *Utilitarian-*

ism) that this subjectivity is "a very tender plant." All subjects are at perpetual risk, Mendus explains, of "being rendered non-autonomous by the world," because autonomy "requires continuous and sustained support." If this is the case, however, then the restrictions that the younger Mill places on liberty cannot be said to be temporary. Political immaturity, or the need for tutelage, becomes the norm. Thus does the binary behind J. S. Mill's justification for empire unravel—colonizer and colonized are both children in need of perpetual schooling.

The ideal of autonomy implies a perpetual work upon the self that remains constitutively incomplete. Only through an active and ongoing disavowal or renunciation of the world, can the subject buffer himself against that world and its tutelary influences. Liberalism, as Amanda Anderson explains, "promotes an ethic of ongoing distance-taking from one's most intimate and meaningful cultural identifications."[109] The liberal knows that we are all mired in particularity, but works to set her particularity aside in the name of a general good. The result is the curiously doubled mode of being that Hadley describes as "abstract embodiment." The mid-Victorian liberal subject was asked to set his particularity aside, training himself to inhabit a position of generality, as through silently introspective procedures like that of devil's advocacy—which demands that the subject become his own opponent, restructuring interiority as a scene of self-agonism. Lived liberalism revolved around such techniques of the self, which grounded its "effort after detachment."[110]

When translated onto the global stage of imperial politics, as Uday Mehta argues, this liberal asceticism guaranteed a form of cultural violence. Where conservatives like Edmund Burke understood human subjects as constitutively embedded in their historically and culturally specific forms of life, liberals took human subjectivity as a tabula rasa, open to vastly ambitious programs of reeducation. For liberals, the life world is always "provisional," a set of contingent accreted customs that are rejected as shackles or restraints on the subject.[111] In this regard, James Mill was firmly of the liberal camp. As he quipped in the *History of British India*, Burke had "worked himself into an artificial admiration of the bare fact of existence; especially ancient existence. Everything was to be protected; not because it was good, but because it existed."[112] Mill, by contrast, hoped to overturn the "tyranny of the dead" so that he could reshape the world "according to the dictates of philosophic reason."[113] Passages like this one suggest the extent to which Mill's fulminations against Hinduism are directed against Britain. William Jones (Mill's Indophilic bogey) becomes a proxy for Burke: both fetishize tradition for its own sake.

To bracket "the bare fact of existence" is to open existence to the critical judgment of the reasoning individual. It is only by standing back from experience that the subject becomes autonomous from, and thus potentially critical of, her world. Mill presents himself as a paragon of just this sort of ascetic refusal. As he infamously claimed, "a man who is duly qualified may obtain more knowledge of India in one year in his closet in England than he could obtain in the course of the longest life, by the use of his eyes and ears in India."[114] Mill never traveled to the colony, and this audacious statement is a way of demoting the knowledge produced by those (like Jones) who might otherwise claim greater scholarly authority. But the statement also, as Sara Ahmed suggests, bears closely on Mill's stoical rejection of the sensory world. Later in the *History*, Mill describes the "first religion" as consisting of a primitive fetishism: just as the child attributes agency to the object that has hurt it, so the savage thinks that a "spirit resides in the storm."[115] That the child and the primitive are unable to stand back from objects is a mark of their immaturity. Mill, meanwhile, has just spent a year in his closet, immunized against this savage immersion in things. The "writing of the book," Ahmed argues, thus "becomes an object lesson in happiness, a way of appreciating things without being swayed by things."[116] Here, to be happy is to be closeted, sealed off from the world and the objects within it.

Discussions of liberal selfhood in colonial India have tended, with Mehta, to present this abstract individualism as complicit with empire. By stressing how self-abstraction functions as an embodied practice, Anderson and Hadley suggest a somewhat different approach. Rather than roundly dismissing liberalism's pretensions to abstract individuality, we find ourselves faced instead with the question of how liberal asceticism confronted other forms of asceticism in colonial India. Liberals were not the only people in colonial India subordinating the world to transcendent ideals. A variety of actors—Hindu, Muslim, Christian, and otherwise— were doing much the same. In other words, instead of equating religion to tradition (i.e., the organically accreted habitation of the subject that is disrupted by colonialism, capitalism, the state, etc.), we would do well to view it too as a disruptive force that can be used to rationalize and remake the world. Religious and secular asceticisms are not as different as one might think.

In the above, we have seen how James Mill's *History of British India* sits at the intersection of several seemingly discrete discursive fields. Tracing a series of concentric circles around this canonical text, I have considered its imbrication with missionary evangelicalism; Enlightenment atheism; the search for the spirit of the Reformation; and lived liberalism as a style of ascetic self-government. By situating Mill's *History* in this way, I have called attention to the shared theoretical framework that accrues around the notion of priestcraft. For the writers considered above, priestcraft denoted a highly diffuse mode of power that became nightmarishly absolute insofar it was able to integrate transcendent or extraneous rule with immanent or capillary government. At times, such writers imply that to displace the priest, the state would have to become like the priest; it would need to rule the soul. At other times, they herald the dawn of an allegedly new species of radically untutored subjectivity. The favorite metaphor for this allegedly spontaneous emergence was the Protestant Reformation—hence the search for the Indian Luther.

By opening *Spiritual Despots* with Mill, I mean to suggest modern Hindu thinkers' experiments in ascetic selfhood need to be read in transnational perspective, so that we can better see how they were reimagining Protestant and liberal norms. At the same time, I also mean to suggest that British thinkers like Mill need to be read in relation to India, which was essential to how they conceptualized self-rule. Whether in Britain or India, nineteenth-century theorists of priestcraft were shaped by the imperial encounter; they thus need to be studied contrapuntally.

TWO

A Popular History of Priestcraft in All Ages and Nations

Thus we have traversed the field of the world. We have waded through an ocean of priestly enormities. We have seen nations sitting in the blackness of darkness because their priests shut up knowledge in the dark-lanterns of their selfishness. . . . . We have listened to sighs and the dropping of tears, to the voice of despair, and the agonies of torture and death; we have entered dungeons, and found their captives wasted to skeletons with the years of their solitary endurance, we have listened to their faint whispers, and have found that they uttered the cruelties of priests. . . . All this we have beheld, and what is the mighty lesson it has taught? It is this—that if the people hope to enjoy happiness, mutual love, and general prosperity, they must carefully snatch from the hands of their spiritual teachers all political power and confine them solely to their legitimate task of Christian instruction. WILLIAM HOWITT, *A POPULAR HISTORY OF PRIESTCRAFT IN ALL AGES AND NATIONS* (1833)

William Howitt's *A Popular History of Priestcraft in All Ages and Nations* (1833) ferries its reader from Indian temples to Druid circles, from snowy Siberia to tropical Africa, stopping off in sundry other exotic climes (Assyria, Egypt, America, Greece) before returning home to England to rail against that nation's established church and its allegedly corrupt priestly class. By cataloguing "the basest frauds" and "the most shameless delusions" ever perpetuated under the name of religion, Howitt aims "to shew that priestcraft in all ages and all nations has been the same; that its nature is one, and that nature essentially evil."[1] The *Popular History* signals an important transitional moment in the genealogy of "religion" and related discourses. The book draws on the human sciences that emerged in the eighteenth century and points the way to the comparative study of religion that would fully emerge later in the nineteenth. Writing over local difference in order to render its notion of priestcraft universal, it draws on Protestant and Enlightenment discourses about religious imposture, while resituating those discourses within the intellectual and political world of the early nineteenth century.

Howitt (1792–1879) had been born to a comfortably bourgeois Quaker family in provincial Derbyshire, moving from rural Heanor to industrial Nottingham in 1822 after marrying his "best friend, truest companion," and fellow Quaker Mary Botham (1799–1888) the previous year.[2] A decade later, the aspiring literary couple began to find fame—Mary for such enduringly popular works as the children's poem "The Spider and the Fly" (1834), a parable of predatory male sexuality; William for the inflammatory *History of Priestcraft*, which piqued the interest of Nottingham's political radicals at a moment when this lace and textile manufacturing town was literally ablaze with reformist sentiment. One biographer aptly describes William and Mary as "Victorian samplers."[3] They dabbled in Romantic poetry, Quaker politics, church reform, the antislavery movement, anticolonialism, nature writing, children's books, feminism, Swedish literature, copyright law, spiritualist séances, and, in the final years of their lives, Roman Catholicism. They could boast of having befriended, or at least lunched with, luminaries as eclectic as William Wordsworth, Charles Dickens, Lucretia Mott, Frederick Douglas, D. D. Home, John Ruskin, Elizabeth Barrett Browning, Harriet Beecher Stowe, and Dante Gabriel Rossetti. Mary even met the Pope. Between the two of them, they authored more than one hundred and eighty books that went into more than seven hundred editions. Mary (who remains the better known of the two) was the first English translator of Hans Christian Andersen. Citations of William's work, meanwhile, crop up in landmarks of nineteenth-century thought as varied as Henry David Thoreau's "Life without Principle" (1863), Karl Marx's *Capital* (1867) and Emma Hardinge Britten's *Modern American Spiritualism* (1870).[4] The Howitts, in short, were paradigmatic vectors of nineteenth-century reform culture, interlacing poetry, politics, and religion in a shared body of work that demonstrates the "promiscuous alliances" that interlinked otherwise discrepant cultural fields at this time.[5] The horizontal and vertical linkages that they so energetically established over the course of their forty-plus year career are characteristic of what I describe in the next chapter as the nineteenth-century reform assemblage.

Despite its apparent incoherence, William Howitt's career demonstrates a surprisingly sustained engagement with a single problematic first visible in his work in 1833–34, the period of the *Popular History of Priestcraft*. In these years, Howitt wrote two essays on George Fox (1624–1691), the founder of the Society of Friends. The first, published in a small Quaker annual, extolled Fox's saintly deeds in hagiographic style. The second, appearing in *Tait's Magazine* after the publication of the *History of Priestcraft*, reworked this hagiography through a narrative of Quaker decline.[6] Howitt was highly critical of his Quaker contemporaries. They had, as he wrote, "abandoned the bold and innovating spirit . . . of their ancestors. . . . The effervescence of their first zeal has evaporated with time; and as the spirit has escaped, they have clung more closely to the letter."[7] Howitt firmly rejected Quaker "peculiarities" of speech and dress, including the use of the informal pronoun "thou." Here, couching his critique in distinctly Pauline language, he sets out to displace the empty legalism of these customs with a rejuvenated Quaker "spirit."

The Howitts drifted steadily away from the Society of Friends after 1833, although they did not resign officially until over a decade later, in 1847. Even after leaving the letter of Quakerism behind, however, William Howitt continued to search for (and to find) its spirit elsewhere: in Romantic poetry; in radical politics; in communion with the dead; and, perhaps most surprisingly, in Roman Catholicism. As I will argue, Howitt's effort to decouple the spirit and the letter of Quakerism can be read as a response to the political impasse that he met with in 1833. Recent shifts in the state's policy of tolerance toward religious minorities had substantially circumscribed the ability of religious groups to mount an effective critique of state power or, at least, to do so in terms that were explicitly marked as "religious." By defining religious dissent as constitutively apolitical, secular governmentality prompted the relocation of dissent to other cultural fields. Howitt's long career as novelist, poet, essayist, travel writer, amateur naturalist, magazine editor, German translator, and spiritualist proselytizer should thus be understood as an effort to reimagine dissent for the nineteenth century by blurring the line between religion and culture.

In my discussion of Howitt, I argue for the pliability of "the Protestant" in Victorian Britain, asking how Protestantism was put under pressure from within England and with an expressly English set of concerns at roughly the same time that it was also being rethought from the colonial margins. Even (and perhaps especially) in the metropolitan center of imperial power, Protestantism was not an uncontested discursive property, nor was the Reformation a neatly reified historical event and exportable module of modernization. To see Protestantism (much less "Protestantization") as a discrete and tidy entity, one almost had to be standing in India.

By making this argument, I seek to temper what has become a dominant mode of critique within the field of religious studies. "Protestant bias," as a generation of scholars has demonstrated, severely constrained the Anglophone nineteenth century's ability to imagine religion. As important as this critique has been, my concern is that in learning to unmask the Protestant presuppositions of nineteenth-century texts, we have at times neglected the extent to which those texts, rather than being passive carriers of Protestant norms, were in fact working actively to reimagine those norms. Thus, my purpose here is not to suggest that all of Howitt's literary output was indelibly, uniformly, or insidiously "Protestant." Rather, I claim that Howitt's career disentangled and recombined the several vectors that composed Victorian Protestantism in ways that challenged the integrity of Protestantism as a discrete cultural category. "Throughout life," wrote his daughter Anna, William Howitt "gloried to walk in the footsteps of Fox."[8] In emulating his Quaker predecessor, Howitt hoped to recuperate the spirit of early modern religious dissent. But repetition implied difference: to walk in the footsteps of Fox was, inevitably, to point those footsteps in new directions. Instead of following these tracks back to their presumed Protestant origin, I trace their generative dispersion.

My analysis of Howitt opens with his *Popular History of Priestcraft*, which I take as working through a proto-Foucauldian theory of pastoral power. By reading the *Popular History* alongside Howitt's essays on George Fox from the same period, I suggest that Howitt presents the category of the "Protestant" as figuring a tension between spiritual heteronomy and spiritual autonomy. Next, I turn from Howitt's writings of the early 1830s to their historical context. I follow Howitt from Nottingham to London, where he met with Prime Minister Grey in order to challenge the established Church of England. Circling this encounter, I use it to sketch a short genealogy of the secular state's policy of tolerance toward religion. The history of the Quakers, I suggest, encapsulates the history of privatized religion (and its complement, state secularism) in remarkably succinct form, providing a metonym for larger cultural shifts that took place between the seventeenth and nineteenth centuries. The Quakers thus provide a useful site for rethinking the privatized form of religious subjectivity associated with the secular state. The Quaker notion of the "inner light" can be read as reinforcing the boundaries of the discrete individual by locating the essence of religious selfhood in private experience. Alternately, it can be read as de-privatizing the self: by splitting the subject, and rendering it heteronomic, the inner light opens the self out into the disciplinary community. It is this latter reading that I explore here.

Over the course of his career, I argue, Howitt experimented with various methods for re-politicizing the inner light as a means of opening the individual toward the collective. I conclude the chapter by discussing Howitt's brief foray into anticolonial critique. Where his experiments with the inner light disrupted the norms of secular subjectivity, I suggest, his proposals for a more "moral" empire reinforced the ascendant logic of colonial governmentality.

The Shape of a Priest

"This unfortunate world has been blasted in all ages by two evil principles— Kingcraft and Priestcraft." The "horrors" of the first "are on the face of every nation" and its historians "countless." Its "sister-pest," meanwhile, remains obscure. In fact, writes William Howitt, "I do not know that there has been one man who has devoted himself solely and completely to the task of tracing its course of demoniacal devastation."[9] Hence the need for Howitt's own *Popular History*. By bringing political and ecclesiastical history into a single frame of analysis, Howitt claims to offer a "clear and complete picture" of priestcraft as a distinctive mode of power that operates in the interstices between religion and politics. It works "conjointly" with kingcraft: "the two evil powers have ever been intimately united in their labours."[10]

Howitt's *Popular History of Priestcraft* demonstrates a double allegiance to the twin anticlerical legacies of Reformation and Enlightenment— indicated by its allusions to the Quaker George Fox on the one hand and the Deist Charles Blount (1654–1693) on the other (the title of Blount's book *Great Is Diana of the Ephesians* becomes an anticlerical rallying cry in Howitt's *History*).[11] By granting India pride of place in its narrative, the text also demonstrates its entanglement with nineteenth-century anticlerical concerns. As Howitt explains, India is the land where priestcraft is "at once in full flower and full fruit; in that state at which it has always aimed, but never, not even in the bloody reign of the Papal church, attained elsewhere." It provides a "marvelous spectacle" for the student of priestcraft, with "millions on millions bound, from the earliest ages to the present hour, in the chains of the most slavish and soul-quelling castes, and in the servility of a religious creed so subtilly framed that it almost makes hopeless the moral regeneration of the swarming myriads of these vast regions."[12] In others' hands, such claims directly influenced the emerging "moral mission" of empire. Howitt's eyes, however, were set firmly on Britain: his world tour is a weapon wielded against the Anglican Church.

The *Popular History*'s globalism is nonetheless significant for Howitt in that it positions "priestcraft" as a universal principle of power that can be analytically separated from any one of its empirical manifestations. Only by demonstrating that priestcraft is universal, Howitt implies, can it be brought clearly into view. By Howitt's account, priestly power is both highly diffuse and highly centralized. Priests, he writes, have "a thousand arts to rivet their power into the souls of the people."[13] Like the frogs that plagued Egypt, they "came up and covered the earth; they crept into every dwelling; into the very beds and kneading tubs." Tucked into the most intimate recesses of the body politic, the priests also stand "ready to communicate the earliest symptoms of insubordination to the papal tyranny."[14] Priests are everywhere, and they are organized into a power structure with a clear head or apex: the Pope. It is this doubled structure (absolute diffusion and absolute centralization) that lends the priestcraft narrative its nightmarish appeal as a model for how power works. This is, no doubt, a fantasy: the field of capillary power, radically decentered, is seldom if ever controlled in its entirety by a single sovereign figure. Its very granularity makes such control all but impossible. Nonetheless, precisely as a fantasy, the priestcraft narrative allows writers like Howitt to make certain analytic distinctions with particular clarity.

As Howitt argues, the suffix "-craft" indicates the "selfish cunning" that "perverts" an office by turning it "into a mischievous machine to secure the base ends of individuals or of a party."[15] To contrast bad and good government, Howitt distinguishes between "kingcraft" and "kinghood." Rather than enriching himself, the good king seeks to maximize the happiness of his subjects. The crafty king, on the other hand, subordinates the ruled to the ruler; he begins "at the wrong end of things" by acting as though the state "was not made for man, but man for it."[16] Much the same distinction holds for priests. Like kingcraft, priestcraft implies a "system of domination in the few, and slavery in the multitude."[17] Priest*hood*, on the other hand, seeks the good of the souls under its guidance. In both cases, the end of crafty power is internal to itself; the end of good government is internal to the things that it directs. Here we see how Howitt, as a nineteenth-century theorist of priestcraft, anticipates one of the key distinctions drawn by Michel Foucault in his much later writings on priestly power.[18]

The metaphor with which Howitt begins his *Popular History* anticipates the book's two major arguments. Until priestcraft's "hydra heads are crushed," writes Howitt, "there can be no perfect liberty" on earth.[19] We have seen the hydra metaphor before, in a *Missionary Register* article of 1832. In Howitt's 1833 book the metaphor serves much the same function as in that contemporary publication. There is no use in striking down individual priests, Howitt implies. In order to eliminate priestcraft, the critic must do war with the "principle," or the body of the hydra. This, presumably, is what the *Popular History* is meant to do. Despite being written as a survey of the empirical manifestations of the priest "in all ages and nations," its target is the abstract principle that ostensibly undergirds them.

Of course, priests from all ages and nations are not the same, nor are they controlled by a single master subject. In his better moments, Howitt seems to realize this. The "whole course of this volume," he says, "has shown that this wily spirit has conformed itself to circumstances." In hunting the "the spirit of priestcraft," the critic must expect to find it every time "in a different shape."[20] If Howitt fails to take his own advice, this is because, for him, the "shape" of the priest had in fact already been fixed—determined for all time in the seventeenth century. As the 1834 essay on "George Fox and His First Disciples" indicates, Howitt's anticlericalism was very much a part of his effort to recuperate the lost spirit of the early Quakers. The essay recounts the story of how the young Fox came to true Christianity. Fox's conversion to God began during long hours working alone as an agricultural laborer. "Taught, as the bulk of people are, and ever have been, not to depend upon their own inquiries, but to lean upon somebody in the shape of a priest," Fox decided to visit several neighborhood ministers to learn more about Christianity. These ministers proved less virtuous than Fox had hoped. One recommended that he chew tobacco. Another yelled at him when he stepped on his flowerbeds. Sorely disappointed, Fox retreated to the seclusion of a hollow tree with his copy of the New Testament. Alone at last, he found God.[21]

Howitt explicitly politicizes this tale of emergence from priestly tutelage. It is because Quakers believe in the "civil and religious freedom of all men" that they abhor "tyranny, political or ecclesiastical, in the shape of the despot or priest."[22] The modern democratic revolutions may have neutralized the first of the twin threats; but they had not, Howitt suggests, sufficiently addressed the second. There could be no real freedom so long as the Anglican Church continued to wield authority over Britain.

In trying to revive the spirit of Fox for the nineteenth century, however, Howitt made a crucial mistake. He failed to appreciate how the British state had changed since the seventeenth century: the shift toward "good government" as the dominant idiom of power was already well underway. Howitt realized that state policies of religious tolerance had changed the Quakers; he did not, however, question whether his theory of priestcraft needed to be reworked to account for these changes.

Secularism and the Politics of Dissent

If Howitt's *Popular History of Priestcraft* diagnosed the relations of religious
and secular power as that of the twin oppressions of king and priest, it
did so at a time when the relations of sovereignty implied by those terms
were rapidly changing. In 1828, the Test and Corporation Acts, which had
placed legal disabilities on religious minorities since the late seventeenth
century, were repealed. This was followed in 1829 by the "emancipation"
of Catholics. As Gauri Viswanathan suggests, these reforms, more than
simply an extension of liberal "tolerance," were a means of assimilating
minorities into a national body now organized around "Englishness"
rather than Anglicanism. Under the new system, religious difference was
to be simultaneously effaced and retained. Religious minorities were to
be refigured, in Viswanathan's formula, as non-Jewish Jews, non-Catholic
Catholics, non-dissenting Dissenters, non-noncomforming Noncon-
formists, and so forth.[23] For Howitt, who thought that even the 1689 Act
of Toleration had done too much to incorporate the Quaker minority into
the national body, thereby muffling their radical "effervescence," the new
reforms presented both a significant problem and a significant opportu-
nity. On the one hand, further assimilation of Quakers would also further
remove them from the critical spirit of George Fox. On the other, the destabilizing conjuncture produced by these legislative changes constituted
a possible moment of maneuver for the Quakers. Especially during the
heady days that followed the passage of the Reform Bill of 1832, it seemed
like it might finally have become possible to realize one of Quakerism's
oldest hopes: the disestablishment of the Church of England. As Howitt
later reflected: "If any one will look back to the period between the passing
of the Reform Bill and the end of 1836, he will now observe with surprise
the high state of excitement" with which both the people and the Parliament discussed "the question of church reform."[24]

During the three fiery months in late 1832 when William wrote his *History of Priestcraft*, Mary assured her sister that he would "treat moderately,
comparatively speaking, the subject of priesthood in the present day; that
is, he will war with the principle, and not with the men."[25] But the book,
ardently polemic, proved her wrong. By Howitt's account, the established
Church was not only unfair to Irish Catholics and English dissenters, who
were taxed to support it. It was even bad for Anglicans. It strangled Oxford
and Cambridge with sinecures and foisted the sluggard nephews of the
rich onto parishes already overburdened with corrupt, useless pastors.

The book's comparativist chapters were even harsher. As the Howitts' biographer, Carl Woodring, summarizes, Howitt sought "to demonstrate that phallic, bacchanalian, and similar orgiastic idolaters had direct descendants in the Anglican clergy."[26] The book was, in other words, not calculated to make friends—and indeed it lost the Howitts several.

When Quaker leaders gathered in London in 1833 for their yearly meeting, they reviewed a prospectus of Howitt's *History* and decided to denounce it as a "libelous work" that Friends would be "cautioned" not to read. Mary thought that this was just as well. Their disapproval "would in reality do the book good, the very caution inflaming curiosity and attracting attention to it." George Fox and William Penn, she suggested, would have liked her husband's book very much. If modern Quakers did not, the fault did not lie with William. "Friends," she wrote in a letter of June 1833, "have adopted a more timid policy in these days, and are more inclined to concede to the powers that be than stand boldly opposed to them."[27] Despite the Friends' censure, however, the *History of Priestcraft* proved as popular as its title had forecast. Two editions sold out in the first six months, with three more and an American reprint to follow by 1834.[28] Critical notice veered between the adulatory (the *Athenaeum* compared Howitt's "eloquence" to the "prose of Milton") and the outraged—one reviewer dismissed the book as nothing but a "wretched farrago of audacious falsehoods."[29]

The book's notoriety catapulted Howitt to prominence among Nottingham radicals. The city had been a manufacturing center since the eighteenth century, and its large working-class population made it a major site of urban unrest during the nineteenth. In 1832, when the Earl of Nottingham voted with other members of the House of Lords to block the Reform Bill, the good people of Nottingham torched his castle. William viewed the towering inferno from afar and wrote a widely reprinted account of the event that indicates acute distress at the violence of the angry mob. Little attests to Howitt's own bourgeois upbringing quite as vividly as the image of him standing atop his privately owned roof watching factory workers burn an aristocrat's French-style villa.[30] But despite his reservations, William's populist sympathies soon brought him into alignment with the fiery mob. Before the publication of the *History of Priestcraft* William had, by Mary's account, "lived in great privacy in Nottingham"; after the book's publication, "the Radical portion of the population now claimed him as their champion."[31] In 1835, William was elected a Nottingham city alderman "against his will" as a representative of the "Radical party."[32] During his political tenure, he was a passionate advocate for causes as diverse as the rights of the Irish and the appropriation of aristocratic lands for public parks. He longed, however, to return to his literary pursuits. As he wrote in an 1836 letter, "it is my fate to be dragged into public botheration, and I shall never be free from it till I am free of Nottingham."[33] By 1840, he had left home for the literary limelight of London.

I want to focus attention on a single moment in this brief political career. In January 1834, Howitt led a delegation to London to petition Prime Minister Earl Grey for the full disestablishment of the Church of England. In a letter written that month, Mary described how Lord Grey, after reading the petition, expressed his regret at the "sweeping measures" proposed therein, which could only "embarrass the Ministers, alarm both Houses of Parliament, and startle the country." It would have been better, the Prime Minister opined, had the delegates "confined themselves to the removal of those disabilities connected with marriage, burial, registration, and such matters, for on these heads there existed, both in himself and his colleagues, every disposition to relieve them." Surely they could not "want entirely to do away with all establishment of religion." Howitt responded in no uncertain terms that that "was precisely what they desired." "People," he assured the sneering earl, "are not so easily frightened at changes nowadays."[34]

This is a curious interaction. Howitt, downright woozy with reformist zeal, seems actually to believe that full disestablishment is right around the corner. Earl Grey, meanwhile, appears almost amused at the outlandish proposal put forward by this misguided band of provincial radicals.[35] Politically impossible, it was also, arguably, beside the point. Modern techniques for managing religious difference—tolerance as governmentality, we might say, following Wendy Brown—had already begun to obviate the need for disestablishment.[36] As responsibility for the governance of the English "souls" was transferred from the Church of England to the idea of Englishness itself, the Church lost at least one of its political functions, its pastoral role having been subsumed, at least in part, by secular governmentality.

The sort of shift implicit here is more overt in a concurrent and closely related development in colonial India. As Viswanathan suggests, it is no coincidence that the British hit upon the English literary canon as a means of producing Englishness in India at roughly the same time that they lifted religious disabilities at home. Not only did the same players, including Thomas Macaulay, help frame policy in both places; the structures of subjectivation in colony and metropole were remarkably parallel. The so-called "Macaulay men," "Indian in blood and colour, but English in taste, in opinions, in morals, and in intellect," were meant to become, in effect, non-Indian Indians—and perhaps, still more specifically, non-Hindu Hindus and non-Muslim Muslims.[37] Both English and not, they were the colonial analogues of England's newly reconstituted religious minorities.

As Viswanathan argues, the Englishness that governed souls in one way in India did so in a different, but related, way in Britain. Consider, for example, the implications of Lord Grey's request that Howitt accept the "removal of disabilities" as sufficient recognition of Quakers by the state. Quakers are invited to assume a form of minority identity that would grant them full participation in national political life, even while allowing them to retain a sense of religious difference. But such inclusion comes at a cost. The Quakers would have to suppress some of their most dearly held convictions, including their disdain for the established church. The legal recognition of religious minorities thus provisionally resolves the problem of dissent by neutralizing dissent's substance. Privatized and reified as "belief," Quaker convictions are reduced to merely formal significance, their content rendered inert: what constitutes the minority as minority is the simple fact of divergent belief, not the substance of that belief. In this framework, inwardly held belief is precisely what mediates between the subject and the state. The religious minority qualifies for public protection insofar as it can circumscribe its normative claims on the public good within the privatized domain of a faith reduced to a marker of group identity, and thus a signifier of the tolerant state's protection. Holding a religious belief in such a context is less a means of expressing an unmediated, pre-political inner self than of producing the self precisely through the medium of "belief" as a legal, or public, practice. Howitt's Quakers thus become, in Viswanathan's phrase, a community of "non-dissenting Dissenters," or dissenters who inadvertently uphold the norms of governance precisely by dissenting from them.

Neutralizing religious dissent had, of course, long been the explicit end of tolerance as a political technology. In his *Letter Concerning Toleration* (1689), John Locke maintains that "it is not the diversity of opinions (which cannot be avoided), but the refusal of toleration to those that are of different opinions (which might have been granted) that has produced all the bustles and wars that have been in the Christian world upon account of religion." Religion, not an inherently fractious topic, had been rendered so by the state's woeful lack of managerial savvy. The best way to defang dissent is to tolerate it, and thus to institute a strict separation between church and state. Each must "contain itself within its own bounds": the state will attend to "the worldly welfare of the commonwealth," the church to "the salvation of souls." Their respective domains guaranteed by the borderline dividing the "inner" life from the "outer," the spiritual and the political are securely partitioned so that there can be no "discord" between them.[38]

Locke, the theorist of liberal subjectivity, thus predicates the political regime of "toleration" on a particular model of the believing subject—a subject immunized against the external world insofar as she is defined as a self-contained and autonomous individual in full control of her beliefs. Brown summarizes Locke's move here as the "privatization, individualization, and subjectivization of religious belief": "Tolerance of diverse beliefs in a community becomes possible to the extent that those beliefs are phrased as having no public importance; as being constitutive of a private individual whose private beliefs and commitments have minimal bearing on the structure and pursuits of political, social, or economic life."[39] This may well be a slanted reading of Locke—a thinker whose liberalism, as Elizabeth Pritchard has shown, grew out of his political theology and who never actually insisted that religion be privatized; in fact, the *Letter Concerning Toleration* works to convert religion into a type of public speech that can circulate more freely across bodies.[40] Even so, I do think that it makes sense to situate Locke in relation to the privatized model of the believing subject that gained ground, however diffusely or unevenly, in the seventeenth century. This model of the believing subject was as much Protestant as it was liberal. Locke likely owed his sense that inward conviction is the essence of religion to his own Calvinist upbringing.[41] In this, he was not so far from his Quaker contemporaries. The young George Fox provides a resonant figure in this regard: tucked into the hollow of a tree, reading the Bible in solitude, he is a paradigmatic liberal-Protestant subject. Whether this subject was ever as buffered against the world as is sometimes claimed is a question that I return to below, where I argue (in sympathy with Pritchard's reading of Locke) that it implied new forms of community.

By the nineteenth century, in any case, the liberal state had, as Brown suggests, learned that it could tolerate religion so long as religion phrased its beliefs as having no public importance. Howitt's belief in disestablishment was not of this kind, because it pertained to a public institution. Had Howitt succeeded in eliminating the established church, of course, this would have resulted in an even more thoroughgoing privatization of religion. What I want to suggest, however, is that the seemingly exceptional moment of Howitt's appearing before Earl Grey reveals an otherwise occluded norm: privatized belief remains addressed to and predicated on public institutions.

The persistence of the Church of England even in an era when secular modes of governance were beginning to supersede its pastoral function attests to the uneven articulation of secularist ideals in different national contexts. Not yet a vestigial anachronism, the Church of the 1830s nonetheless found itself caught between two very different political logics. Howitt's miscalculation in demanding disestablishment suggests the ambiguous situation of the Church at this moment and the two mutually contradictory modes of belief implicitly invited by the British state, the one gloriously publicized and the other diligently privatized. It was the latter model that Lord Grey invoked when he requested that Howitt set disestablishment aside by submitting to the removal of disabilities.

Of course, precisely in their ability to dictate the contours of belief, the bylaws of toleration violate one of their own founding principles: the strict separation of "inner" and "outer" life. This, it will be recalled, is also the principle at the heart of the separation of church and state— whereas the former governs the soul, the latter manages the collective welfare of the "commonwealth," or population. In its foundational move (the privatization, individualization, and subjectivization of religious belief) tolerance as a political technology operates more in the mode of the church than the state. It governs souls (telling them how, but not what, to believe) as a means of securing the "worldly welfare" of the population. This is what Brown describes as tolerance-as-governmentality. Tolerance works by establishing a series of correspondences among different levels or sites of governance. Individuals, churches, and states are all, in a sense, analogous. Each must exercise tolerance, developing techniques and habits for regulating aversion and respecting difference; and each can, presumably, borrow techniques developed at one register in this series and adapt them for application at another. In short, and in flat contradiction of Locke's claim that "the care of the soul does not belong to the magistrate," tolerance-as-governmentality establishes "the soul" (or, at least, subjectivity) as a primary site for the articulation of secular rule. Here, the secular state is included within the "interior" space of religious subjectivity as its constitutive limit. So configured, religious interiority is necessarily unstable, teetering between the public and the private—it being precisely its inherent instability that makes it culturally and politically productive.

Simply reviving the early modern anticlericalism of George Fox was not an effective means of critiquing these new forms of governance, not least because of Fox's clear affinity for Locke. Howitt's effort to rethink the species of inward-looking religious subjectivity that undergirded the state's posture of tolerance was thus potentially more politically productive than his direct challenge to the established church. Precisely because the state acted as priest, governing how its subjects understood their relationship to religious belief, it became possible to modulate state power by questioning the privatization of religion—a privatization that, in the Quaker case, centered on the notion of the "inner light."

Communities of Spirit

"It is because I am religious that I feel myself compelled, irresistibly compelled, to be also political."[42] In voicing this political compulsion in his 1835 speech "Politics Inseparable from Christianity," delivered in Nottingham, William Howitt suggests the extent to which the early modern project of disentangling religion and politics had succeeded by this time. Had they not seemed obviously separate to his audience, Howitt would not have pleaded for their inextricability.

Howitt's speech, I suggest, shows how the genealogy of secularism found succinct expression among the Quakers and the problems confronting them in the early nineteenth century. As a religious group that emerged in the seventeenth century—roughly concurrent with the most canonical early articulations of church-state separation—the Quakers came to conceptualize religion in a manner more or less symbiotic with secular modes of governance. They did this partly by invoking much older Christian theological discourses; Quakers were especially fond of the biblical injunction to "be subject unto the higher powers," with its implied division between the temporal and the spiritual, or "Caesar" and "Christ."[43] Quakerism and Lockean secularism are thus both predicated on a sharp demarcation of the inner, spiritual life as distinct from the outer, political life. (So is the modern concept "religion," also arguably a product of the seventeenth century.) Early Quakers demonstrated a consistent affinity for the Lockean minimalist state. In the North American settler colony of Pennsylvania, they eventually established a government on the Lockean model.[44] In England, they tended to withdraw from political affairs, becoming increasingly quietist by the late eighteenth century.

Howitt disapproved of this quietism. "There are those," he proclaimed in his 1835 speech, "who think that religion consists in cultivating certain inward feelings" and who warn "against indulging in politics, as if it were some *sinful* indulgence, like swearing or gin drinking." Politics, they say, will "disturb the serenity of our minds" and "unfit us for religious meditation." Howitt insists that this "inward" form of religion is not "the *Christian* religion" (emphasis original). "A religion of inward feelings is a religion of monks, let its votaries call themselves what they will. The religion of Christ led him out into the highways and hedges, into the streets and marketplaces."[45] Rejecting the foundational distinction between public and private that gave rise to secularism and Quakerism alike, Howitt suggests that, for Quakers, this distinction is necessarily linked to the distinction between the worldly and the otherworldly. As a founding discourse of secular modernity, the command to "render unto Caesar" entails not just the accession to secular rule, but also the renunciation of the world and its immanent goods. Secularism, by this account, is born as much of religion's ascetic abnegation of the political as of the state's tolerant circumscription of religion. The two arose in tandem, each the negative face of the other. By 1835, Howitt seems to have abandoned the project of disestablishing the Anglican Church. Nonetheless, it is clear that by resisting the privatization of religion, he also resists a fundamental precondition of secular governmentality and liberal selfhood.

Howitt explicitly engages the history of this form of subjectivity in his two essays on George Fox. As he explains, the intolerant despotism of the Stuart period provoked an the "orgasm of intellectual intoxication" that subsided once the "boundaries of religious liberty" came to be "better defined." After the passage of the Toleration Act, a "transition" of a "most sedative nature" overtook Quakers, Baptists, Independents, and Presbyterians, such that "no contrast can be greater" than the one between the Dissenters of "that day and this." Today's Quakers, Howitt complains, are "a people submissive to good government, a people unworldly in their appearance, but worldly in their substance."[46] Where Fox had refused to make any "concession to the spirit of the world," less ardent men had "endeavored to bend christianity [sic] down to themselves; to contract it to their own size." The "law of Christ," Howitt insists, is "a literal and unbending law" to which "the world must bow, ere the standard of human virtue is reared to its intended height."[47] It is the principle of reform that bends the world toward its divine potential. Although clearly directed at Quaker bankers and businessmen, Howitt's discussion implies that economic self-interest was not the primary factor in making the Quakers worldly. The rise of tolerance, or good government, had blunted the Friends' dissenting spirit, demonstrating the complicity of inward religion with secular strategies of rule. For Howitt, rethinking the religion of "inward feelings" thus became a means of rethinking secularism.

In the Quaker context, such "feelings" meant something specific. The "inward Light" was a longstanding pillar of Quaker theology that, in the years preceding Howitt's speech, had begun to wobble. The controversial notion that the inner light was more authoritative than scripture, popularized by charismatic preacher Elias Hicks (1748–1830), prompted a schism in the Philadelphia meeting that, by the end of 1828, resulted in the "Great Separation" of American Quakers into two major denominations. Where the Hicksites championed the inner light, "orthodox" Quakers (influenced by English Evangelicalism) defended the priority of scripture. British Quakers mostly rejected the Hicksite heresy, but, in their effort to suppress the schism, they also provoked other secessions. In 1835, Isaac Crewdson (1780–1844) published *A Beacon to the Society of Friends*, which denounced Hicks and described the inner light as a "great deception." Soon, the "Beaconites" were added to the list of schismatics. Meanwhile, John Joseph Gurney (1788–1847) promoted a compromise position that emphasized both scripture and the inner light, while clearly subordinating the latter to the former. The result was yet another sect: the "Gurneyites."[48] The numbers of people involved in these schisms may have been small, but for a community of English Quakers numbering only fourteen thousand at its first census, even three hundred seceding Beaconites seemed a substantial loss.[49] The theological issues at stake were, moreover, significant. Too great a drift in either direction risked collapsing Quakerism's distinctive culture into mainstream British Protestantism on the one side or rationalist deism on the other. Howitt's writings of the 1830s are clearly of this moment. The Howitts had been friendly with Gurney in the 1820s, and his evangelical fervor seems to have recruited them to the cause of reform.[50] Mary was solidly evangelical. William had strong Hicksites proclivities, evident in his abiding interest in the inner light.

To get a better sense of how the inner light was understood in the early nineteenth century, we can turn to Thomas Clarkson's *Portraiture of Quakerism* (1806)—a book known to both Howitts and admired by Mary's father, Samuel Botham. Clarkson, a leading abolitionist who admired the Quakers' unyielding opposition to slavery, wrote his *Portraiture* so that non-Quakers like himself could learn more about the Society of Friends. His semi-ethnographic account offers an especially clear and thorough exposition of the Friends' major customs and beliefs. Clarkson explains the inner light as follows: "When the Almighty created the Universe," he "gave to Man . . . a spiritual faculty, or a portion of the life of his own Spirit to reside within him." Adam's rebellion compromised this inborn "spiritual feeling," but as part of his promise that sin would someday be "subdued," God "poured" a "certain portion of his own Spirit" into Adam for the "regulation" of his "spiritual conduct." A "portion of that Light" persists in Adam's progeny and continues to "enlighteneth every man that cometh into the world," allowing the human person "to hold a heavenly intercourse with his Maker."[51] Three major features of the inner light are evident in this description. First, it enables communication between the human and the divine. Second, it institutes a procedure of discipline that subdues sin so that postlapsarian humanity can recoup its original proximity to God (thus recalling a longer history of Christian theological reflection on spiritual "reform").[52] Third, the inner light abstracts the human person from external networks of religious guidance by insisting that the only true guide is located inside the subject. It is "the only infallible guide to men in their spiritual concerns."[53] By the 1830s, such a claim might have seemed overly Hicksite. Even so, it suggests the importance of spiritual autonomy as Quaker ideal.

While the doctrine of the inner light might appear to privatize religion, thus reinforcing the norms of secular governance, it also calls the coherence of the private individual into question. The light can only release the person from external networks of spiritual guidance by instituting a parallel procedure *within* the individual soul. The "good Spirit takes possession" of humanity; it "resides in their hearts, becomes the mover, enlightener, and director of all their faculties and powers."[54] Quaker self-discipline consists in submission to an indwelling divine spirit that secures individual autonomy through subjective rupture: the Quaker ascetic is other unto her self, and it is her aliveness to the "guide" inside her that constitutes her as an ascetic (which is to say, self-disciplined or self-guiding) subject. The reform of conduct unfurls from the heteronomy of the ascetic soul.

If self is a form of society, then it is fitting that religious introspection was thought to develop best when thoroughly embedded in a community. George Fox taught "that every Christian was bound to watch over another for his [the other's] good." The community would guarantee the "moral conduct of the individuals" that comprised it through constant "vigilance."[55] If one Friend erred, another Friend would correct or "admonish" her. Alongside the "general care" or surveillance of all by each, Quakers also appointed "two or more persons of age and experience" as "overseers," with special responsibility for regulating the conduct of "their respective flocks."[56] The result was a highly ordered system of control that seemed to some observers to violate the Quaker commitment to moral liberty. Clarkson, for example, remarks that, "though the Quakers abhor what they call the authority of priestcraft, yet some overseers possess a portion of the spirit of ecclesiastical dominion." Replacing the crafty priest with the domineering overseer hardly seems a triumph for the freedom of conscience. The difference, Clarkson explains, is that overseers are required to be "upright" and "to exercise their function in a meek, calm, and peaceable spirit"; when they err, they are "liable to be admonished by others."[57] Priestcraft implies a system of external control. Quaker "admonishment," by contrast, ensures that all regulatory agents (overseers, etc.) are internal to the system of control, their power deriving from the goodwill of compatriots who can likewise exercise a disciplinary function.

As is often remarked, Quakers were among the earliest proponents of individuating disciplinary power, interlinking religious technologies of the self to the state apparatus in pathbreaking manner. This was particularly evident at Pennsylvania's Eastern State Penitentiary (est. 1829), where the idea of the inner light was applied to prison architecture: criminals were to be reformed through perpetual solitary confinement, interrupted only by a skylight stationed at the top of each cell to facilitate the contemplation of God. As Thomas Dumm suggests, this prison was "an early attempt to move from the kind of regime in which people are made to act in response to the coercive power of physical violence to the kind of regime in which people are constituted as individuals so that they might behave themselves."[58] The development of spiritual autonomy, in other words, is predicated on externally applied discipline that writes itself onto the body and soul. As Clarkson remarks, Quakers believed "that all persons who live in civil society must give up a portion of their freedom that more happiness and security may be enjoyed."[59] Discipline and freedom go hand and hand, and the Quakers were key innovators in both domains.

In the early nineteenth century, many people were interested in how this Quaker discipline could be adapted for other uses. Clarkson, for instance, hoped that the Quakers' famously ethical character could be generalized so as to bring about the "moral improvement of mankind." Where Quakers attribute their moral uprightness to God, Clarkson looks to the "auxiliary causes" of morality ("Moral Education," "Discipline," etc.), the "combined tendency" of which is to shape character in a particular way. If any "other people were to resort to the same means," they would obtain the same results: "human nature is not so stubborn but that it will yield to a given force."[60] In his effort to generalize Quaker discipline to a non-Quaker population, Clarkson anticipated the crossings between the secular and the sacred characteristic of the reform culture that took shape in the decades following his book's publication. Similar experiments in the deterritorialization of religious discipline would also eventually shape Hindu reform movements in Britain's South Asian colonies.

Howitt goes about broadening the community of Friends by a different means, and one more closely connected to the theology of the inner light. As he proclaimed in the 1834 "George Fox" essay, Quakers must work "to assist our fellow-citizens to cast down the established enormity of priest-craft" so that one day "we shall . . . regard all men as brothers, really made of one flesh, and ordained as one salvation—not as mere machines for us to grow rich upon." Where the priest grows rich on his flock, reducing humanity to "mere machines," the Quaker reformer seeks to reorganize society according to a utopic principle of "illimitable Christian Friendship."[61] As Howitt explains in the *Popular History*, "By declaring that 'wherever two or three were met together in his name, he would be in the midst of them,' [God] cut off, for ever, every claim . . . of priestly dominance."[62] The circle of Friends protects its members against priestly misrule, while also instating a style of rule all its own.

The urban masses of the industrial nineteenth century posed a problem for this Quaker ideal of illimitable Christian friendship. As Howitt pleaded in 1835, it is impossible "to love our neighbors as ourselves, if we see them oppressed, made poor, made miserable, made ignorant and criminal by the measures of a bad government, and this not in individual cases, but by thousands and tens of thousands."[63] A year earlier he had faulted Quakers for treating religion as a thing "to be shut up in your own heart, your own house, or, at most, to regulate your own conduct between man and man in ordinary affairs—not to extend to those great human movements in the mass, on which the happiness of the mass depends."[64] Quakerism, in other words, hinges on a question of governmentality. Where it had previously restricted itself to managing the interrelations among the affective (the "heart"), the domestic (the "house"), and the social ("conduct between man and man in ordinary affairs"), Howitt challenges it to extend its sphere of concern to include "the mass"—a social form still assuming its characteristically modern shape at this time, but already on memorable display in events such as the 1832 Nottingham riots.

If the inner light recasts subjective interiority as a form of a society, a stage upon which the self apprehends itself as other, then it can never be entirely reduced to privatized belief. Or, perhaps more precisely, because both belief and the inner light were simultaneously private and public, subjective and political, each worked to inscribe the self in a larger social collective. As the shape of the collective changed, so too would the shape of divine inspiration.

Taken as a whole, Howitt's career unfolded as an experiment occasioned by these changes. As I suggested at the beginning of this chapter, Howitt set out to follow in the footsteps of Fox. In the process, however, he ended up rethinking Fox and the inner light for the nineteenth century. I would divide Howitt's career into four distinct phases: (1) Romanticism, which dominated in the 1820s and persisted as a major concern of Howitt's work through the 1840s; (2) Reform, which structured the period from 1833 till about 1840; (3) Spiritualism, which consumed the Howitts' attention after the early 1850s; and (4) Catholicism, which the Howitts arrived at via spiritualism, moving to Rome in 1870 (William died and is buried there).

It is beyond the scope of this chapter to explore Howitt's full career in any depth. A brief sketch, however, will suggest how Howitt positioned each of the four phases of his career in relation to the legacy of Fox and the inner light. We begin with poetry. In the 1830s and 40s, Howitt looked to poetic inspiration as a "revelation from heaven" that, like the inner light, "lives in all human hearts, more or less."[65] In 1847—the same year that the Howitts officially resigned from the Society of Friends—Howitt went so far as to assert that the basic doctrines of Fox and the poet William Wordsworth were "identical": "if George Fox had written poetry," Wordsworth's poems ("a very bible of Quakerism") are "exactly what he would have written."[66] This "poetic Quakerism" is, presumably, just the sort of thing that orthodox Quakers had worried the Hicksite heresy would unleash: once uncoupled from scripture, the inner light can be entirely secularized, with the Romantics' Nature its new sacred text. During roughly the same period, reformist political zeal emerged as another possible analogue to religious inspiration. Indeed, it seems plausible to understand the political rally as a sort of refigured Quaker meeting, with the speechifying Howitt moved by the spirit to preach. For example, after one 1836 speech that "seemed to him like inspiration," he wept and "returned thanks to the Almighty that he had been so enabled."[67] By the 1840s, Howitt's poetry and his politics had come into conflict: although he hoped that poetic inspiration could be generalized to the masses, Romantic poetry was increasingly becoming an elite or conservative cultural form.[68] How then could the inner light be spread to the multitude?

Spiritualism, Howitt's third major enthusiasm, suggested a possible answer to this question. As Mary Howitt remarked in 1853, a "feeling seems to pervade all classes, all sects, that the world stands upon the eve of some great spiritual revelation."[69] Rapping their way out from Rochester, the spirits had arrived in England. The Howitts' involvement with spiritualism started slowly, with William's translation of Joseph Ennemoser's *History of Magic*, a project that occupied him while en route to Australia in 1852.[70] (Howitt's son, Alfred William Howitt, stayed on in Australia and eventually wrote a book about its "native tribes" that was one of the principle sources for Émile Durkheim's *The Elementary Forms of Religious Life* [1912]).[71] Within a few years, Howitt became a full-fledged spiritualist convert.

Howitt's spiritualist phase culminated in *The History of the Supernatural in All Ages and Nations* (1863), a thousand-page tome that no less an authority than Emma Hardinge deemed to have "ransacked the ages" and "exhausted the subject."[72] Parallel in form and argument to the *History of Priestcraft*, the book promotes what Ann Taves terms a "spiritualist universalism," arguing that the same spiritual forces have animated supernaturalisms in all ages and nations.[73] It aims to end the "epidemic" of "the anti-spiritual." Toward this end, Howitt sets out to combat the conjoined forces of Protestantism and Enlightenment philosophy. Both deny miracle, the fountainhead of spirit. Although Rome may have begun the process of disenchantment by faking some of its wonders, Protestantism "plucked up the tree" itself.[74] What exactly Howitt means by "Protestantism" in this context is a somewhat fraught question. It evidently should not be taken as inclusive of either Martin Luther (a "genuine spiritualist") or George Fox (who used his "spirit-power" to cure the sick and see the future). Protestantism seems to refer to something more closely aligned with modern disenchantment per se. As Howitt explains in an 1864 letter, spiritualism is "old as the world itself," but "protestantism [*sic*] and philosophy, so-called, have renounced, dismissed, and trodden upon it now for several generations."[75] For Howitt, spiritualism facilitates a populist groundswell of the inner light, distributing the divine to the masses like nothing before it.

Or, at least, like almost nothing. In the fourth and final phase of his career, Howitt flirted with Catholicism, which he interpreted through a spiritualist lens. Even while denouncing "the great papal imposture," he celebrated "pure and primitive Catholicism itself."[76] As he explained in an 1870 letter, "true" Catholicism is radically antihierarchical. "At the top, all is rotten, but at the bottom God, who overrules all things, has caused it to strike its roots into the soil of the common humanity, and send up shoots and crops of an active, a holy, an indefatigable beneficence such as present Protestantism knows nothing of."[77] True Catholicism, in other words, resembles spiritualism. It proliferates miracles from below in a raucous and effervescent manner reminiscent of the early Quakers. Here, Howitt denatures the categories "Catholic" and "Protestant" until they become almost unrecognizable. Fox and Luther are not Protestants, and Catholicism is a sort of sublimated spiritualism—itself already a populist substitute for Romantic (which is to say Quaker) inspiration. It makes little sense, I think, to try to unravel these crossings: for Howitt, the decoupling of the "spirit" from the "letter" of Protestantism was precisely the point.

If tolerance as a technology of governance neutralizes religious dissent by ensuring that all modes of dissent that are legible as properly "religious" serve as markers of the state's benevolence toward religion and thus reinforce state hegemony, then criticism of a tolerant state needs to leave "religion" behind to mount its dissent from elsewhere. Whether coincidentally or not, Howitt's career did this. In the *History of the Supernatural*, Howitt claimed that Quakerism "can never die out. As it never could be circumscribed within the bounds of a sect—George Fox never wished it to be so—so the sect of Quakers may perish, but its principles must eternally remain."[78] This sounds like a mission statement. Howitt's turns to romantic poetry, reformist politics, spiritualist revelation, and Catholic miracle had been so many efforts to separate the spirit or "principle" of Quakerism from the actuality of existing Quakers.

Reforming Empire

There is one last aspect of Howitt's career that I have saved till the end of this chapter, as it points us away from England and toward India—and thus toward the remainder of *Spiritual Despots*. In the late 1830s and early 1840s, Howitt became directly involved in the effort to reform—but, notably, not to end—the British Empire. In 1838, he published a book on *Colonization and Christianity* that took a global view of its subject, with attention to Spanish, Portuguese, Dutch, French, and English imperialisms, as well as the "treatment of the Indians by the United States." The book was meant to "lay open to the public the most extensive and extraordinary system of crime which the world ever witnessed."[79] That this phrasing recalls the *History of Priestcraft* is not surprising; *Colonization and Christianity* was Howitt's next book-length project. Anticlerical critique led Howitt to anticolonial critique, however circuitously. Two years later, in 1840, Howitt was elected to the governing board of the British India Society, a voluntary association that numbered Thomas Clarkson and Isaac Crewsdon among its members. During this phase of his career, Howitt sought to make empire more "moral" by better aligning it with the principles of Christianity. As he insisted, only the "spirit of Christianity living in the heart of the British public . . . can secure justice to the millions that are crying for it from every region of the earth." As humanity's "perpetual watch and guardian," Christian conscience calls for the reform as well as the extension of empire.[80]

This open-ended call for justice could have pointed Howitt in any number of directions. That it ended up pointing him toward what can be anachronistically described as market solutions to moral problems is indicative of broader shifts in the logic of colonial capitalism. Howitt advocated for free trade as a means of moral uplift. He insisted that if the British were to use India to grow commodity crops like cotton, while also developing the subcontinent as an export market for British manufactured goods, they would reduce idleness and starvation in colony and metropole alike.[81] They would also indirectly help to end the slave trade: India's "swarming" labor force would produce cotton and sugar more cheaply than American and Caribbean slave labor; market forces, rather than sovereign decree, would result in the full abolition of slavery.[82] This was partly out of necessity. Britain abolished slavery in 1833, but economic forces assured its survival in non-British territories; finessing the global economy of slave crops was beyond the means of any single sovereign power, so experiments with the emergent technologies of governmentality appeared as the only plausible solution to the impasse. Accordingly, Howitt's colleagues echoed his proposal. To "banish the blood-stained produce of America," as another member of the British India Society put it, all Britain needed to do was to "cherish" and "care for" Indians by "raising them from starving beggars into thriving peasants."[83] Or, in the words of an 1840 resolution, Britain should rule India "on such principles as shall promote the happiness and improvement of the native population."[84] Here, the British India Society asks that the empire assume the mantle of what Howitt had termed "kinghood"—ruling for the good of the governed, not for the good of the sovereign.

The members of the British India Society were obviously not (in the old Quaker adage) speaking truth to power here. At most, they were telling power to adhere to its own clearly articulated best practices. By 1840, "good government" had already begun to consolidate its hold on the British state, with economics its major technical vocabulary, and the colonies a major field for its application. The freedoms promised by the new dispensation of imperial capital were not illusory per se; but they were ambivalent, predicated on new systems of control. We can get a clearer sense of the ambivalences of this system by comparing it to Howitt's own definition of slavery: "Slavery does not consist in being bought and sold—that is *but one mode of making slaves*, not *Slavery* itself. SLAVERY IS THE CONDITION OF PRIVATION *of free will, and being put under the arbitrary will of another*" (emphasis original).[85] According to Howitt, wage laborers who work on a cotton plantation do so of their own free will and thus are not slaves. Such a claim may now seem overly simplistic, if not morally callous. The actions of wage laborers, bound as they are by structural constraints, are seldom if ever "free." Indeed, the conceptual binary "slave-free" cannot quite make sense of the forms of power associated with strategies of rule like the one that Howitt is proposing. At one level, the program of moral "improvement" espoused by the British India Society asks the colonized to submit to the "will" of these metropolitan reformers. At another level, it asks them to internalize this will, learning to govern themselves and their laboring bodies more effectively.

In demanding that empire create self-disciplined, hard-working capitalist subjects, Howitt and company affirmed the ascendance of liberal governmentality as a strategy of rule. Max Weber might suggest that their Quakerism was essential in this regard. By Weber's account, the worldly asceticism of early Quakers played a disproportionate role in the rise of the modern capitalist ethos. Paradigmatic for the Protestant ethic more broadly, Quaker abstemiousness pioneered a form of subjectivity that has since become central to the functioning of the modern world. In the 1840s, we see Howitt trying to extend this ethic to India through benevolent imposition. The British state will arrange the economy so as to refashion subjectivity from on high, making the economically inefficient denizens of India more like England's industrious Protestants. Here, Quaker technologies for disciplining the self and the emergent techniques of secular governmentality coincide all too neatly. The Protestant ethic is remade as an explicitly imperial technology of subjectivation.

Howitt's brief foray into the politics of colonialism thus leaves us with a question that will loom over the rest of *Spiritual Despots*: how else could this problem have been conceived? In closing, I would suggest that we can read the *Popular History of Priestcraft* as implying a reformist project that does not coincide so neatly with the agendas of the colonial state. Surely Howitt meant his *History of Priestcraft*, as its title indicates, partly as a means of allying himself with anticlerical critics in all ages and nations. His subnational Quaker minority affirms its distance from the Anglican nation by gesturing toward transnational connection: because religion is global (or is rendered such during this period), it always carries the potentiality of solidarities beyond the national fold. Indeed, the *History of Priestcraft* demonstrates how empire altered Britain's relationship to its own history. "Little England" eludes Howitt: to recoup the spirit of George Fox, he first has to traverse the world. The English priest, mediated by empire and the comparative disciplines, no longer stands alone; neither, then, can the anticlerical critic. In the remainder of *Spiritual Despots*, I rework Howitt's project to draw out its connective potential. By tracing how the word *priestcraft* traveled between India and Britain during Howitt's lifetime, I literalize his title, asking what it would look like to trace the *Popular History of "Priestcraft" in All Ages and Nations*. How, I ask, did the travels of this term link anticlerical critics across national, cultural, and religious borders?

In 1840, Howitt insisted that the 1832 Reform Bill was not "a final measure by any means." The "same spirit has always been at work in the nation—the spirit of popular liberty." Since the earliest resistance to feudal despotism, "we have ever since been *forming* and *reforming*." Now, he wrote, "we must yet strike fearlessly the lancet of reform deeper."[86] In the following chapters, I ask how reform struck broadly as well as deeply— moving across colony and metropole to form what I describe as the nineteenth-century reform assemblage. The transition from this chapter to the next pivots on the kind of granular transcolonial connection or coincidence that I argue was central to the nineteenth-century reform scene. In 1833, Howitt published his *Popular History of Priestcraft* from Nottingham. The same year, in Bristol, Rammohun Roy lay dying.

THREE

Reform Affinities

May God render religion destructive of differences and dislike between man and man, and conducive to the peace and union of mankind.   RAMMOHUN ROY (1820)

The grammar of modern theology must be condemned by every scientific man as bad grammar. It makes no mention of the copulative conjunction. The disjunctive *Or* reigns supreme; the copulative *And* finds no place.   KESHUB CHUNDER SEN (1881)

"It was," John Estlin later wrote in his journal, "a beautiful moonlight night." But the quiet of the countryside only amplified the bustle of a tragedy unfolding indoors. "On one side of the window," as the doctor "looked out of it, was the calm rural midnight scene; on the other, this extraordinary man *dying*. I shall never forget the moment." Estlin, a prominent surgeon, had been tending to Rammohun Roy since the onset of the celebrated Bengali's fever eight days earlier. Alongside him at the window were Ann Kiddell, one of the many Unitarians who had welcomed Rammohun to the English port city of Bristol, and John Hare, whose late brother David was Rammohun's friend and fellow advocate for English education back home in Calcutta.[1] David's niece, meanwhile, sat "sobbing in a chair" on the other side of the room, as Rammohun's son Ram clasped his dying father's hand.[2] There was nothing else to be done, so at half past one Dr. Estlin yielded to Miss Kiddell's pleas that he get some rest. He retired to his room, lying down with his clothes still on. An hour later, when Mr. Hare woke him up, it was all over: Rammohun Roy was no more. As the doctor reentered the sickroom, he was confronted with what must have been a striking tableau. Ram Rotun, one of the two servants who had accompanied Rammohun to England, was kneeling next to his deceased employer, "holding the Rajah's chin." Grouped around this mournful duo were seven others, plus "one or two" miscellaneous household servants. There were the two Bengalis, Ram Roy and Ram Hurry (a second servant); the two Hares, also with Calcutta connections; and three Englishwomen of a Unitarian bent: Ann Kiddell, Susanna Estlin (the doctor's mother), and Catherine Castle (the young Bristol heiress who owned Stapleton Grove, the now grief-stricken country estate).[3]

In short, it was an eclectic assembly. Convened by a death, it nonetheless had its eyes set firmly on the future. It was, after all, the utopian hopes of nineteenth-century reformism that had brought this unlikely group together to begin with. Rammohun Roy (1774–1833) had risen to prominence in Calcutta starting in the 1810s by trying to reform or eliminate Hindu religious practices that he found corrupt (like image worship) or inhumane (like widow burning). Sparring with Christian missionaries, he translated Hindu scriptures into Bengali and English and ultimately issued his own edition of *The Precepts of Jesus* (1820). This staunchly anti-Trinitarian text earned Rammohun many admirers in Unitarian enclaves like Bristol. When he traveled to Britain in 1831—in part to petition the East India Company to increase the annual living stipend of the nominal Mughal emperor—Rammohun found himself a veritable celebrity, his company sought out by the likes of Robert Owen, William Wilberforce, James Mill, Jeremy Bentham, William Godwin, and Benjamin Disraeli. Poor Thomas Macaulay, for his part, "went away in despair" having been unable to get an audience. Harriet Martineau succinctly stated what many surely felt: "There is something about Rammohan that melts one irresistibly."[4] At least part of Rammohun's fame was clearly due to good timing. The reformist fervor that overtook Britain around the passage of the 1832 Reform Act (which extended the franchise and restructured the electoral system) was happy to claim an Indian ally. But Rammohun did more than simply reaffirm reform's preexisting desires. His charismatic presence suggested the potential for a radically expanded reform scene that could traverse the utopian hopes of colony and metropole. The fulfillment of reform would be found in its partial negation, as it was swept up in cosmopolitan currents that would necessarily transform it.

In the days and years after Rammohun's death, the assembly convened by his loss grew. So did the disagreement about what the legacy of this "Father of Modern India" was to be. Some mourners claimed him as a Christian convert, thus aligning him with the values of the imperial West. Others insisted that he had remained a committed Hindu till the end—and thus a determined champion of precolonial Indic tradition. Both of these positions, however, would seem to reinforce the very lines of religious "difference" that Rammohun, by his own account, had set out to destroy.[5]

Here, I use the assembly gathered around Rammohun's deathbed to open an inquiry into nineteenth-century Anglophone reformism. My topic will not be Rammohun per se, but rather the posthumous "voice" that was "heard impressively from the tomb" even after his death.[6] This "Rammohun," who began life in 1833, cannot be separated from his major interpreters: Debendranath Tagore (1817–1905) and Keshub Chunder Sen (1838–1884). In the 1840s, Tagore (son of the wealthy industrialist Dwarkanath Tagore and father of the poet Rabindranath Tagore) repositioned Rammohun both figuratively, by resurrecting Rammohun's Brahmo Sabha as the Brahmo Samaj, and literally, by traveling to Bristol to exhume and rebury Rammohun's remains. In the 1860s, Keshub reworked this legacy yet again. Although I open this chapter with Rammohun, Keshub is its real subject. After Tagore inducted him into the Brahmo Samaj, Keshub provoked a major schism in the society by controversially laying claim to a quasi-prophetic status. Even as he scandalized the Brahmos, however, he continued to emphasize the style of religious "eclecticism" that was one of the Brahmos' most cherished traditions.

Brahmo eclecticism was important to the making of modern Hindu thought, as Brian Hatcher and others have noted. By adapting Vedanta to the Victorian era, Brahmos provided a powerful theological vocabulary for generations of thinkers keen to promote syncretic recombinations of elements drawn from diverse faiths.[7] This syncretic streak is evident in the second of the above epigraphs, wherein Keshub Chunder Sen complains about the "grammar of modern theology." It is, he says, "bad grammar" in that it emphasizes the "disjunctive *Or*" over the "copulative *And*."[8] Like Rammohun Roy before him, Keshub hoped to use religion to eliminate rather than to reinforce human difference. This project ran into problems, however, precisely around Keshub's copula: the conjunction *and* offers the thrill of transgression only insofar as it is able to reify the entities so conjoined, by presenting them as self-evidently coherent wholes. The same charge can be leveled against syncretism more broadly: it reinforces the very boundaries that it purports to violate in that it must reify the discrete "religions" before it can claim (with great aplomb) to have mixed them. Mere conjunction does not eliminate difference.

To find another approach to this problem, we have to look elsewhere in Keshub's writings. There, I suggest, we find a principle of religious connection that operates by a logic distinct from that of conjunction. Borrowing a term from Keshub, I describe this connective principle as one of spiritual "affinity." Rather than replacing the grammar of cultural disjunction with a grammar of cultural conjunction, the principle of affinity goes one step further: its copulations destabilize the identities of whatever they conjoin so that "conjunction" itself becomes a misnomer, an attempt to impose lines of difference where those lines are no longer clear.

In the following discussion, I introduce several technical terms, but all of them cluster around the notion of "affinity." With this term (which I take from Keshub), I mean to refer obliquely to Max Weber's notion of "elective affinity"—a perennial staple of scholarship on the Brahmo Samaj, with its bourgeois ethos of worldly asceticism.[9] Weber's "elective affinity" is in turn an allusion to Johann Wolfgang von Goethe's novel *Elective Affinities* (*Die Wahlverwandtschaften*) (1807), which uses scientific chemistry to analyze human romantic relationships, showing how a happily bonded married couple predictably separates when two friends come to visit them at their country estate. To recall, an "elective affinity" is the mysterious chemical force that draws unrelated substances together, disembedding each from its previous set of relations to bring a new substance into being. Cross-reading Goethe's novel with Weber's *Protestant Ethic*, Andrew McKinnon distinguishes between two different types of kinship implicit in both texts: the lineal and the spiritual. As Goethe's heroine Charlotte observes, entities joined by means of affinity "seem to me not so much blood relations as related in spirit and soul." Affinity, then, is the means by which "spiritual paternity" displaces or crosses the bloodlines of biological descent.[10] Here, I build on McKinnon's reading of Goethe by developing a notion of a "reform affinity." This type of affinity, as I suggest below, emerges from the split subjectivities produced through the ascetic work on the self so often prescribed by nineteenth-century reform culture. A reform affinity aligns two partial selves; it cuts across subjects that are already fractured by the work of ascetic self-discipline.

Goethe, of course, was neither the first nor the last thinker to experiment with borrowing terms from the physical and biological sciences and launching them to new life in social and political theory. The nineteenth century was rife with such efforts, with Brahmo Samajis quite prominent in this regard. Keshub Chunder Sen, for example, argued that colonialism had produced not just "a mechanical contiguity of races" but "a sort of chemical solution and fusion" of cultural "elements."[11] Whereas classical mechanics as a form of thought can imagine only proximity, chemistry theorizes fusion. Because Keshub and his Brahmo associates arose from within the same world of ideas as their German near-contemporaries, I do not think it makes sense to "apply" the Germans to India, using a Goethe or a Weber to interpret Hinduism; instead, it seems more productive to ask how Brahmos were using some of the same terms (affinity, asceticism) that were circulating in the North Atlantic world during their lifetimes.

I foreground this circulation of ideas between South Asia and the North Atlantic by two principal means. First, I propose the term "reform assemblage" as a lens for interpreting nineteenth-century reform culture. After developing this term in a theoretical register, I shift to a more histori-cist account of the vibrantly transnational reform scene that interlinked Britain and India during the mid-Victorian period. I then turn back to theory to suggest that, for nineteenth-century reformers, the self and so-ciety were difficult to disentangle: the reform of one necessarily implied the reform of the other. Because reform disaggregated or split the self, it rendered selfhood the scene of a social relation, thus blurring the line be-tween the inter-and intra-subjective.

Second, I ask how one denizen of the nineteenth-century reform as-semblage theorized these social/subjective relations. My discussion of the reform assemblage, which starts out broad, thus gradually narrows to the metonymic figure of Keshub Chunder Sen, whom I approach via his English-language lectures and writings. This English material consti-tutes a substantial portion of Keshub's overall corpus and deserves serious study; indeed, by at least one account, Keshub was more at ease lecturing in English than he was in Bengali.[12] In his English works, I suggest, Keshub develops a principle of spiritual affinity that is the basis for the radically egalitarian mode of community that he describes as "spiritual fellowship." He defines this spiritual fellowship against priestcraft or spiritual despo-tism as its principal foil. Like Rammohun Roy before him, Keshub was a staunch critic of Brahmanical authority, predicating the rise of "Young India" on the elimination of priestly power. It was thus more than a little ironic then that, by the late 1860s, he had set himself up as a char-ismatic guru with seemingly despotic powers over his followers—or so it was alleged at the time. Without necessarily trying to clear Keshub of the charges laid against him, I nonetheless want to suggest that we take his writings from this period seriously as offering a theory of religious author-ity. If they do offer such a theory, surely they should be used to interpret Keshub's role within the religious movement or "New Dispensation" that he founded.

Keshub, by my reading, insists on the necessity of religious leaders of a very particular type. The good leader should be like the figure that Keshub terms the "Spirit Christ": a self-emptying signifier that mediates among "little individualities" so that they can join together into a larger fellowship. Unlike the crafty priest, such a leader eschews material self-interest, opting instead for spirit as a principle of self-abnegation; if he stands above the horizontal field of the social, it is only as an ascetic or self-negating mediator. The final section of this chapter thus turns to the theme of asceticism more explicitly, asking whether the generalized attitude of self-negation implied by the Brahmo ideal of the worldly ascetic corresponds to Keshub's Spirit Christ. This ideal has already been well documented by Hatcher and other scholars; my aim here is simply to suggest that worldly asceticism, as a practice of the self, also insinuated the self into a form of society. As a whole, I argue, Keshub's reform project sought to replace a hierarchically ordered society, associated with priestcraft and the guru-follower relation, with a more egalitarian mode of politics that he described as spiritual fellowship. To begin building toward the latter term, I return us to Rammohun's deathbed.

The Reform Assemblage

To describe the group of mourners who clustered around the recently deceased Rammohun Roy as an "assembly" is to construe it as consisting of precisely the sort of individuals that its spirit called into question. Although nineteenth-century reformers frequently established voluntary societies that roughly conformed to the procedures and norms of parliamentary liberalism, reform's stated ideals tended to flout these norms. Where an assembly presumes the fixity of the individual, deriving its claim to public authority from its supposed ability to represent articulable private interests, reform abided by a different logic. It presumed the malleability of the human and set out to remake the individual in a manner that denied it both its privacy and its discreteness. Instead of describing this grouping as an *assembly*, then, we might do better to think of it as an *assemblage*.

As I will use it, "reform assemblage" has two related meanings. First, it refers to the transnational network of people, ideas, practices, objects, and institutions that were strung together by the shifting signifier *reform*. Akin to Simon During's "magic assemblage," it was "not a well-bounded, discrete, and tidy formation" defined by a single "formal or abstract feature" that all its constituent components share.[13] It was, rather, an open-ended network of unstable elements. Like other assemblages, the reform assemblage operated according to principles of connection, heterogeneity, and multiplicity. It consisted of lines of force, rather than constellated points or positions. Thus, in the group gathered around Rammohun's deathbed, just as pertinent as the dozen constellated persons were the vectors running through them: the capital that financed this country estate on the outskirts of Bristol, a thriving center of the slave trade that had been officially abolished one month prior to Rammohun's death; the incipient feminist movement that, in the coming decades, Unitarian women would help to establish; the demand for English education in India that Rammohun and David Hare had so forcibly articulated and that would become official policy two years later.[14] Some of these lines segment the assemblage, articulating it into discrete territories; others disrupt and de-territorialize it. Both types of line, however, remain part of the unstable whole, which is defined by precisely such processes of de- and re-territorialization.[15]

Second, "reform assemblage" suggests that any given element within the larger scene of nineteenth-century reformism can itself be further decomposed into a series of mobile lines or directionalities, which cannot be easily disentangled. Instead of enumerating and trying to separate the cultural and religious vectors that intersected in a given person or event, we should instead ask how such sites merge, dissipate, and scramble these vectors so that they are no longer identifiable as such.

I mean for the word *reform* to indicate this decomposition of the subject in a very particular way. As I discuss in the Introduction, Charles Taylor develops his notion of "Reform" as a reworking of Max Weber's "worldly asceticism." Taylor's "Reform impulse" transposes the conflict between the transcendent and the immanent, the monk and the ordinary believer, into the psyche of a single subject. This subject thus becomes a worldly ascetic, working assiduously to reform both himself and his world by bringing them into closer alignment with the transcendent dictates of the divine. This worldly asceticism accrues yet another set of resonances if we reread it through Michel Foucault. The ascetic internalizes the disciplinary power relation of priest-follower, splitting his subjectivity such that a higher self (aligned with the transcendent) can govern a lower self (aligned with the immanent). But the potential for a confusion of identities ensues: in the scene of self-governance, it is not always clear who is the self and who is the other. Self-discipline necessarily opens the subject to external control, insofar as the rule of disciple precedes and constitutes the subject. To become one's own guide is, in some sense, to cease to be oneself—and thus to reveal that one is always already part of a broader assemblage of networked subjectivities.

When dealing with questions of colonial culture, it might be tempting to describe such subjects as "hybrid." By using the word *assemblage* instead, I aim to bypass what seems to me like a persistent ambiguity in the scholarship on colonial hybridity. For Homi Bhahba, hybridity had meant something very particular: "It is not a third term that resolves the tension between two cultures," as by mixing their content. In fact, it is not about "content" at all. Denoting the doubling and disavowal that structures "the problematic of colonial representation," hybridity points to the process whereby different cultures are demarcated as different and thus is prior to the moment of empirical difference or content as such.[16] By contrast, later invocations of colonial hybridity have tended to resort to the very syncretisms that Bhabha's account would seem to preclude. Here, the hybrid appears as a third term that blends together otherwise distinct cultures, and it is often figured using metaphors (grafted plants, crossbred animals) that naturalize difference as biologically given—thus reifying cultural boundaries in the very moment that it purports to transgress them. Bhabha might say that this is because of this scholarship's refusal to engage with the semiotic question of how difference is produced as such; it is not willing to ask what is prior to the copulative conjunction *and*. My tactic in the following discussion, meanwhile, is step to the side of this debate. I leave the biological language of hybridity behind, opting instead for the Deleuzian language of the assemblage. I hope that, in doing so, I can retain something of Bhabha's poststructuralist energy, while also allowing for greater attention to religion, as one type of "contents" structured by the problematic of colonial representation.

My move away from biological metaphors is inspired in part by the nineteenth-century texts that I am working with. Thus, Goethe's Charlotte rethinks the biology of blood relations by turning to the metaphor of chemical "affinity." An 1880 Brahmo tract does something similar. Defending Brahmo "eclecticism" on the occasion of the society's fiftieth anniversary, Protap Chunder Mozoomdar starts out by using Darwin to narrate the history of religion, appealing to the doctrine of the survival of the fittest to explain why some religions prevail over others. But then he abruptly changes course, defining religion instead (with a metaphor taken from physics) as a field of accumulated "forces." Forces, as he reminds his audience, are always conserved, and this natural law applies to both the "material" and the "spiritual" worlds. "Forces are internally convertible, and may be simplified, added, and consolidated, but they can never be destroyed." The "growth" of the Brahmo Samaj is the result of the "accumulation of these indestructible moral and spiritual forces."[17] A society like the Brahmo Samaj can work to manipulate these forces, augmenting or decreasing them, but it can never destroy them. The most radical intervention one can make in this religious physics is, perhaps, to exploit the "internal convertibility" of a given force, turning that force in an unforeseen direction.

Mozoomdar explicitly contrasts his approach to that of "comparative theology," which juxtaposes "contending systems of faith" to "find out the common principles" that unite them. Comparative theology proceeds from taxonomic principles. It presumes discrete religions and then tries to resolve the apparent contradictions among these religions "intellectually." Mozoomdar gestures to Akbar, Auguste Comte, and Max Müller as cases in point. The Brahmo Samaj, by contrast, takes this problem and tries "to solve [it] in a spiritual and practical manner." It "combine[s] the spirit of every religion in faith, worship, and spiritual discipline."[18] This move, in its way, recalls Max Weber, who likewise sought to analyze how a spiritual discipline or ethic can circulate semi-independently of religious doctrine. As systems of symbols, religions may seem discrete. But as accretions of forces that can be applied to the body as part of a spiritual discipline or practice of the self, the lines between them are far from clear.

Viewing the reform assemblage as composed of forces of this type should preempt certain cultural essentialisms. Here, Hinduism and Christianity are unstable accumulations of movement, of directionalities and accelerations; they are not trees that can be grafted together. If biology renders religions as relatively stable blood lineages, Mozoomdar's religious physics renders them as unstable and dispersive storehouses of forces that they can assemble, but never quite contain.

Reassembling Reform

To further theorize the reform assemblage, I want to return to the distinction that Taylor draws between the transcendent and the immanent. Recall that in Taylor's account, post-Axial religion is defined by its ongoing "quarrel with the immanent." Sometimes this quarrel generates a relatively stable system of two-speed religion, in which certain subjects devote themselves to otherworldly salvation while most people continue to devote themselves to worldly flourishing. At other times, this complementarity breaks down: religion tries to remake the world according to the dictates of the divine. It is this latter orientation, which substantially heightens the tension between the immanent and transcendent, that Taylor describes as "Reform.

Here, Taylor echoes a tradition of Christian theological writing that had understood reform in similar terms. In Latin, *reformatio* denoted Christian penitential practice designed to bend fallen humanity toward the good so that it might recoup its "image-likeness" with God. Where baptism and conversion were "instantaneous and non-repeatable" turnings toward the divine, "the idea of reform" implied "prolongation and repetition": the subject of reform can move "toward" God, but can never close the gap that separates it from the divine.[19] The tension between the worldly and the otherworldly, the actual and the potential, is an irreducible part of human experience.

We find an almost identical sentiment expressed in the early writings of Keshub Chunder Sen. The "destiny of human life," Keshub opines, is "to attain God; or to make constant progress unto Him." Just as the egg "develops itself" until a bird emerges and the "seed develops itself" till it produces a tree, so does the human work to overcome itself in the attainment of the divine. Unlike an egg, however, a human being can never "attain" its destiny; it remains in the state of perpetual becoming that Keshub terms "progress." The result is the constitutive incompletion of the human. "There is a restless character about religion," he writes. "The soul is never stationary; it must move whether it be towards good or evil: *status quo* can never be predicated of the soul."[20] This restlessness, I would suggest, is the abiding spirit of reform. Forever incomplete, reform has a relentless need to claim new objects, entering them into its ever-expanding assemblage.

Something of this constitutive incompletion is evident in the history of the term *reformation* itself. As we saw in chapter 1, this term could denote either a discrete historical event or a more general process of work upon the self and society. John Milton exploited the difference between these two meanings in 1644, when he proclaimed that "God is decreeing to begin some new and great period in his Church, even to the reforming of Reformation itself." As Joanna Innes remarks, the "question of whether the Reformation *was* an event that had finished, or a process that should continue, provided a focus for religious controversy in England and elsewhere for the next few centuries."[21] With perfection being hard to come by, reform would remain an ongoing process.

It seems fair to say that *reform* was the virtual byword of nineteenth-century Britain. At times an empty, or nearly empty, signifier, it took on any number of functions, channeling and containing the destabilizing effects of revolutionary events in France, mobilizing radical impulses in Britain, and cutting across a potpourri of period causes including antislavery, temperance, women's suffrage, Irish nationalism, antivivisection, factory reform, and Chartism, to name just a few. Despite their many differences, reform movements demonstrated considerable unity, benefiting from both "horizontal linkages" that connected the "various types of nineteenth century reformer at any one time," as well as "vertical linkages" that connected reform movements over time. "Continuity of personnel" (the same characters turn up everywhere) was complemented and reinforced by "continuity of technique" (methods successfully applied in service of one cause quickly spread to others).[22] Even the differences among these movements could prove a point of commonality: efforts to distinguish between different kinds of reform and chart their interrelations served as a means of mapping the reform scene as a whole.[23]

Although the rhetoric of "reform" left Protestantism behind, no longer taking the church as its paradigmatic object, it nonetheless continued to invoke the Reformation and associate itself, however nebulously, with the legacy of Luther. Often this was for strategic purposes: citing the Reformation could to win moderates and conservatives over to causes that might otherwise seem dangerously radical. But at other times, and especially with respect to moral causes, the convergence of religion and reform appears more fundamental. This is particularly true with regard to India. Starting in the 1790s, British Evangelicals pleaded for the East India Company to permit Christian missionaries to enter their territories, so that by spreading the gospel they might improve the moral condition of Britain's "Asiatic subjects," as well as of the imperial enterprise itself (morally suspect since the Warren Hastings debacle).[24] While other more "secular" currents of British reform culture (e.g., utilitarianism) also exerted considerable influence in the colony, the rhetorical prominence of Christianity ensured that religion would mediate India's relationship to the broader Anglophone reformist scene.[25] In a similar manner, the rhetoric of empire came to mediate metropolitan reform movements' own hopes for improving Britain. The history of reform, from the abolition of slavery to the foundation of the RSPCA, was regularly interpreted as a testament to Britain's moral preeminence, and thus a justification for the civilizing mission of empire.[26]

Socio-religious reform movements in British India established yet another set of horizontal linkages in this chain. While it is important to study Hindu reformism vertically in relation to the long history of Hinduism, it is equally important to pursue the horizontal connections that it forged within the nineteenth century. Hindu reformers themselves were clearly thinking in such horizontal or transversal terms, noting the concurrent establishment of Brahmoism and Mormonism, for instance, or the near simultaneous births of Karsandas Mulji, Dayananda Saraswati, Robert Ingersoll (the American agnostic), and Charles Bradlaugh (the British secularist)—all in or around 1830, just before Rammohun's demise.[27]

Nor did they stop at merely observing parallelisms. Hindu reformers tried to form concrete alliances with their counterparts in Britain and elsewhere. As Keshub Chunder Sen explained to members of Bombay's Prarthana Samaj in 1870, he had traveled from India to England to "to bring about a closer social and spiritual fellowship" between the two countries so that they could "enter into a sort of moral and spiritual covenant with each other." There are, he informed his audience, "thousands of men and women in that country who live the lives of disinterested reformers—their only object is to bring relief to the poor, the needy, the ignorant, and the superstitious."[28] His hope was that the reform-minded denizens of Bombay would start to conceive of themselves as part of a larger reform enterprise, shared with their British counterparts.

One means of establishing alliances was through the speaker circuit, as Keshub was well aware. In England, he lectured to crowds assembled by various institutions: Unitarian and Congregationalist churches, the Peace Society, the Ragged School Union, the Swedenborg Society, and assorted temperance groups.[29] Sometimes, an event's roster might stage a fleeting encounter among an eclectic group of lecturers, as when Keshub, Dadabhai Naoroji, and Mary Carpenter all expounded on the topic of "female education" at a meeting of the East India Association.[30] At other times, more permanent institutional alliances were proposed. Thus, in speaking against alcohol consumption, Keshub called for "a system of communication between temperance friends in England and temperance friends in India."[31] The practical and political impediments to such "communication" were substantial, and proposals like this one were seldom fully realized. Even so, they seem to have been popular; Keshub's call for temperance "friendship," for instance, elicited a cry of "Hear, hear."

Disassembling the Self

Institutional alliances of this type return us to the argument that I anticipated above. The voluntary association, as quintessential civil society institution, was in many respects the dominant institutional form of the nineteenth-century reform assemblage. Groups like the Brahmo Samaj adapted the major political idioms of the modern state to a civil forum structured discursively by parliamentary procedure and organized institutionally according to a bureaucratic logic.[32] Within any given meeting of such a society, the powers of the deliberative, liberal individual would seem to rule supreme. For example, the "printed covenant" that Keshub Chunder Sen signed in 1858 to become a member of the Brahmo Samaj was a bureaucratic document (requiring more than one signature) that positioned Keshub and his act of conversion in a particular way.[33] Entered into freely by rational individuals whose existence by definition precedes it, this social contract should, in principle, be open to dissolution at any time, thus freeing its composite individuals from their socio-religious bond. In the terms I lay out above, it institutes an assembly, not an assemblage.

Here, I am trying to read this scene against the grain. Such a reading is justified in that it draws out the latent contradictions that were internal to nineteenth-century reformism. At one level, reform was eminently liberal—procedural, reasoned, and predicated on the individual citizen-subject. At another level, it called liberal politics into question, gesturing toward new social forms. As a force that traverses the self-enclosed subject, reform disassembles the self. It establishes a power relation internal to a subject who—through an ascetic work upon the self, an application of disciplinary force—is split into two. In the process, this subject is also incorporated into networked power relations that exceed and to a certain extent subsume it. A reform assemblage brings multiple such subjectivities together in a fissiparous network of constantly shifting affective relations that I describe with the word *affinity*.

Recall Keshub Chunder Sen's stated hope that India and England could "enter into a sort of moral and spiritual covenant with each other" and thus "bring about a closer social and spiritual fellowship" between the two nations. The first of these two phrases ("spiritual covenant") reflects the liberal procedural idiom with which Keshub's audience would have been familiar. Indeed, it seems almost a direct citation of the "printed covenant" that Keshub had signed fourteen years previously upon becoming a member of the Brahmo Samaj. This spiritual covenant operates by a different principle, however—or so I would like to suggest. The printed covenant presumes that its signees preexist it. The spiritual covenant, by contrast, refuses the ontological priority of the subjects who enter into it. Instead, it fuses them together via a principle of spiritual affinity that calls the liberal individual into question.

The second phrase ("spiritual fellowship") points in a different but related direction. Fellowship or friendship was a leitmotif of nineteenth-century reform rhetoric; at times, personal relations seemed to be at the very heart of reform. Asceticism, as a work upon the self, could easily slide into a work upon the friend. From the friend, it would then slide into a work upon the nation. As these slippages suggest, spiritual fellowship was not simply a relation between or among individuals. Rather, it took the individual as a metonym for the larger assemblage—a part that stands in for a whole that cannot be represented as such. (As I suggest in the introduction, I have tried to replicate something of this metonymic principle in the methodology of this book.) If a spiritual covenant is the end goal of Keshub's reform program, spiritual fellowship is the mechanism by which this goal is to be achieved.

In his lecture to the Bombay Prarthana Samaj, Keshub Chunder Sen offered one justification for the symbolic importance of fellowship to his project. Just as "individuals" should "fraternize and cooperate with each other," he proclaimed, so "should nations do. If no individual is infallible no nation is, and unless there is a wholesale interchange of hospitality, unless there is a cordial, full intercourse between man and man and between woman and woman there cannot be anything like reformed society."[34] The scalar confusions in this passage are substantial. Keshub uses friendship as a simile for international relations, while also suggesting that the reform of interpersonal "intercourse" is necessarily prior to societal, national, or international reform. The vertiginous slide among these different registers is characteristic of reform rhetoric more broadly: reform can only proceed if the political-national and personal-social are taken within a single frame, fused together via the connective logic of the "spiritual."

This method is likewise evident in Keshub's lectures about temperance and alcohol. At an 1870 meeting of the East Central Temperance Association in Shoreditch's New Town Hall, Keshub decried the evils of drink by reminding his audience of "facts and figures" with which they were all familiar—"statistics" that prove liquor to be a "gigantic evil." Keshub demands that his listener "do all in your power to call upon the Legislature to suppress by legislation this fatal liquor traffic." But while political exertion within the structure of the state is "necessary," it is not, Keshub argues, sufficient: "Individual exertion of a moral character is necessary too. Let us all individually try to exercise a healthy influence on those around us by means of our example and our personal conduct." Keshub illustrates the causal mechanism behind this "influence" with an example worth quoting in full:

We know now how greatly our actions really influence others. We think that when in our own family circle, and when enjoying the innocent glass of beer, we do not see anything beyond the pale of our domestic sphere; we do not take into consideration whether it is at all probable or possible that the influence of this thing I am taking may extend the evil by next hour beyond the family circle and spread on all sides; and yet such is really the case in the great majority of instances. If one pious man drinks a small quantity of brandy, there are thousands of impious hearts ready to quote the example of that man.[35]

Here, Keshub drops the nation onto the family dinner table, inserting the mass of humanity between the man and his pint. No beer is "innocent" because no beer is private. To fail to recognize the public nature of the domestic sphere and its family circle is to ignore the centrality of behavioral "quotation" to the constitution of the political field. A man becomes a saint by his ability to set an example, entering the mass by iteration—something that anyone, Keshub implies, can do. Newly aware of this fact, the private man's relationship to all of his actions becomes mediated by the mass, open to imitation and thus, by some categorical imperative, rendered impersonal, national, open to legislation. The reference to "statistics" completes this process. Overlaid with "facts and figures," self-conduct becomes simultaneously personal, social, and political. Thus, where "every individual at the present age is trying, as it were, by his very civilization and intelligence to retire into his own family circle, and to close his eyes to the interests of those around him," Keshub refuses the individual its retreat from collectivity. He offers a theory of the subject that can be read as contravening liberal individuality to the extent that the individual is analytically detached from the quotable language of his behavior.[36]

A related model of behavioral mimicry appears to undergird Keshub's theory of colonialism. It is not the case, he argues, that English laws "force" Indians to "buy brandy." It is because of their "imitation of English life" that Indians carouse like drunken sailors and dump liquor bottles in streets, like those of Shimla, which were once the sacred stomping grounds of Hindu philosophers.[37] Here, we can see the basic lineaments of an argument that would achieve full form in the next century: to achieve self-rule, the colonized would have to rid themselves of the English "nature" acquired through behavioral citation and not just of English law.[38] In its nineteenth-century context, this claim suggests that society cannot be reformed through legislation alone. The state's sovereign laws stand too high above the social field to guide behavior in capillary fashion. Other means are needed to govern human conduct. Reform addresses itself to this gap, articulating a mode of power that mediates between the "Legislature" and the "family circle" by refusing the liberal individual his privatizing buffer against the world. Between the man and his pint, it seems, lurks not just one nation but many. Colonial connectivity vastly amplifies the iterability of behavior, thus implicating the entire globe in the "private" English citizen's littlest sip of pernicious drink. If Bhabha's work on colonial mimicry provides one tool for reading this scene of circulatory behavior, Weber's work on the peregrinations of the Protestant ethic provides another. In both cases, the subject fails to coincide with itself; it comes into being via behavioral patterns that connect it to other subjects.

By foregrounding relations of this type, the reform assemblage articulated a mode of politics that bypassed or supplemented the state, reaching for cross-generational and cross-colonial connections that could catalyze a thoroughgoing reform of society. It thus emerges via a principle of affinity as spiritual rather than blood relation. Returning to Rammohun's deathbed, we can see how the personal connections that crisscrossed the body of the dying reformer were central to this scene. The tableau of mourners that confronted Dr. Estlin when he reentered the sickroom is a study in the kinds of horizontal connections facilitated by reform. Moreover, the odd temporality of this tableau—poised among timelines both actual and potential, with its grief addressed as much to what Rammohun could have become as to what he had been—suggests the uncanny verticality of reform, as it clung to its own futures past.[39]

The remainder of this chapter explores this terrain by analyzing Keshub's English-language lectures and writings from the 1860s and 1870s. As I will argue, reform positioned the appeal to otherworldly perfection as one means by which the worldly particularity of colonial difference could be negated and converted into a principle of counter-colonial collectivity. I begin by tracing how Keshub's early writings define the egalitarian bonds of the Indian nation against the hierarchical bonds of priestcraft. I then suggest that, in place of priestcraft, Keshub experiments with a type of religious mediation most succinctly captured in his writings on the "Spirit Christ." Finally, I turn from Keshub to the broader scene of Bengali reform, to ask how the claims of spirit inscribed themselves into daily life via the ideal of worldly asceticism.

Young India: The Nation against the Priest

A pillar of missionary polemics against Hinduism, the rhetoric of "priestcraft" was also quickly adopted by Hindu reformers. Rammohun Roy was an early and ardent critic of priestly power. The figure of the despotic Brahman loomed over the "suttee" debates of which Rammohun was such an integral part, with priests allegedly pushing unwilling widows onto their husbands' funeral pyres. (In this emblematic scene, we see the presumed conflict between what would become Hindu reform's two paradigmatic objects, "priest" and "woman.")[40] Crafty priests likewise lurk behind Rammohun's English and Bengali translations of the Upanishads. As he explained in his *Translation of an Abridgment of the Vedant* (1816), although these scriptures are "most highly revered by all Hindoos," they remain "little known to the public" because they are "concealed within the dark curtain of the Sungskrit language."[41] The Brahmans are mere "self-interested . . . pretended guides" who maintain their authority over their "deluded followers" with the mantra "Believe whatever we may say—don't examine or even touch your scriptures, neglect entirely your reasoning faculties."[42] The Christian public, he argues, has likewise been deluded by "priestcraft," which, by "working on the ignorance and superstition, the bigotry and intolerance of mankind, . . . wrested [Jesus's] words to evil purposes."[43] The "public" only emerges as such, it would seem, once freed from the clutches of the priest.

Much the same contrast structures the early work of Keshub Chunder Sen. By comparing two of Keshub's earliest published essays, we can see how he used priestcraft as foil for defining the nation. *Young Bengal, This Is for You* (1860) was Keshub's first tract, published when he was just twenty-two years old. Its name is the name of Keshub's generation, a demographic (urban, male, and English-educated) that, as the *Bombay Saturday Review* wrote in 1861, consisted of "schoolboys whose sole title to the superiority they claim over their fathers is, apparently, that they have learnt to believe nothing."[44] Keshub was just as scathing in assessing his peers. Through English education, he wrote, Young Bengal had learned to regard religion as nothing but "a phantom conjured up by crafty priests to terrify and gall people in order to satisfy their own lust of lucre." It had begun by doubting only Hinduism, but, via the universalizing priestcraft narrative, eventually came "to doubt religion altogether."[45] What was needed, Keshub implied, was a means of preserving religion in the absence of the priest.

As though to answer this need, *An Appeal to Young India* (1865) presents the nation as the antidote to priestcraft. In 1864, Keshub undertook "a complete circuit of the Indian peninsula" that began the process of recasting the Bengali Brahmo Samaj as an all-India organization comprised (as the tract explains) of Young Bengal, Young Bombay, Young Madras, and Young Punjab.[46] English, with its subcontinental scope, is crucial to the tract's ability to call its presumed audience into being: anyone who can read this appeal is potentially a part of its imagined community. Noting that the "spirit of Western enlightenment" is "at work in the core of Hindu society," busily "revolutionising its entire organism," Keshub enjoins the "rising generation" to labor with it, instead of resisting it.[47] Shifting to the second person, he exhorts his readers to

Look at yourselves, enchained to customs, deprived of freedom, lorded over by an ignorant and crafty priesthood, your better sense and better feelings all smothered under the crushing weight of custom; look at your homes, scenes of indescribable misery, your wives and sisters, your mothers and daughters immured within the dungeon of the zenana, ignorant of the outside world, little better than slaves whose charter of liberty of thought and action has been ignored; look at your social constitution and customs, the mass of enervating, demoralizing, and degrading causes there working. Watch your daily life, how almost at every turn you meet with some demand for the sacrifice of your conscience, some temptation to hypocrisy, some obstacle to your improvement and true happiness.[48]

The series of views presented here moves between social registers in a manner indicative of the reform assemblage more broadly. Keshub moves his reader from the examination of the self, to examination of the home, to examination of society. In doing so, he maps out the three major fields that comprised the colonial Indian reform scene: religious reform, domestic reform, and the reform of the "social constitution" as a whole. Not incidentally, priestly despotism is the first of these, providing the paradigm for the type of spiritual slavery that prevails elsewhere.

Keshub then points to a fourth field implicitly positioned as the site where the other three are to be resolved: "daily life." "Say from your experience," he asks his reader, "whether the *spiritual government* under which you live is not despotism of the most galling and revolting type, oppressive to the body, injurious to the mind, and deadly to the soul?"[49] The imperative, second-person address is essential in that it inscribes Keshub's text into the lived "experience" of the reader. Only by examining his own life, Keshub implies, can the young Indian male see the despotic rule under which he lives and, in seeing it, also escape it. This turn toward the self institutes a new form of spiritual government. As Keshub explains, "those who desire to reform their country must first reform themselves. . . . We should remember that a nation is but the totality of individuals, and that without the reformation of individuals there can be no national reformation." Only "pseudo-reformers," he writes, "forget the individual in the nation." They "preach" and "theorize," but fail to engage in the only kind of "action" that counts: the "care of self."[50] Here, "India" as an imagined nation is positioned as emerging only once spiritual despotism is struck down so that the politics of spiritual autonomy, or self-care, can take hold, beginning at the most granular level: the conduct of daily life.

In condemning the "Brahminical order" for having set its members up as "the very vicegerents of the Deity," Keshub echoes colonial writers like James Mill who had likewise viewed caste as the product of priestcraft. Like these writers, Keshub takes the presumed pervasiveness of caste as a provocation to imagine an equally pervasive political principle, calling on his "fellow countrymen" to "establish and organize a new brotherhood" or "reformed alliance" that will be without "caste distinctions."[51] This "reformed alliance" reorders the social bonds at the base of the nation by unraveling the bonds of priestcraft and allowing new bonds to spontaneously emerge. First, "individuals" will "unite," followed by "families," then "cities and villages." Next regions (Young Bombay, Young Punjab, etc.) will "combine." At last, "the circle [will] gradually widen till it brings the whole nation together within its embrace!"[52] The physical touch of this final embrace is hardly neutral in a discussion that begins with a critique of caste; the same holds for the cross-lineal kinship of the coming "brotherhood."

Priestcraft remained a persistent problem for Keshub throughout his career—not least because he was frequently accused of it. After breaking with Debendranath Tagore in 1865 and splitting the Brahmo Samaj in two, he came to seem more and more like a charismatic guru who commanded intense loyalty from his youthful following. As one Dhaka Brahmo anonymously complained, Keshub's sensational 1866 lectures "Jesus Christ, Europe and Asia" and "Great Men" recast him as a "Saviour" intent on proving his own "greatmanship" in a manner fundamentally at odds with Brahmoism's absolute opposition to religious "mediators"— described here as "monster men." True Brahmos, writes the pamphleteer, are dedicated to "the great work of unmasking imposture that dwells under the guise of religion."[53] Or, as another anonymous "Old Brahmo" crisply declared in an 1869 pamphlet: "Away forever from the regions of Brahmoism, ye so called Saviours, Mediators, Intercessors, Redeemers, Prophets, God-men, Incarnations, *et hoc genus omne*." Here, the priest has become a genus—and, as the author strongly implies, is it a genus that most definitely includes Keshub.[54]

It is not my intention to try to clear Keshub of such charges. Nonetheless, I do think that before we use the stock narrative of priestly imposture to interpret and condemn him, we would do well to ask how he himself tried to rethink this narrative toward particular ends. It is well beyond the scope of this chapter to analyze the relationship between Keshub's writings and his practical experiments in religious community, from the Sangat Sabha to the Bharat Ashram. Keshub and his followers appear to have adapted Hindu and Christian religious technologies so as to produce contagious devotional affects that bonded group members to one another, as well as to Keshub as their charismatic leader. The almost Pentecostal ecstasy of these groups seems a direct inversion of the sober norms of liberal voluntary associations like the Brahmo Samaj.[55]

Keshub's writings on priestcraft, I would argue, bear directly on these experiments. They suggest that he permitted his followers' worshipful attitude toward him because he saw it as a catalyst for the creation of lateral bonds within the community. In other words, he fancied himself a mediator among his followers, rather than between his followers and the divine. Whether or not Keshub lived up to this ideal is a different question. But before we can even pose that question, we have to read Keshub's writings, taking them seriously as theoretical documents that provide an interpretive lens for his religious practices.

Take, for example, the 1866 "Great Men" speech that the Dhaka pamphleteer presents as evidence of priestcraft. With clear echoes of Thomas Carlyle's widely read *On Heroes, Hero-Worship, and the Heroic in History* (1841), the lecture uses the category of "great men" to consider the relationship between aristocratic feudalism and representative democracy. Unlike some of Keshub's other work, the lecture advocates for social hierarchy. Here, the despotic priesthood gives way not to universal brotherhood, but to an "aristocracy of great men" that is "representative, not arbitrary or despotic. Great men rule the masses. . . . because they faithfully represent the interests of those whom they govern." These aristocrats are unlike crafty priests because they "do not live on their own account," exercising an extraneous directive rule; instead, they "live for others." Thus, to honor them is not the same thing as "hero worship." As Keshub insists, in an almost proto-Durkheimian formula, the "people honour themselves by honouring their prophet."[56] The prophet, in other words, is a totem or symbol for society. His representativeness results from his self-abnegation: it is through his denial of self that he becomes a cipher for "the people," a mediatory self-emptying signifier.

There is a clear tension between the radical egalitarianism implied by terms like "human brotherhood," "reformed alliance," and "spiritual fellowship," and the hierarchical republicanism of the "Great Men" speech. I do not think that Keshub's work ever really resolves this tension; it does, however, explore and develop it in productive ways. The structure of authority outlined in "Great Men" recurs elsewhere—most vividly in the figure of the "Spirit Christ." Christ, for Keshub, is a paradigm for the self-abnegating religious leader who mediates the social bond that unites his followers into a single body. As a self-emptying signifier, Keshub's "Christ" implies a distinctly modern political form. It also positions *spirit* as a term indicating self-negation per se. I would suggest that Keshub, as guru, comes to occupy the position of this Spirit Christ or self-negating Great Man. To found the nation, he first has to interlink its discretely particular "little individualities." For this, he needs a mediating term: without a prophet-totem, "the people" cannot come to exist as such.

What I mean to suggest in the following discussion is that the "spirit" in Spirit Christ is related to the "spirit" in spiritual fellowship. In both cases, the spiritual places the particular under erasure in order to allow little individualities to coalesce into a larger assemblage that nonetheless consists only of such interlinked particularities (rather than becoming a reified entity in its own right). The spiritual, as described here, differs from liberal generality in that it signals its own artifice: the position of the Spirit Christ is impossible to inhabit. It is a non-position, a position that negates the subject. Seeking to occupy a position structurally similar to that of the Spirit Christ, Keshub situates this figure as a resolution to the problem of religious tutelage as well as the problem of religious difference. Indeed, it is partly by conjoining these two problems that Keshub lends his distinctive cast to the problematic of reform.

The Spirit Christ

For Keshub, "Spirit Christ" is a technical term. As he explains in a prayer of this title, there are three distinct possible Christs: (1) the physical Christ, "a thing of eyes and ears"; (2) the historical Christ, "a thing of facts and figures"; and (3) the spiritual Christ, "a joy forever." "The first two the world has seen, the last it has yet to see."[57] Generally preferring the abstract title "Christ" to the name of the historical personage "Jesus," Keshub is at pains to distinguish among these figures. His lectures on Christianity can be read an attempt to bring this third, spiritual "Christ" into view.

In the late nineteenth century, to claim Christ as "spiritual" was to claim him for India. Although Swami Vivekananda would not deliver his famous Chicago address until 1893, we can already see the trope of "spiritual India" under development in texts like Keshub's "Spirit Christ," anthologized in 1884. Keshub's use of this discourse is distinctive in that he aligns spirituality with potentiality. As he argued in an 1879 lecture, there is an "Ideal Jesus" that inhabits the historical Jesus in much the same way that the "future tree lies potentially in the small acorn.[58]" Although ontologically prior to the historical Jesus, the ideal-spiritual Jesus is chronologically posterior to it, as the historical Jesus's *telos*, or final cause. To use a term that Keshub develops in a much earlier lecture, the Ideal Jesus is the historical Jesus's "destiny," the principle of movement or "progress" that animates it from within and disrupts the actuality of its empirical existence.[59]

Keshub's first major lecture on Christianity was titled "Jesus Christ, Europe and Asia" (1866). As this title implies, his Christ is a means of uniting

West and East, the conjunctive *and* that sutures Europe to Asia and vice versa. In this lecture, Keshub famously claimed Christ as an "Asiatic," thus eliciting effusive applause. His effort to convert Christ away from Western Christianity did not achieve its full form until several years later, however. Three different lectures given on two continents over the course of a decade bring Keshub's "Spirit Christ" into view: "Christ and Christianity" (London, 1870); "India Asks—Who is Christ?" (Calcutta, 1879); and "We Apostles of the New Dispensation" (Calcutta, 1881).

In "Christ and Christianity," Keshub states the key move that structures his approach to Christian tradition. As he says, he "studied Christ ethically, nay, spiritually"; that is, while "standing aloof" from Christian "dogmas," he formed an "inward attachment to Christ" and tried to become "Christ-like" through the "work of reformation."[60] This is Keshub's major renunciation. He withdraws from the historical particularity of "dogma" so as to align himself with the ethical ideal latent in that dogma as its spirit. As he repeatedly stresses, he aims to surpass the merely "particular ideas" that Christians hold based on their "peculiar circumstances."[61] Keshub goes on to address those who find themselves unresponsive to Christ. Even they, he suggests, can "still accept his spirit" and "try to be Christ-like":

When every individual man becomes Christian in spirit—repudiate the name if you like—when every individual man becomes as prayerful as Christ was, as loving and forgiving towards his enemies as Christ was, as self-sacrificing as Christ was, then these little units, these little individualities, will coalesce and combine together by the *natural affinity of spirits*; and these new creatures, reformed, regenerated, in the childlike and Christ-like spirit of devotion and faith, will feel drawn toward each other, and they shall constitute the true Church according to Christ's ideal.[62]

This, I will propose, is the central passage, not only for this 1870 lecture, but also for Keshub's writings on Christianity more broadly. It opens by suggesting that to become Christian "in spirit" is to "repudiate the name" of Christianity. Once Christianity's dogmatic particularity has been effaced, a new social principle begins to emerge. "Little individualities," stripped of self, undergo a chemical re-composition, drawing together by a principle of spiritual "affinity" to form a new "Church" based on "Christ's ideal"—which is to say, a collectivity founded on the principle of ascetic self-sacrifice.

Keshub uses the word *affinity* only in passing here, quickly shifting to a second term that serves much the same function for him: *sympathy*. If the British Empire has failed to produce a real global community, it is because of its failures of sympathy: just as "England cannot sympathize with

India," so "even one part of England cannot sympathize with another." Here, sympathy is the "electric fluid" that draws people and nations together. The improvisational space of the lecture hall demonstrates how it works: it is along lines of sympathy that Keshub finds himself "drawn to" each of his listeners.[63] Crisscrossing lines of sympathy, we might infer, traverse the little individualities gathered together in the lecture hall, such that each is drawn toward the others through forces that exceed her.

Nine years later, the Calcutta lecture "India Asks—Who Is Christ?" developed this theory of sympathy still further. Opening with a description of an "Asiatic Christ, divested of all western appendages," the speech goes on to argue that India has a *national affinity* to the invisible as well as to the visible Christ."[64] Where his earlier (1866) lecture had turned Christ toward India by dressing him in Oriental robes, this 1879 lecture presents us with a third Christ, "inward" and "invisible," who supersedes both of his visible counterparts, the Eastern and the Western. By Keshub's account, Christ's central teaching was the gnostic claim that "I and my Father are one," which implies the "absorption" of the self into the "Godhead." As Keshub reveals halfway through the lecture, this "doctrine of divine humanity" is "essentially a Hindu doctrine" that "millions of men in this land believe."[65] In becoming a true ascetic, Christ thus also becomes a "true Yogi."[66]

It is no mistake that Christian missionaries took Keshub for a potential agent of mass conversion. His lectures insistently turn India away from Hinduism so that it might "reach Christ."[67] Not unreasonably, missionaries often assumed that such claims were a means of bringing India to Christianity. This, however, was far from the case. In turning India toward Christ, Keshub also turns "Christ" away from Christianity as a historically particular religion. The equation "I and my Father are one," Keshub clarifies, expresses "the philosophical principle . . . of self-abnegation."[68] Through it, Christ achieved the "highest form of self-denial," having "destroyed," "renounced," and "denied his self altogether." Christ, for Keshub, represents "self-sacrifice" as such, and it is only via self-sacrifice that he becomes the paradigm for a "perfect asceticism."[69] This much had already been stated fairly explicitly in the 1870 London lecture on Christianity, which had likewise indicated that the very name of Christianity could and should be renounced in order to realize Christianity's spiritual potential. In the 1879 Calcutta lecture, however, Keshub begins to theorize self-abnegation in historicist terms by appropriating one of the organizing ideas of Christian theology.

In "Who Is Christ?," Keshub recalls "the passage in the Gospel" in which Jesus says "I am not come to destroy, but to fulfill." Keshub goes on to predict that Christ will fulfill not just the "Mosaic dispensation," but also "the Hindu dispensation."[70] For decades, British missionaries had been spreading a hermeneutic of prefiguration in India, claiming that Indian religions were vague presentiments of a Christian truth yet to come. Keshub lays claim to this discourse, but only to put it to an unforeseen use: as a reading strategy that effaces the historical particularity of religion in the name of a spiritual universal, it could also be turned against Christianity.

A strongly worded response to this lecture by the Church Missionary Society's Reverend W. R. Blackett clarifies the lecture's stakes. Blackett begins by protesting that Keshub's Christ is "not the Christ whose history is written in the Gospel records." "Jesus," he pleads, "is a real man amid real scenes, a living Oriental in an Eastern land. Do not attempt, then, to subtilize Him into an abstraction. He is and ever must be . . . a *fact*, clothed with all the circumstances of actuality." Blackett is correct: Keshub's spirit Christ negates history, converting empirical fact into subtle abstraction, actuality into potentiality. Blackett's historical Christ, meanwhile, cannot be budged from "Judea."[71]

But, as Blackett goes on to demonstrate, Christian insistence on Christ's historical "actuality" was fraught. Jesus's Jewishness is one actuality that even Blackett feels the need to "subtilize": "In very truth, while on one side the Lord Jesus can only be really understood as a Jew speaking to Jews in a Jewish way, in another respect He was altogether outside or above the limits of nationality." As several scholars have recently argued, discourses on religion in colonial India frequently made use of the figure of "the Jew" to articulate notions of religious minority and "ethnic" (as opposed to "universal") religion.[72] Fulfillment theology was a clear case in point. Generations of Christian exegetes had developed allegorical reading strategies that allowed them to neutralize the religious particularities of the Hebrew Bible so as to claim its texts as proto-Christian. In the nineteenth century, missionaries redeployed this hermeneutic in the colonies. So, to take one of Blackett's examples, "*Práyaschitta*" (ritual purification) could be said to prefigure the Christian doctrine of "atonement," just as the Passover lamb had prefigured the crucifixion.[73] In both cases, the Christian doctrine is the "fulfillment" of its predecessor; it simultaneously completes and negates it, overturning the flesh of the lamb to release the spirit of Christ.

It somewhat perverse, then, for Blackett to fault Keshub for "putting a double meaning upon Christian language."[74] Christianity had been doubling scriptural meaning for two millennia; Keshub is just following suit. Indeed, Christianity's ability to read its past doubly was at the heart of its claim on the souls of the colonized. As Blackett argues, Christianity's global spread is "one of the proofs" of its "divine origin." That is, Christianity becomes Christian (rather than Jewish) at the moment that it effaces the historical specificity of its beginnings to become a "universal" religion. Its Jewish origins under erasure, it can spread to Syrians, Greeks, Italians, and Saxons, and then on to "Hindus, Africans, Red Indians, Chinese, [and] Polynesians."[75] This achingly imperial chronology underscores the extent to which nineteenth-century Christianity's self-narrative was caught up with colonialism. One could dispute its historical "facts" (to recall Blackett's term), which are certainly suspect. Keshub, however, demonstrates a commitment to theory, exploiting one of missionary discourse's key internal contradictions in order to claim that discourse away from Blackett and his ilk.

Because it purports to deny difference as such, this stratum of Christian theology apparently appealed to Keshub as a means of intervening in colonial ideologies predicated on the maintenance of difference. Already in the 1866 lecture, Keshub had juxtaposed his wish that Jesus might conjoin "Europe and Asia" with the Pauline claim that in Christianity "there is neither Greek nor Jew."[76] Demoting the historical Jesus to a mere local particularity, Keshub does not, however, elevate Hinduism to the status of the universal in Christianity's place. Instead, he insists that a true universal must be devoid of dogmatic (i.e., discursive) content. His "Spirit Christ" is not so much the principle of self-abnegation as it is an operator of self-abnegation, the procedure of negation as such. For Hinduism to "reach Christ" would thus be for it to repudiate its name, ceasing to be "Hindu" but without thereby becoming "Christian."

We see the clearest development of this theme in Keshub's 1881 lecture, "We Apostles of the New Dispensation." The lecture opens by contrasting the "dried bones" of religious dogma to the "living" spirit of true religion. Identifying the "New Dispensation" with this spirit, it enumerates this dispensation's three principle traits: immediacy, synthesis, and subjectivity. These three traits, I suggest, indicate how Keshub positions his Spirit Christ as a resolution not only to the problem of religious difference, but also to the problem of religious tutelage.

The first two traits of the New Dispensation—immediacy and synthesis—appear at first glance to be simple restatements of longstanding Brahmo concerns. On the one hand, the New Dispensation stipulates that everyone approach God directly, without the help of a "prophet-mediator."[77] On the other, it promotes an "all-inclusive and all-absorbing eclecticism."[78] The third trait, subjectivity, provides the framework through which the first two are to be understood. Subjectivity is the principle by which the New Dispensation "endeavors to convert" the "barren outward fact, the dead Christ of history and dogma," into a new Christ that is a "living spirit, a fact of consciousness."[79] This conversion from the outward to the inward (that is, the move from dogma to spiritual force) is what prompts the emergence of the principle of spiritual fellowship, or affinity.

To illustrate how the "principle of subjectivity" reorders social relations, Keshub describes a "practical application" of this principle: the "Pilgrimages to Saints." This was a meditative practice that Keshub promoted among his followers in the years around 1880: they were to concentrate on and thus draw close to a series of past prophets like Moses. When pilgrims approach the saints in this way, says Keshub, they "commune with them in spirit, killing the distance of time and space. We enter into them, and they enter into us."[80] Just as the spirit kills the letter of religious law, so too does it kill the empirical fact of geographical and historical distance. Keshub stresses that this is not a supernatural, but rather "a normal psychological process, to which neither science nor theology can take exception. Here is the subject mind, there is the object—a prophet or a saint. The subject, by a mysterious though natural process, absorbs the object," which is "spiritually *drawn into*" it.[81] As that verb should suggest, it is the "theory of sympathy" or "fellow-feeling" (the electric fluid that draws little individualities together) that explains "the efficacy of saintly communion." Here, sympathy is described as a force that "breaks" the "iron chains" of "selfishness." It "drags us into the bosom of the sorrowing brother" and "makes us one with others."[82] The mental pilgrimage to the deceased saint is a spiritual exercise that trains the subject to develop his capacity for sympathy, traversing the gap that separates subject from object.

The prominence of saints here might seem puzzling. After all, as Keshub insists, the New Dispensation's definitive characteristic is its absolute eschewal of any "prophet-mediator."[83] The New Dispensation, in other words, is fully consistent with Brahmoism's longstanding dislike for "God-Men . . . *et hoc genus omne.*" Here, Keshub presents his own charismatic authority in a manner that recalls his formulation in "Great Men": if the prophet-aristocrat is sufficiently self-abnegating, to honor him is not to indulge in hero worship. By honoring him, the people honor themselves. Keshub concedes that every religious "dispensation has a central personality, and that, therefore, willingly or unwillingly, I must permit myself to be treated as a Moses or a Chaitanya."[84] Even as he permits his followers to turn him into a prophet, however, he insists that "behind the visible 'I' there is an invisible 'We.' It is my Church that speaks through me. . . . Behind and around me are brother-apostles, who think and feel and live as I do, united with me in spirit."[85] Keshub's individuality is a cipher for the collectivity that he represents and that traverses him with lines of affinity or sympathy. The visible (i.e., actual and historical) particularly of his ego conceals the invisible (i.e., potential and spiritual) collectivity of a universal "Church." Keshub is thus, to be sure, a prophet-mediator. But rather than mediating between the human and the divine, he mediates between the human and the human.

As one Brahmo wrote, the "necessity of mediation" is such a universal feature of religion that even some of its staunchest opponents "have themselves been converted into mediators." With regard to Brahmoism, one can thus safely say that "Mr. Sen or some other leader will erelong be converted into a mediator in spite of all the loud talk against mediation associated with it!"[86] Religious mediation is unavoidable. In order to prevent being "converted" into a mediator, then, Keshub had to convert mediation into something other than a byword for exploitative priestcraft. If he did this in one way through his own charismatic authority, he did so in another through his favorite mantra: "The Fatherhood of God and the Brotherhood of Man." Fatherhood, this formula implies, is what allows Brotherhood to emerge. That is, the social field can only be divested of hierarchy if that hierarchy is displaced and projected onto a transcendent referent. The Pauline result is a denial of the "obnoxious distinctions between Brahmin and Sudra, between Hindu and Yavana, between Asiatic and European." In place of "invidious distinction," the New Dispensation "seeks to establish one vast brotherhood among the children of the great God."[87] To become Christ-like is to cultivate this "universal spirit of sonship." By practicing "filial obedience" to the divine father, the follower of the New Dispensation establishes his formal identity with all other such sons—which is to say, all humanity.[88] As a mediator, Keshub simply helps to articulate the lateral bond between these spiritual brothers, rather than standing between those brothers and their shared Father.

We might say here that the transcendent is a converter: by negating the historical differences between persons or nations, it facilitates the combination of otherwise discrete entities. The New Dispensation, says Keshub, is the "mighty absorbent," the chemical precipitant that by altering the internal structure of self-enclosed subjectivities, allows new assemblages to take hold by a principle of "spiritual affinity" or "sympathy."[89] It is a catalyst for the formation of transversal spiritual connections.

Although Keshub's devotion to Christ was often taken as evidence of his sympathy for Christianity, it should instead be understood as an effort to develop "Christ" as a technology for actualizing the internal convertibility of religion—the innate tendency of religion to negate its own historical particularity through an appeal to spirit. If we see this convertibility developed in one way in relation to Keshub as charismatic religious leader, we see it developed in another way among his followers—or, at least, among the culture of worldly asceticism that characterized the Brahmo Samaj more broadly. In the final section of this chapter, I leave the priest behind to ask how Keshub and other Brahmos discussed asceticism as a technology of self-rule. I highlight two key themes: the convergence of religiously eclectic ascetic technologies in colonial India, and the ambivalent position of the ascetic at the margins of freedom and domination. The ambivalent position of the ascetic—situated between subjects and between cultures—is part of what made him such a productive figure for the nineteenth-century reform assemblage. I should clarify that the following discussion departs substantially from the preceding analysis. Nonetheless, it does carry forward Keshub's interest in self-negation. The worldly ascetic suspends his particularity by mediating daily life through the transcendent; by placing the self under partial erasure, the ascetic thus also potentially opens himself to identification with others through lines of spiritual affinity.

The Protestant Ethic and the Spirit of Asceticism

Reflecting back on colonial Bengal in the years just after Independence, Nirad Chaudhuri described the Brahmo Samaj as form of "Hindu Protestantism" that was "based for the most part on Puritan Christianity."[90] Some twenty-five later David Kopf would restate this basic claim: the "this-worldly asceticism" on view in texts like Debendranath Tagore's *Brahmo Dharma* (1850), he suggested, recalls Max Weber's influential account of the Protestant ethic. Like Weber's Puritans, Brahmos stressed values like "self-reliance, perseverance, and the utility of hard work." They even took an interest in Benjamin Franklin's *Autobiography*, Weber's paradigm for post-Protestant self-discipline.[91] There is no denying that Brahmos adopted some of the major cultural forms of Protestantism, such as the Sunday worship service. But to suggest that their worldly asceticism was "based for the most part" on Christianity is surely going too far. Instead, I would propose that we ask whether and how Brahmo asceticism might have been a means to exploit what P. C. Mozoomdar termed the internal convertibility of these assorted religious disciplines.

The question of whether the Brahmo Samaj "Protestantized" Hinduism also returns us to Rammohun Roy. Variously hailed as an "orthodox Vedantist," a "very sound Moulvi," and the "first Brahmin-Hindu converted to Christianity," Rammohun Roy was, as one later enthusiast put it, alternately reckoned a "universal pervert" and a "universal receptacle" of all religious truth.[92] The question of conversion has dogged Rammohun Roy ever since, albeit in altered form. Where some scholars see him as promoting Unitarianism, others argue that his primary debt was to Hindu tradition.[93] Perhaps Rammohun changed religions or religious orientation multiple times during his life.[94] Perhaps he simply seemed to, skillfully pivoting among different audiences during of his thirty-year career.[95]

Conversion, as a set of cultural, institutional, and legal practices, substantially constrained the political possibilities open to religious actors in colonial India.[96] Among other things, it was a means of conceptualizing religious difference. In dramatizing a decisive "turning" from one religion toward another, conversion narratives presume that religions are discrete, stable entities across which human actors can move; such narratives enact connection and disjunction simultaneously, drawing two religions together only to insist on their essential incompatibility. If we want to follow Keshub in rethinking the grammar of modern religion, then we also have to reconsider the grammar of of conversion.

This is the context in which I want to return to the notion of assemblage outlined above. As I suggested, Mozoomdar's rereading of religions as accretions of internally convertible forces suggests one means of thinking past the logic of family relations that usually structures accounts of religious and cultural encounter. Forces are inherently mobile, and their points of origin matters less than the direction they are headed.

By turning from comparative theology to spiritual discipline, Mozoomdar arguably situates the ascetic body as a privileged site for the conversion of these spiritual forces. As a dense transfer point where multiple spiritual forces converge, the ascetic learns to simplify, accumulate, and consolidate those forces, pointing them in novel directions. If the conversion narrative presents religions as fixed discursive or institutional fields across which believing individuals move at will, the convertibility narrative presents religions as unstable fields of forces that migrate across the disciplined body of the religious subject. Indeed, the body becomes religious insofar as it is composed and recomposed of such transversal lines of force. By this account, the claim that the Brahmo Samaj Protestantized Hinduism proceeds under false assumptions. If Brahmos experimented with the Protestant ethic, they necessarily also experimented with converting that ethic away from Protestantism. An ethic is a spiritual force that, when applied to a body, tends to change direction.

The figure of the worldly ascetic that rose to prominence between the 1860s and 1880s thus should not be understood as evidence of Protestantization. This would be, in a sense, to simply "apply" Weber to Indian materials. Instead, we should view this figure as anticipating Weber and giving rise to the problematic that we now mostly associate with him. As we will see in the following chapters, worldly asceticism was a topic of keen interest to Karsandas Mulji, Dayananda Saraswati, and Helena Blavatsky, among others. To lay the groundwork for my discussion of these figures, here I call attention to five essential features of the Brahmo ideal of the ascetic householder. Precisely because the figure of the bourgeois Brahmo figures so prominently in the scholarship on religion in colonial India, it can be used schematize worldly asceticism in an especially clear way. Indeed, it serves as a sort of paradigm for Hindu worldly asceticism more broadly. Where the following chapters work to complicate this paradigm, collapsing it back into the cultural crosscurrents from which it was taken, here I offer a brief sketch of it.

First, the ascetic householder was a norm enjoined on a particular demographic: urban, *bhadralok*, and male. Wife and child are routinely presented as extensions of the Brahmo male body, and the frequent injunctions to treat the workplace as "sacred" indicate the extent to which this class of men adhered to values such as industriousness and "economy."[97] This is the world of what Hatcher has called "bourgeois Hinduism."[98]

Second, the ascetic householder was a norm that drew on multiple cultural traditions. Or, more precisely, it emerged in close relationship to the problematic of colonial difference, demarcating and defining religious differences rather than receiving them as pre-given. Debendranath Tagore, for his part, tended to emphasize a Sanskritic heritage. Sometimes he described the ascetic subject's stance towards the world using the figure of the charioteer, familiar from the *Katha Upanishad*: "As the charioteer restrains his steeds, so shall ye restrain the senses engaged with objects."[99] At other times, he repeated the *Bhagavad Gita*'s demand that the actor guard against attachment to the "fruits" of action, offering these fruits up as a sacrifice to God.[100] Keshub, meanwhile, and in a much more Christian vein, emphasized the power of prayer. The staggeringly large number of prayers and hymns that he authored in Bengali and English include morning prayers, evening prayers, prayers for times of prosperity, prayers for times of affliction, prayers for fortitude, prayers of thanksgiving, school prayers, deathbed prayers, family prayers, and congregational prayers.[101]

Third, as indicated by the thoroughness of Keshub's prayer list, the ascetic householder was a norm that regulated daily life in microscopic detail. Prayer was an ascetic technology of the self (in the Foucauldian sense) that oriented the subject away from the world and toward God throughout the day. "The householder shall rise early in the morning, but not too early, never too late," writes Keshub. "Seven hours' sleep hath the Lord enjoined on his people." Upon rising, the householder is to follow a well-ordered morning regimen. He expresses thanks to the Lord; engages in "moderate exercises"; reads the morning paper; takes his daily bath (while reverently pondering the waters mentioned in the *Rig Veda*); worships in his home sanctuary; eats his morning meal; and, finally, arrives punctually at his work place.[102] This regimen is intensely detailed: Keshub goes so far as to prescribe a particular way of toweling off after a bath. As a disciplinary technique, prayer fractures daily life by orienting it toward the divine. Just as the bathwater is mediated by the waters of the *Rig Veda*, so are other ordinary places and objects abstracted from their immediate context and linked to a transcendent referent.

Fourth, the ascetic householder was a norm that overturned the traditional bifurcation of religious law. Where classical Hinduism had asserted the complementarity of householder and renunciant (as in the four life stages or *ashrama*s), Rammohun Roy and his successors fused the two, holding up "saintly practice" (*shishtachara*) as a religious paradigm for "every woman, man, and child." Like Shaunaka, the "great householder" to whom the *Mundaka Upanishad* is addressed, the layperson should worship the abstract Supreme Being, exercise control over the senses, and live a disciplined, orderly, and moral life.[103] Rammohun's writings thus, as Bruce Robertson suggests, undo the spiritual elitism advocated by Shankaracharya and other thinkers by stipulating "one universal mode of worship for everyone."[104] A *Brahmo Catechism* published in the 1890s makes the case just as forcefully: "God's law is the same for all mankind." It "cannot enjoin some to live in the bosom of families and others to retire to a forest." Neither can it mandate universal monasticism: "If all men became ascetics," then the "human race" would become "extinct."[105] The only remaining alternative is a worldly asceticism that reorders the immanent according to the dictates of the transcendent, but without compromising the bio-productivity of the nation.

Fifth, and finally, the norm of the "ascetic householder" was explicitly addressed to the problematic of spiritual despotism and religious tutelage. To conceive of the self as a charioteer standing apart from the sensory world, or to dissociate the doer from both the deed and its fruits, cultivates a particular type of habitus, a way of being toward the world that buffers the self against whatever lies outside it. The presumed result is an absolute autonomy of the ascetic subject. Tagore puts the matter succinctly: "All that lays a man under the dominion of another, is a source of misery; all that places him under the dominion of himself, is the source of happiness." Thus, "Brahmos must strive for independent lives. Each must practice thinking for himself and depending upon himself. Never be a dependent upon another, if you have power to do otherwise."[106] Self-rule, however, was necessarily imbricated with new regimes of discipline. As suggested by Tagore's proliferating imperatives, the ascetic householder was a norm external to those subjects who opted to inhabit it, submitting to it as an external power. The contradictory kernel at the heart of this discipline shines through in the injunction: "By day and night, instruct yourselves—govern yourselves."[107] Self-government only becomes possible once the self-governing subject has submitted to an external imperative, learning to inhabit this directive as its proper subject position.

Self-government thus fractures the subject. As Tagore dizzyingly remarks, the "self by which the self is conquered—that self is the friend of the self. Self is always friend, and self is always enemy."[108] The ascetic self cannot be self-identical. It is always split, both the subject and the object of its own disciplinary procedures. The result is a doubling or internal spacing of the self that makes subjectivity a form of society. Indeed, in dividing itself so as to become both "friend" and "enemy," the ascetic subject makes itself a first ground for the political as such.

Like so many of his contemporaries, Keshub Chunder Sen sought to distinguish between good and bad forms of asceticism. The otherworldly "yogi" and "faqueer" demonstrate asceticism's "admitted evils": its misanthropic attitude, its excessive attachment to self-punishment, its renunciation of children and family. But even though "modern civilization hates it, laughs at it, and is determined to hunt it out of the world," there is "something good" in asceticism that can and must be recuperated. The "essence" of asceticism, Keshub argues, is "the crucifixion of worldliness" through self-sacrifice.[109] Here, we find echoes of the Spirit Christ: asceticism is the means by which the subject crucifies or negates his worldly particularity so that little individualities can begin to coalesce along emergent lines of spiritual affinity.

––––––––

I want to close this discussion of Keshub's English writings with a final suggestion. Keshub returned periodically throughout his career to the question of how to define *religion*. Early on, he defines it as "the bond that binds 'man to man, and all to God," although stressing the latter aspect: religion is "constancy," the discipline that draws the human toward its divine fulfillment.[110] Later, he returns to the same formula ("the true object of religion is to bind mankind together, and to bind them all to God") but with greater emphasis on "spiritual fellowship" among men.[111]

If religion is primarily a means of binding the social, then it draws remarkably close to another term that assumes considerable importance for Keshub: yoga. The "power of spiritual communion" embodied by the Christian Eucharist, he explained in 1881, is none other than the "yoga faculty" of the Hindus. It is through yoga that we can "annihilate space and time, and bring home to our minds an external Deity and an external humanity." It is through yoga, in other words, that one achieves the "true object of religion"—thus raising the question of whether, for Keshub, *yoga* rather than *dharma* is the best translation for *religion*.

The doubled meaning that yoga assumes here is fitting. It is the yoke of ascetic self-discipline, that which turns the immanent toward the transcendent so that it might reach its destiny in the divine; it is also the conjunctive *and* that intertwines immanent individualities through a logic of spiritual affinity that takes the constitutive incompletion of the human as its ground and precondition. It is the "yoke of religion" that a person must accept in order to become "Christ-like," as well as the principle through which colonial difference is dissolved: "How by yoga one nation becomes another! How Asia eats the flesh and drinks the blood of Europe! How the Hindu absorbs the Christian; how the Christian assimilates the Hindu!"[112] Yoga, as religion, is the bond in spiritual affinity and the principle of transcolonial connection.

In this chapter, we have seen how Keshub Chunder Sen built toward this vision of religion as a principle of connection. We began at the deathbed of Rammohun Roy, which at first glance appears as an assembly of discrete individuals. The longer we circle around this assembly, however, the more it comes to seem like an assemblage—these little individualities aspire to be other than what they are, drawing together along lines of spiritual affinity that disassemble the gathered subjects so that they might be reassembled differently. The desire to transcend the self, by partly negating the subject of reform, helps nudge that subject closer to others. Thus, although I introduced the term reform assemblage partly to capture the expansiveness of the nineteenth-century reform scene, I also used it to read that scene against the grain: running alongside the liberal institutional form of the voluntary association, we find a very different political imaginary predicated on the dissolution of the individual. For Keshub, the relation priest-follower was a crucial if partly disavowed figure for this dissolution. Keshub objected to the accusation that he had become a priestly mediator, who stood between the human and the divine. In doing so, I suggested, he experimented with a different type of mediation—one that links the human to the human. It is only through a mediator or Spirit Christ, he implies, that little individualities can coalesce into an open-ended assemblage.

FOUR

Guru Is God

Sudhārvuṃ, *verb*, 1. To amend. 2. To improve; to ameliorate; to reform; to civilize; to correct KARSANDAS MULJI, *POCKET DICTIONARY OF GUJARATI AND ENGLISH* (1862)

Priestly craft is ever alert to obtain by fair means or foul the wealth needful to the sustentation of its power and self-indulgence. This is a vice not limited in its operations to India, or to the chiefs of the sect of the Hindu religion: it pervades all human society, with greater or lesser energy. KARSANDAS MULJI, *HISTORY OF THE SECT OF MAHARAJAS* (1865)

At Madame Tussaud's Wax Works, while strolling through corridors filled with English monarchs, American presidents, and Indian governors general, Karsandas Mulji (1832–1871) found himself face-to-face with three figures eerily reminiscent of his own recent past: the "great reformers" (*sudhārāwāḷā mahā puruṣ*) Knox, Calvin, and Luther. These wax statues, he later wrote, were like actual people "with only their spirits yet to be put in" (*mātra jīvaj mukvānuṃ bākī che*).[1] Just one year earlier, back home in Bombay, Mulji had himself been acclaimed as "a Reformer, a Martin Luther of the Banian caste" for the role that he had played in the scandalous Maharaj Libel Case.[2] Now he was further challenging the bounds of caste and community by voyaging over the "black waters" to the metropolitan heart of the British empire, surely realizing that when he returned home and refused ritual purification he would be outcasted and ostracized by all but the most radical of his friends and acquaintances. But return was not only inevitable; it came sooner than expected. Ill-health plagued Mulji in cold, wet London, and after refusing a doctor's advice to eat meat during his stay, he resolved to return to the tropics in September, before winter settled over England.[3]

Although Mulji does not expand upon his encounter with the wax Luther in his *Inglaṇḍmāṃ Pravās* (*Travels in England* [1866]), it is a strikingly resonant moment—and not just for Mulji, but also for the Hindu reformist milieu of which he was a signal part. Two Luthers faced off that day in 1863, and in their uncanny doubling they offer a window onto how the Victorian Luther, as a symbolic property, circulated in the colonial nineteenth century. If the wax effigy had inherited the form of Luther, Mulji, it would seem, had inherited the "great reformer's" missing spirit. The German original, meanwhile, remained conspicuously absent: whatever Martin Luther's early modern accomplishments, they bear only a tangential relationship to the nineteenth-century Anglosphere. As the scene at Madame Tussaud's suggests, more important than how either of these latter-day Luthers relates to his early modern referent is how each of them relates to the other, in a web of signification contemporary to both and specific to their historical moment.

In this chapter, I attempt to chart some of the interrelations between metropolitan and colonial citations of Luther by analyzing Karsandas Mulji and his relationship to Protestantism. Mulji's reputation still rests mostly on his status as an "Indian Luther" who liberated his caste fellows from "spiritual tyranny" during the celebrated Maharaj Libel Case (1862).[4] Here, I look past that scandalous trial, driven largely by the English-language press, to consider Mulji's earlier writings in Gujarati and the project of reform suggested by them. During the Maharaj Libel Case, it was said that to depict Mulji as a Luther was to put the "case . . . forward unfairly."[5] In anticlerical English, the tale of Reformation could have only one outcome, with Luther its preordained winner. Here, I use Mulji's early writings to find a different way of narrating his conflict with the Maharaj. Instead of a contest between "Protestant" self-rule and "Catholic" submission to priestly authority, I suggest, we should understand Mulji and the Maharaj as each plying a different kind of ascetic self-discipline geared toward the transformation or reformation of human subjectivity.

Where the preceding chapters of *Spiritual Despots* ask how the Victorian Luther came under pressure within Britain, or in the space between colony and metropole, this and subsequent chapters shift focus to India and the Hindu reform movements that gained ground there between the 1850s and the 1880s. Each chapter takes up a single reformer or reform movement, taking its topic as a metonym for this broader scene. Although each chapter is structured around an invocation of priestcraft, priests are not my primary focus. Instead, I am interested in how the critique of priestcraft framed discussions about technologies of self-rule—technologies that I analyze under the rubric of "worldly asceticism." With this phrase, as I explain in the Introduction, I mean to refigure Weber by way of Foucault, while rerouting both these thinkers through the colonial nineteenth century. Each chapter goes about this project somewhat differently. As a whole, however, they suggest the extent to which Hindu reformers' experiments in self-rule served as a means of exploiting the internal convertibility of religions. By facilitating the circulation of ascetic technologies of the self, these reformers positioned "ethics" as a key ground for reimagining society.

This section of *Spiritual Despots* begins with Karsandas Mulji. I open my discussion with a brief biography of Mulji before turning to his star appearance in the Maharaj Libel Case. Next, leaving the trial behind, I trace the continuities that interlink Mulji's earlier Gujarati essays on seemingly discrete topics: ethics, women, and priests, respectively. Finally, I turn from Mulji to the Maharaj to suggest that these two ostensibly opposed figures can be read as having plied parallel technologies of ascetic self-government.

Karsandas Mulji: A Short Life

Although well known to scholars of nineteenth-century Bombay, Karsandas Mulji is otherwise a relatively obscure figure, his important contributions to Hindu reform culture muted by the persistent personal setbacks that he faced during his short and tragic life. During the 1850s and 60s, Mulji was among the most prominent members of the class that Christine Dobbin has termed the "Bombay intelligentsia." Educated in English, these men quickly came into conflict with the established authorities of what Dobbin calls Bombay's "merchant aristocracy," an alliance of commercial magnates and traditional caste leaders.[6] Mulji's story is in many ways the story of his class. A classic instance of a Macaulay man, Mulji was mocked in his lifetime for "aping" the English by wearing trousers.[7] His fellow Elphinstonians of the 1840s and 50s included Dadabhai Naoroji, Bhau Daji, K. R. Cama, M. G. Ranade, as well as Mulji's close friends and associates, the poet Narmadshankar Lalshankar and the educationalist Mahipatram Rupram. As they graduated from Elphinstone and entered public life, such men formed a new elite that eventually wrested a good deal of power away from their traditionalist competitors.

Unlike his friends, however, Mulji had a precarious class status. Disowned by his family at an early age, he had to work frenetically in order to make ends meet, moving frequently between city and mofussil and working multiple jobs, often at the same time. He served variously as a writer, editor, teacher, cloth merchant, and government administrator. His passionate advocacy for reform causes overextended him still further. Reform brought him renown; but it also, by pitting him against caste elites, significantly limited his ability to find stable work, thus contributing to his persistent ill health and difficult home life.

Mulji was born into an elite commercial caste group; his maternal ancestors had been among the first Bania merchants to relocate from Gujarat to Bombay. But when Karsandas was seven, his mother died. Upon his father's remarriage, the boy permanently shifted to the home of his maternal aunt, who enrolled him in both Gujarati and English schools. In 1848, when he was sixteen, his aunt was widowed. In the same year, he was married to Valibai, a young woman who herself died four years later, in 1852. Both of the young couple's two children predeceased their mother.

Mulji's public life began in 1853, when he was twenty-one years old and a student at Elphinstone. That year, he wrote two essays that would determine the course of his life. One, which advocated foreign travel, was read before the Buddhi Vardhak Hindu Sabha. Meeting with great acclaim, it established him as a rising star of the reform world. The other, which advocated widow remarriage, was discovered in his desk by a prying servant and handed over to his widowed aunt, who, as a religiously orthodox upper-caste woman, was horrified by its argument. She ejected Karsandas from her home, and he soon had to withdraw from Elphinstone.

Mulji found work as a newspaper editor and school administrator. In 1855, in collaboration with the Parsi-run *Rast Goftar*, he founded his own reformist newspaper, the *Satya Prakash* (*Light of Truth*), addressed to Gujarati Hindus. Although it had only five hundred subscribers, the paper was an important voice for extending the criticism of tradition already underway among Marathi-speaking Hindus and Gujarati-speaking Parsis to Bombay's Gujarati Hindu population. Throughout the late 1850s, Mulji worked assiduously. He edited several papers, including the *Satya Prakash*, the *Rast Goftar*, the *Niti Bodhak*, the *Mumbaina Bazaar*, and the women's journal *Stri Bodh*; wrote extensively in article and book form; and cofounded a Chinese cloth shop. For a time, he took up the post of headmaster at the English School in Deesa, in north Gujarat, but was forced to return to Bombay after only ten months due to ill health. In 1857, he married for a second time; his wife died within six months. That December, he undertook his third marriage, but he refused to participate in traditional wedding customs like riding a horse to the bride's house, thus angering his in-laws. Mulji and his third wife eventually had four sons and a daughter, all of whom outlived their father.

In October 1860, Mulji published the article that made him famous. Entitled "The Original Religion of the Hindus and the Present Heterodox Opinions," it criticized the practices of the Vallabhacharyas, the Hindu sect into which Mulji had been born. Because the article mentioned one of the sect's leaders, or "Maharajas," by name, accusing him of sexual misconduct, it opened Mulji to prosecution for libel. The result was the sensational Maharaj Libel Case of 1862. Bombay's reformists celebrated Mulji's role in the trial and presented him with a substantial cash purse; Karsandas's father, meanwhile, complained that the trial had completely ruined the family's reputation.

After the trial, reform-minded commercial magnate Karsandas Madhavdas lent Mulji a substantial quantity of money to extend his Chinese cloth trade to England. In 1863, Mulji left Bombay, but had to cut short his English sojourn due to ill health. Upon his return, he and his family were officially excommunicated from their caste group, after which it was even difficult for them to find servants. Refusing ritual purification, Mulji remained an outcaste for the rest of his life. His financial difficulties were further compounded when the "share mania" financial bubble, induced by a spike in cotton prices during the American Civil War, burst after 1864. Mulji went into debt, but was bailed out by his Parsi and European friends. In the late 1860s, he continued to publish in English and Gujarati. His most significant works from this period are *A History of the Sect of Mahárájas, or Vallabhácháryas in Western India* (1865) and *Travels in England* (1866). In 1867, he was made Assistant Superintendent of the princely state of Rajkot in Kathiawar, where he also oversaw the education of the young Thakore Saheb. Although he had no experience as a government administrator, Mulji used his new post to experiment with reformist policies. He was later hired as Special Assistant to the princely state of Limree (Limbdi), where he earned the handsome monthly salary of Rs. 500.

In 1871, Mulji again shocked his community's mores by arranging the first Kapol Bania widow remarriage, between his good friend Madhavdas Rughnathdas and a young widow named Dhankore. At the ceremony, Mulji performed the *kanyadan* on behalf of the bride, presenting her to Rughnathdas in the role of her godfather. A few months later, in August 1871, he died. His chronic health problems had been compounded by overwork. On his deathbed, Mulji told his Parsi medical advisor that he held no "enmity" toward the Vaishnava Maharajas or their followers. All his "strenuous labours" had been undertaken for "the reformation of the sect of Vallabhacharyas."[8] Nearly three thousand people of various communities attended his funeral, and Limree observed a complete *hartal* to mark the occasion.[9]

A central figure for Gujarati Bombay, Mulji was also an important node in the subcontinental Hindu reform scene. His polemics against priestcraft seem to parallel the anti-Brahmanical movement unfolding in Marathi during roughly the same period.[10] But his influence extended well beyond western India. The memory of the Maharaj Libel Case framed the enthusiastic reception of Keshub Chunder Sen in Bombay in 1864, thus providing part of the context for the Bengal-Bombay connection cemented by the creation of the Prarthana Samaj upon Keshub's return three years later.[11] Keshub in fact met Mulji several times in March 1864, sharing a "hearty dinner" with him and Dr. Bhau Daji at Malabar Hill and later hearing him deliver a paper in which (as Keshub wrote in his diary) Mulji described "the peculiarly miserable predicament of his wife" after his return from England.[12] In 1869, meanwhile, Mulji's supporters Dharmsi and Jaikishendas Khimji visited Banaras, where they met with Swami Dayananda Saraswati and invited him to Bombay; they surely, in the process, mentioned the Maharaj Libel Case, apparent allusions to which appear in Dayanand's magnum opus, the *Satyarth Prakash* (1875). When Dayanand finally arrived in Bombay in 1874–75, the late Mulji's compatriots composed the core of the city's charter branch of the Arya Samaj.[13]

Such lines of influence should not be surprising. Whether in his advocacy of widow remarriage, women's education, and foreign travel, or in his staunch opposition to sacerdotal authority, Mulji was an emblematic vector of mid-nineteenth century Hindu reformism. He was, moreover, understood as such during his lifetime—especially in relation to the Maharaj Libel Case. It is to that controversy that we now turn.

Mulji and the Maharaj

The Maharaj Libel Case of 1862 thrilled scandalmongers throughout India with its tales of a guru gone bad, earning acclaim by the end of the nineteenth century as the "greatest trial of modern times since the trial of Warren Hastings."[14] The controversial contest between reform-minded journalist Karsandas Mulji and Jadunathji Brizratanji, a leader or Maharaj of the Pushtimargi Vaishnavas, had been brewing for years in the Gujarati press. It was not until an especially umbrageous 1860 article spurred Jadunathji to sue Mulji for libel, however, that their row went national with the leap into English. The article in question not only denounced the

Pushtimarg as heterodox, a latter-day corruption of the originary Vedic religion; it also specifically accused Jadunathji of foisting himself sexually on his female devotees.

Although Jadunathji had hoped that the Bombay Supreme Court would clear his good name, he was sorely mistaken. After a grueling hearing that filled a full twenty-four days in court and stretched out over almost three months (January 24-April 22), the British judges decided that Mulji's libel was justified. As alleged, the Pushtimarg was held to be a heterodox debasement of authentic Hinduism, and Jadunathji a libidinous sham of a spiritual guide.

Along the way, there had been many titillating revelations. Followers of the Pushtimarg were said to drink water in which the Maharaj had washed his feet, to eat the dust that he walked on, and to chew his premasticated *paan*.[15] It was further rumored that the Maharaj required his male followers to surrender their body, mind, and property (*tan, man,* and *dhan*) to the Maharaj—and that *property* was construed to include wives and daughters.[16] The gossipy confessions that poured forth from the witness stand that spring included many lurid tales of sexual surrender; and even more shocking to bourgeois male mores than the heady blend of the devotional and the erotic that these tales implied was the sense, evident in so many of the testimonies, that the women involved might actually have been enjoying themselves.[17] The verdict against the Maharaj was cinched when two different doctors, one of them leading Bombay citizen Bhau Daji, testified to having treated the religious leader for syphilis on multiple occasions via the topical application of mercurial "blackwash."[18]

Many people, it seems, enjoyed these smutty disclosures, snapping up copies of the Bombay dailies to follow the scandal. Other onlookers perhaps sided with the *Poona Observer*, which prudishly complained that the trial was "about as disgusting [a one] as can be imagined."[19] Smut, however did serious social work. It fueled the competition between the two English-language newspapers (the *Times of India* and the *Bombay Gazette*) that were vying for dominance of the Bombay market.[20] It also distilled complex historical problems in a public drama as symbolically dense as it was scandalously salacious.[21]

The ruling against the Maharaj was quickly hailed as an epochal event. Sir Joseph Arnould, one of the trial's two judges, emphasized its significance in his much-reprinted closing opinion. Praising "these men" who had at great risk to themselves "done determined battle against a foul and powerful delusion," he expressed his hope "that the seed they have sown will bear its fruit"—that there will be a "steady increase in the number of those, whom their words and their examples have quickened into thought and animated to resistance, whose homes they have helped to cleanse from loathsome lewdness, and whose souls they have set free from a debasing bondage."[22] Since Arnould's confident pronouncement, the Maharaj Libel Case has consolidated its place as a canonical event in the annals of modern Hinduism, distilling and dramatizing key historical shifts of the colonial period. It testifies to the emergence of an Orientalist legal apparatus that displaced traditional structures of religious authority in the process of asserting its own ability to adjudicate Hindu orthodoxy.[23] It highlights the constitutive exclusion of women from public debates that nonetheless took female sexuality and the regulation of the domestic sphere as a primary locus of religious reform.[24] Finally, it exemplifies how an emergent Anglophone bourgeoisie used colonial legal institutions as well as the print public to displace what Amrita Shodhan terms "caste polities," largely evacuating these traditional institutions of their juridical and political functions, so that caste would retain its salience only as a social marker.[25]

In amplifying and refining our understanding of the Maharaj Libel Case, the scholarship on the trial has moved beyond Arnould's archly imperial narrative, which celebrated colonialism for "liberating" the colonized from indigenous religious institutions. But, in focusing on the social and institutional changes that the trial prompted, scholarship has also tended to lose sight of an essential aspect of colonial discourse: its insistence on the reform of subjectivity, which during this period was seen as either a necessary corollary of social reform or a precondition of it. Arnould's judgement is characteristic. To his mind, the trial centered on the freeing of "souls" from "a debasing bondage," on the "quickening" of thought, and the dispelling of "delusion." The reform of society is the presumed outcome of these shifts in, and reengineering of, Indian souls and inseparable from them. As Alexander Duff memorably put it some twenty odd years earlier, to "regenerate" a people "steeped in the very slough of bondage," the colonizing power must first act upon the mind.[26]

By Arnould's account, the Maharaj Libel Case stands as an exemplary instance of what we might, following the lead of Charles Taylor, call a "subtraction story" of modern subjectivity.[27] Mulji heroically liberated the Pushtimargi Vaishnavas from the fetters of their religious bondage so that they could assume political majority as properly autonomous secular subjects. Such stories, as Taylor reminds us, assume that the modern individual preexists its "liberation," rather than being produced through the modern social imaginary itself. During the Maharaj Libel Case, and arguably in colonial India more broadly, the prototypical such subtraction story was that of the Reformation. B. N. Motiwala's 1935 biography of Mulji distills the sentiment prevalent during the scandal: with the "spirit" of Luther, Mulji set forth on his "magnificent crusade" to "free men and women from ecclesiastical slavery" and "priestly tyranny."[28] Whether in Alexander Duff's paean to the "flame of liberty" that would engulf India once the "Indian Luther" was roused, or in James Mill's claim that the Reformation was *the* "great and decisive contest against priestly tyranny for liberty of thought," Luther was routinely presented as the great emancipator.[29] This narrative clearly provides a woefully impoverished account of the Pushtimargi devotees' relationship to the Maharaj, apprehending it in terms of a stereotyped narrative of priestcraft that can see only self-serving veniality on one side of the religious bond and blind credulity on the other. But it also, as I will suggest, provides an inadequate account of Mulji and his own effort to disseminate technologies of ascetic self-discipline among his Gujarati readership.

In 1857, Mulji's newspaper, the *Satya Prakash*, offered a prize for the best essay on the question, "What should be the ideal relation between Gurus (spiritual guides) and their male and female disciples?"[30] This question loomed over the Maharaj Libel Case, where it was shadowed by a second question: is a guru the same thing as a priest? The perils of translation were clear at court: the judges had to ascertain whether Mulji's article had been libelous by examining the English version produced by the official court translator. Translation problems did not, however, stop there. In fact, the entire affair can be read as an effort to establish *priest* as a synonym for *Maharaj* or *guru*. Mulji inaugurated this effort in the 1850s, when he decried the popes as "the Maharajas of Europe."[31] During and after the trial, the Bombay and Poona papers cemented the connection between the Maharajas and the discourse of popery by referencing literary works (e.g., Dryden's "Absalom and Achitophel," which includes the line "In pious times, ere priestcraft did begin") and current events (e.g., Mormonism) that mentioned or connoted religious imposture.[32] The Maharaj, the papers implied, belonged to a global species and must be read as such.

Mulji's quasi-Orientalist monograph *A History of the Sect of Maháráras, or Vallabhácháryas in Western India* (1865) affirmed this classificatory procedure. In the above epigraph, Mulji insists that "priestly craft" is not "limited in its operations to India," but "pervades all human society, with greater or lesser energy."[33] To attack the Maharajas in Bombay, he implies, is to join the global war against priestcraft. The language in which Mulji makes his claim here is important. To name "the priest" as a universal type, he code switches to English and its scholarly genres. This switch implicitly positions the Maharajas and their vernacular followers as merely local subjects, the unwitting instruments of a global phenomenon visible only to the English-literate cosmopolitan critic. Writing against "the priest," Mulji performs his ability to step above the cultural constraints of Gujarati by subordinating Gujarati to the language of imperial command.

This jump to English was, however, only the beginning of the semiotic complexities that confronted the court and the Bombay reading public. As David Haberman notes, the trial hinged on the "ontological hierarchy" of guru and disciple.[34] Where the Pushtimarg held that the Maharaj was an incarnation of Krishna and thus inherently, and even somatically, different from his followers, the Bombay court saw all the trial's litigants and witnesses as formally identical subjects of the crown. In the very act of suing for libel, then, the Maharaj had already begun to undermine his distinctive ontological status by presenting himself before the law as a "private" citizen with an abstract reputation that could be won, lost, and translated into a numerical value via the pecuniary logic of "compensation."[35] Such difficulties are implicit in the fraught testimony of witness for the prosecution Jumnadas Sevaklal. Asked by Mr. Anstey, Mulji's defense attorney, whether "some Banias believe the Maharaj to be a God," he demurs: "We consider him to be our gooroo." "By God," he clarifies, "I mean Krishna." Irritated at this apparent prevarication, Anstey asks again: "Is Gooroo a God?" Sevaklal insists: "Gooroo is gooroo."[36] Is it too much to read this tautological statement (which earned Sevaklal a fine for contempt) as a refusal of all translation? Guru is guru, and that is all.

The tenuous hold of the "priest" on the "guru" is perhaps nowhere more clearly articulated than in the dedication to Mahipatram Rupram's 1877 biography of Mulji, who had died in 1871 at the age of thirty-eight. Rupram commends the late reformer's example to "the rising generation who, emancipating themselves from the thraldom of ignorance, superstition, and priestcraft, have dedicated themselves to promote the elevation of their country."[37] Separated from this English inscription by a blank page, the Gujarati dedication echoes its sentiments, translating *priestcraft* as "the net of foolish and wicked gurus" (*murkh ane duṣṭ gurūonī jāl*). Rupram's dueling inscriptions catch the priest in the guru's net, and vice versa. Mulji's career, it implies, centered on such acts of translation, intertwining the priest and the guru, but never quite eliminating the blank page separating the two. Thus bounded by translation, Rupram's tale of "emancipation" (or, in Gujarati, the "breaking of chains") becomes considerably more interesting. To discover how, we need to turn to a body of texts published twenty years previously, when Mulji's exemplary reformist career was just beginning.

Translated Virtue: Karsandas Mulji's *Moral Training*

In order to understand that Mulji's reform agenda was not simply about liberating subjects but rather producing them, his critique of the Maharaj needs to be situated within the larger body of work that he produced during the late 1850s. Because these writings do not directly bear on the problems addressed by the Maharaj Libel Case, they have not generally been read in relation to the trial. Nonetheless, Mulji's earlier essays on conduct can, in fact, help us to rethink what the trial was about. These essays detail a mode of work upon the self that signals a convergence of Protestant self-discipline, social reform, and the gendered affective economy of the home. Interesting in their own right, they also help reframe Mulji's interest in the Maharaj, and specifically in his failure to do what Mulji indicates is the proper work of priests—to guide and manage their flocks. Taking a holistic view of Mulji's writings during this period (1855–1860) suggests continuities among bodies of work generally held to be distinct: his ethical writings, his women's writings, and his criticisms of priestly religion. These bodies of work correlate roughly to three books: *Nīti-Vacan* (*Moral Training*) (1859); *Saṃsār Sukh* (*Domestic Happiness*) (1860); and the *Nibandhmāḷā* (*Collected Essays*) (1870), which collects newspaper articles first published in the late 1850s.[38] The following discussion will take up each of these texts in turn, beginning with *Moral Training*, which provides the template for the genre of didactic moral writing that Mulji would later pursue in other forms.

Moral Training plies a decidedly Protestant ethic, and this is no coincidence. As its preface explains, more than half of its sixty-five essays are translated from English texts like those of "Bler" and "Gregarī"— presumably the Scottish Presbyterian minister and rhetorical theorist Hugh Blair (1718–1800) and Irish Anglican minister and writer George Gregory (1754–1808).[39] The essays composed by Mulji himself emulate their English models in tone, style, and topic. So, for example, where a translated essay on "The Uses of Time" informs its reader that time "is considered the most invaluable of all things," Mulji's own essays pick up on this theme by embedding it in moral tales about bourgeois men who regret the time they have wasted in frivolous leisure pursuits and vow to dedicate their futures to social uplift.[40] In addition to translations from these unnamed collections of sermons, *Moral Training* also includes extracts from one volume that Mulji mentions by title: Robert Dodsley's *The Oeconomy of Human Life* (1750–51). Reckoned the most widely reprinted book of the eighteenth century, Dodsley's *Oeconomy* was by any measure an extraordinarily popular volume. By 1800, it had gone into two hundred editions, with translations into at least nine different languages and a global fan club that included Thomas Jefferson.[41] Given its global circulation, it is not surprising that at least one copy of the book made it to Bombay by the 1850s, nor is it particularly remarkable the Elphinstone-educated Mulji, steeped in English, would have gotten his hands on it.[42]

Much more interesting, I think, is how Dodsley's *Oeconomy* situates itself—and therefore Mulji—in relation to the behavioral regulations of Protestantism. In form and content, the *Oeconomy* is a work of "didactic morality" composed in a quasi-biblical style so ponderously inflated that Dodsley himself felt the need to apologize for it.[43] It brims over with moral maxims like the following: "The thoughtless man brideleth not his tongue; he speaketh at random and is entangled in the foolishness of his own words."[44] Although not a Protestant text in the strict sense of the word (Dodsley, who was Voltaire's English publisher, seems to have been a Deist), it clearly falls well within the domain of the diffusely ascetic culture that Max Weber associated with the Protestant ethic. Consider, for example, this chestnut: "Idleness is the parent of want and of pain; but the labor of virtue bringeth forth pleasure . . . The slothful man is a burden to himself; his hours hang heavy on his head."[45] This is surely as abstemiously self-denying a piece of advice as anything to be met with in Weber's own Deist paragon of Protestant virtue, Benjamin Franklin.[46] Even though Dodsley recommends that his reader "lyeth down late" after rising early (so as to maximize industriousness), he and early-to-bed Franklin both devise their regimens so as to "preserveth the health" and facilitate the acquisition of wealth.[47]

We see a similarly Weberian set of concerns reflected in Mulji's *Moral Training*—most interestingly in his own original compositions. "Human Pride" ("*Māṇasnuṃ Abhimān*"), for example, describes a rich man who gazes admiringly at himself in the mirror up to fifteen times per day. While in his fancy carriage, he whips his horse with great pomp and circumstance; while seated in his beautiful garden, he relishes the company of his sycophantic "yes men" (*hājiyāo*). Having portrayed this character, the essay presents its reader with "a terrifying and sorrowful thought": as soon as the breath leaves the body the corpse begins to stink and, devoured by worms, dwindles to a skeleton. Mulji instructs his (presumptively male) reader to meditate on this truth by standing in front of a mirror, examining every part of his body, and asking what will become of it. Lest there be confusion, Mulji answers the question: "it becomes dust." Regular performance of this mirror practice is recommended as a cure for vanity. The resultant ascetic subject will forego worldly pleasures and work harder for the benefit of others (his brothers, neighbors, fellow countrymen, and all humanity), if only to secure his good name—the only part of the person that survives his death. The essay concludes by enjoining vigilant awareness of the traps of this world: "You should always remain aware."[48] Where "Human Pride" promotes ascetic denial of worldly pleasure in the name of good reputation, "Now I Realize Everything" (*"Have Badhuṃ Sūjhe Che"*) does so in the name of God.[49] In the essay, a man awakens in the middle of the night and realizes that he has misspent his fifty-one years in laziness, fraud, and treachery. Written primarily as a long first-person lament in which the narrator begs God (*īsvar*) to give him his youth back, the essay concludes with the man vowing to spend his remaining time praising God and working for the benefit of others. The basic lesson imparted by both essays is aptly distilled in advice that Mulji offers elsewhere: "Do not forget your death! Remember death at all times!"[50]

These essays, and others like them, share two characteristics important for understanding how Mulji translates "Protestant" norms of selfhood. First, they recommend worldly asceticism to a bourgeois male readership asked to replace its sensual pleasures with arduous work for social uplift, deferring present gratification for a future gain that is figured as either posthumous reputation or divine reward. Second, they model the cultivation of interiority via agonized solitude. One man is forced to offer an account of himself and his time to God during lonely insomniac hours. Another gazes at his image in the mirror to contemplate his physical impermanence. In both cases, the awareness of death serves as a means of individuation, or what Taylor would call "buffer": although both individuals are ultimately counseled to go forth and help others, the foundational moment for these ascetic subjects remains the moment of introspective crisis (with the mirror scene, I think, serving as the most emblematic illustration of how that moment centers on the subject's awareness of himself as a discrete, and therefore precarious, individual). Not insignificantly, the act of reading sets the stage for this introspection, even while inscribing readerly interiority within the social field constituted by print culture.

Mulji wrote the newspaper article that culminated in his 1860 libel concurrently with the essays later collected in *Moral Training*. In order to understand what was at stake in the Maharaj Libel Case, we need to appreciate the program implicit in this largely neglected body of writing. Simply "liberating" the Pushtimargi Vaishnavas from the "tyrannical" influence of their "priests" was not, it would seem, all that was going on here. Rather, the criticism of priestly religion goes hand in hand with a project of moral reform; freedom from the priest is achieved not by simple subtraction but instead through the institution of a new regime of instruction or discipline. In place of the Maharaj and his followers, we have Mulji and his readers. If the latter are ascetic or self-disciplining subjects, their interior life is thoroughly mediated by the print object itself, and thus enmeshed in a network of disciplinary or ascetic practices. Between the man and his mirror stands Mulji.

The question remains as to whether these practices are specifically Protestant. In the preface to the second edition of *Moral Training*, Mulji explains that in translating English texts he did his best to eliminate any specifically Christian content so that "all people of different religions [*dharm*] and different castes [*jāt*] can use this small book in like manner." His hope, he writes, is that the book will be useful to young men and women in every Gujarati family.[51] Nonetheless, and despite the occasional *Ramayana* reference, Mulji seems to have emulated Dodsley all too well: *Moral Training* is a text with a drearily Protestant ethos. In resisting the Protestantization narrative, I do not mean to deny that Protestant cultural forms found new life in South Asia during the nineteenth century. I simply mean to question the narrative's implied teleology, asking whether the mobility of Protestant discourses and practices at this time might not lead in unexpected directions, seemingly foreclosed by the mechanical language of Protestantization.

Mulji's translations are a case in point. First, there is the inevitable matter of mimicry: the very iterability of the "Protestant" ensured that each citation of the original would diverge from it, thereby calling the unity of that original into question.[52] Does Mulji count as a Protestant in the same way as Dodsley or Franklin, and if all three of these men (Deists and Hindus that they are) qualify as "Protestant," what does that term mean? When Weber attributes a Protestant ethic to Benjamin Franklin, he is obviously not speaking to the latter's theological views, which are largely irrelevant to the genealogical arc that connects Protestant self-discipline and the spirit of capitalism; this is an argument about practice or habitus, rather than doctrine or belief. Franklin is a secularized Protestant insofar as he transfers a Protestant technology of the self into the secular realm of economic affairs, participating in the larger process whereby "asceticism was carried out of monastic cells and into everyday life." Weber is coldly deterministic when parsing the relationship between the monastic and the everyday: Puritan discipline ossifies into an "iron cage" that sustains the capitalist order and constrains the humanity of its prisoners.[53] But is this determinism warranted? Or might there be other ways of reading the Protestant signature on modernity? Such questions become especially pertinent if, with Peter van der Veer, we want to develop a "post-Weberian" project that leaves the sixteenth century behind and looks instead to the colonial nineteenth century as laying the groundwork for Weber's inquiry into worldly asceticism (see Introduction).

In order to loosen the grip of early Puritans on capitalist modernity, we need only look a little closer at the conceptual move that grounds *The Protestant Ethic*. It is only when the Protestant ethic ceases to be specifically Protestant, Weber suggests, that it assumes its characteristic or ideal form. It is an ethic that emerges fully only once it has detached from its point of origin, putting the "Protestant" under erasure, and dispersing beyond it. Weber charts one route taken by this mobile set of ascetic technologies, but there is no reason to think this was its sole itinerary. If modernity emerged when religious asceticism "escaped from the cage" of Christian theology, then it behooves us to ask where that asceticism went—not just retracing the line linking Calvin to Franklin, but also looking for other, more unexpected ascetic crossings. To put the point slightly differently, it seems worth asking whether a third movement should be appended to the classic Weberian narrative. If (1) the Reformation generalized monastic asceticism to lay Christians, and then (2) capitalism secularized the resultant form of Protestant asceticism, thus generalizing it beyond Protestantism, what happens when (3) this secularized Protestant asceticism (which both is and is not Protestant) is taken to the colony and generalized yet again via its crossings with other ascetic traditions?

This is a large question, and Mulji's *Moral Training* is only of limited help in answering it. The text promotes asceticism (enjoining its readers to relinquish worldly pleasures), but it does not explicitly engage with Hindu materials, and so any claim to its having established cross-ascetic connections remains highly speculative—caught up with fraught questions of reader reception. These questions are, to be sure, foregrounded by the essays themselves, which address their reader directly and instruct him in how to apply the moral lessons of the book in daily life. Although we cannot know who was reading *Moral Training*, and even less what they were thinking about when they read it, it seems likely that Mulji's readers would have understood his emphasis on the impermanence of the flesh in relation to a set of religious references internal to Hindu tradition, and perhaps specifically the Pushtimarg. If this was the case (and, again, this remains necessarily speculative), Mulji's book should be understood not so much as Protestantizing Hinduism as gesturing toward a set of possible connections between Protestant asceticism and Hindu asceticism.

The book's preface frames this gesture. In addressing his essays to all Gujarati readers regardless of their religion or caste and insisting that everyone can "use this small book in like manner," Mulji not only hails a reading public that subsumes Bombay's many discrete caste polities. He also, in effect, separates religious belief from religious behavior. Mulji scrubs his essays of all theological particulars, but does not do so in order to conflate those religions' truth claims, as in some forms of neo-Vedanta. His strategy, rather, is to bracket out "ethics" (*nīti*) from "religion" (*dharm*) so that technologies of the self can circulate independently of community, identity, and belief. Hence, these discourses on ethics open with a claim to the specificity, and thus the mobility, of ethical practices of self-formation—which are related to but distinct from "religion" proper.[54] Mulji's move here seems to parallel Weber's: an ethic emerges as such once it is disencumbered of its theological and communitarian trappings. Where Weber asked how the Protestant traversed the line between the religious and the secular, Mulji poses the question of how it should traverse the line between the Christian and the Hindu. This is not to say that it would make the Hindu Christian, or vice versa. It is simply to suggest that, as an eminently mobile ascetic technology, the "Protestant" had the potential to enter into assemblage with other forms of asceticism.

Dodsley's *Oeconomy of Human Life* is a remarkably fitting accoutrement for such a project. First published anonymously, the *Oeconomy* was prefaced by a fictional letter explaining the book's provenance. It was, allegedly, a translation of an ancient Indian manuscript discovered in Tibet, in the closely guarded scriptoria of the despotic lamas (Tibet, "like Italy, abounds with priests"). Its discoverer, an emissary of the Chinese court named Cao-tsou, translated the manuscript from the language of "the ancient Gymnosophists, or Brachmans [*sic*]" into Chinese and brought it back to Beijing, where it was acquired and translated for a second time by an anonymous Englishman who also arranged for its publication. Patently untrue, this "Oriental tale" would probably have been received as such by contemporary readers, who were already accustomed to faux-Eastern texts of various kinds.[55]

As a frame story, however, this tale is more than a simple marketing technique. The *Oeconomy*, it implies, is a text with no clear original, which can pass as Indian, Chinese, or English. Many of the Chinese scholars who examine Cao-tsou's translation hypothesize that the Sanskrit manuscript must itself have been a translation of Confucius. Others attribute it to "Dandamis," Alexander the Great's Brahman traveling companion. Still others note that the overall "plan" of the work seems suspiciously "European." The point, presumably, is to underscore the universal appeal of these ethical precepts. No doubt this universal claim levels local difference. But it does so in a very particular way. One might contrast it, for example, with Herbert of Cherbury's *De Veritate* (1624), a foundational work for the comparative study of religion, which asserts that a set of "Common

Notions" underlie the world's various faiths. Where Herbert produces his notion of the "common" through dehistoricized comparison, Dodsley playfully suggests that the universal emerges through the concrete circulation of particular texts and persons.

The physical fact of the book is key here: it is the plot device that structures this comedy of circulation. There is, of course, a certain poetic justice in this text's "return" to the land of its ostensible origin. Its Orientalist fantasy becomes transcolonial fact, as Mulji adapts Dodsley to argue for ethics as a form of common culture that crosses communal boundaries. This tale of circulatory ethics should also, I think, prompt us to revisit Weber's problematic of worldly asceticism. Where Weber divided the world up into discrete areas open to comparison, Dodsley and Mulji call attention to the messy crossings between cultures and the mutual affinities that bring disparate texts and practices into assemblage. This connective rather than comparative approach cues a critical shift in how we approach worldly asceticism; it asks not only that we reroute Weber through empire, but that we also allow his ideas to become denatured along the way.

The colonial milieu, of course, was one of the background conditions that enabled the emergence of Weber's comparative sociology in the first place. Empire was, among other things, a fact-gathering machine, harvesting data from around the globe to fuel the armchair speculations of social theorists back in the European capitals. In doing so, it established an unequal system of knowledge production in which North Atlantic thinkers had disproportionately greater voice than their colonial counterparts. But it also, if only inadvertently, produced textual intimacies that connected world regions in sometimes surprising ways.

It is in this latter vein that I want to call attention to the clear textual line that connects Karsandas Mulji to Max Weber. Weber's *The Religion of India* (1916) explicitly mentions the Maharaj Libel Case in its discussion of the Pushtimarg and quotes the trial transcript via a later text.[56] It also draws on H. H. Wilson's influential formulation, read aloud during the trial proceedings: "Vallabháchárya taught that privation formed no part of sanctity, and that it was the duty of the teacher and his disciples to worship their deity not in nudity and hunger, but in costly apparel and choice food; not in solitude and mortification, but in the pleasures of society and the enjoyment of the world."[57] Versions of this idea dominated accounts of the Pushtimarg for the rest of the century, as when Bartle Frere dubbed it a "Sect of Hindu Epicureans."[58] Very much in this vein, Weber argues that Pushtimarg negated ascetic otherworldliness through simple inversion, rejecting Hindu "contemplative" culture, but without the creative synthesis of the "Puritan model," with its "this-worldly asceticism." Instead, it produced an "orgiastic" form of religion that embraced the world in all its sensuality.[59] If Mulji's worldly asceticism has a Weberian feel to it, this perhaps attests to his indirect influence on Weber: Weber inherited a problematic that Mulji had, in his small way, helped to shape.

By returning to Mulji, then, we may be able to arrive at a more satisfying account of worldly asceticism in modern India. Throughout this period, from Wilson to Weber, commentators on the Pushtimarg focused on the early modern writings of the sect's founders. To discover the "truth" of the Pushtimarg, they implied, one should study Vallabhacharya, just as one studies Luther and Calvin to get at the "truth" of Protestantism. Mulji's appropriation of Dodsley, I suggest, implies a different approach — one that turns us away from the search for religious essences and origins to highlight the multiple ascetic crossings produced by the scene of colonial encounter. We should study worldly asceticism, not in the writings of Vallabha and his immediate successors, but rather in the Pushtimargi texts most proximate to Mulji: the published writings of the Maharaj. I turn to these writings at the end of this chapter. First, however, I linger a little longer with Mulji, asking how he understood the term that anchors Dodsley's disquisition on human life: *oeconomy*.

The Oeconomy of Domestic Happiness

In its earliest uses, the word *oeconomy* referred primarily to the good governance of the household. By 1750, when Dodsley published his *Oeconomy of Human Life* (with its suggestively Foucauldian title), the term could refer to governance at the very different registers of self, household, society, and state, as well as the movement of techniques of governance between and among these registers.[60] Dodsley's *Oeconomy* is structured around such correspondences, suggesting an upward movement that begins with the government of self and then extends to the government of society. Where the earlier chapters of the book treat specific virtues (compassion, contentment) that the reader is enjoined to cultivate within his own person, later chapters focus on the familial and social duties that should govern individuals occupying particular roles (woman, husband, son) or involved in specific types of relationship (e.g., between "rich and poor" or "master and servant"). Work on the self, this organization implies, precedes and facilitates the proper fulfillment of social duty. The interrelations among self-discipline, familial discipline, and social discipline, meanwhile, are what constitute "the oeconomy of human life."

Mulji's *Moral Training* replicates this organizational scheme, suggesting similar relations among the different registers of self-government and the government of society. In order to trace how he develops the implications of this scheme, however, we need to turn to a different text from the same period in his career: *Saṃsār Sukh* (*Domestic Happiness*), an ethical manual for women that grew out of Mulji's involvement with the periodical *Strī Bodh* (*Knowledge for Women*). In the nineteenth century, "Hindu woman" was more than just one possible object of reform; she was arguably the quintessential such object, whether as the hapless victim of practices like widow burning and female infanticide, or as the key vector for the transmission of "superstition" across generations. The vernacular-language women's magazines produced and distributed during the second half of the century were a key vehicle whereby bourgeois men hailed women as objects of reform. These publications expanded female literacy; but, as a number of scholars have argued, they did so as a means of extending male hegemony into the home. Founded in 1857 by a group of young Hindu and Parsi social reformers, *Stri Bodh* is typical of this genre.[61] A representative issue (January 1861) seeks to educate its readers on topics ranging from slave markets in the American south to the current emperor of China, from the kangaroo to William Penn. Fictional and non-fictional stories relate the experiences of women worldwide, highlighting the sorrows of war and the difficulties of travel, and castigating those women who bring hardship on themselves with their superstitious belief in ghosts and other imaginary beings.

The essays in *Domestic Happiness* (1860), although similar in aim to those in *Stri Bodh*, are in form and content closer to *Moral Training* (1859), constituting a sort of women's counterpart to that text.[62] Alternating between second-person address of its presumed female readership and didactic moral tales, this conduct manual for housewives accords the bourgeois wife and mother a special role in fostering societal happiness through her work in the home. If *Moral Training* highlights technologies of self-conduct, *Domestic Happiness* clarifies how ascetic self-discipline facilitates the proper management of the conduct of others.

This relationship is evident from the first story in the collection, "Jivkor and Her Family" ("*Jīvkor ane Tenuṃ Kutumb*"). Jivkor, we are told, is the wife of a merchant. Due to her "wicked disposition," she angrily grumbles and mutters from morning till night, whether cooking, sewing, or sitting, whether with her husband, her children, or her servants. She learned her bad behavior by watching her own mother, who was also a perpetual grumbler. By the time she had grown up, this learned behavior had become a fixed "habit" (*ṭev*). Jivkor is not a bad person: she is compassionate and loving. Nonetheless, she will not give her family even a second of peace. As a result, her husband spends most of his time at a friend's shop in the bazaar, and her children, their hearts hardened from too much scolding, start to grumble too. "Her husband," writes Mulji, "would rather go sit in a cave somewhere than be in a house with an irritable, grumbling woman." Her children would rather live in the jungle. Switching to direct address, Mulji counsels his readers to purge their own dispositions of any irritability lest their homes descend into this unfortunate state. It is the housewife's job to arrange things so as to increase her family's happiness (*kuṭumbnuṃ sukh*), and so she must cultivate in herself a graceful and smiling disposition (*svabhāv*).[63]

It is easy to imagine Mulji or his social equivalent as the "persecuted" husband high-tailing it to the bazaar to escape his grumbling, overworked wife. The essay, by this account, is his backhanded means of reestablishing dominance in the home by regulating his wife's behavior. This is only part of the story, however. Jivkor is more than simply the object of reform; she is also its agent, playing a privileged role in the production of domestic happiness and, indeed, the oeconomy of human life. As Dodsley writes in his own chapter on "Woman," the good housewife "commandeth with judgment, and is obeyed. She ariseth in the morning; she considers her affairs; and appointeth to everyone their proper business." The care of the family is for her an object of "study" and of prudent "management" (she governs the domestic space according to reasoned technique), and it proceeds from her careful self-regulation. She cultivates virtue instead of beauty so as to curb her husband's "passion," and she fashions her children's "manners from the example of her goodness."[64] Here, women are invited to become objects of power by submitting to Dodsley's vision of feminine virtue. But at the same time the housewife is also established as a crucial site for the dissemination of power, as she commands and manages the home. Mulji's essays operate in roughly analogous manner. Jivkor's inability to master her own habits, and thus her character, indicate her larger inability to manage her family. Ascetic self-rule precedes and provides critical practice for the prudent government of others.

This self-rule can be achieved via religion, as explained in the essay "Remember God at Every Moment" ("*Harghaḍī Īśvarne Yād Karta Rehejo*"). A hapless housewife asks her upright older neighbor how she can worship God when she has to spend all of her time doing housework. The old lady recommends her own method, which is to correlate domestic tasks to religious ideas. She prays constantly, asking God to clean her heart of sin just as she cleans her house; to kindle the fire of virtue just as she lights the cooking fire; and to wash her heart just as she washes her body of dirt while bathing.[65] The housewife is enjoined, in short, to become a worldly ascetic, dedicating mundane tasks to the divine through a perpetual prayer that comes to mediate daily life. This cultivated distance from everyday affairs is presumably of a kind that will allow the housewife to stand over and control those affairs more effectively; not fully immanent to or immersed within the domestic field, she is able to master that field just as she masters her own dispositions.

Domestic Happiness's program of ascetic self-discipline is strikingly similar to the program that *Moral Training* recommends to a more general (which is to say, presumptively male) audience. Reading these two texts together, in fact, reveals Jivkor and her ilk to be exemplary self-regulating subjects—and not only for other bourgeois women, but also for bourgeois men. Just as the housewife must regulate herself to serve the home, the bourgeois male must regulate himself to serve his community and nation. Consider *Moral Training*'s essay on "Mutual Happiness" (*"Parasparnuṃ Sukh"*).[66] God, Mulji explains, created men that they might help each other. Society works by mutual cooperation and support, as in the complementary relations among various economic functions: the weaver, the farmer, and the dhobi all need each other to survive. It is this "mutual help" that prevents society from devolving into a "savage state" (*jaṅglī hālat*), and it is also what drives social progress according to the logic of reform. "All people," Mulji writes, "need to help each other, for without each others' help there is no means of reforming humanity's condition."[67] If we place this essay in the larger context of Mulji's writings from this period, the call for mutual "help" (*madad*) begins to look less like an anodyne plea for neighborly uplift and more like the managerial skill of the ascetic housewife. We might call this reform in the "oeconomic" mode. It unfolds at the interface of subjectivity and sociality, of the conduct of self (working hard, regulating one's disposition, giving an account of one's time) and the conduct of others, and it relies on the connections or relays among these different registers of good governance in order to produce its effects.

Taken together, *Domestic Happiness* and *Moral Training* situate subjective reform, domestic reform, and social reform as a set of overlapping and interlinked spheres, with the good wife as the paradigmatic self-disciplined subject overseeing the transfer of affect among them. Her ability to self-regulate in spite of adversity (no matter what troubles befall her, she must maintain a cheerful disposition) is a model of a this-worldly ascetic practice designed to increase the world's stock of "happiness." Her "character" (*svabhāv*) is the double object of Mulji's reformism and her own self-regulatory practice. In addition to being an object of reform, however, it is also an instrument—a tool for regulating the behavior, and thus eventually the character, of others. These persons' characters are, in turn, themselves instrumentalized: ascetic interiority is a tool for governing the conduct of one's friends and neighbors. The housewife is a pivotal node in this regulatory network. Her private habitus is a public good, mediated by her consumption of vernacular print media. She is, in exemplary manner, managed into becoming an effective manager. The irresolvable tension between autonomy and heteronomy is expressed here in the ambivalent relation produced by ascetic practices that render the self simultaneously the subject and the object of discipline.

In sum, although the Maharaj Libel Case excluded actual women from its proceedings and thus rendered them, in Usha Thakkar's concise phrase, "puppets on the periphery" of the trial, the abstracted figure of the ideal woman was nonetheless central to the controversy, and in at least two different ways. The court may have seized on the sensational cross-gender identifications of Krishna bhakti, where Radha and the gopis serve as paradigmatic devotees and thus provide an example to male worshippers of Krishna. But, for Mulji and his fellow reformists, the ideal housewife was the more important role model. It would be too much to claim that it was only through his ability to identify with the disciplined housewife that the bourgeois male reformer was able to imagine the kind of subjectivity that he himself aspired to. Even so, it seems clear that women's literature was central, rather than peripheral, to the articulation of Mulji's larger reform project. Written by men, these essays can be read as being in some sense for men. They articulate technologies of social and subjective reform that could then be applied elsewhere—as in the case of the Pushtimargi "priest."

"Our Priests and Their Duties"

If the housewife was the first paradigmatic object of nineteenth-century Hindu reform culture, the priest was the second. As one early twentieth-century colonial administrator quipped, "The priests and the women are the most important influences in India . . . and I am not much afraid of the politicians until they play on these two."[68] How these two powers should relate to one another was a different question. At times the potential connection between priests and women was concretely and scandalously realized, as in the scenes of sacerdotal seduction that gripped the Bombay public during the Maharaj Libel Case (or, in a similar vein, Calcutta's Tarakeswar Murder Case [1873], which likewise dramatized a libidinous priest disrupting the sexual economy of the bourgeois home).[69] The plotline of violated chastity was not, however, the only way of configuring the connection between "priest" and "woman" during this period. Karsandas Mulji's writings from the late 1850s suggest another.[70]

As I will argue, Mulji's essays imply that the good priest, or *dharmguru*, should act like a good housewife. That is, he should cultivate virtue in himself so as to better tend to his flock, fostering the virtue of those in his care. He should also, importantly, submit to the authority of vernacular print media and the public opinion that it represents. As we have seen, in 1857 Mulji advertised a prize in the *Satya Prakash* for the best essay on the topic, "What should be the ideal relation between Gurus (spiritual guides) and their male and female disciples?"[71] It is this question, I suggest, that Mulji's own essays sought to answer.

Most modern-day priests, Mulji repeatedly claims, are corrupt. Thus, in order to understand how a priest should act, nineteenth-century Hindus must look to the past. Where contemporary Brahmans are lazy ignoramuses who excel only at cheating people out of money, the learned and wise "original" Brahmans (*asalnā brāhmaṇo*) were selflessly committed to reforming their country.[72] They cultivated their own virtue so that they could cultivate virtue in their followers: only if Brahmans are "virtuous" (*sadguṇī*), "upright" (*sadācaraṇī*), and "ethical" (*nītivān*) can they effectively lead others toward virtue through "religious instruction" (*dharmno upadeś*) and work for "the good of the country" (*deś*).[73] As the 1857 essay "Our Priests and their Duties" suggests, these responsibilities apply to Hindu priests and Parsi dasturs alike. The *dharmguru* should disseminate virtue among his followers by educating them about religious books, as through regular sermons that draw out the ethical implications of the Hindu epics.[74] Mulji's allegedly libelous 1860 article is of a piece with this project. Its call for a return to "primitive" Hinduism predicates the restoration of religion on the reform of priests. The Maharaj, writes Mulji, can either "delude simple people still more" or he can "personally adopt a virtuous course of conduct" that will alter his relationship to his followers.[75] Ascetic virtue and priestly fraud are presented here as stark alternatives, temporally differentiated. Virtue is for the past and the future, fraud for the present.

Although Mulji presents himself as trying to restore "primitive" Hinduism, what he actually promotes is, of course, necessarily novel. Mulji's essays erode the ontological distinction between the guru and his followers by positioning the priest as a vocation like any other. The Maharajas, he argues, are fully human, having the same faults, the same hungers, and the same body parts as other mortals. "There is," Mulji writes, "no difference between man and Maharaj." The "Maharajas are not gods, but religious teachers" (*māhārājo īsvar nathī, paṇ dharmgurū che*), and it is a "sin" (*bhul*) to think otherwise. Instead of pretending to divinity, they should focus on doing their jobs: instructing their flocks in "ethics and religion" (*nīti ane dharm*). They should also spend their own money to alleviate the sufferings of the poor, thus augmenting the general stock of human "happiness" (*sukh*).[76] Mulji's Maharajas are not avatars of Krishna, immanent manifestations of the transcendent divine. As religious teachers or *dharmgurus*, inhabitants of a particular vocational role, they are fully embedded in the entirely immanent networks of humanity's "mutual happiness." Indeed, one of Mulji's articles on the Brahmans draws very close to the essay by that title from *Moral Training*. God, it suggests, created humanity so that each person can help all others. The rich man becomes useful by giving money to the poor; the laborer by doing labor; the doctor by giving medicine; and the businessman by doing business in a way that keeps his subordinates satisfied. The role of the Brahman, as a part of this general system, is to give instruction in "religion and ethics" and develop expertise in the shastras and Puranas.[77]

This claim echoes traditional discourses on caste, which posit the complementarity of the different professional groups that join together organically to form the social body. It differs from this traditional schema, however, in Mulji's recurrent emphasis on work. The more that "Maharajness" is defined as a job rather than a state of being, the more the Maharajas become vulnerable to charges of "laziness." It is industriousness, for example, that is said to separate the hard-working founders of the Pushtimarg from their insouciant heirs.[78] These latter-day priests are indolent like male buffalo calves. They go from house to house and window to window demanding alms, shamelessly sponging off of others' "hard work" (*mehenat*), as though begging itself was their "business" (*dhandho*). The sarcasm is telling. So is Mulji's claim that Brahmans will not be worthy of receiving gifts until they learn the scriptures properly and starting teaching.[79] Here, the structural dimorphism of clergy and laity (Taylor's two-speed religion) begins to dissolve. Religious virtuosi are no longer worthy of receiving ritual gifts because of who they are. They can only earn wages based upon what they do; the word *gift* (*dān*) simply indicates payment for services rendered. Mulji also, and in a related vein, seeks to delegitimize most ritual services proffered by Brahmans, dismissing them as ruses for extorting people of money. The only religious service that counts as worthy of remuneration is ethical instruction. The Brahmans are not the only group that Mulji wants to see more fully incorporated into the economy of mutual uplift. He also, for example, proposes methods for productively employing blind people.[80] Nonetheless, the Brahmans are the most prominent group for him and the one that, in his view, is in most urgent need of reform.

By incorporating religious professionals into the economy of mutual help and happiness, Mulji opens them to policing by the laity. Even as he stipulates that it is the duty of religious professionals to improve the ethical situation of the people, he calls for civil society to take on the ethical direction of those professionals.[81] In part, this is a function of the position that Mulji assumes for himself as critical journalist, telling the Brahmans how to behave and how to manage one another. He is especially concerned that they decline offers of lavish feasts hosted by wealthy patrons and instead use the money to establish a fund to educate Brahman children in the scriptures. He likewise advises would-be patrons that today's Brahmans are in such a sorry state that hiring them for religious purposes will do no spiritual good. Money that could have been spent on religious rituals should instead be dedicated to Brahmanical education.[82] The lay donor is remade here as a religious instructor, guiding his guru into the proper performance of his professional duty.

This change in roles does not so much invert the ontological hierarchy of priest and follower as indicate a new distribution of tutelary power. Where the priestcraft narrative posits an unguided subject who stands outside the network of tutelary guidance and controls that network, here all parties are internal or immanent to the networked system of moral instruction. The priest or *dharmguru* is an object of reform; but, once reformed, he will go on to reform others. He is more like the disciplined housewife, who exercises control from within the field of power, and less like the puissant pope of the priestcraft narrative who controls the field of power from without. Reformist bourgeois men thus assert their power over and above both bourgeois women and traditional religious elites. But the effect of this is not to produce themselves as unmitigated masters of the new society. Rather, if we take Mulji at his word, he fully expects to be instructed and managed by both priest and housewife, a node in a behavioral network that fully subsumes him and his interior life.

We have, in short, arrived at a very different narrative than the one put forward by Judge Arnould at the conclusion of the Maharaj Libel Case. Instead of acquiescing to the prescriptive plotline of the Indian Luther liberating the Hindus from their despotic priests, we would do better to catalogue the multiple technologies of self-regulation that intersected before and during this trial. This was a moment when religious technologies of the self seemed open to new uses and seemed to gesture toward new potentials in human persons and collectivities. Arnould's narrative foreclosed some of these potentialities by delimiting the field of possible technologies of the self and reducing the kinds of available selfhood to the easily plotted duo, "slave" and "free." Mulji, meanwhile, explicitly engages with Protestantism as a cultural problematic, repurposing it yet again by pushing it onto novel linguistic, cultural, and religious terrain.

Before leaving the Maharaj Libel Case behind, I want to turn from Mulji to his supposed nemesis: Jadunathji Maharaj, the priest whom Mulji most wanted to manage. To compare the writings of these two colonial Gujaratis is to adjust Weber's comparative project in a useful way: here, the categories "Hinduism" and "Protestantism" appear only as negotiated from within very particular histories. As such, they suggest ascetic affinities that are obscured by Weber's comparative method. By my reading, both Mulji and the Maharaj use print media to disseminate religious technologies of ascetic self-rule.

Reading the Maharaj: Bhakti as Asceticism

In 1860, to respond to Mulji's attacks on the Pushtimarg, Jadunathji Brizratanji founded his own magazine, the *Svadharm Vardhak ane Saṃśay Chedak* (*Propagator of Our Own Religion and Destroyer of Doubt*; henceforth referred to as "the *Propagator*"). Amid polemical swipes at its reformist opponents (and especially the "fool" who edits the *Satya Prakash*), the journal offers a fairly complete course in bhakti devotionalism, designed to educate the Maharaj's erring followers in the ways of their sect. Although I will be able to provide only the most cursory account of the journal, I want to argue that what we find in its pages suggests a way of analyzing the relationship between Mulji and the Maharaj that helps refigure the question of Protestantization. The *Propagator* presents bhakti as a mode of worldly asceticism that, although unquestionably different from the asceticism outlined in Mulji's *Moral Training*, appears analogous to it. Instead of fully opposed religious worlds, we find two print-mediated technologies of the self that draw on different religious traditions but remain functionally parallel.

It had not previously been the custom for Pushtimargi Maharajas to print devotional matter, and you can watch Jadunathji work through his discomfort with the medium, repeatedly commenting that he will not print selections from the Vedas or other shruti literature because the printed text could easily end up in the hands of a low-caste person. But, determined to counter the reform party's denigration of the "shastras," especially Narmadshankar Lalshankar's claim that they were of human rather than divine origin, he does publish selections from this somewhat nebulously defined class of smriti literature (most quotations seem to come from the *Bhagavad Gita* and the *Bhagavat Purana*)—offering them up to his necessarily anonymous readership, even while repeatedly asserting that sacred texts cannot be understood without the help of a guru. It would not, for any number of reasons, make sense to treat this text as a "pure" instance of precolonial "tradition" in valiant contest with colonial forms of knowledge. The *Propagator*'s formidable marshaling of Sanskritic material derives its meaning and its energy more from its polemic context than its classical sources; the zone of colonial debate is what is setting the agenda here, guiding this energetically argumentative text as it veers among topics in what can seem a rather haphazard manner. Rather than trying to map the *Propagator*'s relationship to its textual predecessors, then, we would do better to chart its points of intersection with the nineteenth-century reform scene.

Bhakti, according to Jadunathji, is one of several disciplinary practices (*sādhanas*) enumerated by Hindu tradition. These include renunciation (*tyāg*), yoga (*yog*), self-mortification (*tap*), spiritual knowledge (*brahmgyān*), and the performance of ritual duty (*karmkāṇḍ*). All of these other disciplines, however, are *saguṇa* (literally, "with qualities"): they remain enmeshed in the material substrate of the cosmos, and so while they can secure a happy rebirth (in a heaven, say), they cannot deliver the soul to the abode of God himself. Only bhakti, as the lone *nirguṇa* ("without qualities") discipline, can free the soul entirely from worldly things. It is therefore the best of disciplines. Its governing ideal, much discussed during the Maharaj Libel Case, is "self-surrender" (*ātmanivedan*). The devotee is to achieve this ideal by practicing the *navadhā bhakti*, or nine types of devotion. The list, as described in the *Propagator*, suggests a progressive work upon the self. Devotion begins by establishing habitual practices (hearing, singing, remembering the deity at all times); proceeds by extending these practices into pervasive attitudes (servility, friendliness); and culminates in the complete loss or surrender of the self to God.[83] As Richard Barz explains, Shri Vallabhacharya (founder of the Pushtimarg) inverted the conventional order of the nine bhaktis by placing self-surrender first. What had been the ecstatic end-point of devotional practice was refigured as its prerequisite, minimizing the agency of the devotee by emphasizing the grace (*anugraha*) of the divine.[84]

To the Bombay Supreme Court, this spelled trouble: such doctrines were presented as undermining the autonomy of the liberal subject and thus facilitating the despotic rule of the Maharajas over their servile devotees. By extension, they were also held responsible for the scenes of ritual abasement that so enthralled the Bombay public. John Wilson's English rendering of a pertinent Sanskrit verse gives a good sense of how the ideal of self-surrender played in translation: "I consecrate to thee my life, my soul, my organs, my property, myself, &c. I am thy slave, oh Krishna."[85] Mr. Anstey, the defense attorney, was more direct, alleging that the Pushtimarg's "doctrines" about "the deliverance of the soul and its re-absorption into the Divine essence" help "enforce the culture of adulterine love and sensual lust towards" the Maharaj and thus facilitate his "engaging in hot love with his devotees!"[86]

Without denying that such scenes were one outcome of the doctrine of self-surrender, I want to suggest that there are other possibilities implicit here. For example, one might note the apparent lack of fit between bhakti as a mode of self-discipline and Arnould's narrative of "spiritual bondage." After defining *atmaniveden bhakti* ("to entrust the body and soul to the Lord"), Jadunathji relates it to the notion of *karmayoga* outlined in the *Bhagavad Gita*. Just as Arjuna is counseled to relinquish the fruits of his actions and surrender them to God, thereby disencumbering himself of those actions' karmic consequences, so is the *bhakta* counseled to entrust himself to Krishna.[87] Only the devotee who practices self-surrender has no "desire for the fruit of his discipline," and so only he avoids rebirth.[88] In the *Gita*, the notion of *karmayoga* reconciles the competing imperatives of *dharma* (worldly duty) and *moksha* (release from the world) by infusing worldly action with a renunciant spirit. In the world but not of it, the *karmayogi* does his socially ascribed duty as a means of service to God, always standing aloof from a field of action mediated and conditioned by awareness of the transcendent.

This worldly asceticism is particularly well suited, as Jadunathji repeatedly affirms, to Hindu householders. Renunciant yogis may have unlimited time to ponder divinity in all its otherworldly abstraction, but householders require shortcuts. Krishna provided images of himself so that ordinary people can more easily keep him in mind during daily affairs. When going to the market to buy vegetables, the devotee should reflect that each item is worthy of being offered to the highest god. When going to do business, he should remember that now is his time to do service. Devotees are to remember God constantly in this way.[89] Pushtimargi practice is meant to supplant the "worldly" (*laukika*) with the "otherworldly" (*alaukika*); but the sect departs dramatically from other Indian religious traditions by discouraging full renunciation as the means of pursuing its otherworldly ends.[90] As Jadunathji reminds his reader, it is in order to demonstrate that the *bhaktimarg* was made especially for householders that the "sect's guru is also a householder."[91] The sect is thus ascetic, not in the sense that it refuses the duties or pleasures of worldly life, but rather in its reorienting those pleasures and duties toward the divine.

Since the founding of the Pushtimarg at the turn of the sixteenth century, loving worship of Krishna icons (especially in the form of Shrinathji) had been the primary technique for orienting daily life toward God. By 1860, however, the rising popularity of print media had suggested another means of devotional self-discipline. Jadunathi explains that he founded the *Propagator* in order to educate his followers: because they are ignorant of the scriptures, they have fallen into "superstition" (*vehem*).[92] But the Maharaj's readers are unruly. Not everyone in the community, he complains, is taking the journal; and even among those who are, many are reading it like they would read a newspaper, pushing through it quickly without full understanding and without learning to keep it in their hearts.[93] People are too infatuated with business to take time to read their sect's scriptures; Jadunathji directs them to set aside two hours every evening to do so, as a supplement to their preexisting regimen of image-based worship.[94] Rather than a "Protestant" refusal of visual or material religion, here we see print and image snugly aligned as complementary ascetic practices joined in opposition to the mundane pressures of daily life.

Jadunathji's anxiety about his recalcitrant readership is, I would argue, of crucial importance for understanding the kind of power he wielded over his followers. The disciplinary technologies detailed in the *Propagator* are procedures of *self*-discipline. They exert their influence not by subordinating a duped mass to a priestly despot, but rather through a process of ascetic dissemination. The Maharaj may control his flock in part; but, as with his distracted readers, he can never control them in full. This is due in part to the vagaries of media reception. But it also, I think, owes something to the ascetic logic of the Maharaj's bhakti. Because the ideal of self-surrender implies a work upon the self as much as it does a relationship with a human other (i.e., the Maharaj), the submission it demands of devotees is more than simple "spiritual bondage." If we take the Pushtimarg as staging scenes of self-discipline, the Maharaj should be understood as a tool used by the follower for her own spiritual ends, rather than the follower appearing as the simple instrument of her guru's pleasure. Or, more plausibly, we might say that within the Pushtimarg, self-control and priestly control (or autonomy and heteronomy) were irreducibly intertwined. This substantially alters how we conceive of the conflict between the Maharaj and Mulji. The question is thus not one of how freedom replaced control, nor even one of how one system of control replaced another. Rather, we should ask how these two mobilized ascetic technologies intersected and overlapped, and how both entered into networks of horizontal exchange in colonial Bombay, and well beyond it.

Arguably, bhakti itself suggests a model of subjectivity more amenable to this altered set of questions. The word *bhakti*, as is well known, derives from a Sanskrit root meaning "to share." As Jack Hawley and Mark Juergensmeyer have suggested, "it points to the importance of relationship—both to God and to human beings—in the kind of enthusiastic, often congregational religion it describes."[95] Bhakti, in short, implies community. "It is not necessary," taught Vallabhacharya, "to take the vow of *sannyāsa* (world-renunciation) in order to practice the ninefold *bhakti*, for in the practice of that bhakti the help of other bhaktas is essential."[96] Accordingly, the type of human-divine relationship prescribed by bhakti was, in Barz's words, "based on the strong emotional ties already present in human beings."[97] The ideal pairings typically used to describe how the devotee is to approach God (friend-friend, mother-child, lover-beloved) orient the transcendent and immanent worlds toward each other.

The Bombay court resisted such confusions between the human and the divine. This was particularly true with regard to the emotion that the court salaciously translated as "adulterine love" (*jārbhāv*)—a devotional affect that could not help but run afoul of Victorian sexual mores, not least for how it encouraged Pushtimargi men to imagine themselves as women in relation to God.[98] The *Propagator* tries to redeem this "adulterine" affect in the public eye. As Jadunathji explains, the "adulterous woman" (*jārbhāvnī prītivāḷī strī*) does the housework, but day and night her mind remains stuck on her paramour (*jār*). If her beloved goes abroad, the pain of separation (*viyog*) ruins her appetite and destroys her appearance until she eventually dies from surfeit of suffering.[99] Just as this ideal female figure pines for her lover, so should the devotee, whether male or female, pine for the divine.

As an ideal subject, the figure of the adulterine woman disrupts the integrity of the self. The self should become porous in relation to the divine or, better yet, realize that it is always already porous, as the more metaphysical passages in the *Propagator* imply. The soul (*jīv*), writes Jadunathji, is just "a part of God"; human selves spray out from the divine like sparks from a fire pit.[100] What we see here is perhaps akin to the distinction that Leela Gandhi draws between Kantian "reflective faith," which reinforces the self-sufficiency of the autonomous human subject, and modes of faith that trigger the "interruptive unraveling" of the self by opening it to the unwavering demand of the divine other.[101]

If we take the scene of the mirror practice as characteristic of Mulji's religion, the difference is striking: on the one hand, a bourgeois man looks anxiously at himself in the mirror. On the other, a devotee looks lovingly at an icon of Krishna or imagines himself as pining for the dark Lord. The first practice produces the subject through isolated interiority, the second through the exteriority of devotional address. Both, however, are ascetic practices disseminated via print artifacts that become tools for transforming the self and bringing it into closer accord with the divine. The pining lover's self-relation is arguably more important than her relation to the divine beloved: she assiduously cultivates longing as devotional affect. Likewise, Mulji's mirror is inscribed in a network of intersubjective relations: in gazing at himself, the bourgeois male orients his inner life toward a print-mediated discipline for which Mulji is a kind of reformist guru. Thus do the Indian Luther and his priestly counterpart converge: spiritual autonomy and spiritual heteronomy intersect at the mediatory figure of the internalized religious teacher.

FIVE

Pope-Lila

In the Aryan country too the Pope-ji has taken on who knows how many thousands of avatars in order to spread his lila. Keeping the king and his subjects ignorant and preventing them from associating with good men, the popes do no work, day or night, aside from duping and misleading others.[1] DAYANANDA SARASWATI, *SATYARTH PRAKASH* (1883)

The religious life of Swami Dayananda Saraswati (1824–1883) began the night he lost his faith. One boyhood evening, he followed his father to temple to keep the vigil of Shivaratri. Late that night, while his father and the other devotees dozed, he had an experience that would change him forever. There was to be no divine vision, only mice scampering across the stone icon of Shiva to eat the offerings arrayed before the deity. As the rodents clambered onto the unprotesting god, the boy (not yet Dayanand) had a revelation: the dumb matter of the *murti* was not divine. Something changed in his heart that night, and although when he left the temple he returned home to his mother, it would not be long before he left his family behind. The mice had made him a man, and as man (born again under a renunciant's name) he resolved to take on the mouse's mantle. He would travel India, exploding ritual illusions to bring his countrymen to the transcendent truths of disenchanted religion.

Years of ascetic wandering brought this boy from rural Gujarat to a series of teachers. One taught him yogic austerities. Another initiated him into *sannyas* and gave him his religious name. A third, Virajanand the "blind sage of Mathura," trained him in Sanskrit grammar and the proper classification of the Vedas and, fatefully, directed him to disseminate this knowledge to the mass of Hindus, who, the great sage believed, had long left Vedic religion behind. Years roving the wilderness, fending off wild bears and boars, armed the young renunciant with the combative manner that would shape his post-Mathura career as a religious polemicist. At first, he challenged orthodox Hindus in traditional settings, decrying image worship at the Kumbha Mela at Allahabad in 1867 and joining in a classically structured debate at Banaras in 1869. But after an 1873 visit to Calcutta, where he met with Keshub Chunder Sen and the members of the Brahmo Samaj, as well as other men from the colonial metropolis's reform-minded middle class, Dayanand's methods changed decisively. Trading his erudite Sanskrit for populist Hindi (itself on the rise as a *lingua franca*), he founded a reform society, the Arya Samaj, which proved at least as influential as its Brahmo model. He also wrote a book, the *Satyarth Prakash* (*The Light of Truth*, 1875), which contained a comprehensive statement of his reform program. During the last eight years of his life, Dayanand was finally in a position to reform the Hindus, bringing them back to the Vedas, as his guru Virajanand had commanded. Celebrity brought Dayanand a new public. But when fame finally arrived, it did so partly in a language that neither Dayanand nor his guru could understand.[2]

Luther at the Least

It was as a "Luther of India" that Dayanand exploded onto the national Anglophone scene in the late 1870s—becoming, arguably, the quintessential Indian Luther by the end of the century. Theosophist Henry Steel Olcott's 1879 address to the Meerut branch of the Arya Samaj is indicative. He positioned Dayanand as the latest in a line of Indian Luthers stretching from Gautama Buddha to Rammohun Roy. Like his predecessors, claimed Olcott, Dayanand was the sworn enemy of India's "crafty and selfish priesthood."[3] Or, as Olcott later broadened this claim, Dayanand "reviles the orthodox Pope-ji from east to west."[4] In the 1890s, the *Indian Evangelical Review* acclaimed Dayanand for having freed himself from "the Brahmanical Church" just as "Luther became emancipated from the authority of the Church of Rome." Where the one's "watchword" was "Back to the Bible," the other's was "Back to the Vedas."[5] By the early twentieth century, Arya Samajis had appropriated this rhetoric as part of their own political semantics, making savvy use of the English language's religious lexicon in order to garner influence in the colonial public sphere.[6] Durga

Prasad's widely circulated 1908 English translation of the *Satyarth Prakash*, for example, claimed Dayanand as "The Luther of India" in its very title.[7]

One might infer from the ubiquity and seeming self-evidence of the Luther comparison that Dayanand was a simple agent of Protestantization, his reforms inspired wholly or in part by the British colonial milieu—and, indeed this has been a standard gloss on Dayanand since the early twentieth century.[8] It is a gloss, however, that overlooks some inconvenient facts. Dayanand did not even speak English when he died, much less when he embarked upon the path of reform as a disillusioned boy in Gujarat. Even though this primal scene (which first appeared in print in English in 1879) is clearly shaped by Dayanand's adult concerns, it also strongly implies that some part of the great reformer's drive to disenchant Hinduism predated his encounter with Protestant rhetoric.

One standard response to this interpretive impasse would be to argue that, by describing Dayanand as an "Indian Luther," colonial writers were imposing British categories onto Indian content in classically imperial fashion.[9] But how to be rid of Luther? Some interpreters have retained the comparison and used it to assert Dayanand's superiority. This is the tactic adopted by a 1912 Arya Samaji pamphlet, which describes Dayanand as "Luther at the least." Where his German counterpart had only taken on a single Pope, Dayanand resisted the "priestcraft and idolatry" of "thousands" of them.[10] Here, arguably, we see a classic ideological procedure in action: colonialism secures the consent of the governed by soliciting identification with the cultural forms of the colonizer, while also denying the possibility of full identification. By virtue of being himself, Dayanand can never entirely equal his German namesake, or at least not without some point of difference or remainder. The aim of this pamphlet is to render this remainder as a sign of surplus ("Luther at the least"), rather than of lack.[11]

Another method is to bypass Protestantism entirely. In this vein, Timothy Dobe has argued that Dayanand should not be understood as a Luther, but rather as an "irascible rishi." As Dobe explains, previous scholarship has overstated Dayanand's dependence on Protestant models, thereby not only oversimplifying his relationship to the Sanskrit textual canon, but also neglecting the title of "Maharishi" bestowed on him by the Arya Samaj. Given the centrality of rishis to how the *Satyarth Prakash* imagines religious authority and religious textuality, we would do well, Dobe advises, to take seriously Dayanand's continuity with earlier tradition. By rereading the *Satyarth Prakash* "in indigenous terms," Dobe sets out to resist dominant scholarly narratives that take modern Hinduism as primarily "derivative" of Western, colonial, and Protestant cultural forms.[12] And in doing so, Dobe is not alone. A growing body of recent work in South Asian studies has countered an earlier scholarship's enthusiasm for cultural hybridity by insisting on the integrity of precolonial cultural forms during and beyond the colonial period.

While Dobe's is a valuable corrective that calls attention to important aspects of the *Satyarth Prakash*, to insist too much on this text's continuity with Sanskritic tradition is to obscure important aspects of Dayanand's intellectual trajectory. As J. T. F. Jordens argues, the 1873 Calcutta trip was transformative for Dayanand. Prior to it, he championed Vedic religion "completely within the context of Hinduism itself." It was only afterwards, however, that he articulated the reform program that made him famous.[13] Of a piece with this later moment, the *Satyarth Prakash* indicates Dayanand's broadening sphere of concern, especially in the much-revised second edition of 1883, which extends Dayanand's criticisms of Hinduism and Jainism to Christianity and Islam.[14] Some of the text's most emblematic passages are those that imagine a giddily global Hinduism, with descriptions of the ancient Aryans' worldwide empire, and mention of Krishna and Arjuna traveling to America in a steamboat (*agniyān naukā*).[15] Dayanand goes to great lengths to position Hinduism (or, more precisely, the *Vedmat*) as universal in its address, neither limited to India nor hermetically sealed within its own textual canon. This universalism is suggested by the episode at the close of chapter 11, in which a neutral arbitrator decides which of the representatives of the world's 999 faiths espouses the true religion (victory, nor surprisingly, is awarded to the representative for the Vedas).[16]

Thus, although the reform program articulated in the *Satyarth Prakash* does clearly emerge from and draw on Hindu tradition, the text inevitably refigures that tradition and its geographic and cultural moorings by refitting it to the nineteenth century. Scholarship on the text should, of course, recognize its continuities with the Sanskrit textual canon. It should also, however, avoid replicating the kinds of claims made by colonial Arya Samajis who were keen to assert the purity of Hindu tradition against its British and Muslim counterparts. Dayanand's biographer Ghasiram, for instance, denies the common charge that Dayanand drew on Western philology by insisting that "with Dayanand, everything was his own; he wasn't any foreigner's debtor." He never learned English and so his reform project must be drawn entirely from the "treasury of Sanskrit literature" (*saṃskr̥tsāhityabhaṇḍār*).[17]

Here, I try to think around the presumption that comparing Dayanand to Luther implies that Dayanand was derivative. I suggest that rather than framing a comparative question (i.e., "Was Dayanand like Luther?"), we should instead pose a connective question that moves us from the study of cultural and religious diversity, in which cultures and religions are presumed as pre-given facts, to a study of cultural and religious difference that traces how the very effort to study culture or religion works to define and delimit cultural and religious worlds that are only apparently discrete.[18] Take, for example, the tale of the mouse and the *murti*. That the "original" version of this story was published in English might be interpreted as incidental to it. After all, the story is so persuasive in positing the roots of Dayanand's reform agenda in his Gujarati childhood that one is inclined to separate the story from its linguistic medium. Dayanand, of course, would have related the tale to *The Theosophist* in some language other than English (probably Hindi). But especially if he did so with English readers in mind, then what we see in this story is an effort to produce cultural difference through the act of autobiography, rather than difference as inert or pre-given fact. The story actively works to situate the origins of Dayanand's reform program in his precocious boyhood. The implied claim to cultural purity is belied, however, by the performative context in which that claim is enunciated: this story is addressed to and thus shaped by the 1870s. Something similar, I think, holds in the case of Dayanand-as-Luther. Rather than starting from a question of comparison, which presumes that Dayanand and Luther preexist one another, we should start with a connective question that foregrounds the generative potential of this odd pairing. How, one might ask, did both Dayanand and Luther come to be reinvented in the moment of their conjunction?

As I discuss in chapter 2, I worry that recent scholarship in religious studies affords too much power to Protestantism as a cultural force. Instead of assuming that Protestantism indelibly shapes all that it touches through seamless self-replication, it seems more productive to ask whether the multiple iterations of the Protestant in the nineteenth-century worked to unravel the Protestant. With iteration comes reinvention. Thus, as I suggest in chapter 1, by distinguishing between the spirit and the historical facts of the Reformation, Victorian writers rendered reformation constitutively unstable, caught between empirical particulars and general norms. We can see how this instability shaped the search for the Indian Luther, a figure who became increasingly dissociated from Christianity over the course of the century. This instability is apparent in another way in the contested symbol of "reform," which circulated widely in the nineteenth century, crisscrossing sacred and secular, colony and metropole. By asking how such ideals circulated within what I describe in chapter 3 as the nineteenth-century reform assemblage, we can potentially move beyond a diffusion model of colonial culture that would consistently return us to questions of influence and derivativeness. Instead, by placing Hindu reformers within a contrapuntally interconnected world of circulatory forces, we can see how they posed a question that recurred throughout this period at a number of different sites: what did *Protestant* mean, anyway?

As Jordens's periodization suggests, in 1873 (if not before) Dayanand entered the nineteenth-century reform assemblage.[19] His writings after that date, including the *Satyarth Prakash*, need to be understood as constitutively embedded within a broad constellation of colonial reform cultures that were never exclusively Hindu. Instead of constraining him within the hermetically sealed "treasury" of Sanskrit, we would do better to ask how he forged connections that dispersed Sanskrit's riches into a broader cultural sphere. Neither derivatively Protestant nor pristinely Hindu, the *Satyarth Prakash* is also more than a site where Protestant and Hindu vectors simply intersect, their cultural worlds remaining easily identifiable and analytically distinct. Instead, as I will argue, the *Satyarth Prakash* refigures the question of the "Protestant Hindu" by refracting it through a reform project that interlinks the pastoral regulation of the populace, the ascetic control of the self, and the biopolitical production of the nation. The text inscribes both the "Protestant" and the "Hindu" within a problematic of self-regulation or brahmacharya.

My close reading of the *Satyarth Prakash* unfolds from a curious compound term—"pope-lila" (*poplīlā*)—that anchors Dayanand's lengthy disquisition on the history of Hinduism as a corruption of Vedic religion. Evidently a translation of the word *priestcraft*, *pope-lila* is an especially suggestive stop on that term's nineteenth-century itinerary. Dayanand seems to have first developed it in his controversialist speeches and public debates; reportedly, the crowds that he addressed were "delighted at his novel use in vernacular of the word 'pope' for the ignorant Brahmins."[20] Notably, the term does not appear in the 1875 version of the *Satyarth Prakash*; its prominence in the 1883 revision thus suggests Dayanand's increasing engagement with Anglophone religious reformism during the last eight years of his life.[21] As is further suggested by the 1912 pamphlet cited above, this trajectory continued after Dayanand's death. His Hindi-language denunciation of the "Pope-ji" and his "thousand avatars" facilitated, if not exactly a rapprochement between Hindi and English, then at least further productive slippages between the two. These "thousand popes" serve a function for Dayanand very similar to the function that they served for James Mill and Charles Grant. *Pope-lila* indicates a mode of power that is specific to religion and that contrasts with technologies of self-rule. Dayanand's program of Vedic reform displaced the priest by establishing a new pastoral order where spiritual and temporal sovereignty are dispersed throughout the body of the nation.

It did this, I will suggest, through a principle of asceticism, or brahm-acharya, that somaticizes the problematic of self-government by associating it with a set of techniques for regulating the body in accord with virtue. Aurobindo Ghosh, in his panegyric to Dayanand ("a very soldier of Light, a warrior in God's world"), writes that the reformer's career exemplifies a "spiritual practicality" that synthesizes "Matter" and "Spirit" by triumphing over the "difficulties" that the former always presents to the latter.[22] To translate this synthesis to the Weberian lexicon, we would say that Dayanand was a worldly ascetic, turning the spirit to practical ends, while also subordinating the merely physical or worldly to the dictates of the transcendent. Unfolding from a concern with religious leaders as bad pedagogues, and entangled with Dayanand's own educational program, brahmacharya as a means of perfecting character proves central to the project of the *Satyarth Prakash* as a whole. It is the antidote to the exploitative misrule of "popes." Eliminating priestly charisma, Dayanand, in effect, sets out to bureaucratize brahmacharya. His use of asceticism certainly draws on and is imbued with Hindu tradition; but it also has a clear affinity for Protestantism. My hope here, as in the rest of this book, is that by generalizing "Protestantism" to the point of its dissolution into a broader field of mobilized ascetic and pastoral technologies, we can deny it its presumed singularity. Instead of embracing the Indian Luther, or trying to displace him entirely, we can use the *Satyarth Prakash* to reimagine the Victorian Luther as a cultural sign.

Who Are the "Popes"?

The *Satyarth Prakash* is a polemical book, and its sharpness of tone is never clearer than in the many dialogues that pepper the text and convey much of its argument. This mode of exposition surely owes something to classical Hindu philosophy, with its dialogic form. Closer by, there was the arena of public debate and religious controversy within which Dayanand had honed his polemic idiom.[23] Indeed, as Dayanand's first real venture into the realm of vernacular print, the *Satyarth Prakash* feels poised between the oral and the written, its staged debates less invocations of classical textual precedent than snippets of overhead or imagined arguments—and arguments of the most caustic kind.[24]

One such dispute is at the heart of my reading of the *Satyarth Prakash*. It comes toward the beginning of the long history of Hinduism that constitutes the book's eleventh chapter. After remarking that most contemporary Brahmans are Brahmans in name only, Dayanand shifts from argumentative exposition to a fictive interchange with one of these pretended priests. The dialogue opens with an accusation: "But you are not a Brahman." It then continues in a question and answer format:

Q: So who am I?
A: You are a pope.
Q: Who is called a pope?
A: Actually, in the Roman language, influential people and fathers were called popes, but now *pope* refers to those who make use of others by duping them with tricks and deceits.

Dayanand, having offered a fair definition of *popery*, if not *pope* itself, goes on to provide a concise history of priestly fraud in Europe. The Roman popes, we are told, would rob their disciples or *chela*s of all their rupees by selling them bills of exchange (*huṇḍi*). The pope would lay the paper contract in front of an image of Jesus or Mary, and then instruct the devotee to carry it with him to the grave, so that he can hand it to the angel who will lead him to heaven. There, the pope said, the paper will purchase celestial amenities, including a house, a garden, and servants. Here in this world, it costs a sizeable fortune of one hundred thousand rupees. Dayanand distills this system of fraud and oppression with the evocative term *pope-lila*, going on to explain that the popes' regime persisted so long as "idiocy" (*murkhtā*) prevailed in Europe. But although widespread education may have helped contain its evils, it has never been entirely uprooted. Next, Dayanand turns his attention to India. "In just this way," he writes, the "Pope-jī" spread his lila in the "Aryan country" by taking on countless avatars. Popes have ensnared all India with lies, illusions, and trickery. Under their guidance "blind tradition" (*andhparampara*) has overtaken the world.[25]

Dayanand wrote most of the *Satyarth Prakash* in a primly Sanskritized Hindi, and so the inclusion of the "pope" as an Anglophone interloper in the text is notable. Apparently a translation of the word *priestcraft*, *pope-lila* certainly derives from the anticlerical milieu of which *priestcraft* was a signal part. Indeed, Dayanand's depiction of an India groaning under the all-pervasive rule of despotic priests would be worthy of James Mill or any number of other imperial writers. But Dayanand also signals a significant point of departure from Anglophone anticlericalism by translating *craft* as *lila*. This highly resonant term, closely associated with Krishna devotion and Vaishnava thought, usually denotes God's mischievous play in the world of creation, as through miracles or the taking of avatars. Equating lila with craftiness is a highly tendentious move on Dayanand's part, as it reduces the theological substrate of this rich devotional tradition to mere fraud, perpetrated by wily humans. The word *pope-lila* was thus a double-edged weapon within Dayanand's polemic arsenal. It marked his affinity for Protestant opponents of popery, while also marking his point of departure from the well-trod terrain of anti-Catholic invective, edging Anglophone anticlericalism onto specifically Hindu theological ground.

The chief function of the hundred-page history of Hinduism that follows Dayanand's spat with the pope is to enumerate and traduce the many heterodoxies that, by Dayanand's account, have accrued since ancient times, all but burying the Vedas in the process. The golden age of Vedic truth and Aryan empire was brought to an abrupt close by the massive war recounted in the *Mahabharata*, which, by killing off good, learned men in unprecedented number, allowed the "sprout" of wickedness that had existed even before the war to bear fruit. Self-serving, ill-educated Brahmans conspired together and resolved to convince the members of the other castes that "we alone are the gods you should worship." Those who refuse to do so will fall into a horrible hell. "Blind of eye and full of purse," their credulous followers adopted the dictum that whatever a Brahman says is like the command of God, and they stupidly heaped luxuries on these pretended deities.

Not everyone, however, accepted the authority of the popes. Occasionally in Dayanand's history, a "man of truth" (*satpuruṣ*) like Shankaracharya arises to challenge their divine pretensions and plead for the Vedas. For millennia, the popes and their truth-loving critics vie for supremacy, with the popes always taking the upper hand. They co-opt and pervert criticisms of their rule, infiltrate rival movements, and proliferate new techniques for amassing and controlling followers. The result is the history of Hinduism and related movements, with each sect or path either a popish ruse or an effort to thwart priestly power that is eventually commandeered by it. Dayanand casts a wide net: Tantra, Jainism, Buddhism, Charvaka, Shavism, Vaishnavism, and Shaktism are all condemned. The Puranas are dismissed as popish fabrications, and Krishna culture excoriated as an abyss of abominations. Even Kabir and Guru Nanak are called up for critique. In the *Satyarth Prakash*, truth recedes to a prehistoric past, buried behind a seemingly endless history of lies.

This grand narrative has a decidedly nationalist tinge, and, as has been much noted in the scholarship on Dayanand, its basic elements were in fact taken up and further developed by twentieth-century Hindu nationalist ideologues.[26] Even so, Dayanand's distinctive concern with the politics of heterodoxy marks his ideological distance from twentieth-century communalism. The incipient discourse of the Hindu nation serves here primarily to refract and heighten the stakes of heterodoxy, rather than constituting a clear political agenda in its own right. The *Satyarth Prakash* sets out to critique the religions of "the Aryan people" (*āryya log*), or "the people who live in the Aryan country" (*āryyavartt deś*), thus overlaying territory, population, and religion.[27] Touring the subcontinent to expose priestly frauds at Hindu temples, the book implicitly reinforces the mutual determination of national and sacred geography. That the latter is almost always Hindu is significant, especially given the organization of the book, which carefully separates its criticisms of the four "anti-Vedic religions" (*vedviruddh mat*): the *purāṇī* (Puranic religion), the *jainī* (Jainism), the *kirānī* (Christianity), and the *kūrānī* (Islam). Some disagreements, this schema implies, are intra-religious family quarrels; others mark the fundamental divisions between religious communities. Cataloguing the history of Hindu heterodoxy thus, and somewhat counterintuitively, ultimately reinforces the boundaries of Hinduism as a whole: by exhaustively listing all types of "bad Hindus," the *Satyarth Prakash* makes it clear who falls entirely outside this raucously argumentative fold. Nonetheless, the text does mark certain Hindus for symbolic expulsion from the nation. Even as it underlines the association of Hindu heterodoxies with Aryan geography, the *Satyarth Prakash*, through its use of the neologism *pope-lila*, also expatriates allegedly false Hindus from this territory. To insist that a Brahman is not a Brahman, but rather a pope, is to effect a semantic exile. No longer truly Indian (or, in Dayanand's terminology, Aryan), he is a resident alien in a national territory that must eject him in order to restore itself to spiritual and political health.[28]

In addition to this proto-nationalist function, the compound term *pope-lila* also serves an important epistemological role for Dayanand. Like many other anticolonial figures of the late nineteenth century, Dayandand asserted India's parity with Britain by staking a claim to the ostensibly universal, value-neutral discourse of science. The Vedas, in his view, were texts of universal significance not so much because they were religious, but because they were scientific, anticipating the major discoveries of modern Western science millennia in advance and attesting to the technological sophistication of Vedic civilization. By tethering the Vedas' transcendent claims to their alleged mastery of empirical fact, Dayanand blurs the line between the secular and the sacred and also attempts (as per Aurobindo's claim) a conciliation of "Spirit" and "Matter." Determined empiricism was, after all, one of the hallmarks of Dayanand's thought and career. This attitude is distilled in the episode from his autobiography where he finds a corpse washed up on a riverbank, and throws all of his classical medical treatises in the water so that he can examine the human body as it actually is.[29]

Lila poses a problem for Dayanand's Vedic science, and thus for his Vedic nationalism. A Sanskrit noun meaning "sport" or "play," *lila* first appears in theological usage in Badarayana's *Vedanta Sutra* (ca. third century), where it resolves an apparent conceptual impasse: how could the Absolute, which is by definition complete unto itself, have given rise to the world without thereby indicating some kind of need or lack? Creation, the text suggests, occurred through the exuberant surplus of divine play, or lila. The precise implications of this play for the resultant cosmos were, however, left open to interpretation. The major commentators on the *Vedanta Sutra* were of two minds on the matter. Philosophical dualists, like Ramanuja, held that God's lila (i.e., the cosmos) actually exists and is ontologically distinct from the divine. Non-dualists, like Shankara, disagreed: lila is not a metaphysical category, but just a metaphor underscoring the freedom of the Absolute. It needs to be understood in conjunction with the properly metaphysical category of maya, or cosmic illusion, which can account for the apparent (not actual) existence of the cosmos. Without conflating lila and maya, this tradition does closely associate them, using both to undermine the ontological integrity of the phenomenal world.[30]

In Dayanand's lexicon, *lila* and *maya* pull even closer together, with the semantic range of each much circumscribed. Both become, in effect, synonyms for fraud, plain and simple. Denigrating both concepts, Dayanand also rejects the theological traditions with which they were most closely associated. With lila went Krishna and the world of folk performance (also called lilas, these popular plays stage the very tales from the *Ramayana* and the *Bhagavat Purana* that Dayanand was trying so hard to eliminate). With maya went Vedanta. As Jordens explains, although Dayanand was initiated into asceticism by Vedantins and would have been trained extensively in Vedantic thought, he broke with this philosophical school starting around 1860, when he committed himself to Virajanand's program of Vedic revival. The break was gradual, and there are important differences in this regard even between the first (1875) and second (1883) editions of the *Satyarth Prakash*. But by the time he had finished revising the book, his disdain for Vedanta was nothing less than scathing.[31]

Dayanand distills Vedantic thought in the following formula: "The ultimate being is true, the world illusion, and the soul one with the ultimate being."[32] To a man of Dayanand's "practical" constitution, contemplative discussion of illusion seemed morally suspect. In one dialogue, a "pope-ji" informs Dayanand that Vishnu created the world through his maya. Dayanand strenuously objects. God could not have made the world through the purposeless power of his maya, because maya is merely human, the same as commonplace trickery (*chal-kapaṭ*). To be an illusionist (*māyāvī*) is to be a cheat, and God cannot be a cheat. The same cannot be said for the popish Brahmans, whom Dayanand accuses of having invented the idea of Vishnu's divine illusion. It is a fraud (*dhoka*) devised to distract from true religion.[33] Here, in a characteristically "practical" move, Dayanand converts metaphysical speculation into *ad hominem* attack. The elimination of lila is, first and foremost, a procedure for disciplining the world and the people in it so that nothing seems to be other than what it is or speaks anything other than the truth. Cleared of divine mystery, the phenomenal world is declared to be the real world, epistemologically accessible to the perceiving subject and thus open to instrumental manipulation by this same masterful agent.

According to Robert Goodwin, one of the main historical functions of the concept of lila has been "to recuperate the phenomenal world in the face of a radical ascetic drive to renunciation" of that world.[34] As in Krishna devotion, the human person should embrace the world lovingly because it is a playful manifestation of God; the otherworldly impulse to unite with Krishna is thus channeled back into immanent affairs. In reducing lila to deceit and popery, Dayanand rejects this solution to the problem of renunciation. But he does not thereby reject the world: quite the contrary. If the concept of lila had provided one means of reconciling the dueling desires for the worldly and the transcendent, Dayanand's "spiritual practicality" would prove another. Indeed, perhaps it makes sense to understand his impassioned rejection of lila as a ground-clearing act: precisely because lila solves a problem akin to the problem addressed by his own reform project, it has to be eliminated.

Dayanand's project centers, as I have suggested, on a revised notion of brahmacharya, which is developed in the first ten chapters of the *Satyarth Prakash*, and which thus provides the context for the polemics against other religions that follow in chapters 11–14. Construction of a reform program precedes Dayanand's destruction of his popish rivals, and these two aspects of his book need to be read in relation to one another. In their intersection, pope-lila and brahmacharya indicate a mode of politics that is specific to Dayanand, but that also suggests the resonance of his reform Hinduism with nineteenth-century reform cultures more broadly construed.

The Science of Making a Better Man

In his preface to a 1915 biography of Dayanand, the prominent Arya Samaji leader Munshi Ram observes that "Dayananda has been compared with the apostle of Protestant Reformation in Europe" and "dubbed . . . the Luther of India." But despite the "wonderful similarity" between these two "greatest all-round religious reformers of the last thousand years and more," there nonetheless remains "one significant difference" between them. This difference has to do with their "characters," and it "has always distinguished the Aryan ideal of *Dharma* from the non-Aryan conceptions of religious duty." It can be summed up in a single word: *brahmacharya*. A complicated and multidimensional term within Hindu tradition, *brahmacharya* can be variously defined as asceticism, chastity, or the initial student phase of the four life stages (*ashrama*s) prescribed by classical scriptures. Elements of all of these definitions are evident here. Where the "non-Aryan apostle" married a nun and became a householder, the "Aryan apostle" renounced "all worldly pleasures" at the outset of his career and so bypassed "the first three stages of human life" to enter the fourth "directly," dedicating himself to hard work and "ascetic practices." Accordingly, as Munshi Ram explains, the "sum total of his teachings" was the "truth of Divine Brahmacharya": "There is no purity without Brahmacharya and, divorced from the purity of body and mind, there is no salvation."[35]

Linking together the ascetic refusal of worldly pleasure, the rejection of marriage, and mental and physical "purity," Munshi Ram touches on a cluster of themes central to the reform program of the *Satyarth Prakash*. He also explicitly links these themes to the question of Protestantism. As C. S. Adcock glosses Munshi Ram's argument, brahmacharya is what makes Dayanand "a *specifically Vedic* reformer."[36] Leaving aside the question of whether there is anything especially "Vedic" about the renunciant ideal, or whether the ascetic desire for world-transcendence postdates and challenges the Vedic world of ritual sacrifice, it seems safe to say that this use of brahmacharya is novel, distinctively modern, and very much at the heart of Dayanand's own neo-Vedic program.[37] Where brahmacharya had previously been the preserve of a narrowly demarcated segment of society, whether student or renunciant, Dayanand generalizes it to the population as a whole—it being through this generalized ascetic practice that the national body is to be reconstituted and reformed. This extension of brahmacharya is likewise implicit in Munshi Ram's comments. The normative force of the claim that there is no salvation and no truth apart from brahmacharya enjoins even householders to regulate their conduct and character on an ascetic model. If they cannot be like Dayananda in degree, then at least they can be like him in kind.

This worldly asceticism rearticulates the relationship between laity and religious professionals, placing Vedic brahmacharya squarely in the realm of the sorts of mobilized disciplinary and pastoral technologies that in this book I have been describing as participating in the logic of reform. As any post-Weberian theorist of the Reformation would insist, Luther's marriage to a nun did not make him *less* of an ascetic; rather, by conjoining marriage and monasticism, he simply transformed the relationship between the two, making the wedding bed a site for a modified form of ascetic self-regulation. Dayanand did something similar. His extension of brahmacharya and his insinuation of ascetic norms into the lives of householders are central to his larger project of the reform of subjectivity—a project that one late twentieth-century Arya Samaji tract memorably terms "the science of making a better man."[38]

The mobilized asceticism characteristic of this vision is succinctly expressed by the 1912 "Luther of India" pamphlet discussed above. Gokal Chand, the pamphleteer, suggests that had it not been for Virajanand's command that Dayanand go forth into the world to preach the Veda, the great swami would have retired to a remote cave somewhere to practice yogic austerities. Virajanand's command repurposed his yogic resolve, turning it outward into the world. It is thus precisely as a *worldly yogi* that Dayanand assumes the status of a "veritable Luther" and "enters the field of reform." Moreover, it is his yogic work upon the self that renders Dayanand, in Gokal Chand's words, "a man of character"—"character," as I will suggest, being the axis along which the generalized practice of brahmacharya remakes the nation. "Having achieved the perfect self-control by the practice of yoga," writes our pamphleteer, Dayanand was "invulnerable to temptations of all kinds," and "even his bitterest critics" could not impugn "the purity of his life."[39]

These biographical pamphlets were published at a time when Arya Samajis took particular interest in the example of their society's founding figure. As Adcock explains, Arya Samajis in the 1910s and 20s placed "brahmacharya at the heart of a moral politics centered on the cultivation of character." This discourse, which developed alongside the anticolonial and communal politics of the same period, predicated national self-rule on "the prior recrafting of national character, person by person."[40] This crafting of character, Adcock suggests, participated in what Joseph Alter has termed the "moral politics" of twentieth-century Indian nationalism. Most famously on view in the career of M. K. Gandhi, this mode of politics sees the political management of the mass and the ethical management of the self as inseparable. Whether through his spectacular fasts or his strenuous celibacy, Gandhi took his own body's ascetic capabilities as a point of intimate access to the national body politic, and he likewise demanded that his followers join the struggle for swaraj through scrupulously somatic self-regulation.[41] Gandhi was not alone in appreciating the productive convergence of the ascetic and the biopolitical; moral politics is now more closely associated with the muscular Hinduism of the RSS and other such organizations. But in the early twentieth century the differentiation among these disparate political agendas was just beginning to take shape. Indeed, if Gokal Chand's pamphlet is any indication, it would seem that the colonial conflict between Hinduism and Protestant Christianity remained the more fully articulated point of tension in the 1910s.

In the 1870s and 80s, yet a different set of tensions seems to have shaped the politics of asceticism. For the *Satyarth Prakash*, the major conflict is not between the Hindu and the Protestant; still less is it between Gandhianism and Hindutva. The text is much more concerned with claiming asceticism away from Vedanta. In some ways anticipating Gandhi's and Aurobindo's much later writings on the *Bhagavad Gita*, or even the warrior ascetics of Bankimchandra Chatterjee's *Anandamath* (1882), Dayanand is intent on redefining renunciation as a fundamentally worldly project. In order to do so, he has to invalidate Vedanta, and he goes about doing this with great gusto.

In one of the book's many dialogues, Dayanand's straw-man opponent describes renunciants as not having any obligations. They should obtain food and clothing, but having done so, should relax without wracking their brains about the ignorant world. "Realizing that they are the Ultimate [*brahm*], they should rest content. . . . Sin and merit do not stick to them. . . . The world is an illusion, and the business of the world is likewise imaginary—which is to say a lie."[42] Dayanand answers these claims irately: "Do they too not have a duty to do good works [*acche karm*]?" If they take food and clothes from householders without doing good deeds in return, then they have sinned. Renunciants who do not preach Vedic truth are a useless burden on the world. Anyone who says otherwise is just spreading lies. The Vedantins are, moreover, wrong to claim that the soul can be disencumbered of its actions. "Whatever deeds are done by the body, they all belong to the soul [*ātmā*]. It is the soul itself that will enjoy their fruits."[43] Dayanand is not particularly interested in working through the metaphysical niceties of this claim or how it might contravene the teachings of other Hindu texts (e.g., the *Gita*'s presentation of *karmayoga* as a "moral Teflon that blocks the consequences of action").[44] His orientation, to return to Aurobindo's formula, is much more practical.

"Whereas a strong strain of Hinduism," writes Jordens, "tends to draw man away from both the world and active involvement" in it, Dayanand's neo-Vedic religion drives hard in the opposite direction.[45] He reorients asceticism toward worldly action by rejecting traditional forms of renunciation. These, he implies, inevitably abet pope-lila. Again, his penchant for *ad hominem* attacks is telling. Dayanand is much more interested in the behavior of modern-day Vedantins than in their philosophical claims. Idlers whose unkempt hair is a testament to their dubious moral constitution, they are clearly of the party of the popes. Religious knowledge is less important than action, and so Vedantins can be disbarred based on their behaviors alone.

Dayanand dismantles two-speed religion by delegitimizing two major classes of religious virtuosi (Brahmans and ascetics). He then devises means for redistributing ascetic technologies of self-regulation to the population at large, above all through his ambitious educational proposals. If later Arya Samajis took the robust physical frame of Dayanand the skilled polemicist as the primary symbol of brahmacharya, thus locating the politics of asceticism in the fully public realm of interreligious debate (and, eventually, communalism), Dayanand himself looked to a different set of ascetic figures—above all the child—to articulate how brahmacharya would transform the social order.[46] The primary locus of brahmacharya as a reform practice is thus, within the *Satyarth Prakash*, the spaces of school and family. Inserting asceticism into the home produces its own breed of conflict, however. Ascetic virtue, as we will see, calls into question the primacy of the heterosexual couple's reproductive function as the key means of sustaining the social body.

The *Satyarth Prakash* implies that an educated populace is immune to the deceptions of the "pope." Because the ascetic subject rules herself, she can resist the lure of the false Brahman. Does this make her akin to the autonomous or buffered individual of liberal political thought? Jordens, for his part, suggests that the Vedantic renunciant is "the supreme individualist, for whom only *moksha* counts." That is, as in Louis Dumont's quasi-Weberian account of the history of Hindu renunciation, the search for salvation from the world disembeds the subject from the world and establishes him as a discrete individual. The *Satyarth Prakash* is generally less concerned with soteriology than it is with social reform, but the few passages that do treat the afterlife explicitly use it to isolate the person from his social network in much this way. In the next world, Dayanand writes, there is "neither mother nor father, neither son or wife, nor can relations support you; dharma alone is a support there. Look! The soul is born alone and dies alone, and it enjoys or suffers the fruit of one single dharma."[47] Here, neo-Vedic religion appears as a technology of individuation. But, as I hope suggest, the larger project of the *Satyarth Prakash* moves in a different direction by situating this isolate religious subjectivity within a network of controls. The self-regulating individual is always embedded in social and institutional structures that entail highly complicated relations between individual and society, autonomy and heteronomy, self-rule and tutelage.

Somatic Virtue and the Body of the Nation

When Munshi Ram suggests that brahmacharya "has always distinguished the Aryan ideal of *Dharma* from the non-Aryan conceptions of religious duty," he speaks somewhat disingenuously. Although Dayanand may himself have cleaved to a strict celibacy, this was not to be the case for most of his followers. Like Luther, criticized by Munshi Ram for his having married, most Arya Samajis are part of the *grihastashrama*, or the order of householders (following one of the translators of the *Satyarth Prakash*, I generally translate *ashrama* as *order* and *varna* as *class*).[48] The relationship of householders to renunciants (a category that I will use to refer primarily to *sannyasi*s, or members of the fourth order, but with a sense for the way in which this late-life renunciation echoes and overlaps with the early celibate student phase of brahmacharya) is a major issue for the *Satyarth Prakash*. In redefining brahmacharya, the *Satyarth Prakash* addresses and interweaves several distinct thematics: asceticism, the family, education, and caste. Partly conflating the figures of the renunciant (*sannyasin*) and the Brahman, the text articulates a mode of spiritual inheritance that both complements and supersedes the material lineages defined by heterosexual reproduction.

Brahmacharya, as Alter and Adcock suggest, somaticizes virtue. It thus, in Aurobindo's terms, fuses spirit and matter in a way that modifies the animal functions of the body so as to qualify the body as properly human.[49] Good deeds, as Dayanand frequently reminds his reader, actually alter the flesh. In the *Satyarth Prakash*, at least, this principle of somaticized virtue poses a problem for caste hierarchies. Instead of being written indelibly into the body at birth, class or *varna* becomes much more volatile in that it can be changed by behavior. A person's class is not necessarily the class of her parents. It is instead created by her practice of virtue—learned through tutelary networks that extend well beyond the family unit. Those who teach virtue become, in effect, surrogate parents. As the head of the body politic, the renunciant signals an alternate principle of biopolitical production, subordinating mere natality to ascetic self-rule as the chief means of producing the body politic and thus ensuring the spiritual and material health of Vedic nation.

This, at least, is the solution that emerges to a puzzle posed in a discussion of the orders of forest-dwellers and full renunciants. Dayanand's interloctuor complains that "taking *sannyas* goes against the intentions of God," which is to "increase humanity." Renunciants do not produce offspring, so if everyone were to renounce the world, it would mean the extinction of the human race.[50] Dayanand strenuously disagrees. Quickly noting that by this standard childless couples would also be classed as against the divine order, he goes on to argue that renunciants have a distinctive role to play in society. Householders are constantly fighting amongst themselves and thus depleting the population. By "preaching Vedic dharma," the renunciant generates "mutual affection" (*paraspar prīti*) among hostile householders, thus reducing violence and increasing the population in a manner "comparable to a thousand householders."[51]

If householders provide the raw biological matter of the Vedic nation, renunciants shape and govern that matter so that it becomes morally, politically, and even biologically productive. "Just as the body requires a head, so do the other orders require *sannyas*."[52] Elsewhere, the text invokes the Rig Vedic verse that explains caste through the tale of Purusha, the primal person, sacrificed by the gods to create the cosmos: his mouth becomes the Brahman, his arms the Kshatriya, his thighs the Vaishya, and his feet the Shudra. Dayanand cites this classic passage in a context that partly conflates the Brahman and the *sannyasi*. The organicist metaphor, meanwhile, clearly implies that these religious professionals are the mind or spirit that rules the limbs of society.[53] Members of the other castes and orders must remain engrossed in affairs, but the renunciant's leisure time allows him to act for the general good like none of the others can.[54] While householders engage in hard work out of self-interest (*svārth mem*), renunciants work even harder, but for the good of others, and it is only when they do so that all the orders improve.[55] In other words, it is the special role of the renunciant to exercise a pastoral power over an organically interlinked social body for the mutual benefit of all.

In doing so, the renunciant establishes a principle of inheritance that complements biological reproduction. Anyone, Dayanand writes, who becomes a religious person (*dharmik manuṣya*) under a renunciant's influence should be considered that renunciant's child.[56] As we shall see, this principle of filiation is simultaneously spiritual and somatic: the virtue learned from renunciants inscribes itself on the body. Renunciants thus shape the biological material that composes the Vedic nation by two means: (a) by guiding the actions of householders, using pastoral techniques for governing and pacifying the population, and (b) by disseminating ascetic technologies of self-regulation that, in addition to their pastoral function of properly arranging the behavior of the mass, also directly shape the latent tendencies of the individual body so that it becomes more virtuous—which is to say, more like a renunciant.

The *Satyarth Prakash* thus does more than simply rearticulate the longstanding complementarity of householders and renunciants by explicitly charging the renunciant with the pastoral management of the bio-reproductive flock. It also redistributes renunciation throughout the social body by detailing an ambitious pedagogic program that refigures the ascetic technologies of brahmacharya so that they can be taken up by householders. As a generalizable technology that mediates between the two orders of householder and renunciant, brahmacharya positions the child-student as the paradigmatic human subject. Some children will go on to become householders, while others will not; but either way the habits of self-regulation formed during their early celibate years should continue to shape how they inhabit the world. Parents are to inaugurate their child's formative course in brahmacharya, strengthening the child's mind and body by teaching him or her self-restraint.[57] The resultant child-ascetic should avoid useless playing, crying, laughing, fighting, joy, and sorrow; should not indulge in greed, jealousy, or ill-will over any matter; and should never touch the reproductive organs, as doing so results in loss of strength (*vīrya*), impotence, and stinky hands.[58] The child should cultivate a manner of speech that is ever truthful, respectful, and economical, restraining his anger, saying only as much as is necessary, and always eating a little short of his appetite.[59]

The mother should train the child-ascetic until age five, and the father from six to eight. At age nine, the child is to be transferred to a special school (*ācaryakul* or *pāṭhśālā*) with an emphatically ascetic orientation.[60] Schools are to be created for both girls and boys, with strict separation of the two. A set of rules restricting access to sexual stimuli is imposed in each (or so one assumes: the text focuses on the boys' schools).[61] Teachers must also abide by ascetic norms, perfecting their own knowledge, disposition, and bodies so that they can better guide their students. The curriculum is to include physical, ritual, and academic training (in, for example, yoga, the homa sacrifice, and Sanskrit grammar), thus suggesting the integrative nature of an educational project bent on shaping both body and soul. Dayanand established some schools during his lifetime, but it was not until after his death that the Arya Samaj educational program really took shape, with the Dayanand Anglo-Vedic College opening its doors in Lahore in 1886 and the rival Gurukul Kangri in Kangra in 1902.[62] The latter in particular emphasized the ascetic component of education so visible in the *Satyarth Prakash*.[63]

In Dayanand's book, schools serve several functions, with one of the most important being to disrupt the caste and class structures rooted in the family. Visits from home are severely restricted, and all students are to dress alike in the style of ascetics (*tapasvī*), "whether they are princes or princesses or the children of beggars."[64] The text goes on to propose the creation of a brave new world in which caste will be ascribed to students based on ability rather than birth. At an appropriate age (twenty-five for men, sixteen for women), students are to be tested on their "qualifications, accomplishments, and character" and then assigned to the correct class (*varna*) and a set of parents within that class. They will perform traditional filial duties to their assigned parents, not their biological ones.[65] Likewise, men and women are to choose their marriage partners from within their assigned class, not their birth class.[66] In addition to establishing a new social structure by rationalizing and bureaucratizing caste, the proposed schools are also meant to help eradicate pope-lila. As the text states a number of times, universal education prevents Brahmanical fraud. This is why the Brahmans oppose it, and why they have proliferated so many rules to keep members of the other castes ignorant. If children are taught properly— trained in Sanskrit and foreign languages, Vedic literature, truth and virtue, and correct behavior, and steered away from superstition—they will not "be misled by any scoundrel."[67] Charisma and sacerdotal hierarchy are thus replaced by rule-driven bureaucratic institutions.

Importantly, the text uses the category of the guru to help distinguish between the role of instructor and that of the pope. Dayanand has little patience for the *Guru Gita*, which he dismisses as nothing but a pope-lila. Where that text declares that the guru is greater than God himself (if God is angry, the guru can save you, but if the guru is angry, no one can save you), the *Satyarth Prakash* is more inclined to emphasize the immanence of the teacher to the social body. Thus, the true gurus are father, mother, teacher (*ācārya*), and guest, and the real "work" of the disciple is to serve this quartet of mundane authorities. By rendering religious authority immanent to society, Dayanand assures that it will not be extractive in nature. Greedy gurus are to be avoided. "They are not gurus at all, but are like shepherds [*voh gurū hī nahīṃ kintu gaḍariye jaise haiṃ*]. Just as shepherds keep their sheep and goats for the purpose of taking their milk, so do [these so-called gurus] keep their students and followers in order to steal their money."[68] Shepherd-gurus, like popes, are "selfish" (*svārthī*).[69] Where the good teacher manages the flock for *its* benefit, the bad teacher manages it for his own benefit. He stands outside the social field in an extractive relationship to it.[70] The educational program laid out in the *Satyarth Prakash* thus intervenes directly against the shepherd-guru by establishing a mode of pedagogy geared toward producing students who can ultimately regulate themselves.

When they enter adulthood, students leave their schools behind and, along with them, the official strictures of brahmacharya. The ascetic practices that the student has cultivated in her formative years will already have shaped her body and her daily habits, however, such that brahmacharya in some sense stays with her into adulthood. Celibacy builds up bodily, mental, and ethical strength, which is why men especially should delay marriage until at least the age of twenty-five.[71] It also founds habits that come in handy in married life—it being, Dayanand implies, their self-regulatory abilities that allows the couple to manage the level of "happiness" in their home.[72] Elsewhere in his corpus of writings, Dayanand further elaborates precisely how religion steps in to mediate the married couple's relationship to its sexuality and the other material accoutrements of life. The *Sanskār-Vidhi*, for example, details sixteen lifecycle rituals that constrain worldly life by subordinating it to the dictates of religion. Marital sex is not only a primary site for the regulation of the immanent by the transcendent; it is the site where this regulation is most explicitly figured as a question of asceticism. "The house-holding man who does not carry out the sexual intercourse with his wife in those eight nights which have been previously prohibited for impregnation is in a real sense a celibate (brahmacharya), leading even the life of a householder."[73] The *Satyarth Prakash* describes how members of all four orders (*ashramas*) are to practice yoga to cultivate firmness of mind.[74] In the familiar metaphor, they are to control their senses just as the skilled charioteer controls his horses and keeps them on the correct path. The ascetic subject does not rejoice when applauded or grieve when censured; he neither delights at beauty, nor feels disgust at disagreeable odors.[75]

Such prescriptions disassociate brahmacharya from particular classes of persons, such that it comes to denote ascetic self-regulation per se. It also suggests parallels between the government of self and the government of others. The slippage between the two is clearest in the statement quoted above: "Just as the body requires a head, so do the other orders require *sannyas*" or renunciation.[76] The renunciant governs the social body in the same way that he governs his own body. It seems likely that a similar principle would inform household management. The celibate student learns to regulate his body at school so that once he joins the order of householders he can transfer these skills to a different domain, regulating his children and the objects of his household: it is insofar as the husband or wife has internalized the self-regulatory norms of renunciation that he or she can assume the role of "head" of household. By a similar logic, members of all four orders or *ashrama*s are enjoined to give instruction in truth (*satyopadeś*). They may never do so as effectively as their fully renunciant counterparts, but that they are called upon to do so at all suggests that householders differ from renunciants in degree rather than in kind.[77]

As a worldly ascetic, every householder in effect plays two roles. On the one hand, qua householder, he builds the body of the nation by breeding; on the other hand, qua ascetic, he builds the national body through the cultivation of somaticized virtue, both in himself and in his children. The householder, just as much as the renunciant, operates at the double register of spirit and matter, although the precise distribution of functions differs in the two cases. The figure of the worldly ascetic, at least within the reading that I am proposing here, thus assumes very particular dimensions. Asceticism stands in for the regulatory functions of governmentality per se by simultaneously indicating the governance of the self and of the population (the renunciant is the head of both his own and also the social body). The metaphor of the chariot serves roughly the same function here that the ship does for Foucault: one is a renunciant insofar as one can stand sufficiently aloof from the affairs of life so as to determine how those affairs are to be best "disposed of" (in Foucault's sense). It is thus via the ascetic renunciation of the world that the subject constitutes itself as subject, set against a field of objects. These objects are renounced as that which is not self, and thereby made available for control and regulation. Likewise, it is the (always partial) renunciation of the merely biological that separates the ascetic subject from bare life and thus constitutes that subject as the sort of political-spiritual entity that can direct its own biological substrate as well as the biology of others.

At the same time that the *Satyarth Prakash* reconfigures the four orders (*ashrama*s) of classical Hindu social theory, it also reconfigures the four classes (*varna*s). *Varnashrama* remains here, if not exactly a coherent "system," at least a unified means of imagining the social. The word *caste*, as is now well known, derives from a Portuguese root (*casta*) that in its English usage conflates two different concepts (*jātī* and *varṇa*), thereby reifying both in keeping with the bureaucratizing pressures of the colonial state.[78] Dayanand's intervention into caste norms is of this colonial moment; it remobilizes a social structure already in flux and already opened to bureaucratic regularization. His trademark move is to re-engineer caste as meritocratic, assigning individuals to social classes based on their abilities and virtues rather than their birth. In doing so, he affirms some established norms, while upending others. For example, in one interchange, Dayanand concedes that only Brahmans have the right to proceed sequentially through all four life stages prescribed by orthodoxy and culminating in full renunciation. But he immediately redefines a Brahman as a person from any of the four classes (*varnas*) who is learned, virtuous (*dharmik*), and loves public service.[79] A similar move structures the dialogue in which the notion of pope-lila is first introduced. When Dayanand accuses his fictive interlocutor of not being a Brahman, the man so accused protests: he must be a Brahman, because he was born one. A person is always of the same caste as his mother and father. Dayanand sternly corrects him. Birth does not make a Brahman, but rather virtue (*gun*), deeds, (*karm*) and disposition (*svabhāv*). Those who claim religious authority but lack these qualities are to be called "popes."[80]

That a non-Brahman can be born to a Brahman should not be surprising, he suggests, insofar as wicked children are born to virtuous parents all of the time. And just as a person can lose caste through the nonperformance of duty (as when a Hindu converts to Christianity or Islam), so can a person gain caste through his or her behavior. If you perform the duties of a Brahman, you become a Brahman.[81] These responses puzzle the interlocutor, who obdurately asks how a body formed from male and female reproductive elements from one caste can be physically transformed so that it belongs to another caste.[82] Embodied caste, the objector implies, derives solely from heterosexual reproduction and not from ascetic virtue. Dayanand responds by arguing that a Brahman body is made, not through the union of reproductive elements, but through ritual observance and ethical behavior. Action permanently conditions the flesh, and it is this principle, rather than the principle of biological reproduction, which ultimately determines a person's caste status. The purely biological body has no qualities that could situate it within the social whole. It is only, Dayanand suggests, through an ascetic work upon the self that the body is able to discover the truth about its own caste identity. Or, in an alternate and partly contradictory formulation, it is only via ascetic self-regulation that the social norms of caste are imprinted on the body.

This refigured caste body is meant, at least in theory, to provide for greater social mobility and to reduce discrimination against those of lower castes. Insofar as all castes come from a single undifferentiated biological substrate, there is no need to fret about pollution born of other people's bodies. Even in theory, however, this effort at caste reform begins to break down. Or, at least, because caste remains inscribed in the body, the *Satyarth Prakash* is unable to fully extricate itself from the somatic logic of caste pollution. For example, the text defends foreign travel, insisting that it does not affect the virtuous conduct (*ācār*) of an Aryan to break caste rules by going abroad. At the same time, it worries about foreigners' lack of virtue. They eat meat and drink liquor, and their bodies contain traces of these polluting substances, particles of which could jump from their corrupted flesh onto the globetrotting Aryan.[83] Behavior, not birth, is the problem here, but the outcome is the same. Likewise, even as the text recommends that low-caste cooks prepare food for high-caste persons (in part so that the latter can focus on their caste-specific professions), it worries that the sharing of food, even between husband and wife, could result in one person's contracting the other's "nature" (*svabhāv*), just as sharing food with a leper can spread leprosy. For similar reasons, the text prescribes vegetarianism: eating meat changes a man's nature by making him violent.[84] Ultimately, this logic circles around to the question of birth. Parents who keep to Dayanand's strict dietary regimen, who follow the "rules of sexual intercourse," and who are generally abstemious about their bodies will ensure the high quality of their "reproductive elements" and thus of their progeny.[85] Virtue, it seems, can be inherited. It is built into the flesh with which we are born.

Despite the conventionalism of this outcome (even after being reformed, caste is still determined by birth), caste is nonetheless configured within the *Satyarth Prakash* in a manner that at least in principle should substantially alter the arrangement of the national body. Renunciants upstage householders as the order most necessary for the survival of the nation. They are the pastoral head that manages the biopolitical body constituted by the other orders. This arrangement, I would suggest, has some dramatic implications. First, the principle of *ethical reproduction* that emerges in the text threatens to displace biological reproduction (and hence the reproductive heterosexual couple) as the primary bearer of the social good. As we have seen, renunciants can have "children" via spiritual instruction; those whom they educate into virtue are to be counted as their progeny. Biological lines of family descent are crisscrossed by other, far more unpredictable, lines of ascetic inheritance.

Second, with renunciation redistributed across the entire social field, so that even householders are able to regulate their character via ascetic self-discipline, the metaphor of head-body begins to seem an inadequate means of conceptualizing the political function of brahmacharya. A rough synonym for the capacity of governance per se, it effectively situates the householder as the renunciant-manager of her own biological being. She stands aloof from her corporeal "chariot" so that she can better govern it. Brahmacharya gains political traction through its ability to establish linkages among multiple sites of governance and self-governance, ranging from child, to mother and father, to head of school, to beneficent worldly ascetics, to king or emperor. It thus articulates a mode of power every bit as capillary as that of pope-lila—which is, after all, precisely the point. It is via the dissemination of ascetic technologies for the control of the self that the Hindus are to be immunized against the seductions of the priest.

Pope-Rajya

If the *Satyarth Prakash* is important chiefly because of its influence on twentieth-century Hindu nationalist politics, this begs the question of how the political is conceptualized within the *Satyarth Prakash*. It is sometimes implied that as religious reform gave way to nationalist politics after 1885, the political simply shed the religious. It had used the private space afforded religion by the British state's policy of non-interference to incubate anticolonial sentiments that, given the hostile environment of the Raj, could only go public once they had become fully grown—maturely political, rather than merely cultural or spiritual. This is a type of secularization narrative or subtraction story. No one, of course, would deny that religious symbols remained integral to Indian politics into the twentieth century and beyond. But, as the standard narrative would have it, these symbols (submerged Ganeshas, parading Rams, etc.) are objects out of place, *content* badly suited to the *form* of modern politics. If religious reform culture lives on after 1885, it is, precisely, as content not form, symbol not structure.

What I would like to suggest is that this narrative ignores a crucial aspect of nineteenth-century reformism. For the thinkers surveyed in this book, religion was not only or even primarily a content, a thing that could be placed either in public or in private. It was, rather, a means of reimagining the social field. Religious power was distinctive. It crisscrossed the subjective, the domestic, the national, and the global along lines of disciplinary force that were neither reducible to nor entirely separate from the state. In narrating the transition from nineteenth-century reformism to twentieth-century nationalism, then, we need to be careful not to collapse the distinctive social imaginary of the earlier era into the categories of the nationalists, but rather to explore it in its conceptual specificity.

How then does the *Satyarth Prakash* conceptualize the political? As I have argued, it is principally concerned with a form of religious power that pivots on ascetic virtue and popish imposture. The pope, with his thousand "avatars," suggests the immanent principle of a governmentality that organizes the social field from within rather than above. The "Pope-ji" who gives rise to these avatars is mentioned, but never seen. His unitary, transcendent authority is always already dispersed into the network of his countless mimics and ministers, whose ability to guide their flocks derives precisely from their simultaneous ubiquity and uniformity. The popes are legion, but they are also one.

Dayanand's teachers operate by a parallel principle. If the renunciant is the head of the social body, he is also simultaneously dispersed throughout that body, localized in those who have sworn off the world entirely (i.e., *sannyasis*), but also present (if only partly so) in householders. These biologically reproductive individuals become political insofar as they are able to hold back from the world sufficiently that they are not simply reducible to it, the kind of brute "matter" that needs to be governed by "spirit" (to recall Aurobindo). As the 1892 *Indian Evangelical Review* put it—telescoping spiritual liberation from priestly rule and political liberation from colonial rule—Dayanand aimed to "fit the people of India" for "Self-Government" by educating them away from their need for external guidance.[86] In other words, the popes serve a crucial conceptual function for Dayanand. They carve out the immanent political space that his good teachers and self-governing ascetics step into as they displace the priests, those quintessential bad pedagogues.

The *Satyarth Prakash* thus calls for a shift in the order of religious tutelage, rather than the outright abolition of that order. Indeed, the Arya Samaj itself can be said to have instituted a new kind of pastorate. During his lifetime, Dayanand rejected honorific titles that connoted "gurudom." For example, when the Lahore branch of the Arya Samaj tried to elect him its *"Parama Sahayaka"* (chief helper), he declined the honor, remarking "What will you call God if you call me by this name?"[87] Denouncing "the smell of gurudom" (*gurūpan kī bū*), he explained that his mission was to abolish sects and gurus, not to establish a new sect by becoming a guru himself. He is not an ultimate support, but the Arya Samajis are welcome to consider him an ordinary support of the society. "Just as other people are helpers, I too am a helper [*sahāyak*]."[88] Here, the principle of "help" (or, in the Kantian idiom, tutelage) is retained, even as it comes to indicate a scene of mutual support substantially different from the ontologized hierarchy of the guru-disciple relationship. As a spiritual guide, Dayanand is just like anyone else—which is also to say that everyone is a spiritual guide, at least potentially. To consider whether the Arya Samaj actually distributed the capacity for spiritual guidance in this manner is beyond the scope of the present discussion. I simply mean to suggest that the fact this question arises indicates the persistence of spiritual guidance as a problematic in Arya Samaji thought.

It thus also underscores the importance of this problematic to the *Satyarth Prakash* and how that text understands the political. The text's most sustained discussion of politics is in its sixth chapter, which outlines the contours of the ideal "Vedic kingdom" (*vaidik rājya*), with its various governmental bodies and political ideals. In closing, I would note that among the most prominent characteristics of the Vedic nation is how its political functions depend on the careful cultivation of physical, intellectual, and spiritual virtue. Ministers are to practice yoga. The king is to refrain from vices like hunting and to cleave to a demanding daily regimen. Rising early, he is to perform the homa sacrifice, consult his ministers, inspect his house, go to the gym (*vyāyāmśālā*), dine with his wife, and watch his diet—regulating the affairs of state and self in a roughly parallel, or at least closely integrated, manner. There is a familiar correspondence here between the royal body and the social body: "as the king, so the people."[89] This vision of the perfect ruler departs from secular norms not because it presents a religious figure like Rama as the ideal king (it mostly does not), but rather because it refuses to divorce the public realm of politics from the private realm of somaticized virtue.

The king is paradigmatic in this regard; but, especially if we understand this chapter within the context of the *Satyarth Prakash* as a whole, it is clear that he is not alone. As we have seen, the *Satyarth Prakash* presents the self-regulating body of the ascetic renunciant as a transfer point between different sites and registers of rule. The ascetic educates the nation toward the ideal of Vedic virtue, thus disrupting the rule of the "popes." By laying claim to virtue of this type, the Vedic king may anchor this biopolitical field. In its dispersion, however, it necessarily, exceeds him.

SIX

Astral Ethics

India is not yet spiritually dead through it is fast dying. We still have even men amongst us—secure from the molestation of haughty British officials and impertinent missionaries, in dark mountain caves and trackless impenetrable forests—those who have almost reached the shores of the ocean of Nirvana. . . . It should be strongly impressed on the minds of the English theosophists that these men are not very anxious to get their existence recognized by them.   T. SUBBA ROW (1882)

[W]e have come to the conclusion that it is useless to strain the Psychical eyes toward the Himalayas. . . . we need not run after Oriental mystics who deny their ability to help us.   JOSEPHINE CABLES AND W. T. BROWN (1886)

Sleeping in a tent near Lahore in November 1883, Colonel Henry Steel Olcott (1832–1907) awoke when he felt "someone putting his hands upon me." Alarmed, the expatriate American grabbed the intruder by the upper arms and demanded his identity in rudimentary Hindustani. The stranger replied in a kind, familiar voice: "Do you not remember me?" It was, Olcott realized, Koot Hoomi, his spiritual master, whom he had never before met in the flesh. "In the next moment I was in full consciousness, and let go my hold of him, slipping my hands down the whole length of his arms to his hands." The two talked for some time, possibly in this intimate position. Then Koot Hoomi pressed his fingers against Olcott's palm until he "felt growing up, as it were, some substance." Closing his disciple's fist upon the strange extrusion, the Master left the tent. Alone, Olcott found himself holding a small package wrapped in Chinese silk. In it was a letter, a secret message addressed to the disciple from his guru.[1]

Four years previously, in May 1879, Olcott had had an encounter of a very different sort with a very different kind of guru, an encounter that happened by day, turning on a public address, not on private whispers. Even so, the parallels are striking: Olcott was meeting his spiritual master for the first time after a prolonged exchange of letters. Their physical union, moreover, was to be celebrated by "clasped hands." Or so Olcott hoped. The American, recently arrived in India, delivered his speech to an assembly of Arya Samajis arrayed on cotton carpets and Persian rugs beneath a blue-and-white-striped canopy "under a blue Indian sky." Swami Dayananda Saraswati (the guru in question) was among them; a handful of Westerners sat slightly higher, preferring chairs. His enthusiasm stoked by the coincidence of the near-simultaneous establishment of the Theosophical Society and the Arya Samaj half a world apart in 1875, Olcott had written to Dayanand two years previously declaring the theosophists the Swami's students. Thirsting for the wisdom of the East, they would submit themselves to Dayanand's spiritual guidance. Henceforth, he would be their master. That May in Meerut, however, Olcott seems to have had a more egalitarian kind of relationship in mind. The theosophists had come, he said, to "clasp hands as brothers long separated" and "to exchange . . . mutual pledges of our devotion to the cause of humanity."[2]

Two competing gurus: Koot Hoomi and Dayanand. Two seemingly incompatible modes of alliance: teacher-student and brother-brother. The first of these conflicts was resolved fairly quickly. In March 1882, Dayanand gave a speech in Bombay's Framji Cowasjee Hall decrying the "humbuggery" of the theosophists. Koot Hoomi's many miracles, he proclaimed, were nothing but hokum, a charlatanic spectacle designed to dupe credulous occultists. Koot Hoomi, apparently, was not pleased: the note he slipped Olcott the next year predicted the death of two of theosophy's critics, a prophecy that Olcott later interpreted as referring to Dayanand (who had died in October) and Keshub Chunder Sen (who died the following January). With its ties to its Hindu reformist contemporaries strained or severed, theosophy would necessarily be guided solely by Koot Hoomi's order of "Masters" or "Mahatmas"—the collective of spiritual adepts based in the Himalayas, from which remote location its members guide humanity via "astral projection" and other occult means.

But how was it that theosophy, heavily invested in these spiritual hierarchies, could also speak of "brotherhood"? Among its most cherished ideals, after all, was "the cause of humanity," a cause that it pursued by forging alliances (as with Dayanand) that seem, at least in retrospect, to have been as much political as spiritual. In India, theosophy had a decidedly anticolonial tinge. Its Orientalist celebration of ancient Asian wisdom flew in the face of imperial ideology's determined denigration of "native" culture. As a consequence, elite Indians flocked to the society, keen to assert India's cultural parity with Britain—and to do so, no less, in English. In 1885, former theosophist A. O. Hume cofounded the Indian National Congress, the group that would go on to spearhead the independence movement. Years later, Annie Besant became an even more prominent nationalist leader. Nonetheless, theosophy and nationalism were always somewhat at odds. The society hoped "to form a nucleus of the universal brotherhood of humanity, without distinction of race, creed, sex, caste, or colour." Nations divide; theosophy, at least in principle, did not.

In practice, however, there was one key "distinction" upon which this theosophical brotherhood was predicated: the difference between its universal brotherhood's general membership and the spiritual elect that formed its "nucleus." Fraternity, for theosophy, did not necessarily imply equality. As Gauri Viswanathan suggests, the doubled articulation of equality and hierarchy implied by the discourse of brotherhood (with its brothers both "big" and "little") anticipates the political logic of the British Commonwealth, which simultaneously positions its members as equivalent and as arrayed into junior and senior positions.[3] What this reading glides past, however, is an important feature of early theosophy's political project: its global brotherhood bypasses the nation-state in utopian manner, articulating a principle of association happily conveyed by Olcott's "clasped hands." The mode of politics espoused by early theosophy was thus roughly continuous with that of other reform movements of the period. It unfolded from a doubled practice of asceticism and pastoral guidance articulated in close relationship to the figure of the crafty priest. Madame Helena Petrovna Blavatsky (1831–1891), the cofounder and chief theorist of the Theosophical Society, was famously adjudged "one of the most accomplished, ingenious, and interesting imposters in history" for having so successfully fabricated (at least allegedly) Koot Hoomi and the other Mahatmas.[4] But Blavatsky was not only among the most prominent objects of the discourse of priestcraft and religious imposture; she was also among its more forceful proponents.

My overarching argument about Blavatsky and the theosophists is a reformulation of the three "objects" of the Theosophical Society: "(1) to form a nucleus of the universal brotherhood of humanity, without distinction of race, creed, sex, caste, or colour; (2) to encourage the study of comparative religion, philosophy, and science; (3) to investigate the unexplained laws of nature and the powers latent in man."[5] I suggest that theosophy posed the following question: how can comparative religion be used to articulate a new principle of political cosmopolitanism by opening up new potentialities in human subjectivity? My discussion traces how theosophy brought Christian, Spiritualist, and other North Atlantic technologies of subjectivation into assemblage with certain Hindu technologies of subjectivation. It did so, I suggest, via a problematic of asceticism that is distilled in the body of the astral Mahatma. Simultaneously a figure for the split ascetic self and the tutelary priestly other, the Theosophical Master is central to how theosophy articulated its vision of "brotherhood."

Masters and Disciples

Inaugurated in 1875 in a New York City drawing room by an American journalist (Olcott) and a Russian occultist (Blavatsky), the Theosophical Society was from the start a transnational affair. Its cosmopolitanism was further amplified when its founding duo left New York for Bombay in 1879 and established their world headquarters in the Madras suburb of Adyar in 1882. Although now obscure, the movement was influential on a global scale during the late nineteenth and early twentieth centuries. Primarily the province of social elites, theosophy nonetheless disseminated its occult sensibility well beyond its relatively circumscribed roster of formal members, insinuating itself into the work of major Anglophone writers like W. B. Yeats, James Joyce, and M. K. Gandhi, and establishing chapters in locations as far-flung as Russia and Indonesia. Associated with socialism and feminism in the nineteenth century, it pointed toward literary modernism, Indian nationalism, and even (via its German offshoot, Ariosophy) National Socialism in the twentieth. In its worldwide spread, theosophy echoed the spiritualist movement that had rapped its way outward from upstate New York starting in 1848, inspiring séances in parlors across England, France, Germany, the US, Brazil, and elsewhere. If anything, theosophy was even more globalized than its spiritualist predecessor. But its globalism was also, and not incidentally, more carefully ordered. Where spiritualism had been highly demotic, and even anarchically so, theosophy prized esoteric forms of knowledge that by definition were available only to a spiritual elect. Accordingly, it governed access to its truths with a hierarchical structure that organized the globe bureaucratically into national "branches" and "lodges"—thus, suggests Viswanathan, replicating and at times parodying the bureaucratic obsessions of empire.[6]

Shadowing the Theosophical Society in its global spread was the hidden order of the Masters, likewise arranged into lodges and sections. Communications between the esoteric and exoteric exponents of divine truth occurred mostly by mail, or, at least, through the miraculous "precipitation" of letters. Olcott received one of the first of these missives in March 1875. Penned in gold ink on green paper and tucked into a black envelope, it was signed by one Tuitit Bey of Luxor, Egypt. This "Copt," Olcott later avowed, was his "first Guru"; but he was not to be his last. Letters from a second Egyptian "Brother" (Serapis Bey) were to follow soon after. Eventually, however, Olcott's apprenticeship was transferred from the Brotherhood's "African" to its "Indian section," headquartered in Tibet.[7] From this time, two new Masters assumed responsibility for the society: Koot Hoomi Lal Singh, a Punjabi with family connections in Kashmir, who had studied at Leipzig; and Master Morya, a "kingly Rajput."[8] Once the mythology of the Masters was fully developed, the Brotherhood's roll call of notables swelled to considerable size, eventually including the Buddha, Manu, Maitreya, Lao Tzu, Jesus, Abraham, Moses, Plato, Cagliostro, and Anton Mesmer, to name just a few. Blavatsky's *The Secret Doctrine* (1888) details the intricate hierarchy that structures this august company. In the early days, however, things were simpler. In fact, as Bruce Campbell notes, the term *Mahatma* does not even enter Blavatsky's writings until around the time of the move to Bombay, at which point the Indic Orient begins to displace the Egyptian Orient as the primary repository for theosophy's ancient wisdom. The full systemization of the Mahatmas was, in other words, yet to come.

Much can be said about these Masters. First, they are male—the homosocial composition of the "brotherhood" being somewhat surprising, given theosophy's strong following among British feminists and the prominence (symbolic, if not always numerical) of women in the movement.[9] Second, they reflect the Orientalist hope that the West would find its spiritual complement in the "mystic East."[10] Indeed, their phantasmatic form seems an apt figure for the ontology of Orientalist desire more generally. Third, and consequently, the basic conceptual form of the Mahatmic Brotherhood is not "Eastern" at all, but an adaptation of the "Adepts" of Rosicrucian lore, as popularized by Edward Bulwer-Lytton's novel *Zanoni* (1842).[11] One would not go to the Masters for "authentic" knowledge about Hindu tradition. Nonetheless, the Mahatmas were important to colonial Hinduism and have appeared prominently in most major surveys of nineteenth-century Hindu reform movements.[12] The question, then, is how one parses the relationship between the astral Masters and this broader Hindu reform scene.

The Masters, as I will suggest, presented a something of a problem for theosophy. Theosophy hated priests, and the basic tale it told about them is a familiar one. Long ago, priestcraft corrupted the pure original religion, and the adulterated result is to be seen in the world's many historical creeds.[13] To recover lost truth, the seeker must first strip these modern religions of priestly perversion. This is what I have elsewhere described as theosophy's "epistemology of the veil"—theosophical occultism implied a critique of print media's epistemology of exposure by unsettling the presumption that knowledge of hidden affairs could ever be made fully present to the critical tribunal of the print public.[14] Distaste for clerics shaped theosophical life in more mundane ways as well. For example, Olcott and Blavatsky kept a "scrap-book into which [they] used to paste paragraphs from newspapers telling of the crimes of clergymen and priests who had been brought to justice." Blavatsky, Olcott explains, hated "clergymen as a body . . . because, being themselves absolutely ignorant of the truths of the spirit, they assumed the right to lead the spiritually blind, to keep the lay conscience under control, to enjoy revenues they had not earned, and to damn the heretic, who was often the sage, the illuminatus, the adept."[15]

Accordingly, theosophy had no priests per se. In their place, it offered up the Mahatmas. Like their clerical counterparts, these ethereal beings assumed the right to lead the spiritually blind. Whether or not (as Blavatsky insisted) they did so from a position of unique wisdom is arguably beside the point. What matters most about the Mahatmas is their astral form—which is to say, the peculiarly spectral structure of their bond with their followers.

A Mahatma is never fully present. He is always partly in Tibet. The Mahatmas thus remain, as Viswanathan suggests, a "calculated absence" in theosophical literature.[16] Even when Koot Hoomi did appear in the flesh, he did so in secret, as in Olcott's nighttime encounter. As a guide, he thus intensified the lonely interiority of the theosophical subject, guiding the theosophist from within as much as from without. The Mahatma thus refigures the master-disciple relation by splitting the theosophical subject in two, blurring the line between self and other and between autonomy and heteronomy. In place of spiritual despotism, theosophy develops what might best be described as "astral ethics." Here, thanks to the spectral ontology of the Mahatmas, spiritual self-rule and spiritual discipleship become semi-indistinguishable.

This Mahatmic experiment in the fracturing of subjectivity drew on the earlier experiments of the spiritualist movement, even while departing from spiritualism in important ways. As a rich scholarship now attests, Victorian séances and other seemingly marginal spiritualist practices were culturally productive, playing a significant role in the later emergence of expressionism, modernism, and psychoanalysis.[17] The spiritualist "cult of the self" extended the neo-Romantic interest in deep interiority by inviting the subject to peer into the depths of her psyche, so as to locate the principle that links "the individual to the transcendent cosmos."[18] Elsewhere, as in séances and hauntings, spiritualism was more interested in how subjectivity could be transgressed from without, as by possession.[19] Shared preoccupations with literary modernism (arcane symbols, automatic writing, displaced authorship, inverted temporality) suggest the extent to which spiritualism sought to overturn the norms of the everyday, disrupting social convention and hierarchy, and causing selves to erupt into multiple voices and even persons. As a prominent site for the exploration of human consciousness, spiritualism piqued the interest of Victorian scientists keen to determine the precise limits of the mind and to document the altered states associated with the use of alcohol and other drugs.[20] It also, and just as importantly, opened up new political possibilities for subjects previously denied public voice. Not surprisingly given that women comprised a majority of England's acting mediums, spiritualism's prototypical fractured subject was gendered female, and séances' gender-bending ventriloquism was closely bound up with shifting gender norms of the period.[21] The séance medium underscored her conventionally feminine passivity by opening herself to a foreign spirit, often male. Speaking in that spirit's voice, she then assumed the mantle of male authority in order to claim her own right to public speech.

A related structure of identification and disavowal is evident in the attitude of theosophists to their Mahatmas. Blavatsky was at great pains to distance herself from séance mediums, but one wonders if she protests too much. After all, she herself had worked as a medium on several occasions, most notably in Cairo, and her career as the doyenne of the Theosophical Society began when she met Olcott at Vermont's Eddy homestead, a spiritualist hotspot. The duo went on to spend the first year of their friendship in pursuit of revenant human spirits, including the notorious celebrity ghost, Katie King. It was only in 1875 that the spirits gave way to the Adepts. Even then, the contrast was not necessarily so great: the racially othered Egyptian brothers recall the Native American, Arab, Indian, and African spirits that had long been staples of the séance scene.[22]

Nonetheless, as Blavasky insists, there are important differences between ghosts and Adepts. "Mediumship," as she explains in the concluding chapter of *Isis Unveiled* (1877), "is the opposite of adeptship." Where "the medium is the passive instrument of foreign influences, the adept actively controls himself and all inferior potencies."[23] Adeptship thus hinges on what Blavatsky terms the "imperial will."[24] What an overpowering external intelligence ("whether it be spirit or living mesmerizer") is to the medium, "the simple exertion of his *will* power" is to the Adept.[25] The mention of mesmerism here is notable. The spectacle of the mesmerist-performer controlling the will of his female subject had attracted widespread attention in Victorian England as entertainment, pseudoscience, and site for coded discussion of a variety of social struggles—including those of colonialism.[26] Blavatsky demonstrates familiarity with the racist notion, common since James Esdaile's mesmerist experiments in Calcutta in the 1840s, that "Orientals" were particularly susceptible to hypnosis due to their weak wills and passive natures.[27] Indeed, the Mahatmas' "imperial will" seems an inversion of this trope. To render the Mahatma-disciple relationship in terms of mesmerism is clearly to foreground the centrality of power imbalance to that relationship. Once this imbalance is clarified, however, the difference between theosophy and spiritualism becomes much murkier. If a medium is "a person through whom the action of another being is said to be manifested and transmitted . . . by the either consciously or unconsciously active will of that other being," then it follows that a "Chela" (disciple) is a medium controlled by a Mahatma.[28] In other words, mediumship may be the opposite of adeptship, but it is therefore the same as discipleship. The relations between the various purveyors of "will" (ghosts, mesmerists, Mahatmas) and that will's passive recipients (mediums, the hypnotized, chelas) are apparently uniform. Or so, at least, Blavatsky implies.

Further consideration of the role of the Mahatmas, however, suggests otherwise. The Mahatma is different from the ghost or the mesmerist. He is not only a Master. He is also, at least potentially, a Brother. The disciple apprentices himself to the Mahatma so that one day, in principle, he too can join the order of the Adepts. Theosophist A. P. Sinnett explains as follows: "the great fraternity is at once the least and the most exclusive organization in the world, and fresh recruits from any race or country are welcome, provided they possess the needed qualifications. The door, as I have been told by one who is himself an adept, is always open to the right man." In order to join the Brotherhood, the aspirant must submit to "initiation" and a course of "training." Brotherhood, in other words, is preceded by an intensification of hierarchy; but at least by Sinnett's account, this hierarchy's principle of control is more internal than external. "The adept is not made: he becomes, as I have been constantly assured, and the process of becoming is mainly in his own hands."[29] If the chief task of the theosophist is to reconstitute the self around its always-deferred possibility of becoming-Mahatma, then, Sinnett implies, the force relations that traverse the disciple should be understood as produced from within this "process of becoming."

The Mahatma, then, is not a spiritual despot in the sense of the missionaries (i.e., a despotic external guide). Rather, it is a spiritual despot in the sense of Ekalavya's clay guru: the "Master" is a cipher that doubles the subject by facilitating its self-negation, its desire to be other than what it is. Less an entity than a function, it is a sign of the aspirant's own internally differentiated self. This sign then institutes a pedagogic relation in which the self becomes a stranger and the stranger another self. Olcott's relationship with Master Koot Hoomi, in short, is doubled by a self-relation: whatever else Koot Hoomi may have been, he was also an alter ego for Henry Steel Olcott. This relational structure, which is simultaneously inter- and intra-subjective, is at the heart of what I am describing as theosophy's astral ethics.

This play of identities is perhaps nowhere clearer than in the text of the *The Mahatma Letters to A. P. Sinnett*—the 1880–1885 correspondence among Blavatsky, Sinnett, Hume, and Mahatmas Koot Hoomi and Master Morya that, consisting of thirteen hundred odd pages of stationery and scrap paper now deposited at the British Library, was published in book form in 1923. Much of the sophistication of the *Mahatma Letters* as a literary text derives, as Joy Dixon notes, from its self-conscious play with its own "fictitiousness."[30] The text's refusal to confirm or deny itself as fiction—simultaneously soliciting and beggaring belief—facilitates a crosswiring of projected and disavowed identities. The *Mahatma Letters*, writes Viswanathan, are a "composite of voices, actors, writers, and interpreters." They upend imperial hierarchies and flirt with a mode of hybrid subjectivity in which races and genders overlap and converge. That this reassemblage takes place in the ethereal realms of the spirit is not coincidental: physical mingling would quickly run afoul of empire's racial mores. Spirit offered a safe space for experiments in new forms of community that would be forbidden elsewhere.[31]

Theosophists wrote fairly extensively about the relationship between spirit and matter. Within the theosophical imaginary, physicality tends to connote the actual, while spirituality connotes the potential. Again, the Masters are the key symbol. Although the body may be "the prison of the soul for ordinary mortals," writes Sinnett, the Adepts have achieved a limited independence from it. A Master is a sort of "aëronaut," who can send his spirit out like a "captive balloon."[32] Mahatmas were not the only ones with such powers. Olcott reported having seen Blavastsky's astral form on the streets of New York and watched the body of young Indian theoso-phist Damodar Mavalankar go rigid on its train berth as its spirit traveled to Tibet.[33] Such feats do not, however, suggest a complete abandonment of physicality. "Spirit," Sinnett reminds us, is a "material reality," but one "enormously subtler and more ethereal" than that of the physical body.[34] Electricity was a common analogy here. At once physical and ethereal, it skipped across the earth as fast as thought itself.

Theosophy rejected regnant nineteenth-century "materialism" (a term that generally implied some admixture of atheism, techno-science, and industrial capitalism) in favor of a renewal of spirit. But, as the insistence that spirit was itself a form of matter should imply, the goal was not to leave bodies behind, but to reform them, subordinating them to higher orders of matter. "I *will*, and my limbs obey. I *will*, and my thought, tra-versing space, which does not exist for it, envelops the body of another individual who is not a part of myself, penetrates through his pores, and superseding his own faculties, if they are weaker, forces him to a prede-termined action. It acts like the fluid of a galvanic battery on the limbs of a corpse."[35] Here, writing in the late 1870s, Blavatsky presents her "impe-rial will" as facilitating the despotic rule of others' bodies and minds. Its primary function is to found an intimate and power-laden form of inter-subjectivity.

By the late 1880s, however, Blavatsky's thinking on this matter seems to have changed. The imperial will returns to its own flesh, becoming a technology of *self*-governance. Blavatsky's late writings psychologize the Masters to a remarkable degree. The "Master," she claims in one essay, is the "Higher Self," the divine spirit that inhabits the human and derives its consciousness entirely from the "Human Soul." The "Mind" mediates between this higher "spiritual Soul" and the lower "animal Soul" that gen-erates the gross passions. More superego than guru, here the "Master" is almost entirely internal to the aspirant, even if he in principle links the in-terior life to a larger cosmic sphere.[36] Blavatsky's late writings thus explic-itly frame the Mahatmas as an ascetic technology that facilitates the rule of self *as* other. These astral guides channel theosophy's utopian reform impulse, making the self better than it is. They also dramatize how reform takes shape from within a particular type of power relation. The transcen-dent's claim on the actual, its drive to convert matter into spirit, cannot be analytically separated from power differentials and technologies of con-trol. If this set of concerns is evident in one way in the quasi-literary text of the *Mahatma Letters*, it takes a different form in a genre of theosophical writing that took shape after the Mahatmas fell conspicuously silent. It is to that genre—the theosophical conduct manual—that we now turn.

The Care of the Theosophical Self

The Coulomb Affair of 1884–85 brought the formative period of theosophical history to an abrupt close.[37] When disgruntled secretary Emma Coulomb delivered a batch of incriminating letters to the *Madras Christian College Magazine* so that they could be published as proof that Blavatsky had faked the Mahatmas and their miracles, a major scandal erupted. Within a year, Blavatsky resigned her official post with the Theosophical Society, left India for England (never to return), and found herself branded one of history's greatest charlatans by the Society for Psychical Research.[38] Ignominy did not, however, end her career. During the remaining six years of Blavatsky's life, she wrote extensively, producing some of her most enduring work, including *The Secret Doctrine* (1888), *The Key to Theosophy* (1889), and *The Voice of the Silence* (1889), as well as launching the London-based journal *Lucifer* (1887) to compete with the Adyar *Theosophist*.

The post-1885 writings, inevitably, differ from those prior to the Coulomb Affair in a variety of ways. Not surprisingly, these include a relative de-emphasis on the empirics of the Mahatmas' astral appearances. As one reader of *Lucifer* queried in February 1888, "How is that we now hear nothing of the signs and wonders with which neo-Theosophy was ushered in? Is the 'age of miracles' past in the Society?"[39] Theosophical charisma, at least for a time, settled into an all-too-familiar routine. This shift had a number of effects. As Dixon suggests, it seems to have contributed to theosophy's drift toward the institutional form of the "gentleman's club," where predominantly male elites discussed properly "masculine" metaphysical topics.[40] But it also, I will argue, prompted the emergence of what was for theosophy a novel literary genre: the conduct manual or ethical guide. The eclipse of the Masters implied a new dawn for the disciple as an object of theosophical knowledge. The continuity with the Coulomb Affair was in one sense striking. What Emma and Pierre Coulomb claimed to have done theatrically—costuming themselves into an ascetic identity, to the delight of their credulous audience—ordinary theosophists would now attempt through less spectacular means, via a sustained work upon the self.

The resulting problematic can be summed up by the phrase "practical occultism," which Blavatsky redefined in the late 1880s. Previously, the phrase had denoted magic; Blavatsky used it to denote ethics, or the practice of the self via the ascetic regulation of everyday behavior. The concept of "magic" had long been an important site through which the category "religion" was demarcated and defined.[41] Victorian thinkers had used it as a lever to pry religion away from science, and, in particular, to clarify that only the latter could claim to produce real effects in the world; magic was a category error, religion's mistaken attempt to do the "practical" things reserved for technology.[42] Like magic, ethics is a mode of religion that is "applied" or "practical," addressed to the production of worldly effects rather than to otherworldly belief. It may not have occasioned much discomfort in Victorian theorists of religion; but it did pose potential problems for theosophists.

We can see the significance of the shift from magic to ethics by comparing Blavatsky's 1888 article on "Practical Occultism" to Franz Hartmann's 1884 "Practical Instructions for Students of Occultism" (a series of articles that appeared in *The Theosophist* and was republished in book form the next year as *Magic, White and Black*). Hartmann, who defines magic as the "Highest Science or Wisdom, based upon knowledge and practical experience," explicitly states that he did not want to write "merely a *code of ethics*."[43] By differentiating between magic and ethics, Hartmann implicitly affirms their parallelism as modes of practical religion. By siding with the supernatural, he aligns himself with his enchantment-hungry fellow theosophists, many or most of whom had "joined the society . . . in the hope of mastering the secrets of magic."[44] They wanted the wonders that Blavatsky had begun to deny them.

But Blavatsky was difficult to deter. In "Practical Occultism," she insists that "occultism is not magic."[45] Too many theosophists, she explains, are unable to control their desire for magical powers. They should therefore renounce their desire to become Mahatmas. The aspirant should not "take a burden upon himself too heavy for him to carry. Without ever becoming a 'Mahatma,' a Buddha, or a Great Saint, let him study the philosophy and the 'Science of Soul,' and he can become one of the modest benefactors of humanity, without any superhuman powers."[46] This is practical occultism. It is mundane (or, in Blavatsky's words, "modest"), but it nonetheless remains oriented toward the superhuman.

One might say that this practical occultism is born of two interlocking forms of self-abnegation. First, the aspirant develops the desire to become superhuman, thus recognizing her ordinary human life as limited and unsatisfying. Second, she renounces her desire for the superhuman, returning to ordinary life, but with a difference. The ordinary world remains ghosted by the spiritual domain to which the aspirant has denied herself access. Hers will be a worldly asceticism, which refuses the subject full presence in an immanent domain that nonetheless remains the self's only possible habitation.

As though to facilitate this worldly asceticism, theosophists in the late

1880s began to publish texts that I will describe as conduct manuals. *The Voice of the Silence* (1889) is transitional in this regard. Ostensibly consisting of translated fragments from the ancient *Book of the Golden Precepts*, this slim volume is, its subtitle suggests, designed for "the Daily Use of Lanoos (Disciples)." Blavatsky's preface, in addition to describing the "discs" on which the original text in the "Senzar" language was written, explicitly situates its teachings as constituting an "exalted ethic" which cannot be placed before the world in full, but only in part. "And yet such ethics fill volumes upon volumes in Eastern literature, especially in the Upanishads."[47] The "fragments" that follow are a sort of Orientalist *Interior Castle*, enumerating the various stages of the disciple's spiritual progress in inflated Victorian prose (e.g., "Three Halls, O weary pilgrim, lead to the end of toils").[48] The presumed end point is religious ecstasy. (Appropriately, the book earns a mention in William James's *Varieties of Religious Experience* [1901–1902]).[49]

Two texts published the next year, although more prosaic in their aims, further develop the form of the daily devotional manual. Indeed, precisely because they are more mundane, they can be said to consolidate this emergent theosophical genre. Blavatsky compiled *Gems from the East: A Birthday Book of Precepts and Axioms* (1890) "chiefly from Oriental writings."[50] As its preface explains, the book contains "a Precept or Axiom for every day of the year" accompanied by "drawings from the pen of F.W., a lady Theosophist."[51] Alongside each daily precept is a blank space on the calendar page, presumably for the reader to record her thoughts on the day's reading. The prevailing ethos is that of a worldly asceticism. During the first four days of January, for example, the reader is told to do her duty "unflinchingly," to keep her heart from "rambling" with her senses, and to avoid using bad language. As we learn on January 3, "He who casts off all desires, living free from attachments, and free from egoism, obtains bliss."[52] As the year progresses, sentimental drawings of sunsets, butterflies, hieroglyphs, and magic lamps adorn nuggets of general advice ("Great works need no great strength, but perseverance"; April 23), as well as extracts from Hindu and other "Eastern" religious texts. The core message of the book, arguably, comes during summer: "Theosophy is the science of life, the art of living" (June 5).

Some Practical Suggestions for Daily Life, Some Hints on the Theosophical Training of Children (1890) is likewise comprised of quotations.[53] Its preface recommends that readers "take the hint, and make daily books of extracts for themselves, thus preserving a lasting record of the books read, and render their reading of practical value." One should read "a set of quotations each morning, trying to live up to them during the day, and meditating upon them in leisure moments."[54] This particular book of extracts is divided into sections for each of the seven days of the week. It opens energetically: "Rise early, as soon as you are awake, without lying idly in bed, half waking and half dreaming. Then earnestly pray that all mankind may be spiritually regenerated." The prevailing sense is that everyday activities should be oriented toward the transcendent. Thus, the theosophist should "will" that his "moral impurities" be washed away as he bathes his body (a practice remarkably parallel to one of the prescriptions in Karsandas Mulji's *Domestic Happiness*, discussed in chapter 3). "Saturday" distills this sentiment: "There is no more valuable thing possessed by any individual than an *exalted ideal* toward which he continually aspires, and after which he moulds his thoughts and feelings, and forms *as best he may* his life."[55] Sound though this advice might be, it is clearly not specifically theosophical. Although continuous with some of theosophy's longstanding preoccupations, this homespun asceticism has left most of theosophy's trademark concerns far behind. There is nary a Mahatma in sight.

But the Mahatmas, of course, were still there in principle. The practical asceticism prescribed by these conduct manuals was predicated on the desire to become Mahatma and on the simultaneous disavowal of that desire. The result was an intensified form of ascetic interiority. As Blavatsky wrote in an essay of October 1884 (one month into the Coulomb Affair), the chela or student is an "unfortunate man": "Instead of being the constant mouthpiece of his Guru, he finds himself left more alone in the world than those who are not Chelas." In the absence of his Master's "constant and friendly guidance," all he can do is strive to "divest himself of that overmastering sense of personality" that precludes knowledge of the "real" self: "His work is hard, his road stony, the end far away."[56] What Foucault might call a hermeneutics of the subject structures the resulting ascetic practice: only through assiduous work upon the self can the subject gain access to truth. But, as truth recedes continually farther into the distance, all that the theosophist is left with is ascetic practice itself. Thus, in a partial inversion of Foucault's formula, we have "spirituality" without "philosophy," discipline without truth.[57]

The Mahatmas also cued how this asceticism would be interpreted. Theosophy closely associated asceticism with India. This was partly for the ususal Orientalist reasons: during the nineteenth century, the stereotyped figure of the emaciated fakir was routinely used to exoticize Hinduism, Islam, and other Indian religions.[58] These Orientalist assocations do not, however, entirely account for the prominence of this figure in theosophical thought. Consider, for instance, Blavatsky's 1886 defense of "The Theosophical Mahatmas." Complaining that aspiring theosophists expect the Masters do all of their work for them, she suggests that they owe their spiritual passivity to the "blind unphilosophical faith" of the "Protestant Church," with its emphasis on salvation by faith alone rather than by works. True theosophy, by contrast, endorses the "doctrine of salvation by *personal* merit and *self*-forgetfulness that is the cornerstone of the teaching of the Lord Buddha."[59] Blavatsky is keen on Buddhism not for its metaphysical claims, but rather because of how it emphasizes the spiritual agency of the ascetic practitioner. Buddhism is appealing because it looks like hard work; indeed, there are moments in Blavatsky's writings when she almost seems to be using *Buddhism* and *asceticism* as synonyms. I am less interested in the question of whether this is a fair representation of Buddhism (it is not), and more interested in the apparent invisibility of a specifically Protestant form of self-discipline to theosophy. It is as though the putative dichotomy of "faith" and "works" has blinded Blavatsky to how faith is itself a deed. Or, to opt for a more Weberian narrative, she neglects how the doctrine of "faith alone" institutes a practice of the self: the worldly asceticism of the anxious Calvinist. The Orientalist figure of the Indian ascetic thus becomes a means of bringing worldly asceticism back into view.

Much the same seems to hold for Olcott. In an 1892 article on "Asceticism," he surveys "the Roman Catholic monk and nun, the Mohammedan fakir, and the Hindu ascetic," criticizing all three groups for holding to the "delusion" that mere "physiological restraint" can "bring the postulant to the threshold of" divine knowledge.[60] The Hindu ascetic embodies this mistake more acutely, however, than his Muslim and Catholic counterparts. His "tortures," says Olcott, "surpass Western belief." Olcott describes Hindu ascetics eating moss, wearing tree bark, inhaling fire, staring at the sun, and walking on their knees. The lesson taught by these misguided ascetics is that physical austerity ("Hatha Yoga," in Olcott's terms) is inferior to mental self-rule ("Raja Yoga") as a means for "self-conquest" or "the liberation of the flesh-prisoned Higher Self."[61]

Here, extreme austerity gives way to a more ordinary form of ascetic self-discipline, fully consistent with the practices prescribed by theosophical conduct manuals. Olcott explains this move with a reference to the *Mahabharata*. As the sage Markandeya explains to Yudhishthara in the *Vana Parva*, "Asceticism, again, is not mere abstinence from the pleasures of the world. He that is always pure and decked with virtues, he that practices kindness all his life, is a *Muni* [sage], even though he lead a domestic life."[62] Here, the householder and the renunciant converge. True asceticism does not lie in the otherworldly rejection of the flesh, but in the careful regulation of worldly behavior. Blavatsky, for her part, concurs: "As it is not the cowl that makes the monk, so no long hair with poetical vacancy on the brow is sufficient to make of one a faithful follower of *divine* Wisdom."[63] Vegetarianism, celibacy, and reading the *Gita* "upside down" are not enough to make a person "a theosophist according to the Masters' hearts." Even elephants and cows, after all, are strict vegetarians.

Theosophy's ideal worldly ascetic thus both is and is not Hindu. Even as theosophists embraced Sanskritic vocabulary and imported it into their "Guru English," they also disavowed the forms of Hindu asceticism with which this vocabulary was associated.[64] In theosophical writing, Sanskrit came to serve other functions. At times, it seems to have been a means for turning asceticism into a domain of technical knowledge with a specialized terminology appropriate to a "science" of the self. Thus, as Patience Sinnett counsels, to gain "complete mastery over all the material desires either of the body or the mind," the theosophist must practice the four "Saddhanas [*sic*]."[65] Here, linguistic experimentation lends the prescribed spiritual exercises an air of authoritative mystery. Technical Sanskrit imposes itself on mundane English, just as ascetic discipline imposes itself on worldly life.

But if Sanskritic exercises were to transform the mundane world of the ordinary theosophist, they too would be changed in the process. Indeed, Blavatsky's jibe at those who read the *Gita* upside down is, at one level, disingenuous: she and her fellow theosophists were busily inverting the meanings of Sanskrit texts through innovative reading strategies. The allegorical method of interpretation that they developed for the *Bhagavad Gita* in particular would, moreover, eventually shape the larger global reception of this textual corpus.

The Astral *Gita*

After 1885 the theosophists found their astral Masters even more absent than usual, and the resulting void was filled by an intensified interest in the ascetic self-discipline of the ordinary theosophist. Where the earlier period had sought to forge ascetic subjects by making them into Mahatmic mediums, rendering their inner lives a site for gregarious communion between master and disciple, the later period placed a higher value on the lonely routine of the everyday. Henceforth, the theosophist would embrace spiritual solitude. What is more, the ordinary practitioner would strive to remain ordinary—holding up the Mahatmas, or at least a stock figure of the trans-Himalayan renunciant, as an image of what *not* to become.

That is, of course is to overstate the case—the continuity between these two moments, before and after the Coulomb Affair, being more pronounced than the rupture. But the infamous "Collapse of Koot Hoomi" inevitably rearticulated, at least in part, an earlier set of tensions.[66] A. P. Sinnett's *Occult World* (1881) frames this tension clearly when it stresses that the regimen of "absolute physical purity" incumbent on the theosophical neophyte should not be confused with "the loathsome asceticism of the ordinary Indian fakeer, the *yogi* of the woods and wilds, whose dirt accumulates with his sanctity." This physical *"Hatti yog"* is inferior to *"Ragi yog,"* "the discipline of the mind." For the theosophist, there should be neither "obtrusive asceticism, nor withdrawal from the world." A "gentleman in ordinary society" could begin his occult training "without anybody about him being the wiser."[67] Emulate the Mahatmas, in other words, but without retreating to the mountains or marking the body with the signifiers of asceticism (the same signifiers that, not incidentally, mark the Mahatmas as Indian; this refiguring of asceticiscm is also about race). Early theosophy had tried to integrate the marvelous and the everyday, but in the late 1880s the marvels mostly stopped, prompting intensified interest in the mundane and an accordant distancing from the otherworldly "fakeer." Sinnett's "gentleman" is emblematic of the type of figure who steps into the foreground around this time. An ascetic within, he remains a consummate gentleman without, his dissemblance being a sign of his fidelity to occult truth.

The late 1880s also saw a pronounced increase in theosophical interest in the *Bhagavad Gita*. This was partly for reasons that had nothing to do with theosophy, but rather with the "Krishna renaissance" underway in Bengal (associated with Bankimchandra Chatterjee, among others).[68] Nonetheless, the *Gita* did serve an important function for theosophy at this time by rearticulating the category "Hindu asceticism." T. Subba Row's first lecture on the *Gita* (generally held to have inaugurated the period of acute theosophical interest in the text) was delivered at the December 1885 annual convention, the first major meeting of theosophists after the S.P.R.'s exposé of Blavatsky. The coincidence is suggestive. With the Mahatmas on the decline, a new mode of Hindu asceticism was needed, and the *Gita*'s *karmayoga* fit the bill.

Until the 1880s, English translations of the *Bhagavad Gita* had been few and far between. Charles Wilkins's *Bhagavat Geeta or the Dialogues of Kreeshna and Arjoon* (1785) had circulated for a full century with almost no rivals.[69] Despite a clutch of influential admirers like Ralph Waldo Emerson, it remained mostly obscure. Kashinath Trimbak Telang's 1882 translation, published as part of Max Müller's *Sacred Books of the East* series, began to broaden the *Gita*'s audience, but it was Edwin Arnold's *The Song Celestial* (1885) that finished the job. Building on the massive success of the author's earlier poetic the life of the Buddha (*The Light of Asia* [1879]), the popular *Song Celestial* helped to establish the *Gita* as "a naturalized Victorian text" by the end of the century.[70] Theosophists were among its most avid readers, and their fervor for it spread to others—including, most famously, the young M. K. Gandhi (see conclusion, following chapter 6).

The history of the Anglophone *Gita* was also shaped by theosophy's peculiar reading strategies, especially its allegorical approach to texts. T. Subba Row's 1885–86 lectures are essential here, laying the terrain taken up by later theosophical commentaries like Mohini Chatterjee's *The Lord's Lay* (1887), William Quan Judge's *Essays on the Gita* (1890), and Annie Besant's *Hints on the Study of the Bhagavad Gita* (1905). If it was Besant's politicized *Gita* that ultimately proved most influential (Eric Sharpe speculates that it was her translation that Aurobindo Ghosh read in jail), it needs to be understood in relation to earlier theosophical approaches to this classic text.[71]

As Mishka Sinha suggests, theosophical interpretations of the *Gita* were, generally speaking, both allegorical and universalist. That is, in decoding what was presumed to be the esoteric symbolism of the text, the-osophists also oriented the *Gita* away from the religious particularities of Hinduism and toward the (in principle) unbounded audience hailed by theosophical English. Besant's expansive claim that "to speak of the Gita is to speak of the history of the world" is representative of this reading strategy.[72] Sharpe, meanwhile, distinguishes among four different and, in his view, sequential modes of interpretation: the esoteric, the allegorical, the nationalist, and the universal.[73] I would expand this list to include the ascetic, it being the relationship between the ascetic *Gita* and the esoteric-allegorical *Gita* that will concern me here. As I will suggest, even as the notion of *karmayoga* ("the discipline of action") oriented theosophy toward the world, allegory suspended worldly particularities as a means of decoding occult truth. Working in tandem, allegory and *karmayoga* thus intertwined the worldly and the otherworldly, not renouncing the world exactly, but putting it under erasure as a sign of that which exceeds it.

Blavatsky's brief mention of the *Gita* in *Isis Unveiled* (1877) already links the text to the problematic of asceticism: "'Be unselfish, subdue your senses and passions, which obscure reason and lead to deceit,' says Christna [*sic*] to his disciple Arjuna, thus enunciating a purely Buddhistic principle. . . . Worship by deeds predominates over that of contemplation."[74] This short passage interleaves several of Blavatsky's concerns. It tendentiously equates Krishna and Christ.[75] It contrasts worship by deeds with worship by contemplation (in the *Gita*'s terms, *karmayoga* and *jñānayoga*), correlating this binary in the next paragraph to the Protestant distinction between "faith" and "works." (Again, by positioning her stress on the necessity of "works" as marking a departure from Protestantism, Blavatsky signals the extent to which the Protestant ethic—or faith as a practice of the self—remained invisible to her). Finally, it describes a major Hindu scripture as "purely Buddhistic," thus using *Buddhism* as a rough synonym for asceticism per se: Krishna's message is "Buddhistic" insofar as it prescribes the self-denying regulation of the senses and passions. Precisely through its apparently careless confusion of distinct religious traditions, then, the passage delineates the sphere of what Blavatsky would later identify as practical occultism, aligning "works," "Buddhism," and *"karmayoga"* as three different ways of configuring the ascetic regulation of the self. The "ascetic *Gita*" is thus almost as old as the Theosophical Society itself.

The "esoteric-allegorical *Gita*," meanwhile, took shape a few years later. Blavatsky's scattered references to the *Gita* during the early 1880s generally treat it as interchangeable with other occult texts. For example, she claims that both the *Gita* and the Book of Job are a "record" of the ancient "Mystery of Initiation."[76] In 1883, she marked the beginning of *The Theosophist*'s fifth year of publication by affirming the importance of "the esoteric meaning of the text of the *Bhagavad Gita*" and promising that each monthly issue to follow would feature the explication of a single chapter of that text. The promised exposition never came, nor perhaps was it really necessary. If there actually was an "almost perfect identity" between the "concealed sense" of the *Gita* and the "Arhat Tibetan Doctrine" already known to theosophy, then why belabor *this* text in particular?[77] This is what Sharpe terms the *esoteric* mode of interpretation. It insists on hidden inner meaning in all texts, but does so by effacing textual particulars. So, for example, in her defense of A. P. Sinnett's *Esoteric Buddhism* (1883) (which was heavily criticized for its almost total disregard of actual Buddhism as an object of philological study) Blavatsky insisted that "positively *all* the doctrines given in *Esoteric Buddhism* . . . are to be found in the *Gita*."[78] This "defense" effectively confirms the critics' chief complaint: to equate Buddhism and the *Gita* is to disregard most or all of the content of both. For the esotericist, however, religious actualities are beside the point. Truth hides behind the discrete religions; to know them, one first has to husk them, peeling back their material differences to reveal them as spiritually equivalent.[79]

T. Subba Row's 1885 lecture on the *Gita* unites these two strands of thought, the ascetic and the esoteric-allegorical. Tiruvalum Subba Row

(1856–1890) had been an influential theosophist since first inviting Olcott and Blavatsky to Adyar in 1882, and although he eventually broke with the Society in 1888 in order to pursue his interest Sanskrit philosophy without the liability of Blavatsky and her dubious phenomena, his collected writings speak eloquently of his attachment to the Mahatmas and theosophical teachings.[80] The success of his December 1885 lecture on the *Gita* led to an entire series of lectures the next year. Much longer, the 1886 lectures veer far from the *Gita* itself onto more metaphysical terrain. The 1885 lecture paves the way for them, suggesting that the *Gita* be read allegorically, and thus positioning it as a prime site for the kind of abstract speculation that dominates the 1886 lectures.[81]

The 1885 lecture suggests the following convergence: just as Arjuna is asked to renounce the material particularities of the world, so is the reader of the *Gita* asked to renounce the particularities of the text. Asceticism as a mode of practice parallels allegory as a mode of reading. The first particularity that we are asked to relinquish is that of Arjuna and Krishna themselves. Among the various epithets granted Arjuna elsewhere in the *Mahabharata* is, apparently, one that provides the crucial "clue" to his real identity: he is "Nara" or "Man." Subba Row explains that Vyasa (the traditional author of the epic) "looked upon Arjuna as man, or rather the real monad in man; and upon Kṛṣṇa as the Logos, or the spirit that comes to save man."[82] Here, Arjuna is an everyman caught in a curious chain of equivalences: Arjuna-man-monad meets Krishna-spirit-Logos. These twin sequences work via progressive abstraction. A named individual is replaced by a general category, which is then placed at a further remove from the everyday by translation into the polyglot esotericist argot characteristic of theosophical writing.

The interpretive principle that Subba Row brings to bear on the *Gita* is also in evidence elsewhere in his work. For example, in his review of Mabel Collins's occult novel *The Idyll of the White Lotus* (1884), he outlines the allegorical significance of the text's major characters and events in considerable detail. It is, presumably, in its "allegorical aspect" as a description of "the trials and difficulties of a neophyte" that he considers the novel to be a "true story." By Subba Row's reading, the novel dramatizes the soul-monad's subordination to the Logos such that "the man becomes liberated from the bondage of matter. In short, he becomes an adept."[83] Subba Row's allegorical reading strategy mirrors this process: just as the novel's hero Sensa is liberated from gross matter (as well as a cabal of wicked Egyptian priests) by the goddess of light, so is he also liberated from the novel's plotline by allegorical reading. Once "the veil of allegory" is removed, he is no longer just Sensa, but stands in for something much greater than a particular individual. Subba Row cannot, obviously, remove Sensa from the world of signification entirely, so that he might somehow step beyond the veil of language. Instead, allegory translates the novel's characters, shifting their meaning from one set of signs to a second, more arcane set. Often, Sanskrit is the idiom of elevation. For example, Subba Row glosses the novel's "dark goddess" as "Avidyā," or ignorance.

Subba's Row's 1885 lecture on the *Gita* incorporates a reading of a second occult novel, Bulwer-Lytton's *Zanoni* (1842), and it likewise insists on reading occult fiction "in a figurative sense." Thus, the novel's "Dweller on the Threshold" (a monster that menaces the spiritual aspirant) represents the "despair and despondency of the neophyte, who is called upon to give up all his old affections for kindred, parents, and children, as well as his aspirations for objects of worldly ambition." Ascetic renunciation of worldly particulars and allegorical renunciation of textual particulars combine. What Subba Row adds to the mix here is a chain of textual equivalencies, not unlike those pursued by Blavatsky in her esotericist mode. The neophyte's "despair" depicted in *Zanoni* is the exact same despair that paralyzes Arjuna in the *Gita*. The two texts, moreover, demand the same thing of their readers: the renunciation of the world and its affections.

Soon, the textual colloquy convened on the field of battle grows larger still. Arjuna and Krishna welcome none other than John Stuart Mill, suffering from a parallel bout of depression. Mill, says Subba Row, "analyzed the whole man into nothing." His "habit of analysis" wore away his "feelings" until he could no longer take "pleasure" in any of his previous passions. Subba Row equates this depression to Arjuna's uncertainty: Mill "indicates what the chela must experience when he has determined to renounce all old associates and is called to live for a bright future on a higher plane."[84] Reading a little farther into Mill's posthumously published *Autobiography* (1873), however, suggests a different interpretation. Mill explains that his elaborate education at the hands of his father and Jeremy Bentham had led him "to believe that all mental and moral feelings and qualities, whether of a good or a bad kind, were the results of association." Experience leads us to "love one thing and hate another." It follows that, in proto-Pavlovian style, the virtuous subject should strive to condition himself such that he finds "pleasure" in those things that are "beneficial to the great whole" and "pain" in those that are "hurtful to it."[85] Mill was unable to force association in this way; "analysis" could dissolve the affective bonds that link the self to its objects, but could not forge new bonds. Hence his depression. But, even in its failure, his mental exercise is an interesting one. Utilitarianism, as we see here, experimented with ascetic practices of the self, asking the subject to release his hold on particular things in the name of a general order of happiness. Mill's depression indicates the difficulty of such a procedure: the ascetic break with objects can preclude the very happiness that the utilitarian calculus appears to promise. The key term, for Mill, is association: once organic association is analyzed away, new associations are not so easy to synthesize.

It is this crisis, I would argue, that theosophical allegory attempts to resolve. By abstracting his characters away from particularity, Subba Row seeks to insert them into new constellations of terms and new sets of associations. This gestures toward something like a politics of brotherhood, as I will discuss below. But it is a brotherhood the form of which is avowedly immaterial. It is no mistake that Subba Row stops Mill's tale before, spurred on by a copy of Wordsworth, he reimmerses himself in the sensual forms of nature, which restore him to mental health. For Subba Row, this is an undesirable outcome. The theosophist wants to arrest the analytic subject in it its state of dissociation from the world.

He does not, however, want the subject to reject the world entirely. The *Gita* prescribes a "kind of mental abnegation," but not full renunciation. This, argues Subba Row, is a fact of crucial importance. The *Gita* answers the "great objection" against "Hinduism and Buddhism." Where it is often thought that these religions "render void the lives of men engaged in ordinary avocations," the *Gita* shows that the mental abnegation of the man in the world is more powerful than the ascetic retreat into the "jungle." As Subba Row puts it, "it is not the nature of the act, but the mental attitude of the performer that is of importance." His *karmayogi*, much like A. P. Sinnett's "gentleman," can make spiritual strides "whilst there is nothing in his mode of life to distinguish him from his fellows." His "separation from the world" is mental, not physical.

Notably, Subba Row's reading of the *Gita* does not engage with the third of the text's great "disciplines": *bhakti*, or theistic devotion. In fact, Subba Row explicitly dismisses the idea that the *Gita* supports "the doctrine of a personal god." His Krishna is a "Guru," and Arjuna a "chela." The power differential between the two is the occasion for instruction, not worship. This is instruction, however, of a very particular kind. The *Gita*, by Subba Row's account, narrates the instruction of the self by the self. Krishna, as "Parabrahman," is immanent within "almost every entity in the Cosmos," including Arjuna. Thus, Krishna as Logos "only calls upon Arjuna to worship his own highest spirit, through which alone he can hope to attain salvation." The "'I' is a sort of fiction." Its "individuality is connected with the Logos," much like Christ was "one with the Father." The Advaitic reduction of Arjuna-Krishna to Self-Cosmos echoes Subba Row's other allegorical interventions into this text. But it also at the same time echoes

Blavatsky's effort to psychologize the Mahatmas. The external spiritual guide becomes the "higher self," a superegotic internal principle that governs the ascetic impulse. It is in this sense, as an allegorical meditation on self-governance, that the *Gita* can be read as a text that explains "the science of spiritual ethics."[86] If, with M. K. Gandhi, we are inclined to read the *Gita* as a "dictionary of conduct," or a text that prescribes an ethics of self-rule, we would do well to consider how an earlier moment in the genealogy of this ascetic *Gita* grew out of theosophy's concern with the effacement of the particular.[87] For theosophy, as I have been arguing, asceticism was simultaneously an ethics and a hermeneutic, both of which sought to subordinate the immanent, material, and particular to the transcendent, spiritual, and general-universal.

Spiritual Hermeneutics, or, Is Theosophy a Religion?

Theosophy's spiritual hermeneutics, its desire to cancel particularity in the name of the "higher life," is not only related to its investment in asceticism (worldly or otherwise) as a set of technologies for the regulation of the self. It also taps into theosophy's anticlericalism. Although heavily invested in anticlerical rhetoric and discourses of religious imposture, theosophy was nonetheless highly resistant to the atheist materialism that such discourses tended to produce. As a letter to the Archbishop of Canterbury published in Blavatsky's journal *Lucifer* put it, the "world is being rapidly brought to the conviction that god is a mythical conception . . . and that the immortal part of man is the silly dream of ignorant savages, perpetuated by the lies and tricks of priests."[88] If theosophy was to counter materialism, it had to find a way to counter the idea that the entire spiritual world was nothing but a ruse supporting worldly regimes of power. Esotericism was the apparent solution. It solved the problem of priestcraft by building a second lie into the mythos of priestly imposture. Behind the first curtain lurks the conniving priest; behind the second waits the wise adept, guardian of Truth itself.

As an 1884 article argued, the modern West may have awakened "to find out that it has been led by the nose by the priests," but this raises an important question: "if all these theological fables are nothing else but stupid tales, at the absurdity of which a child would laugh, how could they dominate for so many centuries the minds of the people?" The masses, the article proposes, "intuitively perceived" the truths hidden behind these lies, which is why the lies had persuasive power.[89] A few years later, Patience Sinnett proffered a similar narrative. Even in ancient Egypt, priests and oracles were "too transparently fraudulent to deceive any but the most illiterate adherents." Behind them, however, stood an order of Adepts who had no need for "jugglery and imposture." They used the smokescreen of priestly lies to shield religious truth and protect it from possible corruption.[90]

Theosophists were not the first to reject priestly fraud as an explanation for ancient miracles. Spiritualist Newton Crosland, for instance, had denied that the Greek oracles could have been "the machinery of priestcraft." That the rationalist Greeks believed in them, he argued, proves the reality of the supernatural: the "wisest and most enlightened nation that ever existed" could not have been "tricked" in this way. In fact, says Crosland, the Delphic oracle operated through the same principles as modern séances.[91] More distinctively theosophical was the cryptographic obsession with hidden meaning. Complaining that academic philology fixates on the outer meaning of sacred texts, Sinnett completes her priestcraft narrative by calling for a "symbology" that looks for "hidden meaning" behind the text. She emphasizes, however, that only the self-disciplined person with "a life of absolute purity" can access these meanings.[92] The ascetic work upon the self must precede the cryptographic search for coded truths. As Blavatsky remarks elsewhere, for an ordinary person to access this truth would be like reaching the "moon on a bicycle."[93]

Asceticism and esotericism both "spiritualize" in that they press pass physical forms, but without eliminating those forms entirely. The "Atma-Vidya," or "Knowledge of the Soul," is the highest kind of knowledge because it takes the lower, merely "material" forms of knowledge and transforms them by "purifying them of their dross."[94] By placing material forms under erasure in this way, the esotericist project negated religious particularities to produce a "universal" secret that, insofar as it consisted only of such negations, was necessarily empty. More a function than a concept, the esoteric served to rearticulate the relations among the various particularities that it so determinedly abstracted from context.

This process, it could be said, is what Blavatsky meant by "religion." In her 1888 editorial "Is Theosophy a Religion?," Blavatsky answers her titular question with a resounding negative.[95] The great growth of the Theosophical Society has, she says, led many to describe it as a new religion—a "sect" or "ism"—thus providing themselves with a "peg on which to hang their . . . slanders" of it. Such critics, Blavatsky claims, fail to recognize that theosophy fundamentally rethinks the category "religion." From the beginning, the Society's "very *raison d'être*" was to "lead an open warfare" against "the intellectual extinguishers known as dogmatic creeds."[96] Consequently, theosophy is entirely without creed. It "can be practiced by

Christian or Heathen, Jew or Gentile, by Agnostic or Materialist, or even an Atheist."[97]

Two closely related conceptual moves allow Blavatsky to make this claim. First, she sharply distinguishes between "*a* religion" (as a singular noun that necessarily implies the plural *religions*) and the article-free general noun *religion*. In W. C. Smith's remarkably parallel account of the history of these terms, *religion*, in the sense of piety, gradually gave way during the modern period to the discrete *religions*—reified, externalized systems that are regulated or mapped by particular forms of knowledge, whether theological or historical-anthropological, and which hail a distinct kind of believing subject that differs in important ways from its premodern predecessor.[98] Blavatsky is similarly concerned with etymology and the analytic potential of playing the general and discrete senses of *religion* against each other. Theosophy, she insists, "is not *a* Religion." Rather, "Theosophy *is* Religion itself. A Religion in the true and only correct sense is a bond uniting men together—not a particular set of dogmas and beliefs. Now Religion per se, in its widest meaning is that which binds not only *all* MEN, but also *all* BEINGS and all *things* in the entire Universe into one grand whole." It connects every "speck," every "blade of grass and atom," into a "Universal Brotherhood." This, Blavatsky says, is her "theosophical definition of religion."[99]

This "definition" looks more like a post-humanist political manifesto than it does, say, Max Müller's effort to define religion etymologically in his Gifford Lectures of the same year.[100] But Blavatsky's definition is clearly a riff on one of the two most commonly proposed etymologies for the Latin *religio*. As Müller explains, the theologian Lactantius, rejecting Cicero's rival etymology, derived *religio* from *religare*, "to bind." "We are tied to God and bound to Him (*religati*) by the bond of piety."[101] If Smith attempts a return to "piety" as a means of securing the interiority and authenticity of the believing subject in its bond to God, Blavatsky chooses instead to invert the directionality of religion's bond. Religion is not that which binds the believer vertically to God; it is that which proliferates horizontal bonds so as to bind all beings to one another in a radically egalitarian federation of humans and "things."

But creeds, fissiparous though they might be, are not so easily dispensed with. In order to liberate "religion" from "the religions" Blavatsky has recourse to a second conceptual move—one that, roughly allegorical in the sense detailed above, produces *religion* by suspending the particularities of *religions*. Theosophy, she writes, is like an alchemical alembic. "It transmutes the apparently base metal of every ritualistic and dogmatic creed (Christianity included) into the gold of fact and truth."[102] The lower metal gives way to the higher, which is, in the theosophical view, no longer properly physical at all: transmutation pushes matter beyond itself into the more ethereal reaches of the astral. Or, more to the point of "religion," it pushes past the immanent sign toward its transcendent referent. "Tearing off with no uncertain hand the thick veil of dead-letter with which every old religious scripture was cloaked, scientific Theosophy, learned in the cunning symbolism of the ages, . . . opens new vistas beyond the old horizons of crystallized, motionless and despotic faiths." It displaces "sham Christianity" (or, as Blavatsky jibes, "Churchianity") to reveal the religion's esoteric core.[103] All extant religions are "true at the bottom" and "false at the surface." The same holds for theosophy. "Theosophy is the soul of its Society; the latter the gross and imperfect body of the former"[104]

The endpoint of this basic procedure—articulating a universal truth that exists only by putting particular truths under erasure, thus in itself remaining void of content—is implied by Annie Besant's 1889 conversion statement. A prominent feminist, secularist, and socialist, Besant provoked a minor scandal when she became an occultist after meeting Blavatsky. In responding to her critics, Besant notes that they have set up "a new infallibility, as indefensible, and less venerable, than that of Rome. . . . It is to do what Churches in all ages have done, to set up their own petty fences round the field of truth." Secularism cannot just oppose itself to religion. This would make the National Secular Society (of which Besant had been a founding member) a mere "Anti-Theological Society."[105] Secularism should instead oppose itself to anything that takes on the function of the religious—that is, anything that becomes, in Edward Said's words, "an agent of closure, shutting off human investigation, criticism, and effort in deference to the authority of the more-than-human, the supernatural, the otherworldly."[106] What theosophy calls for, in short, is heterodoxy—it being heterodoxy, as Viswanathan has argued, that is theosophy's answer to secularism.[107] Maurice Davies, in his *Heterodox London* (1874), put the matter succinctly, defining heterodoxy as "the special 'doxy' of those who lay no claim to orthodoxy whatever, who elect to be heretical, and who would resent the imputation of doctrinal soundness as a personal affront."[108]

Theosophy, Blavatsky claims, is opposed to all creeds. It is thus, in Davies's terms, constitutively heterodox. If secularism, as Besant suggests, tends to set itself up as a new Church that holds to a particular set of beliefs, then it is, in Blavatsky's sense, a religion. What theosophy calls for, we might say, is something that approaches Said's "secular criticism." Inherently "oppositional," it is marked by its "suspicion of totalizing concepts" and its "discontent with reified objects."[109] By trying to rethink the legacy of Saidian secular criticism through the framework of heterodoxy, Viswanathan signals how the criticism of religion can only proceed in the negative. Heterodoxy can only function as critique if it has a "doxy" to react against. This, I want to suggest, is one function of theosophy's spiritual hermeneutics. It discovers "Religion" by putting "the religions" under erasure, retaining traces of them as the ground against which ethereal truth can emerge. The resulting network of partial presences that crisscross theosophical selves and texts are what give rise to the kind of community that Blavatsky claims her Religion is productive of. It is in this sense that the "theosophical definition of religion," which strings discrete religions together by effacing their particularities, gives rise to "Universal Brotherhood."

In this regard, theosophy's spiritual hermeneutics operates conjointly with its astral ethics. The goal of occult training, as Blavatsky describes it in her essay on "Practical Occultism," is best expressed by the Delphic injunction to "know thyself." To know the self, the aspirant first has to change the self so that it is worthy of occult knowledge. One does this through such ascetic practices as meditation, abstinence, and the cultivation of good thoughts, words, and deeds. If rigorously pursued, these practices will produce "goodwill to all and entire oblivion of Self," the necessary prerequisites for "the reception of higher wisdom."[110] This "goodwill to all," of course, echoes the ideal of universal brotherhood. As Blavatsky clarifies in a companion essay, "true Occultism or Theosophy is the 'Great Renunciation of SELF,' unconditionally and absolutely, in thought as in action. It is ALTRUISM, and it throws him who practices it out of calculation of the ranks of the living altogether."[111] This radical self-negation necessarily entails a renunciation of everyday relationships. The aspirant should unbind his "daily and hourly thoughts" from "worldly things" like the family. Even "the holy love of a mother for her child, or that of a husband for his wife," is insufficient; "there is still *selfishness* in the first, and an *égoisme à deux* in the second."[112] If the soul is "entirely occupied with its own privileged tenants," writes Blavatsky, there will be no room in it for the "great orphan" of "Humanity *en bloc* . . . without distinction of race, complexion, religion, or social status. It is *altruism*, not *ego-ism* . . . that can lead the unit to merge its little Self in the Universal Self."[113] Here, the quasi-Vedantic merger of self with the transcendent Absolute bleeds into the merger of self with universal humanity. Cosmic unity and sociopolitical unity are the convergent aims of ascetic practice.

Just as the connective principle of religion only emerges after the particularities of discrete religious traditions have been renounced, the possibility of a global society only emerges through the ascetic disavowal of inherited social bonds. The biological relations of husband-wife and mother-child give way before a radically dispersed principle of sociality that Blavatsky conjures under the sign of religion or spiritual reform.

Only Connect: Theosophy's Brotherly Politics

In closing, I want to return to where I began: Henry Steel Olcott's hands, alternately entwined with those of Koot Hoomi and Swami Dayananda Saraswati. Olcott, as we have seen, remained unsure of whether he was reaching out for a brother or for a guru. Either type of connection, however, would surely have seemed suspect to the British colonial state. When Olcott delivered his address in Meerut in May 1879, his audience included a police spy who had trailed him across north India, shaving his mustache along the way to confuse the increasingly suspicious theosophists.[114] What exactly did the spy think was going on here? Was he worried that Blavatsky was a secret Russian agent, sent to obstruct British power in central Asia? Or was he more concerned with theosophy's implicitly anticolonial rhetoric, its advocacy for India?

Whatever his agenda, it seems likely that this clean-shaven police spy would have assumed that his chief interpretive task was to separate theosophy's spiritual trappings from its latent political content. To detach the political and the spiritual too quickly here, however, is a mistake. Blavatsky could be and was political without being a secret agent. Her cryptopolitics, her interest in the hidden and encoded, did not necessarily imply that her religious writings were simply a veneer or mask, a veil that must be pulled aside to reveal her as a government agent. Nor does it seem sufficient to suggest that, after 1885 and the creation of the Congress, anticolonial gestures that had been rehearsed in the relatively safe schoolroom of "the spiritual" could at last emerge onto the world historical stage of politics proper. This classic coming-out story, which inscribes religion into history by rendering it the closet of anticolonial desire, remains a persuasive and essential hermeneutic device for interpreting nineteenth-century religious reform. But, insofar as it functions as a subtraction story, a *Bildung* narrative that predicates political maturity on the full exfoliation of the religious, it also remains incomplete. It not only fails to provide a sufficient account of the sacred's "citational" hold upon the secular.[115] It also tends to occlude the complex interrelations between the political and the social foregrounded by religious reform movements themselves. These movements arrest the political in the unstable and experimental field of social relations, such that their apparent "immaturity" should be understood as essential to their overall political project.[116]

"Clasped hands" imply a principle of association that bypasses the state en route to what Olcott terms the "cause of humanity" and what Blavatsky calls "Universal Brotherhood." In fact, theosophy's "brotherly" politics seems to have been articulated less against the state than against the figure of the priest, one of its principle foils. As Olcott declaimed in Meerut, India's millions "blindly follow the lead of a debauched, ignorant, selfish priesthood, who fatten on their substance, multiply ceremonies for gain, encourage ignorance, often set an example of hard brandy-drinking, and split the people up into innumerable useless castes." Shared opposition to the priest is, by Olcott's account, what will bring the Theosophical Society and the Arya Samaj into alliance. Here we have the classic elements of the priestcraft narrative, little changed since its earlier iterations in the work of Evangelicals like Charles Grant and William Ward.

What had changed, however, was the context in which this story was told. As we have seen, Hindu reformers from Rammohun Roy to Dayanand Saraswati had made strategic use of Anglophone anticlericalism in articulating their own reform projects in Bengali, Gujarati, and Hindi. Theosophical English repurposed this narrative yet again, but it did so against the backdrop of adjustments to the discourse of priestcraft that had happened on English's margins. Chief among these was the elaboration of a distinctively South Asian mode of governmentality that took the history of Hindu asceticism as one of its primary points of reference.

Theosophy's politics unfolded along the immanent axis of spiritual tutelage, its attempted resolution of the apparent conflict between egalitarian brotherhood and hierarchical guidance coalescing in the figure of the astral ascetic. Theosophy's Mahatmas conjoin ascetic autonomy and priestly heteronomy by displacing the self into the spiritual guide. Simultaneously interior to the theosophical subject and inaccessibly distant from it, the Mahatmas figure "spirit" as a principle of partial presence whereby the self is opened to the other. They thus, in Blavatsky's terms, potentially establish religion as a "bond uniting men together," instead of positioning it once again as a force for social fission. Theosophy, writes Blavatsky, shows "the necessity and actuality of the connection between man and all things in the universe with each other."[117] It does so, I have been arguing, by using asceticism to demonstrate the inherent sociality of the self.

Doomed though it might have been, the reform alliance between the Arya Samaj and the Theosophical Society is nonetheless significant. By aligning North Atlantic and South Asian religious reform cultures, how-

ever fleetingly, it brought into view some of the social and political potentialities that structured transnational religious movements of this time.
To attend more closely to the specific mode of politics outlined by theosophists, Arya Samajis, and others certainly tells us more about the particular historical conjuncture of nineteenth-century reform. But it also, I
would wager, opens up an important chapter in the genealogy of the kind
of disciplinary power that emerged as central to political religion in the
latter years of British colonial rule in India, as in Gandhi's somatic politics. If the larger story of political religion in modern India tends to rush
proleptically to fascism, theocracy, and the manipulation of religion by
the state, then in order to rethink the problematic of South Asian secularism, we would do well to return to an earlier moment in its genealogy (and
before "Indian secularism" even emerged as such) to ask what "political
religion" looked like at a moment when the political, arguably, did not
take sovereign state and the rights-bearing individual as its primary referents. It sought instead, to establish, although in partly inarticulate term,
a coming utopian community that would establish itself in the immanent
political field opened up by the priest.

For its part, theosophy sought to amplify the disjuncture between
spirit and matter, the transcendent and the immanent, the potential and
the actual. "No man," writes Blavatsky, "however gross and material he
may be, can avoid leading a double existence; one in the visible universe,
the other in the invisible."[118] We all, in other words, lead unstable lives,
caught between the anchor of what is and the pull of what could be. Stated
otherwise, "form" (the actual) is always doubled and ghosted by "reform,"
the potential that animates it from within and points it toward its own
self-transcendence.

The Circulation of Self-Rule

When thy firm soul
Hath shaken off those tangled oracles
Which ignorantly guide, then shall it soar . . .
Troubled no longer by priestly lore
EDWIN ARNOLD, *THE SONG CELESTIAL* (1885)

When M. K. Gandhi read the *Bhagavad Gita* for the first time, he did so in English translation. The year was 1889, and Gandhi was studying law in London. Refusing to eat meat, he had fallen in with the city's growing circle of vegetarians and other assorted radicals, and it was two of these new acquaintances that loaned Gandhi a copy Edwin Arnold's popular *Gita* translation, *The Song Celestial* (1885). Gandhi devoured the book and soon thereafter broadened his religious reading to include the New Testament and *The Light of Asia*, Arnold's 1879 poem about the life of the Buddha. This fin-de-siècle reading list seems to have shaped Gandhi significantly; indeed, one could plausibly look here to find the beginnings of his later theorization of worldly asceticism as swaraj or self-rule. "My young mind," he wrote as an adult, "tried to unify the teaching of the *Gita*, the *Light of Asia*, and the Sermon on the Mount. That renunciation was the highest form of religion appealed to me greatly."[1]

Standing as he does at the intersection of the previous chapters, Gandhi provides a fitting coda for this book. The acquaintances who loaned Gandhi their *Gita* were theosophists (probably Bertram and Archibald Keightley); shortly thereafter, they also introduced him to Annie Besant and

Madame Blavatsky, who had relocated to London a few years previously on the heels of the Coulomb Affair. As Gandhi later reported, it was Blavastky's *Key to Theosophy* (1889) that "disabused me of the notion fostered by the missionaries that Hinduism was rife with superstition."[2] Gandhi's travels in England, meanwhile, echo those of his fellow Gujarati Karsandas Mulji thirty years earlier. Like Gandhi, Mulji was keenly interested in self-rule (or in his terms, *svatantrata*), a trait that he thought characterized the British. Where Gandhi's religious eclecticism recalls Keshub Chunder Sen and the Brahmo Samaj, his strenuous asceticism recalls Dayananda Saraswati and his effort to make brahmacharya the moral basis of the Hindu nation. Finally, although Gandhi did not court the Quakers until relatively late in his career, it is hardly a stretch to claim William Howitt—an avowed pacifist and the author of *Mad War Planet* (1871)—as having anticipated his commitment to the politics of nonviolence.[3] The scene of fin-de siècle radicalism was, after all, an extension of the mid-Victorian reform assemblage.[4] I do not mean to imply that Gandhi was somehow the necessary culmination these variegated histories. Nonetheless, he does succinctly distill a set of themes that has run throughout this book, bringing them from the nineteenth century into the twentieth.

Gandhi's experiments in self-rule shared in the diffusely transnational "ethical turn" that, as Shruti Kapila suggests, characterized global public culture in the early decades of the twentieth century.[5] Where Kapila points to psychoanalysis as one transnational counterpart to the anticolonial Indian "culture of the self," I would point to Max Weber's *The Protestant Ethic and the Spirit of Capitalism* as another. Weber's book took shape between 1904 and 1920, thus overlapping with the early phase of Gandhi's transformation into an icon of political asceticism. Both Gandhi and Weber launched a critique of what Gandhi called "modern civilization" by asking how the history of subjectivity shapes larger social, political, and economic forms. In particular, both challenged what, following Kapila, we might describe as the liberal "cult of the individual."[6] Where Weber called attention to the religious genealogy of capitalist selfhood to demonstrate its historical contingency, Gandhi experimented with how religious asceticism could be used to reform the capitalist subject: science was Weber's vocation, politics was Gandhi's.

In recent years, Gandhi has been the subject of a substantial scholarly revival. As Tridip Suhrud remarks, *Hind Swaraj* (*Indian Home Rule*, 1909) in particular has come to seem like a book written for the twenty-first, rather than the twentieth, century.[7] Like Michel Foucault, Gandhi was heavily invested in biopolitics, or what Joseph Alter terms "biomorality."[8] Gandhi's dedication to hygiene, fasting, celibacy, and homeopathy once seemed embarrassing to scholars otherwise keen to claim him as an anti-colonial hero. Now, it is precisely those experiments that make him so interesting. Rather than an idiosyncratic personal indulgence, Gandhi's ascetic experiments were the means by which he positioned his body as a dense transfer point for the dissemination of technologies of self-rule. For Gandhi, the body was a public site, a node in a networked circuit of horizontal governmentality. His own highly publicized flesh was the icon for this emergent biopolitical regime. Here, body and nation become critically analogous. A person should govern her body and behavior in much the same way that a nation governs its territory—it being the transferability of technologies of self-rule between these different registers that comes to constitute the domain of the political as such.

In *Spiritual Despots*, I have traced the contours of a specifically nineteenth-century culture of the self that anticipated many of Gandhi's concerns. The Gandhian problematic of self-rule, I suggest, both drew on and refigured this earlier material. In effect, Gandhi came to occupy a site that emerged gradually over the course of the nineteenth century in relation to several seemingly discrepant discourses or cultural fields: the Luther of India, the spirit of Protestantism, reform, ethics or moral training, generalized brahmacharya, and astral discipleship, to name just a few. None of these terms are entirely equivalent to the others. As a set, however, they suggest the extent to which spiritual tutelage became a key problematic for nineteenth-century thinkers in India as well as Britain.

Repeatedly, we have seen how "self-rule"—a notion that I gloss via a set of intertwined terms drawn from other theorists, notably Weber's "ethic," Foucault's "discipline," and Charles Taylor's "Reform"—comes to relocate the spiritual guide into the self to articulate a structure of subjectivity perhaps best described by Thomas Carlyle. In place of priestcraft, as I suggest in the Introduction, Carlyle offers "auto-popery." Self-rule splits the subject into two, rendering subjectivity the site of what Foucault describes as "a sort of permanent political relationship between self and self."[9]

In the same movement that it disassembles the self, however, self-rule also insinuates the subject into a larger assemblage of split subjectivities. In the Introduction, I used the character of Ekalavya to illustrate this process of subjectivation. Asceticism, even if it appears as a practice of freedom, induces in the subject a posture of obedience that, at least potentially, can open the subject to external discipline. In my reading of the Ekalavya story, I stressed how the clay guru becomes a third term that mediates between teacher and pupil by facilitating a projection and confusion of identities. Importantly, this third term doubles and overlays identities but without ever synthesizing them (or hybridizing them, in the biological sense of that term). Rather, by exposing the space internal to any given subject, the tutelary encounter works to disseminate subjectivity into an expansive assemblage of tutelary relations. Tutelage, in other words, indicates a dialectic of a particular type: it mediates particularities but without thereby producing a synthesis that transcends those particularities; the transcendent appears here only as the contingent negation of the immanent, a mediatory function rather than a totalizing being.

This tutelary encounter is at the heart of the process that I have described as "reform." By disassembling the self along the immanent-transcendent axis, reform establishes a power relation that can be either intra- or inter-subjective. If intra-subjective, it establishes the political relation of self to self that Foucault calls asceticism. If inter-subjective, it establishes the tutelary relation that Foucault calls pastoral. It is this latter relation, I have argued, that colonial missionaries discussed under the rubric of "priestcraft." For the missionaries, priestcraft denoted spiritual despotism in the sense of absolute heteronomy: priests, as James Mill had it, are the "uncontrollable masters of human life." Part of the work of this book has been to redefine spiritual despotism away from Mill and the missionaries. Taking the story of Ekalavya as paradigmatic, I have suggested that asceticism and pastoralism converge on the figure of the clay guru, entering a zone of indistinction in which the difference between self and other is unclear. When I discipline myself according to an externally derived norm or rule, who is the actor or agent?

Asceticism necessarily situates the subject within a larger network of disciplinary or tutelary relations. This open-ended structure of overlapping tutelage is what I have described as a reform assemblage. Ethics, or techniques for conducting life, circulate within this assemblage; they are among the accreted forces (to recall Protap Chunder Mozoomdar's definition of religion) that simultaneously hold the assemblage together and pull it apart. Precisely because the self-ruling subject is never self-equivalent, it is also always imbricated with others, a node in the circulation of ethical technologies for managing the conduct of life. We might say, with Keshub Chunder Sen, that self-rule spreads by behavioral quotation; or, to take a slightly different term, it spreads via behavioral mimicry. Because the self-ruling subject aspires to become other than what it is, it submits to an external rule that, once internalized, opens the subject to the rule of others.

The Highest Form of Religion

The scene of ascetic self-rule suggests a structure of religious subjectivation quite different from the structure implied by the scene of priestly despotism as described by the missionaries. To make this structure visible, anticolonial thinkers like Gandhi thus had to rethink the figure of the priestly despot. Priestcraft is not a term often associated with Gandhi, but it does appear twice in *Hind Swaraj*; the first of these appearances, moreover, marks a significant moment in the text. Before Gandhi can position ethics as the basis for politicized religion, it seems, he first has to exorcise the specter of the priestly charlatan.

Hind Swaraj unfolds as a dialogue between an Editor and a Reader, thus indicating its debt to Gandhi's early experiments in newspaper publishing.[10] Broadly speaking, the Editor speaks for Gandhi, while the Reader functions as a devil's advocate. It is notable, then, that it is the Reader who mentions priestcraft. In the early chapters of *Hind Swaraj*, the Editor has begun to develop his argument that in order to truly attain independence from Britain, India has to rid itself of "the tiger's nature" as well as the tiger. That is, it has to do more than just expel the British; it also has to eliminate their modern ethic of economic "base self-interest" by reforming Indian subjectivity. "Real home-rule is self-rule or self-control." It is "one's rule over one's own mind."[11] To cultivate this ascetic self-rule, the Editor argues, India needs religion (*dharm*); but, as he goes on to clarify, he is "not thinking of the Hindu, the Mahomedan, or the Zoroastrian religion, but of that religion which underlies all religions."[12] This latter formula could be taken to imply to a transcendent truth of the kind that theosophists, neo-Vedantins, and others had posited as the universal substrate of apparently divergent religious traditions. I would suggest, however, that the better interpretation would return to Gandhi's 1889 reading list: the highest form of religion is renunciation. It is the worldly practice of the self, rather than otherworldly truth.

Such an interpretation is supported by what the Editor says next. He contrasts the "industrious and enterprising" spirit of the "Europeans" with the passivity taught by Hinduism, Islam, Zoroastrianism, Christianity, "and all other religions," which subordinate "worldly pursuits" to "godly pursuits." It seems as though he is about to propose a synthesis of these two apparently contradictory orientations—that is, he seems as though he is about to propose some form of worldly asceticism. But before the Editor can finish his thought, the Reader interrupts him: "You seem to be encouraging religious charlatanism [*pākhaṇḍī*]. Many a cheat has by talking in a similar strain led the people astray."[13] This apparent non sequitur is revealing. At the junction of the "worldly" and the "godly," it seems, stand two competing figures: the self-interested charlatan and the self-abnegating ascetic. Before he can endorse the second of these figures, Gandhi has to dispense with the first.

He does not, however, do this directly. Instead, the text takes yet another abrupt turn. "Humbug there undoubtedly is about all religions," the Editor concedes; but he then insists that the "humbug of civilization" is far worse than any religious humbug. His aim, he says, is to "fight" both kinds of "superstition," the religious and the secular.[14] Here, Gandhi seems to affirm the old Marxist adage that the criticism of religion is the premise of all criticism. To expose the priest is to rehearse a critical procedure that can be reenacted in the exposure of secular ideologies. This move recurs a few chapters later, when the Editor compares "selfish and false religious teachers" to the British, "who usurp the function of the Godhead . . . and hypnotise us into believing them. We, in our ignorance, then fall at their feet."[15] In both these passages, charlatanism, or *pakhandi*, denotes a power structure that is analytically separable from religion per se. Indeed, the second passage could almost be taken as a play on the frontispiece of this book: just as the devotee falls at the feet of his guru, so does India fall at the feet of Britain. To see through priestcraft, then, is to see through the ideologies of empire.

After the 1780s, as Nicholas Dirks has shown, the scandal of the Warren Hastings trial prompted a shift to a new style of imperial rule structured around a moral or civilizing mission.[16] Religion was of key importance to this moral empire, as texts ranging from Charles Grant's "Observations on the State of Society among the Asiatic Subjects of Great Britain" (1792) to William Howitt's *Colonization and Christianity* (1838) suggest: Christianity, they argued, would ensure that Britain ruled India for *its* benefit, sacrificing the interests of the colonizer for the good of the colonized. This shift, Gandhi implies, never happened. In fact, colonialism made extractive rule even more widespread: modern civilization works to make *all* subjects analogous to self-interested priestly charlatans.

For Gandhi, then, the charlatan and the ascetic are antonyms in a fairly direct sense: where the former is a figure for unalloyed self-interest, the latter is a figure for dutiful self-abnegation. The former characterizes "modern civilization" (*ājkālnā sudhāro*). The latter characterizes civilization proper: "Civilization is that mode of conduct which points out to man the path of duty. Performance of duty and observance of morality are convertible terms. To observe morality is to attain mastery over our mind and our passions."[17] Here, Gandhi enumerates several terms that he claims are "convertible": civilization, duty, morality, and self-mastery or self-rule. One more term, I would argue, is implicit in this list. In the English text, Gandhi points out that the "Gujarati equivalent for civilization means 'good conduct.'" This is a slightly misleading translation, as Gandhi well knew.[18] A more usual English rendering of *sudhāro* would be "reform." We have already encountered this word in the epigraph to chapter 4: it was the banner beneath which Karsandas Mulji and other reformers unfurled their Hindu modernity. That Gandhi chose this word to denote his vision of a good society is surely notable; other words, after all, were available (e.g., *sabhyata, sanskriti*).[19] By opting to equate *sudharo* to *civilization*, I would suggest, Gandhi repositioned the legacy of nineteenth-century Hindu reform culture. Where reformers like Mulji had opened themselves to charges of complicity with the British, Gandhi inverted the resonance of "reform." Modern reform is not true reform. True reform is neither British nor Indian. It is, in Suhrud's words, a "movement toward virtue."[20]

While the general thrust of Gandhi's text is to separate this virtue from nationalist rhetoric, he does sometimes present it as specifically Indian. Thus, the Editor asserts that ancient Indian villagers knew "that kings and their swords were inferior to the sword of ethics, and they therefore held the sovereigns of the earth to be inferior to the Rishis and Fakirs."[21] Ethics emerges here as another term that is "convertible" to self-rule, and it does so via the religiously plural figure of the ascetic (both Hindu *rishi* and Islamicate *faqir*). Although probably coincidentally, this passage revisits James Mill's claim from the previous century: priests, not kings, are India's real rulers. At first glance, Gandhi seems simply to restate Mill's argument: religious virtuosi claim power away from princely sovereigns. The difference, however, is critical: in the place of the priest, we find the worldly ascetic. As practitioners of the highest form of religion, these renunciants stand above both temporal sovereigns and priestly sovereigns, with the "sword of ethics" the icon of their rule. This oxymoronic phrase, then, is of central importance. Gandhi was, of course, a pacifist whose guiding principle was nonviolence or *ahimsa*. Like "soul force" (a term Gandhi that introduces later on in *Hind Swaraj*), the "sword of ethics" denotes a principle of worldly action that departs from and undoes the efficacy of "brute force" or violence.

In this passage, we see how the "sword of ethics" provides a means of rethinking sovereignty, as the theoretical basis for the political as such. The sword of the ethical renunciant nullifies the sword of the sovereign king in a manner that recalls Leela Gandhi's argument that swaraj entails a principle of "non-sovereignty." As an ascetic practice, it indicates an "anti-care of the self, aimed at making common cause with both the victims and abettors of unjust sociality."[22] The English *sovereignty* derives from the Latin prefix *super-* ("over" or "above"): it indicates rule from on high. The Sanskrit *svarajyam*, meanwhile, corresponds to Latin *suum regnum* or self-rule (as Shyamji Krishnavarma, who claimed to have coined the term, pointed out in 1907).[23] Self-rule might seem to raise the self to the heights of the sovereign. But, as Gandhi shows, it in fact entails a disavowal of those heights. For him, somewhat paradoxically, the highest form of religion involved reducing the self to nothing—making it less than one and double, both the object and the subject of governance.

Religion without Principle

Perhaps the clearest articulation of this principle of non-sovereignty comes in the closing pages of the *Autobiography*, where Gandhi states his desire "to reduce myself to zero."[24] This reduction of self, he explains, is the essence of nonviolence. In describing how to reduce the self, Gandhi appeals to a "Truth" that, at first glance, seems to indicate precisely the sort of transcendent principle that he elsewhere disavows. Upon closer examination, however, this Truth reveals itself to be chronically inaccessible; it thwarts the subject's desire for transcendence. Gandhi thus asserts both that "there is no God other than Truth" and that "a perfect vision of Truth can only follow a complete realization of Ahimsa" or nonviolence.[25] If all action entails violence, then a complete realization of nonviolence is by definition impossible. So then is "Truth." It is an unattainable object of desire that, precisely because it can never be perfectly realized, necessarily entails an unceasing work upon the imperfect self.

In one of his later lecture courses, Foucault sketched a thumbnail genealogy of Western thought that hinges on the gradual disarticulation of "philosophy" (the search for truth) from "spirituality" ("the search, practice, and experience through which the subject carries out the necessary transformations on himself in order to have access to the truth"). Where the ancient Greeks viewed the imperatives to "know yourself" and to "care for yourself" as inseparable, the moderns separated them. Thus, as Foucault argues, the "history of truth enters its modern period" when philosophy and spirituality are divorced, such that the philosopher or scientist "can recognize the truth . . . solely through his activity of knowing, without anything else being demanded of him and without him having to change or alter his being as subject."[26] Gandhi, we could say, inverts this formula: he gives us a spirituality, or work upon the self, that never arrives at knowledge or Truth. The transcendent here becomes a sort of MacGuffin—ever receding, it drives the continual reform of the self, the immanent particularity of which is nullified in the process. As Akeel Bilgrami has suggested, Gandhi, proposes a religion stripped of propositional "principles and truths."[27] The closing paragraphs of the *Autobiography* gesture to this religion without principle. Here, Gandhi's "experiments in truth" appear as a form of purely immanent practice. They render the self iterable, canceling its particularity by opening it to behavioral quotation; but this quotable behavior never quite results in principles or truths that stand above the domain of practice.

By separating practice from principle, I would argue, Gandhi again echoes Weber's *Protestant Ethic*. As Weber insists, religious doctrine and religious practice or *habitus* have distinct, if overlapping, trajectories. Religion, by Weber's account, establishes "psychological sanctions" that function to establish a particular "attitude" in the religious subject. "Only insofar as these sanctions work, and, above all, in the direction in which they work, which is often very different from the doctrine of the theologians, does such an ethic gain an independent influence on the conduct of life and thus on the economic order." He goes on to complain that many of his critics "completely overlooked" this aspect of his argument, which was, "to speak frankly, the point of the whole essay."[28] Techniques for managing the "conduct of life" (*Lebensführung*) may take shape in religious contexts; but, once developed, they circulate semiautonomously of religious doctrine or principles.

Weber's title thus contains an unresolved tension: his "ethic," as a set of mobile techniques for managing the conduct of life, pulls ineluctably away from the "Protestant" as a doctrinally defined religious community. The title *Hind Swaraj*, I would suggest, contains a parallel tension. The word *Hind* (or *Indian*) works to tether the practice of the self to a particular nation; but self-rule is not so easily contained. It circulates across bodies and continents and bears only a tenuous relationship to markers of national, cultural, or religious community. What matters most about swaraj, as Ritu Birla and Faisal Devji put the matter, are its "itineraries." Gandhi's "techniques of self-rule" were "deeply situated in bodies, intimacies, and localities, and at the same time ever moveable. The call to swaraj was the call to the performative power of iteration, to the power of citation to make new contexts."[29] To become like Gandhi is to cite Gandhi. Such citations, by disarticulating the ethical ideal from the particular man, reveal that "Gandhi" was never self-identical. Behavioral quotation thus reduces the particular Gandhi to zero, rendering his iconic flesh an empty node for the circulation of techniques of self-rule.

Thus do we return to Gandhi's *Gita*—as apt a figure for this circulation of the ethical as one is likely to find. Gandhi's *Gita* was constantly spilling outward from itself—its verses stuck to the wall opposite where he brushed his teeth, for example, so that he could memorize them during his "morning ablutions."[30] As though to distinguish more clearly between fixed Hindu principle and his own itinerant ethics, Gandhi described the *Gita* as a "dictionary of conduct."[31] That is, it is less a statement of unified doctrine than a series of discrete and separable entries, the chief function of which is to regulate practice. For Gandhi, one entry in this dictionary was clearly most important: *karmayoga*, or the "discipline of action." In the Gandhian context, as I will argue, this term can be productively translated into English as "worldly asceticism."

Gandhi, as Simona Sawhney notes, was an "activist reader" of the *Gita*.[32] As he himself explained, even in 1889 he "felt that it was not a historical work, but that, under the guise of physical warfare, it described the duel that perpetually went on in the hearts of mankind.[33] This allegorical reading strategy recalls the theosophists and, in a different way, Keshub Chunder Sen. As Gandhi insisted, "I am not a literalist. . . . Therefore I try to understand the *spirit* of the various scriptures of the world."[34] At the same time, Gandhi's interpretation of the *Gita* also echoes Foucault: it was only insofar as Gandhi could render the battle between the Pandavas and Kauravas as a scene of heautocratic self-combat that he could render the *Gita* a manifesto for nonviolence. As he argued, "instead of teaching the rules of physical warfare, [it] tells us how a perfected man is to be known."[35]

The perfected man who emerges through Gandhi's reading of the *Gita* suggests a resolution to the contradiction between the immanent desire for worldly flourishing and the transcendent desire for release from the world:

While on the one hand it is beyond dispute that all action binds, on the other hand it is equally true that all living beings have to do some work, whether they will or no. Here all activity, whether mental or physical, is to be included in the term action. Then how is one to be free from the bondage of action, even though he may be acting? The manner in which the *Gita* has solved the problem is to my knowledge unique. The *Gita* says: "Do your allotted work but renounce its fruit—be detached and work—have no desire for reward and work.[36]

This "renunciation of the fruits of action," claims Gandhi, is "the centre round which the *Gita* is woven."[37] In a remarkably similar vein, Weber describes Protestants as anxious that their work ethic could be taken to imply a doctrine of salvation by works (rather than by "faith alone").

Martin Luther, says Weber, "could not but suspect the tendency to ascetic self-discipline of leading to salvation by works," and so he downplayed it.[38] John Wesley, meanwhile, attacked the doctrine of works by insisting, with his Puritan forbearers, that good deeds produce no fruits; they are simply the sign of divine grace, "and even this when they are performed solely for the glory of God."[39] Weber's Wesley, like Gandhi's Krishna, asks that the devotee sacrifice the fruits of action to God. Worldly asceticism consists of acting in the world while renouncing worldly objects; action follows from a duty (*svadharm*) or calling (*Beruf*) that becomes the vehicle for self-abnegation.

In *The Song Celestial*, Edwin Arnold translated key *Gita* passages pertaining to *karmayoga* into an English idiom that strongly evokes the Protestant work ethic. Here, the discipline of action centers on the command to "do thine allotted task" because "work is more excellent than idleness," and Krishna instructs Arjuna to "live in action! Labour! Make thine acts/ Thine piety, casting all self aside."[40] Gandhi's early encounter with *The Song Celestial* thus suggests the proximity of his project to the cultural field that Weber had set out to analyze. Gandhi, in effect, follows through on the provocation only implied by Arnold's text: how could one use the *Gita* to imagine a Hindu worldly asceticism? Gandhi's gloss on the *Gita* provides a persuasive response: "renunciation does not mean abandoning the world and retiring into the forest. The spirit of renunciation should rule all the activities of life."[41] Where otherworldly asceticism entails abandoning the world in the search for the transcendent, worldly asceticism entails mediating one's mundane activities through the transcendent such that "there is no line of demarcation between salvation and worldly pursuits."[42]

According to one classic line of thought, *karmayoga* buffers the self against its environs. Thus, in the *Gita*'s own metaphor, the sage or "true Recluse" withdraws his senses just as the "wise tortoise draws its four feet safe under its shield."[43] Here, worldly asceticism becomes a means of pulling back from the world to render the subject as a self-enclosed individual. Gandhi's reading of the *Gita*, I would propose, suggests a different model of the subject. Gandhi, as we have seen, understood the *Gita* allegorically: as a pacifist text, it does not narrate a literal battle, but rather than spiritual struggle that takes place inside the self. Here, Gandhi's reading recalls that of T. Subba Row, whose interpretation of the *Gita* rendered the dialogue between Krishna and Arjuna as a heautocratic encounter between self and self. If the self is doubled in this way, however, it is different in kind from the self-enclosed tortoise. Instead of presenting a model of self-enclosed subjectivity, Gandhi's *Gita* uses asceticism to open the subject into a broader network of tutelary relations.

Hind Swaraj can be read as working through the implications of this model of subjectivity. Like the *Gita*, *Hind Swaraj* is structured as a dialogue: in it, Editor and Reader replace Krishna and Arjuna. Earlier, I identified Gandhi with the Editor. In fact, the text is more complicated than this simple equation would suggest. In his foreword to *Hind Swaraj*, Gandhi partly disavows his own views: "These views are mine, and yet not mine. They are mine because I hope to act according to them. They are almost a part of my being. But, yet, they are not mine, because I lay no claim to originality. They have been formed after reading several books."[44] The Editor is Gandhi's alter ego; he is the ideal self that Gandhi aspires to become. *Hind Swaraj* thus emerges as an experiment in self-rule, a dramatic enactment of the tutelary relation between self and self: Gandhi is both Editor and Reader. This heautocratic relation is not, however, a closed circuit. In stressing his unoriginality, Gandhi insists that the rule he inhabits is not of his own devising. The Editor speaks in a composite voice. He is a site where multiple teachers overlap and intersect. In canceling the self to become the Editor, Gandhi thus seeks to occupy a subject position that is not just unstable, but perhaps ultimately impossible. The Editor is less a subject position than a subject-function that opens the self out toward a wider assemblage of tutelary relations.

By claiming the *Gita* as a seminal text for contemporary political theory, Gandhi was engaging in a quintessential move of anticolonial politics, for which "culture" had long been a key battleground. Where Thomas Macaulay had demoted the entire combined literatures of India and Arabia to a status less than that of a single good British bookshelf, Gandhi insisted on the modernity of Sanskrit—seizing on the *Gita* as a vital thing from the past that could be used to construct a philosophical account of the present.[45] Thus, while Gandhi did at times seem keen to isolate Indian tradition as a counterweight to British tradition, his "India" was always already imbricated with empire. Gandhi's own bookshelf was emphatically eclectic, with his *Gita* oriented as much toward Tolstoy and Thoreau and as toward Tulsidas and Tilak. To be modern (or oriented toward the present) the *Gita* also had to be secular, circulating in the flow of worldly time, rather than set apart as sacred. In contrast with the civilizational gridlines of Weber's comparative method, then, Gandhi foregrounds the lateral slide empire. Like self-rule, the *Gita* comes into itself as it crosses between religions. Or, more precisely, it reveals itself as a dictionary of conduct precisely insofar as it can travel semi-independently of religious doctrine.

Gandhi thus adjusts the question that we ask with Weber. Instead of simply tracing the single line of movement from Protestantism to capitalism, we should append a third movement to the Weberian narrative. After it escaped the monastery, worldly asceticism did not end its career with the self-denying capitalist. It continued to travel, and we should study its ongoing itineraries. After all, as I suggest in the Introduction, it is this ongoing circulation that marks asceticism as worldly or secular.

It has been suggested that the recent "return of religion" is in actuality simply a return of spiritual exercises or "anthropotechnics"—that "religions" themselves are nothing more than "misunderstood spiritual regimens," with the distinction between the "practicing and the untrained" displacing the distinction between believers and unbelievers.[46] Without going quite this far, I would like to suggest that Gandhi makes a similar move. By articulating a religion without principle, he isolated the semi-autonomous circulation of ethics as the practice of the self. This "new moral language for a politics of the self," as Kapila suggests, challenged Victorian liberalism's "cult of the individual."[47] This critique had ambivalent results—as Gandhi's enthusiasm for Mazzini suggests, there is a thin line separating him from his fascist contemporaries. Later in the twentieth century, meanwhile, the politics of self-care would discover an affinity for the managerial style of neoliberalism.[48] Fully cognizant of these longer histories, I have sought in this book to excavate the conceptual contours of one moment in the travels of ascetic self-rule.

If we look to transnational religious reformism in the nineteenth century, we find a means of shifting the story we usually tell about twentieth-century selfhood. In the late nineteenth century, self-rule was an eminently circulatory property. It cut across multiple cultural and religious archives, stringing together the liberal, the Protestant, and the Hindu—to name only three. Rather than fixed cultural "traditions," these three archives of possible selves were storehouses of accreted forces waiting to be remobilized, dictionaries of conduct that could be cited and, through citation, reinvented and remade.

Precisely because the trope of spiritual despotism was important to the dissemination of the liberal norm of the autonomous individual in India, it was also an important means of rethinking that norm. The liberal narrative of emancipation from priestly despotism tended to draw an overly stark distinction between intersubjectivity (surrender to external influence) and intrasubjectivity (individual autonomy). Religious reformers offered an important corrective to this narrative by showing how ascetic self-rule necessarily entails a form of sociality. In the world of the nineteenth-century reform assemblage, the liberal ideal of the self-sufficient or autonomous individual simply failed to find firm footing. In this regard, the reform assemblage remains much more than a historical curiosity. In an era when the liberal ideal of the autonomous subject is still very much with us, it reminds us of how religion has been used to promote a counter-ideal of the inherent sociality of the self.

Notes

INTRODUCTION

1. Keshub Chunder Sen, "God-Vision in the Nineteenth Century," in *Keshub Chunder Sen's Lectures in India*, 2nd ed. (Calcutta: Brahmo Tract Society, 1886), 306. The lecture was delivered on the occasion of the fiftieth anniversary of the Brahmo Samaj at the Town Hall, Calcutta, on Saturday, January 24, 1880.
2. See, for example, Randall Styers, *Making Magic: Religion, Magic, and Science in the Modern World* (Oxford: Oxford University Press, 2004).
3. Max Horkheimer and Theordor W. Adorno, *Dialectic of Enlightenment: Philosophical Fragments*, ed. Gunzelin Schmid Noerr, trans. Edmund Jephcott (Stanford, CA: Stanford University Press, 2002), 90.
4. Keshub Chunder Sen, "Behold the Light of Heaven in India," in *Keshub Chunder Sen's Lectures in India*, 183–84.
5. See, for example, Susan Buck-Morss, *Hegel, Haiti, and Universal History* (Pittsburgh: University of Pittsburgh Press, 2009).
6. Peter Berger, *The Sacred Canopy: Elements of a Sociological Theory of Religion* (New York: Doubleday, 1967), 106.
7. Max Weber, *The Protestant Ethic and the Spirit of Capitalism*, trans. Talcott Parsons (New York: Routledge, 2001 [1920]), 140.
8. Ibid., 40.
9. Ibid., 123–24.
10. James Mill, *Political Writings*, ed. Terence Ball (Cambridge: Cambridge University Press, 1992), 39; Thomas Carlyle, *On Heroes, Hero-Worship and the Heroic in History*, ed. Michael K. Goldberg, Joel Brattin, and Mark Engel (Berkeley: University of California Press, 1993 [1841]), 106.
11. Weber, *The Protestant Ethic*, 49.

12. Ibid., 5, 117.
13. See, for example, Tomoko Masuzawa, *The Invention of World Religions: Or, How European Universalism was Preserved in the Language of Pluralism* (Chicago: University of Chicago Press, 2005).
14. Peter van der Veer, "Smash Temples, Burn Books: Comparing Secularist Projects in India and China," in *Rethinking Secularism*, ed. Craig Calhoun, Mark Juergensmeyer, and Jonathan VanAntwerpen (Oxford: Oxford University Press, 2011), 270–71.
15. Peter van der Veer, *Imperial Encounters: Religion and Modernity in India and Britain* (Princeton, NJ: Princeton University Press, 2001), 11.
16. Bhikhu Parekh, *Colonialism, Tradition, and Reform: An Analysis of Gandhi's Political Discourse* (New Delhi: Sage, 1989), 12.
17. Lloyd I. Rudolph and Susanne Hoeber Rudolph, *The Modernity of Tradition* (Chicago: University of Chicago Press, 1967), 216–40.
18. Richard F. Gombrich and Gananath Obeyesekere, *Buddhism Transformed: Religious Change in Sri Lanka* (Princeton, NJ: Princeton University Press, 1988).
19. Brian Hatcher, *Bourgeois Hinduism, or the Faith of the Modern Vedantists: Rare Discourses from Early Colonial Bengal* (Oxford: Oxford University Press, 2008), 8.
20. See Andrew M. McKinnon, "Elective Affinities of the Protestant Ethic: Weber and the Chemistry of Capitalism," *Sociological Theory* 28, no. 1 (March 2010): 108–26, at p. 121.
21. Quoted in McKinnon, "Elective Affinities," 114. See also Johann Wolfgang von Goethe, *Elective Affinities: A Novel*, trans. David Constantine (Oxford: Oxford University Press, 1994).
22. For further discussion of how the identification of textual affinities can structure postcolonial literary criticism, see J. Daniel Elam, "The 'Arch Priestess of Anarchy' Visits Lahore: Violence, Love, and the Worldliness of Revolutionary Texts," *Postcolonial Studies* 16, no. 2 (2013): 140–54.
23. M. K. Gandhi, *Hind Swaraj and Other Writings*, ed., Anthony J. Parel (Cambridge: Cambridge University Press, 2009), 74.
24. Eric Stokes, *English Utilitarians and India* (Oxford: Clarendon, 1959), 54.
25. For efforts to historicize liberalism more thoroughly see, for example, Karuna Mantena, *Alibis of Empire: Henry Maine and the Ends of Liberal Imperialism* (Princeton, NJ: Princeton University Press, 2010); and Elaine Hadley, *Living Liberalism: Practical Citizenship in Mid-Victorian Britain* (Chicago: University of Chicago Press, 2010).
26. Shruti Kapila, "Self, Spencer and *Swaraj*: Nationalist Thought and Critiques of Liberalism, 1890–1920," *Modern Intellectual History* 4, no. 1 (2007): 109–27.
27. See Ajay Skaria, "Gandhi's Politics: Liberalism and the Question of the Ashram," *South Atlantic Quarterly* 101, no. 4 (Fall 2002): 955–86.
28. My discussion here draws on Uday Mehta, *Liberalism and Empire: A Study in Nineteenth-Century British Liberal Thought* (Chicago: University of Chicago Press, 1999), as well Karl Marx's "On the Jewish Question," in *Early Writings*,

trans. Rodney Livingstone and Gregor Benton (London: Penguin, 1974), 211–42. For a further discussion of the latter, see J. Barton Scott and Brannon Ingram, "What Is a Public? Notes from South Asia," in "Imagining the Public in Modern South Asia," ed. Brannon Ingram, J. Barton Scott, and SherAli Tareen, special issue of *South Asia: The Journal of South Asian Studies* 38, no. 3 (2015): 357–70. For a related discussion of what I call "print asceticism," see J. Barton Scott, "Unsaintly Virtue: Swami Dayananda Saraswati and Modern Hindu Hagiography," *Journal of Hindu Studies* 7, no. 3 (2014): 371–91.

29. M. K. Gandhi, *Autobiography* (New York: Dover, 1983), 454.

30. My argument here draws on Leela Gandhi, "The Pauper's Gift: Postcolonial Theory and the New Democratic Dispensation," *Public Culture* 23, no. 1 (2011): 27–38.

31. Carlyle, *On Heroes*, 106.

32. Charles Taylor, *A Secular Age* (Cambridge, MA: Harvard University Press, 2007).

33. Carlyle, *On Heroes*, 99–100.

34. Michel Foucault, *Security, Territory, Population: Lectures at the Collège de France, 1977–1978* (New York: Picador, 2007), 149–50. Emphasis added.

35. In the late 1970s, Foucault's key interlocutors (Daniel Defert, Pasquale Pasquino, Paul Rabinow, and Paul Veyne) pointed out his work's similarity to Weber's, prompting Foucault to read Weber during the final years of his life. In his 1982–83 lecture series, he went so far to list Weber as part of the lineage of thinkers (including Hegel, Nietzsche, and the Frankfurt School) who had, like him, attempted an "ontology" of the present. The similarity between Weber and Foucault may be due in part to Nietzsche's significant influence on each of them. It might likewise derive from their respective interests in the sixteenth century: as Philip Gorski suggests, it is possible to read Foucault's intellectual trajectory of the 1970s as "a sort of extended circumlocution, in which he repeatedly approached the chronological boundaries of the Reformation from various directions without ever transgressing them." While Foucault's debt to Weber is sometimes acknowledged, the accident of the two theorists having entered Anglophone academia at opposite ends of the disciplinary and ideological spectrum has tended to inhibit a full recognition of their commonalities. See Michel Foucault, *The Government of Self and Others* (New York: St. Martin's, 2010), 21; David Owen, *Maturity and Modernity: Nietzsche, Weber, Foucault, and the Ambivalence of Reason* (London: Routledge, 1994); Arpád Szakolczai, *Max Weber and Michel Foucault: Parallel Life-Works* (London: Routledge, 1998); Philip S. Gorski, *The Disciplinary Revolution: Calvinism and the Rise of the State in Early Modern Europe* (Chicago: University of Chicago Press, 2003), 25.

36. Giorgio Agamben, *The Kingdom and the Glory: For a Theological Genealogy of Economy and Government* (Stanford, CA: Stanford University Press, 2011), 3–5.

37. Michel Foucault, "On the Genealogy of Ethics," in *Ethics: Subjectivity and Truth*, ed. Paul Rabinow (New York: New Press, 1997), 272.

38. Michael Foucault, *The Use of Pleasure*, trans. Robert Hurley (New York: Vintage, 1990), 65-70.

39. Taylor, *A Secular Age*, 146-58; Weber, *Protestant Ethic*, 60.

40. Quoted in Szakolczai, *Max Weber and Michel Foucault*, 72.

41. Louis Dumont, "Renunciation in Indian Religions," in *Religion, Politics and History in India: Collected Papers in Indian Sociology* (Paris: Mouton, 1970), 33-61.

42. See, for instance, Peter van der Veer, "The Foreign Hand: Orientalist Discourse in Sociology and Communalism," in *Orientalism and the Postcolonial Predicament: Perspectives on South Asia*, ed. Carol A. Breckenridge and Peter van der Veer (Philadelphia: University of Pennsylvania Press, 1993), 23-44; Nicholas Dirks, *Castes of Mind: Colonialism and the Making of Modern India* (Princeton, NJ: Princeton University Press, 2001), 55-59.

43. *The Offering of Srimat Maharshi Devendranath Tagore*, 2nd ed. (Madras: Brahmo Orphan Asylum Press, 1898), 35.

44. *Keshub Chunder Sen's Lectures* (Calcutta: Brahmo Tract Society, 1888), 12.

45. Foucault, "On the Genealogy of Ethics," 277.

46. Foucault, *Security, Territory, Population*, 174-79.

47. K. M. Ganguli, trans., *The Mahabharata of Krishna-Dwaipayana Vyasa: Adi Parva* (Calcutta: Bharata Press, 1883), pp. 393-95; J. A. B. van Buitenen, trans., *The Mahabharata: Book 1: The Book of the Beginnings* (Chicago: University of Chicago Press, 1973), pp. 270-72.

48. Ganga Prasād Śarmā, *Mahān Gurū Yogya Śiṣya: Pāvan Paramparā kī Alaukik Prastuti* (Delhi: Manoj, 2007), 62.

49. Leela Gandhi, *Affective Communities: Anticolonial Thought, Fin-de-Siècle Radicalism, and the Politics of Friendship* (Durham, NC: Duke University Press, 2006), 180, 184-85.

50. Justin Champion, *The Pillars of Priestcraft Shaken: The Church of England and Its Enemies, 1660-1730* (Cambridge: Cambridge University Press, 1992).

51. Surely "priestcraft" was translated into other languages as well, but these are beyond the scope of this project. If Rosalind O'Hanlon's translations from Jyotirao Phule are any indication, however, the word "priestcraft" did make it into Marathi, thus suggesting a relationship between Phule's critique of caste and the critique of priestly power that is the topic of this book. See Rosalind O'Hanlon, *Caste, Conflict, and Ideology: Mahatma Jotirao Phule and Low Caste Protest in Nineteenth-Century Western India* (Cambridge: Cambridge University Press, 1985), 154-55.

52. Srinivas Aravamudan, *Guru English: South Asian Religion in a Cosmopolitan Language* (Princeton, NJ: Princeton University Press, 2005).

53. See, for example, Vasudha Dalmia, *The Nationalization of Hindu Tradition: Bhāratendu Hariśchandra and Nineteenth-Century Banaras* (New Delhi: Oxford University Press, 1999); Arjun Appadurai, *Worship and Conflict under Colonial Rule: A South Indian Case* (Cambridge: Cambridge University Press, 1981); C. J. Fuller, *Servants of the Goddess: The Priests of a South Indian Temple* (Cambridge: Cambridge University Press, 1984); Brian A. Hatcher, "What's Become of

the Pandit? Rethinking the History of Sanskrit Scholars in Colonial Bengal," *Modern Asian Studies* 39, no. 3 (2005): 683–723.

54. Kenneth W. Jones, *Socio-Religious Reform Movements in British India*, New Cambridge History of India, vol. 3, no. 1 (Cambridge: Cambridge University Press, 1989).

55. Brian Hatcher "Situating the Swaminarayan Tradition in the Historiography of Modern Hindu Reform," in *Swaminarayan Hinduism in History, Theology, and the Arts*, ed. Raymond B. Williams and Yogi Trivedi (New York: Oxford University Press, forthcoming).

56. For two different versions of the argument that modernity is not a content but a formal operator that orients the subject in time via a performative declaration of rupture with the past, see Simona Sawhney, *The Modernity of Sanskrit* (Minneapolis: University of Minnesota Press, 2008), 17; and Frederic Jameson, *A Singular Modernity: Essay on the Ontology of the Present* (London: Verso, 2002), 34.

57. Partha Chatterjee, *The Nation and Its Fragments: Colonial and Postcolonial Histories* (Princeton, NJ: Princeton University Press, 1993).

58. Yogi Aurvind Ghosh, *Dayananda: The Man and His Work* (Delhi: International Aryan League, n.d.), 11.

59. Indrani Chatterjee, "When 'Sexuality' Floated Free of Histories in South Asia," *Journal of Asian Studies* 71, no. 4 (November 2012): 945–62.

60. Nicholas Dirks, *The Hollow Crown: Ethnohistory of an Indian Kingdom* (Cambridge: Cambridge University Press, 1987). For an effort to excavate the political economy of the early modern ascetic body, see William Pinch, *Warrior Ascetics and Indian Empires* (Cambridge: Cambridge University Press, 2012).

61. See, for instance, Michael C. Behrent "Liberalism without Humanism: Michel Foucault and the Free Market Creed, 1976–1979," *Modern Intellectual History* 6, no. 3 (2009): 539–68.

62. C. A. Bayly, *Recovering Liberties: Indian Thought in the Age of Liberalism and Empire* (Cambridge: Cambridge University Press, 2012).

63. Viewing the "moment of theory" that stretched from the 1970s to the 1990s (and for which Foucault serves as a useful metonym) as continuous with earlier social theory also forces us to reevaluate the claim that we are now in a moment "after theory." At one level, of course, it is clearly true that there have been significant shifts in the culture of the academic humanities since the early 2000s. How these shifts are to be understood is a different question, however—and one related to how we understand the temporality of theory to begin with. If we follow theory's own rhetoric of historic rupture (evident, for example, in its frequent recourse to the prefix "post"), then it becomes relatively easy to dismiss it as a late-century fad. If we take it as continuous with a lineage of thought that stretches from Bentham to Weber and beyond, however, this becomes harder to do: theory is always with us. For further discussion of these themes, see Terry Eagleton, *After Theory* (New York: Basic Books, 2004); Ian Hunter, "The Time of Theory," *Postcolonial Studies* 10, no. 1

(2007): 5–22; and Jane Elliot and Derek Attridge, eds., *Theory after 'Theory'* (New York: Routledge, 2011).

64. Michel Foucault, *Security, Territory, Population*, 153, 191.

65. Mithi Mukherjee, *India in the Shadows of Empire: A Legal and Political History* (New Delhi: Oxford University Press, 2010); A. Azfar Moin, *The Millennial Sovereign: Sacred Kingship and Sainthood in Islam* (New York: Columbia University Press, 2012).

66. See, for example, Shabnum Tejani, *Indian Secularism: A Social and Intellectual History, 1890–1950* (Bloomington: Indiana University Press, 2008).

67. Carol Gluck and Anna Lowenhaupt Tsing, eds, *Words in Motion: Toward a Global Lexicon* (Durham, NC: Duke University Press, 2009).

68. Edward Said, "Traveling Theory," in *The World, the Text, the Critic* (Cambridge, MA: Harvard University Press, 1983), 226–47.

69. See Giorgio Agamben, *Homo Sacer: Sovereign Power and Bare Life*, trans. Daniel Heller-Roazen (Stanford, CA: Stanford University Press, 1998), 22.

70. Johannes Quack, *Disenchanting India: Organized Rationalism and Criticism of Religion in India* (New York: Oxford University Press), 92–93; Osho, *Priests and Politicians: The Mafia of the Soul* (Delhi: Full Circle, 1983).

71. Shruti Kapila, "Self, Spencer and *Swaraj.*"

72. Talal Asad, *Formations of the Secular: Christianity, Islam, Modernity* (Stanford, CA: Stanford University Press, 2003), 16.

CHAPTER ONE

1. Thomas R. Trautmann, *Aryans and British India* (Berkeley: University of California Press, 1997), 117.

2. James Mill, *The History of British India*, vol. 2, 4th ed., ed. Horace Hayman Wilson (London: James Madden, 1840), 187.

3. Charles Grant, "Observations on the State of Society among the Asiatic Subjects of Great Britain, Particularly with Respect to Morals; and on the Means of Improving It—Written Chiefly in the Year 1792" (London: House of Commons, 1813), 46.

4. For arguments against the claim that missionaries were complicit with empire, see Jeffrey Cox, *Imperial Fault Lines: Christianity and Colonial Power in India, 1818–1914* (Stanford, CA: Stanford University Press, 2000); Robert Frykenberg, *Christianity in India: From Beginnings to the Present* (New York: Oxford University Press, 2008).

5. Michael C. Behrent "Liberalism without Humanism: Michel Foucault and the Free Market Creed, 1976–1979," *Modern Intellectual History* 6, no. 3 (2009): 539–68.

6. See, for example, C. A. Bayly, *Recovering Liberties: Indian Thought in the Age of Liberalism and Empire* (Cambridge: Cambridge University Press, 2012).

7. Javed Majeed, *Ungoverned Imaginings: James Mill's* History of British India *and Orientalism* (Oxford: Clarendon, 1992), 8.

8. See, for example, Jonathan I. Israel, *Radical Enlightenment: Philosophy and the Making of Modernity, 1650–1750* (Oxford: Oxford University Press, 2001).

9. Geoffrey Oddie, *Imagined Hinduism: British Protestant Missionary Constructions of Hinduism, 1793–1900* (New Delhi: Sage, 2006), 95. As Andrew Nicholson and others have argued, the consolidation of Hindu dharma as a discrete "religion" seems to have begun in the early modern period, probably in relation to Islam. Despite having coined the neologism "Hinduism," then, the British cannot be said to have "invented" this religious object; instead, colonialism intensified a reification of Hindu tradition that was already underway prior to British rule. My point here is simply that the specter of the crafty priest was important to this intensification. See Andrew Nicholson, *Unifying Hinduism: Philosophy and Identity in Indian Intellectual History* (New York: Columbia University Press, 2010).

10. John Statham, *Indian Recollections* (London: Samuel Bagster, 1832), 101.

11. Alexander Duff, *India and India Missions: Including Sketches of the Gigantic System of Hinduism, Both in Theory and Practice*, 2nd ed. (Edinburgh: John Johnstone, 1840), 63.

12. Samuel Stennett, *The Life of the Rev. William Ward, Late Baptist Missionary in India* (London: J. Haddon, 1825), 146.

13. William Ward, *A View of the History, Literature, and Mythology of the Hindoos, including Minute Description of Their Manners and Customs, and Translations from their Principal Works*, vol. 1 (London: Kingbury, Parbury, and Allen, 1822), xxx, cxv.

14. *Missionary Register* (London: L. B. Seeley, 1822), 175.

15. Statham, *Indian Recollections*, 69.

16. "Notices of Hindoo Superstition and Cupidity," *Missionary Register* (L. B. Seeley, 1832), 525.

17. Thomas Maurice, *Indian Antiquities*, vol. 7 (London: John White, 1800), 801.

18. Perry Anderson, *Lineages of the Absolutist State* (London: NLB, 1974), 462–549; Mia Carter and Barbara Harlow, *Archives of Empire*, vol. 1 (Durham, NC: Duke University Press, 2003), 89–130.

19. Élie Halévy, *The Growth of Philosophic Radicalism*, trans. Mary Morris (London: Faber, 1972 [1928]); William A. Thomas, *The Philosophic Radicals: Nine Studies in Theory and Practice* (Oxford: Clarendon, 1979).

20. Majeed, *Ungoverned Imaginings*, 180–82.

21. Trautmann, *Aryans and British India*, 117.

22. Grant, "Observations," 46.

23. Ibid., 74.

24. Peter Harrison, *"Religion" and the Religions in the English Enlightenment* (Cambridge: Cambridge University Press, 1990).

25. Grant, "Observations," 44.

26. Ibid., 110.

27. Ibid., 44–45.

28. Mill, *History of British India*, vol. 1, pp. 202–3.

29. Ibid., 218–20.
30. Slavoj Zizek, "How the Non-Duped Err," *Qui Parle* 4, no. 1 (1990): 1–20.
31. Mill, *History of British India*, vol. 1, pp. 188, 179.
32. Ibid., 188, 329.
33. Bentham to Rammohun Roy, in John Bowring, ed., *The Works of Jeremy Bentham*, vol. 10 (Edinburgh: William Tait, 1843), 589–92.
34. James E. Crimmins, *Secular Utilitarianism: Social Science and the Critique of Religion in the Thought of Jeremy Bentham* (Oxford: Clarendon, 1990), 17–18.
35. Ibid., 207–9. Bentham's writings on religion have mostly been neglected in the scholarship because of their omission from the first edition of his collected *Works*, which were prepared by his executor John Bowring—a Unitarian who shied away from Bentham's atheism. As Crimmins remarks, it is strange to think that while Bentham was writing an atheist treatise, Bowring was nearby composing Unitarian hymns (ibid., 3–6).
36. Justin Champion, *The Pillars of Priestcraft Shaken: The Church of England and Its Enemies, 1660-1730* (Cambridge: Cambridge University Press, 1992). For greater contextualization of eighteenth-century anticlericalism, which at the popular level often implied a strong respect for sacerdotal authority, see W. M. Jacob, *The Clerical Profession in the Long Eighteenth Century, 1680-1840* (Oxford: Oxford University Press, 2007), 291–92.
37. Philip Beauchamp [Jeremy Bentham], *Analysis of the Influence of Natural Religion on the Temporal Happiness of Mankind* (London: R. Carlile, 1822), 34.
38. Ibid., 126, 116.
39. Ibid., 33.
40. Ibid., 68–70.
41. Ibid., 114.
42. Ibid., 55.
43. Mirin Božovič, "Introduction: An Utterly Dark Spot," in Jeremy Bentham's *The Panopticon Writings* (London: Verso, 1995), 1–27.
44. Bentham, *Panopticon Writings*, 31.
45. Ibid., 42.
46. Crimmins, *Secular Utilitarianism*, 186.
47. James Mill, *Political Writings*, ed. Terence Ball (Cambridge: Cambridge University Press, 1992), 1–42.
48. Compare the discussion in Giorgio Agamben, *The Highest Poverty: Monastic Rules and the Form-of-Life*, trans. Adam Kotsko (Stanford, CA: Stanford University Press, 2013).
49. For a discussion of the modern moral order of mutual benefit, see Charles Taylor, *Modern Social Imaginaries* (Durham, NC: Duke University Press, 2004).
50. Harrison, *"Religion" and the Religions*, 73, 78. See also Frank Manuel, *The Eighteenth Century Confronts the Gods* (Cambridge, MA: Harvard University Press, 1959).
51. Mark Goldie, "Priestcraft and the Birth of Whiggism," in *Political Discourse in*

Early Modern Britain, ed. Nicholas Phillipson and Quentin Skinner (Cambridge: Cambridge University Press, 1993), 217.

52. Crimmins, *Secular Utilitarianism*, 3, 211.
53. See Champion, *Pillars of Priestcraft Shaken*.
54. Alexander Bain, *James Mill: A Biography* (London: Longmans, Green, and Co., 1882), 51-52, 61.
55. Mill, *Political Writings*, 39.
56. Jennifer Pitts, *A Turn to Empire: The Rise of Imperial Liberalism in Britain and France* (Princeton: Princeton University Press, 2005), 127.
57. Mill, *History of British India*, vol. 1, p. 172.
58. Ibid., 175-76.
59. Ibid., 178 (emphasis added).
60. Ibid, 178.
61. Ibid., 179.
62. Ibid., 179-81.
63. Mill, *Political Writings*, 228-29; cf. 50-51.
64. Elaine Hadley, *Living Liberalism: Practical Citizenship in Mid-Victorian Britain* (Chicago: University of Chicago Press, 2010).
65. David Gilmartin, "Towards a Global History of Voting: Sovereignty, the Diffusion of Ideas, and the Enchanted Individual," *Religions* 3, no. 2 (2012): 407-23.
66. Mill, *History of British India*, vol. 1, p. 184.
67. Ibid.
68. Mill, *Political Writings*, 37-39.
69. Champion, *Pillars of Priestcraft*, 25-52.
70. Charles Villers, *An Essay on the Spirit and Influence of the Reformation of Luther*, trans. James Mill (London: C. and R. Baldwin, 1805), ii.
71. Giorgio Agamben, *Homo Sacer: Sovereign Power and Bare Life*, trans. Daniel Heller-Roazen (Stanford, CA: Stanford University Press, 1998), 22.
72. Villers, *Essay on the Spirit and Influence of the Reformation*, 26-30, 4-5.
73. Ibid., 295-96.
74. Ibid., 396. In the French, this is "*Il sort tout à fait de tutelle.*"
75. Ibid., 401.
76. Ibid., 405.
77. Charles Villers, *Essai sur l'ésprit et l'influence de la réformation de Luther*, 2nd ed. (Paris: Henrichs, 1804), iii.
78. Villers, *Essay on the Spirit and Influence of the Reformation*, 288.
79. Ibid., 18-19.
80. Gerhart B. Ladner, *The Idea of Reform: Its Impact on Christian Thought and Action in the Age of the Fathers* (Cambridge, MA: Harvard University Press, 1959).
81. Villers, *Essay on the Spirit and Influence of the Reformation*, 51.
82. D. G. Paz, *Popular Anti-Catholicism in Mid-Victorian England* (Stanford, CA: Stanford University Press, 1992).

83. James Fergusson, *Tree and Serpent Worship, or Illustrations of Mythology and Art in India, from the Topes at Sanchi and Amravati* (London: India Museum, 1868), 65; Sophia Dobson Collet, ed., *Keshub Chunder Sen's English Visit* (London: Strahan & Co, 1871), 495; Monier Monier-Williams, "Indian Religious Thought," *Contemporary Review* (August 1879): 843–61; W. W. Hunter, *The Indian Empire: Its People, History, and Products* (New Delhi: Asian Educational Services, 2005 [London, 1886]), 345; John Murdoch, *The History of Civilization in India: A Sketch, with Suggestions for the Improvement of the Country* (London: Christian Literature Society for India, 1902), 53.

84. See, for example, Richard King, *Orientalism and Religion: Postcolonial Theory, India, and the "Mystic East"* (London: Routledge, 1999), 144–45.

85. Kenneth W. Jones, *Socio-Religious Reform Movements in British India*, New Cambridge History of India 3, no. 1 (Cambridge: Cambridge University Press, 1989); Amartya Sen, *The Argumentative Indian: Writings on Indian History, Culture, and Identity* (London: Allen Lane, 2006).

86. Dipesh Chakrabarty, *Provincializing Europe: Postcolonial Thought and Historical Difference* (Princeton, NJ: Princeton University Press, 2000), 28.

87. Gauri Viswanathan, "Secularism in the Framework of Heterodoxy," *PMLA* 123, no. 2 (2008): 466–76.

88. Chakrabarty, *Provincializing Europe*, 16.

89. *Christian Observer, Conducted by Members of the Established Church for the Year 1834* (London: J. Hatchard and Son, 1834). Within the year, the *Observer's* comparison was quoted elsewhere, and it is likely the origin point for Buchanan's persistent association with the phrase. See Samuel Charles Wilks, *Memoirs of the Life, Writings, and Correspondence of Sir William Jones, with the Life of Lord Teignmouth, Selections from Sir William Jones's Works, and Occasional Notes*, vol. 1 (London: John W. Parker, 1835), 49.

90. Duff, *India and India Missions*, 351–53. Similarly, as the *Calcutta Christian Observer* reflected in 1833, it was "cheering to reflect that the beautiful groves on the banks of the Indian rivers may one day be noted, not as the ancient abode of some dumb idol, but as the spot where an Indian Luther or John Knox commenced his labours." Review of Rev. J. Hay and Rev. H. Belfrage, *A Memoir of the Reverend Alexander Waugh*, in *Calcutta Christian Observer* (January 1833), 30.

91. Tomoko Masuzawa, *The Invention of World Religions, or How European Universalism Was Preserved in the Language of Pluralism* (Chicago: University of Chicago Press, 2005), 11.

92. Charles Friedrich Neumann, *Catechism of the Shamans; or the Laws and Regulations of the Priesthood of Buddha in China* (London: Oriental Translation Fund, 1831), xxvi.

93. For the rejection of the Buddha as Luther, see *Asiatic Journal and Monthly Register for British and Foreign India, China, and Australia*, vol. 6, n.s., September–December 1831 (London: Parbury, Allen, and Co, 1831), 262.

94. Philip Almond, *The British Discovery of Buddhism* (Cambridge: Cambridge University Press, 1988), 34–35, 69–74.

95. For Coleridge, see Daniel E. White, *From Little London to Little Bengal: Religion, Print, and Modernity in Early British India, 1793–1835* (Baltimore: Johns Hopkins University Press, 2013), 111. For a contemporary comparison of Rammohun to Luther, see *The Asiatic Journal and Monthly Register for British India and Its Dependents*, vol. 6 (June–December 1818), 177.

96. See, for example, La Belle assemblée: *Bell's Court and Fashionable Magazine* (November 1820); *Calcutta Journal of Politics and General Literature* (February 22, 1823); Lant Carpenter, *A Review of the Labours, Opinions, and Character of Rajah Rammohun Roy: In a Discourse on Occasion of his Death, Delivered in Lewin's Mead Chapel, Bristol; A Series of Illustrative Extracts from His Writings; and a Biographical Memoir, to Which Is Subjoined an Examination of Some Derogatory Statements in the Asiatic Journal* (London: Rowland Hunter, 1833), 21. At least one article referred to Rammohun, however confusingly, as a "Hindoo Christian Reformer": *London Morning Chronicle* (January 26, 1824). For obituary coverage concerned with the conversion question, see "Rammohun Roy," *Bristol Mercury*, September 14, 1833; *Bury & Norwich Post*, October 2, 1833; "Rajah Rammohun Roy," *Bristol Mercury*, October 5, 1833.

97. Mary Carpenter, *The Last Days in England of the Rajah Rammohun Roy* (London: Trübner & Co., 1866), 52–53.

98. George Smith, *The Life of Alexander Duff*, vol. 1 (London: Hodder and Stoughton, 1879), 112–13.

99. *The Standard* (London), Thursday, 14 April 1870.

100. Henry Steel Olcott, "An Address to the Arya Samaj of Meerut, Delivered May 5th 1879, on the Occasion of a Public Welcome to a Committee of the Theosophical Society, by the Revered Swami Daya Nand [*sic*] Saraswati and the Meerut Samaj" (Roorkee, India: Thomason Civil Engineering College Press, 1879), 3–4.

101. Masuzawa, *Invention of World Religions*.

102. To my mind, the best discussion of the Protestantization model remains Richard Gombrich and Gananath Obeyesekere, *Buddhism Transformed: Religious Change in Sri Lanka* (Princeton, NJ: Princeton University Press, 1990). Not incidentally, their account is heavily Weberian.

103. The *Oxford English Dictionary*'s first attested use of the verb is from 1829, with that illustration and those that follow from the 1830s pertaining to the question of "Protestantising Ireland." It suggests that the English verb derives from the French *protestantiser*, which itself dates to 1827. The *OED* does not include any definition of the term that could make sense of the statement "Dayanand protestantized Hinduism."

104. Quoted in Stokes, *English Utilitarians and India*, 32.

105. John Stuart Mill, *On Liberty, with The Subjection of Women and Chapters on Socialism*, ed. Stefan Collini (Cambridge: Cambridge University Press, 1989), 13.

106. Uday Singh Mehta, *Liberalism and Empire: A Study in Nineteenth-Century British Liberal Thought* (Chicago: University of Chicago Press, 1999), 102.
107. Pitts, *A Turn to Empire*. For further efforts to complicate the claim that liberalism was complicit with empire, see Karuna Mantena, *Alibis of Empire: Henry Maine and the Ends of Liberal Imperialism* (Princeton, NJ: Princeton University Press, 2010), and Andrew Sartori, *Liberalism in Empire: An Alternative History* (Berkeley: University of California Press, 2014).
108. Susan Mendus, "Liberty and Autonomy," *Proceedings of the Aristotelian Society*, n.s. 87 (1986-87): 107-20, at p.112.
109. Amanda Anderson, *The Way We Argue Now: A Study in the Cultures of Theory* (Princeton, NJ: Princeton University Press 2005), 17.
110. Hadley, *Living Liberalism*, 20, 11.
111. Mehta, *Liberalism and Empire*, 191.
112. Mill, *History of British India*, vol. 5, p. 201.
113. Majeed, *Ungoverned Imaginings*, 142.
114. Mill, *History of British India*, vol. 1, p. xxi.
115. Ibid., 331.
116. Sara Ahmed, *The Promise of Happiness* (Durham, NC: Duke University Press, 2010), 126.

1. William Howitt, *A Popular History of Priestcraft in All Ages and Nations* (London: Effingham Wilson, 1833), 14.
2. Carl Ray Woodring, *Victorian Samplers: William and Mary Howitt* (Lawrence: University of Kansas Press, 1952), 9.
3. Woodring, *Victorian Samplers*. Other biographical accounts include Anna Mary Howitt Watts, *The Pioneers of the Spiritual Reformation: Biographical Sketches* (London: Psychological Press Association, 1883); Margaret Howitt, ed., *Mary Howitt: An Autobiography*, 2 vols. (London: W. Isbister, 1889); and Amice Lee, *Laurels and Rosemary: The Life of William and Mary Howitt* (London: Oxford University Press, 1955).
4. Henry David Thoreau, "Life without Principle," in *The Portable Thoreau*, ed. Jeffrey S. Cramer (New York: Penguin, 2012), 600; Karl Marx, *Capital*, vol. 1 (New York: Penguin, 1976), 916; Emma Hardinge, *Modern American Spiritualism* (New Hyde Park, NY: University Books, 1970 [1870]), 12.
5. They thus anticipate the fin-de-siècle radicalism analyzed by Leela Gandhi in *Affective Communities: Anticolonial Thought, Fin-de-Siècle Radicalism, and the Politics of Friendship* (Durham, NC: Duke University Press, 2006), 177.
6. William Howitt, "George Fox and His Contemporaries," *The Aurora Borealis: A Literary Annual* (Newcastle upon Tyne, UK: Charles Empson, 1833), 1-20; William Howitt, "George Fox and His First Disciples: Or, the Society of Friends as It Was, and as It Is," *Tait's Edinburgh Magazine*, October 1834: 577-85. This second version was then reprinted as *George Fox and his First Disciples; or, the*

Society of Friends as It Was, and as It Is (Philadelphia: Merrihew and Gunn, 1837) and consolidated in 1839 for the article "Quakers" in the Seventh Edition of the *Encyclopedia Britannica* (further expanded for the Eighth Edition, it was replaced in the Ninth). See Woodring, *Victorian Samplers*, 42.

7. Howitt, "George Fox and His First Disciples," 582.

8. Watts, *Pioneers of the Spiritual Reformation*, 163.

9. Howitt, *Popular History of Priestcraft*, 13–14.

10. Ibid.

11. Ibid., 48, 124, 196. The text opened Howitt to accusations of having become a Deist. In an indignant reply to the accusation by Archdeacon Wilkins, Howitt insists that to question his religious orientation would be to "charge the whole Society of Friends with Deism." There might be more truth than Howitt realizes in what he presents as an absurd claim: Quakers are not Deists, but Howitt's text foregrounds the extent to which the two groups emerged from a shared seventeenth-century culture of anticlericalism. See William Howitt, *Vindication of his 'History of Priestcraft,' Against the Attack of Archdeacon Wilkins*, 2nd ed. (London: Effingham Wilson, 1833); reprinted as "William Howitt's Vindication," in *A Popular History of Priestcraft in All Ages and Nations*, 3rd ed., revised and enlarged (London: Effingham Wilson, 1834), 407–27.

12. Howitt, *Popular History of Priestcraft*, 1st ed., 74–75.

13. Ibid., 119.

14. Ibid., 106–7.

15. "Advertisement to the Seventh Edition," in William Howitt, *A Popular History of Priestcraft in All Ages and Nations*, 8th ed. (London: Effingham Wilson, 1847), i.

16. Howitt, *Popular History of Priestcraft*, 1st ed., 13–15.

17. Ibid., 42.

18. Michel Foucault, *Security, Territory, Population: Lectures at the Collège de France, 1977–78*, ed. Michel Sennelart, trans. Graham Burchell (New York: Palgrave, 2007), 98–99.

19. Howitt, *Popular History of Priestcraft*, 1st ed, i.

20. Ibid., 196–97.

21. Howitt, "George Fox and His First Disciples," 578.

22. Ibid., 581.

23. Gauri Viswanathan, *Outside the Fold: Conversion, Modernity, and Belief* (Princeton, NJ: Princeton University Press, 1998), 4–5.

24. William Howitt, *A Popular History of Priestcraft in All Ages and Nations: Eighth Edition, with Large Additions* (London: Effingham Wilson, 1846), 317.

25. Mary Howitt, letter of December 19, 1832; in *Autobiography*, vol. 1, p. 231.

26. Woodring, Victorian Samplers, 48.

27. Mary Howitt, letter of 15 June 1833; in *Autobiography*, vol. 1, pp. 233–34.

28. In May 1834, an abridgment of the book was published without Howitt's permission, on the grounds that a much shorter and cheaper version would

make the work available to a far wider audience (at ninety pages, it is much shorter indeed). Howitt was incensed at the publishers and accused them of copyright violation. They cited the law to argue that a "fair and bona fide abridgment of any book is considered . . . as a new work." "Vindication of an Abridgement," from the *True Sun*, p. 4. Published as a preface to *A Popular History of Priestcraft; Abridged from William Howitt's Work* (London: John Cleave, 1834). See also William Carpenter, *A Reply to William Howitt's Preface to the Abridged History of Priestcraft* (London: John Cleave, 1834). Howitt's complaints about copyright law are discussed in Woodring, *Victorian Samplers*, 30–31.

29. Howitt includes snippets from the reviews at the very back of the fifth edition. William Howitt, *A Popular History of Priestcraft in All Ages and Nations*, 5th ed. (London: Effingham Wilson, 1834), 429.

30. Lee, *Laurels and Rosemary*, 86–87. Howitt's vivid description of this event can be found in Mary Howitt, *Autobiography*, vol. 1, pp. 226–28.

31. Mary Howitt, letter of January 1834, *Autobiography*, vol. 1, p. 237.

32. Mary Howitt, letter of 29 December 1835, *Autobiography*, vol. 1, p. 247.

33. William Howitt, letter of 9 February 1836, in Mary Howitt, *Autobiography*, vol. 1, p. 248.

34. Mary Howitt, letter of January 1834; in *Autobiography*, vol. 1, pp. 237–39.

35. Howitt's Nottingham radicals were not alone in challenging the established church at this time. A variety of factors, including the successful revolution of Protestant New England in the 1770s and the lifting of religious disabilities in the late 1820s, made it seem for a short moment in the early 1830s that disestablishment might be possible. The resulting challenge to the Anglican Church contributed to the substantial institutional reforms of the late 1830s. See W. M. Jacob, *The Clerical Profession in the Long Eighteenth Century, 1680–1840* (Oxford: Oxford University Press, 2007), 20–23.

36. Wendy Brown, *Regulating Aversion: Tolerance in the Age of Identity and Empire* (Princeton, NJ: Princeton University Press, 2006).

37. Viswanathan, *Outside the Fold*; Thomas Babington Macaulay, "Minute on Indian Education," in Barbara Harlow and Mia Carter, eds., *Archives of Empire: Volume 1: From the East India Company to the Suez Canal* (Durham, NC: Duke University Press, 2003), 237.

38. John Locke, *A Letter Concerning Toleration* (London: Huddersfield, 1796), 63, 65.

39. Brown, *Regulating Aversion*, 32.

40. Elizabeth A. Pritchard, *Religion in Public: Locke's Political Theology* (Stanford, CA: Stanford University Press, 2013), 16.

41. John Dunn, *The Political Thought of John Locke: An Historical Account of the Argument of the "Two Treatises of Government"* (Cambridge: Cambridge University Press, 1969), 259.

42. "Politics Inseparable from Christianity," afterword to seventh edition of *Popular History of Priestcraft*, 1847, p. 349.

43. Romans 13:1. Quoted in Henry Tuke, *The Principles of Religion, as Professed by the Society of Christians, Usually Called Quakers; Written for the Instruction of their Youth, and for the Information of Strangers*, 9th ed. (York: W. Alexander, 1827).

44. Thomas Dumm, "Friendly Persuasion: Quakers, Liberal Toleration, and the Birth of the Prison," *Political Theory* 13, no. 3 (August 1985): 387–407.

45. Howitt, "Politics Inseparable from Christianity," 50.

46. Howitt, "George Fox and His First Disciples," 582.

47. Howitt, "George Fox and His Contemporaries," 8–10.

48. See especially Rufus Jones, *The Later Periods of Quakerism*, vol. 1 (London: Macmillan, 1921); Elizabeth Isichei, *Victorian Quakers* (London: Oxford University Press, 1970); and Pink Dandelion, *An Introduction to Quakerism* (Cambridge: Cambridge University Press, 2007).

49. Isichei, *Victorian Quakers*, 44.

50. Woodring, *Victorian Samplers*, 44–45.

51. Thomas Clarkson, *A Portraiture of Quakerism, As Taken from a View of the Moral Education, Discipline, Peculiar Customs, Religious Principles, Political and Civil Oeconomy, and Character of the Society of Friends*, vol. 2 (London: Longman, Hurst, Rees, and Orme, 1806), 2, 113–17.

52. Gerhart B. Ladner, *The Idea of Reform: Its Impact on Christian Thought and Action in the Age of the Fathers* (Cambridge, MA: Harvard University Press, 1959).

53. Clarkson, *A Portraiture of Quakerism*, vol. 2, p. 151.

54. Ibid., 192.

55. Clarkson, *A Portraiture of Quakerism*, vol. 1, pp. 181–82.

56. Ibid., 191.

57. Ibid., 197.

58. Dumm, "Friendly Persuasion," 402.

59. Clarkson, *A Portraiture of Quakerism*, vol. 1, p. 188.

60. Ibid., 6–7.

61. Howitt, "George Fox and His First Disciples," 585.

62. Howitt, *Popular History of Priestcraft*, 1st ed., 101.

63. Howitt, "Politics Inseparable from Christianity," 349.

64. Howitt, "George Fox and His First Disciples," 583.

65. William Howitt, *Visits to Remarkable Places: Old Halls, Battle Fields, and Scenes Illustrative of Striking Passages in English History and Poetry* (London: Longman, 1840), 347.

66. William Howitt, *Homes and Haunts of the Most Eminent British Poets*, vol. 2 (London: Richard Bentley, 1847), 273–84.

67. Mary Howitt, letter of 6 March 1836, *Autobiography*, vol. 1, p. 250.

68. In fact, Howitt wrote a series of literary travel guides that invited city dwellers to tour the countryside so that they could have greater access to poetic inspiration. This attempt at a "democratic extension of transcendental experience" eventually led to a conflict with Wordsworth. See Donald Ulin,

"Seeing the Country: Tourism and Ideology in William Howitt's *Rural Life of England*," *Victorians Institute Journal* 30 (2002): 41–64; and Donald Ulin, "Reforming Wordsworth: William Howitt and the 'great Republican Conservative,'" *European Romantic Review* 20, no. 3 (2009): 209–325.

69. Quoted in Woodring, *Victorian Samplers*, 190.
70. Joseph Ennemoser, *The History of Magic, to which is Added an Appendix of the Most Remarkable and Best Authenticated Stories of Apparitions, Dreams, Second Sight, Somnambulism, Predictions, Divination, Witchcraft, Vampires, Fairies, Table-Turning, and Spirit-Rapping*, trans. William Howitt, ed. Mary Howitt, vol. 2 (London: Henry G. Bohn, 1854), 416.
71. Alfred William Howitt, *The Native Tribes of South-East Australia* (London: Macmillan, 1904).
72. Hardinge, *Modern American Spiritualism*, 12.
73. Ann Taves, *Fits, Trances, and Visions: Experiencing Religion and Explaining Experience from Wesley to James* (Princeton, NJ: Princeton University Press, 1999), 190–93.
74. William Howitt, *The History of the Supernatural in All Ages and Nations, and in All Churches, Christian and Pagan: Demonstrating a Universal Faith*, vol. 2 (London: Longman, 1863), 67.
75. Letter of October 1864 to Mrs. Harrison, Ht 2/2, Papers of William and Mary Howitt, Manuscripts and Special Collections, University of Nottingham.
76. [William Howitt], *The Religion of Rome Described by a Roman*, trans. William Howitt (London: Balliere, Tindall, and Cox, 1873), iii–v, xi–xii.
77. Quoted Woodring, *Victorian Samplers*, 214.
78. Howitt, *History of the Supernatural*, 308.
79. William Howitt, *Colonization and Christianity: A Popular History of the Treatment of the Natives by the Europeans in All their Colonies* (London: Longman, 1838), i.
80. Ibid., 507.
81. [William Howitt], "The Present Condition of British India," *Eclectic Review* (March 1840): 304–26. The article is published anonymously; Woodring identifies the author as Howitt.
82. See William Howitt, *A Serious Address to the Members of the Anti-Slavery Society on Its Present Position and Prospects, for and in Behalf of the Advocates of the Free Labour of British India, as the Grand Means for the Extinction of Slavery* (London: William Henry Cox, 1843).
83. *British India: Proceedings at a Public Meeting in Darlington. Held in the Friends' Meeting House, on Thursday Evening, February 14th, 1839* (Darlington: J. Wilson, 1839), 23–25.
84. *Report of the British India Society, Read at the First Annual Meeting, Held at Freemasons' Hall, Monday, July 6th 1840* (London: British India Society, 1840), 3.
85. Howitt, *A Serious Address to the Members of the Anti-Slavery Society*.
86. William Howitt, "A Copious Historical Sketch of the Progress of Parliamen-

tary Reform, from the Attempt to Repeal the Septennial Act in 1734 to the Passing of the Reform Bill in 1832," in John Saunders, *Portraits and Memoirs of Eminent Living Political Reformers* (London, 1840), 213–15.

CHAPTER THREE

1. Surnames were not customary in Bengal in the early nineteenth century; Rammohun's "Roy" should be understood more as a hereditary honorific (*rāī*) than as a family name. In keeping with cultural custom and scholarly convention, I refer to him in this chapter as "Rammohun" (his own Anglicized spelling)—despite the awkward aparallelism with "Estlin" and other characters. See D. H. Killingley, *The Only True God: Works on Religion by Rammohun Roy* (Newcastle upon Tyne, UK: Grevatt & Grevatt, 1982).
2. Mary Carpenter identifies Miss Hare as David Hare's daughter, but David Hare's biographer points out that he was never married and had no children; Miss Hare must be his niece. See Peary Chand Mitra, *Biographical Sketch of David Hare* (Calcutta: W. Newman & Co., 1877), 2.
3. Mary Carpenter, *The Last Days in England of the Rajah Rammohun Roy* (London: Trübner & Co., 1866), 144–46.
4. Lynn Zastoupil, *Rammohun Roy and the Making of Victorian Britain* (New York: Palgrave Macmillan, 2010), 1–6, 47.
5. Rammohun Roy, *The Precepts of Jesus, The Guide to Peace and Happiness, Extracted from the Books of the New Testament, Ascribed to the Four Evangelists, to Which are Added, the First and Second Appeal to the Christian Public in Reply to the Observations of Dr. Marshman of Serampore* (London: Unitarian Society, 1823), 130.
6. Lant Carpenter, *A Review of the Labours, Opinions, and Character of Rajah Rammohun Roy: In a Discourse on Occasion of His Death, Delivered in Lewin's Mead Chapel, Bristol; A Series of Illustrative Extracts from His Writings; and a Biographical Memoir, to Which Is Subjoined an Examination of Some Derogatory Statements in the Asiatic Journal* (London: Rowland Hunter, 1833), 46.
7. Brian A. Hatcher, *Eclecticism and Modern Hindu Discourse* (New York: Oxford University Press, 1999).
8. Keshub Chunder Sen, *Lectures in India*, 2nd ed. (Calcutta: Brahmo Tract Society, 1886), 25.
9. See, for example, Brian A. Hatcher, *Bourgeois Hinduism, or Faith of the Modern Vedantists: Rare Discourses from Early Colonial Bengal* (New York: Oxford University Press, 2007).
10. Andrew M. McKinnon, "Elective Affinities of the Protestant Ethic: Weber and the Chemistry of Capitalism," *Sociological Theory* 28, no. 1 (March 2010): 108–26.
11. *Keshub Chunder Sen's Lectures* (Calcutta: Brahmo Tract Society, 1888), 143.
12. Much of Keshub's public life transpired in English. His friend and biographer Protop Mozoomdar described him as "out of element" in Bengali, noting

how crowds never warmed to the stilted language of his Bengali lectures. See P. C. Mozoomdar, *The Life and Teachings of Keshub Chunder Sen*, 3rd ed. (Calcutta: Nababidhan Trust, 1931), 97–98.

13. Simon During, *Modern Enchantments: The Cultural Power of Secular Magic* (Cambridge, MA: Harvard University Press, 2002), 66–69.

14. Kathryn Gleadle, *The Early Feminists: Radical Unitarians and the Emergence of the Women's Rights Movement, 1831–51* (New York: St. Martin's, 1995).

15. Gilles Deleuze and Félix Guattari, *A Thousand Plateaus: Capitalism and Schizophrenia*, trans. Brian Massumi (Minneapolis: University of Minnesota Press, 1987).

16. Homi Bhabha, *The Location of Culture* (London: Routledge, 1994), 162–63.

17. Babu Protap Chunder Mozoomdar, *Will the Brahmo Samaj Last? The Substance of an Extempore Lecture Delivered at the Fiftieth Anniversary of the Brahmo Samaj* (Calcutta: Indian Mirror Press, 1880), 6.

18. Mozoomdar, *Will the Brahmo Samaj Last*, 7–8.

19. Gerhart B. Ladner, *The Idea of Reform: Its Impact on Christian Thought and Action in the Age of the Fathers* (Cambridge, MA: Harvard University Press, 1959).

20. *Keshub Chunder Sen's Lectures*, 6–7.

21. Joanna Innes, "'Reform' in English Public Life: The Fortunes of a Word," in *Rethinking the Age of Reform, 1780–1850*, ed. Arthur Burns and Joanna Innes (Cambridge, UK: Cambridge University Press, 2003), 76.

22. Brian Harrison, "A Genealogy of Reform in Modern Britain," in *Anti-Slavery, Religion, and Reform: Essays in Memory of Roger Anstey*, ed. Christine Bolt and Seymour Drescher (Hamden, CT: Dawson-Archon, 1980), 119–20.

23. Arthur Burns and Joanna Innes, "Introduction" in Burns and Innes, eds., *Rethinking the Age of Reform*, 63.

24. Charles Grant, *Observations on the State of Society among the Asiatic Subjects of Great Britain, Particularly with Respect to Morals; and on the Means of Improving It. Written Chiefly in the Year 1792* (London: House of Commons Sessions Papers, 1813); Nicholas Dirks, *The Scandal of Empire: India and the Creation of Imperial Britain* (Cambridge, MA: Belknap Press of Harvard University Press, 2008).

25. Eric Stokes, *The English Utilitarians and India* (Oxford: Oxford University Press, 1959).

26. Harrison, "Genealogy of Reform," 122.

27. Ram Chandra Bose, *Brahmoism; or, History of Reformed Hinduism from Its Origin in 1830, under Rajah Mohun [sic] Roy, to the Present Time, with a Particular Account of Babu Keshub Chunder Sen's Connection with the Movement* (New York: Funk & Wagnalls, 1884), 7; B. N. Motiwala, *Karsondas Mulji: A Biographical Study* (Bombay: Karsondas Mulji Centenary Celebration Committee, 1935), 63.

28. *Keshub Chunder Sen's Lectures*, 123–26.

29. Mozoomdar, *Life and Teachings*, 139–40.

30. *Keshub Chunder Sen in England*, vol. 1 (Calcutta: Brahmo Tract Society, 1881), 110.

31. Ibid., vol. 2, p. 102.
32. John Zavos, *The Emergence of Hindu Nationalism in India* (New Delhi: Oxford University Press, 2000); Gauri Viswanathan, "The Ordinary Business of Occultism," *Critical Inquiry* 27, no. 1 (2000): 1–20.
33. Mozoomdar, *Life and Teachings*, 68.
34. *Keshub Chunder Sen's Lectures*, 127.
35. *Report of a Special Meeting at the New Town Hall, Shoreditch, of the East Central Temperance Association, on May 29, 1870, with the Speech in Full of the Baboo Keshub Chunder Sen of Calcutta. John Robert Taylor, Esq., The President, in the Chair* (London: Heywood & Co., [1870]), 5–6.
36. Ibid., 7.
37. Ibid., 9–12.
38. I am, of course, thinking here of M. K. Gandhi's claim that India wants the "tiger's nature" without the tiger, in M. K. Gandhi, *Hind Swaraj and Other Writings*, ed. Anthony Parel (Cambridge: Cambridge University Press, 2009), 29.
39. I borrow this last phrase from Molly McGarry, *Ghosts of Futures Past: Spiritualism and the Cultural Politics of Nineteenth Century America* (Berkeley: University of California Press, 2008).
40. See, for example, Lata Mani, *Contentious Traditions: The Debate on Sati in Colonial India* (Berkeley: University of California Press, 1998).
41. Rammohun Roy, *The English Works of Raja Rammohun Roy*, ed. Jogendra Chunder Ghose, vol. 1 (Calcutta: Oriental Press, 1885), 3–4.
42. Ibid., 23–24, 79–83.
43. Ibid., vol. 2, p. 167.
44. *The Bombay Saturday Review of Politics, Literature, and Commerce*, vol. 2: October 5, 1861-March 29, 1862 (Bombay: Exchange Press, 1862), 3.
45. *Keshub Chunder Sen's Essays: Theological and Ethical*, 2nd ed., vol. 2 (Calcutta: Brahmo Tract Society, 1892), 18–19.
46. Mozoomdar, *Life and Teachings*, 98.
47. Keshub Chunder Sen, *An Appeal to Young India* (London: Christian Literature Society, 1897), 1.
48. Ibid., 4.
49. Ibid., 4, emphasis added.
50. Ibid., 6–7.
51. Ibid., 9.
52. Ibid., 12.
53. S.C., *The Indian Prophet, or A Review of Babu K.C. Sen's Lecture, Entitled 'Am I an Inspired Prophet' Being a Lecture Delivered at the E. B. Theatre Hall, Dacca, Feb. 8th, 1879* (Dacca: New Press, 1879), 2, 35.
54. *Brahmic Advice, Caution and Help, by an Old Brahmo* (Allahabad: Carbery Brothers, 1869), 6–7.
55. For descriptions of these groups, see Mozoomdar, *Life and Teachings*.
56. Keshub, *Lectures in India*, 53–56.

57. "The Spirit Christ," *Keshub Chunder Sen's Prayers: Part 1* (Calcutta: Brahmo Tract Society, 1884), 20–21.
58. Keshub, *Lectures in Inda*, 292.
59. "The Destiny of Human Life," *Keshub Chunder Sen's Lectures*, 2–29.
60. Keshub, *Lectures in India*, 165–67.
61. Ibid., 168.
62. Ibid., 180–81, emphasis added.
63. Ibid., 182–83.
64. Ibid., 283, 301; emphasis added.
65. Ibid., 300.
66. Ibid., 302.
67. Ibid., 300.
68. Ibid., 287.
69. Ibid., 290.
70. Ibid., 300.
71. W. R. Blackett, *Who Is Christ? Can India Rest Satisfied with Babu Keshub C. Sen's Answer to This Question?* (Calcutta: Advertiser Press, 1879), 5–6.
72. Aamir Mufti, *Enlightenment in the Colony: The Jewish Question and the Crisis of Postcolonial Culture* (Princeton, NJ: Princeton University Press, 2007); Robert Yelle, "The Hindu Moses: Christian Polemics against Jewish Ritual and the Secularization of Hindu Law under Colonialism," *History of Religions* 49, no. 2 (2009): 141–71.
73. Blackett, *Who Is Christ?*, 20–21.
74. Ibid., 13.
75. Ibid., 1–7.
76. Keshub, *Lectures in India*, 29.
77. Ibid., 351.
78. Ibid., 354.
79. Ibid., 365–66.
80. Ibid., 366–67.
81. Ibid., 367, emphasis added.
82. Ibid., 369.
83. Ibid., 351.
84. Ibid., 351.
85. Ibid., 345.
86. Bose, *Brahmoism*, 22–23.
87. Keshub, *Lectures in India*, 362–63.
88. Ibid., 293, 379.
89. Ibid., 381.
90. Nirad C. Chaudhuri, *The Autobiography of an Unknown Indian* (Reading, MA: Addison-Wesley, 1989 [1951]), 195, 217.
91. David Kopf, *The Brahmo Samaj and the Shaping of the Modern Indian Mind* (Princeton, NJ: Princeton University Press, 1979), 107–8, 110.

92. Mozoomdar, *Will the Brahmo Samaj Last*, 1–3.
93. Kopf, *Brahmo Samaj*, 14; Bruce C. Robertson, *Raja Rammohan Ray: The Father of Modern India* (Delhi: Oxford University Press, 1995).
94. See Rajat K. Ray, "Introduction," in V. C. Joshi, ed., *Rammohun Roy and the Process of Modernization in India* (Delhi: Vikas, 1975).
95. Dermot Killingly, *Rammohun Roy in Hindu and Christian Traditions: The Teape Lectures, 1990* (Newcastle upon Tyne, UK: Grevatt and Grevatt, 1993).
96. Gauri Viswanathan, *Outside the Fold: Conversion, Modernity, and Belief* (Princeton, NJ: Princeton University Press, 1998).
97. Keshub Chunder Sen, *The New Samhita, or, Sacred Laws of the Aryans of the New Dispensation* (Calcutta: Brahmo Tract Society, 1884), 18; *The Offering of Srimat Maharshi Devendranath Tagore*, 2nd ed. (Madras: Brahmo Orphan Asylum Press, 1898), 12–13.
98. Hatcher, *Bourgeois Hinduism*.
99. *Offering of Srimat Maharshi Devendranath Tagore*, 35, 48–49.
100. Ibid., 41.
101. Keshub Chunder Sen, *The Theist's Prayer Book* (London: Philip Green, 1904).
102. Keshub, *New Samhita*, 7–16.
103. Bruce Carlisle Robertson, ed., *The Essential Writings of Raja Rammohan Ray* (New York: Oxford University Press, 1999), xxviii–xxx.
104. Robertson, *Raja Rammohan Ray*, 171.
105. Babu Raj Narain Bose, *Brahmo Catechism*, trans. Babu Eshan Chunder Bose (Allahabad: Sukh Sambad Press, 1890), 7–9.
106. *Offering of Srimat Maharshi Devendranath Tagore*, 12.
107. Ibid., 24.
108. Ibid., 13.
109. "Asceticism," in *Keshub Chunder Sen's Essays: Theological and Ethical: Part 1*, 2nd ed. (Calcutta: Brahmo Tract Society, 1885), 84–87.
110. *Keshub Chunder Sen's Lectures*, 7.
111. *Keshub Chunder Sen in England*, vol. 2, p. 121.
112. Keshub, *Lectures in India*, 170–71, 376.

CHAPTER FOUR

1. Karsandas Mulji, *Inglaṇḍmāṃ Pravās: Travels in England* (Gandhinagar, India: Gujarat Sahitya Academy, 2001 [1866]), 143.
2. *Report of the Maharaj Libel Case and of the Bhattia Conspiracy Case, Connected With It. Jadunathjee Brizrattanjee Maharaj, vs. Karsandass Mooljee Editor and Proprietor, and Nanabhai Rastamji Ranina, Printer, "Satya Prakash"* (Bombay: Bombay Gazette Press, 1862), 83.
3. B. N. Motiwala, *Karsondas Mulji: A Biographical Study* (Bombay: Karsondas Mulji Centenary Celebration Committee, 1935), 42.
4. *Bombay Gazette*, May 1, 1862, p. 412.

5. *Report of the Maharaj Libel Case*, 83.

6. Christine Dobbin, *Urban Leadership in Western India: Politics and Communities in Bombay City, 1840–1885* (London: Oxford University Press, 1972).

7. Motiwala, *Karsondas Mulji*, 55.

8. Ibid., 50.

9. The above biographical summary is based on Motiwala, *Karsondas Mulji*, ix–xii, 17–50.

10. Rosalind O'Hanlon, *Caste, Conflict, and Ideology: Mahatma Jotirao Phule and Low Caste Protest in Nineteenth-Century Western India* (Cambridge: Cambridge University Press, 1985).

11. J. K. Majumdar, *Raja Rammohun Roy and the World* (Calcutta: Sadharan Brahmo Samaj, 1975).

12. Keshub Chunder Sen, *Diary in Madras and Bombay: From 9th February to 8th April 1864* (Calcutta: Brahmo Tract Society, 1887), 47–48, 57, 60, 65, 67.

13. There are a number of arguments to be made for Mulji's influence on Dayanand. Dayanand was living in Mathura, the epicenter of Krishna devotion, during the 1862 Maharaj Libel Case and thus may well have heard about Mulji's criticism of Vaishnava devotional practices at this time. He definitely heard about them in Banaras in 1869, when he was visited by Mulji's associates. Whether coincidentally or not, shortly before his 1875 death, Mulji published a small Gujarati pamphlet entitled *Ved Dharm*, which advocated for two causes now closely associated with Dayanand: rejecting the Puranas in favor of an *"Arya Dharma"* contained only in the Vedas; and promoting Hindi as a *lingua franca*. Finally, there is there is the strikingly similarity in title between Mulji's newspaper, the *Satya Prakash*, and Dayanand's book, the *Satyarth Prakash*—both beacons of the light of truth. See Dobbin, *Urban Leadership*, 154–55; J. T. F. Jordens, "Dayananda and Karsondas Mulji: Their Condemnation of the Vallabhacharyas," in *Dayananda Sarasvati: Essays on His Life and Ideas* (New Delhi: Manohar, 1998), 140–62.

14. Motiwala, *Karsondas Mulji*, 33. The comparison to the Hastings trial was made by F.S.P. Lely in 1897 at a celebration of the Mulji anniversary.

15. *Report of the Maharaj Libel Case*, 173–74.

16. Ibid., 125.

17. See, for example, ibid., 123.

18. Ibid., 138–39, 226.

19. *Poona Observer*, 30 January 1862.

20. Competition between the *Bombay Gazette* and the *Times of India* shaped the development of both papers after the 1861 amalgamation of the latter from the *Bombay Times*, the *Bombay Standard*, and the *Telegraph and Courier*. As the *Poona Observer* implied, it was primarily these two papers that drove coverage of the trial, their columns being "occupied, to the exclusion of better matter, by the disgraceful revelations of the abominations of which the Maharaj is accused" (February 13, 1862). In the coming weeks, the *Observer* would con-

tinue to chide the *Times of India*, in particular, for its "religious frenzy about this wretched libel case" (February 22; March 11).

21. Cf. Robert Darnton, *The Devil in the Holy Water, or the Art of Slander from Louis XIV to Napoleon* (Philadelphia: University of Pennsylvania Press, 2010).

22. *Report of the Maharaj Libel Case*, 234.

23. David L. Haberman, "On Trial: The Love of the Sixteen Thousand Gopees," *History of Religions* 33, no. 1 (1993): 44–70.

24. Jürgen Lütt, "From Krishnalila to Ramarajya: A Court Case and Its Consequences for the Reformulation of Hinduism," in *Representing Hinduism: The Construction of Religious Traditions and National Identity*, eds. Vasudha Dalmia and Heinrich von Stietencron, (New Delhi: Sage, 1995), 142–53; Amrita Shodhan, "Women in the Maharaja Libel Case: A Re-examination," *Indian Journal of Gender Studies* 4, no. 2 (1997): 123–39; Usha Thakkar, "Puppets on the Periphery: Women and Social Reform in 19th Century Gujarati Society," *Economic and Political Weekly* 32, nos. 1–2 (January 4–11, 1997): 46–58.

25. Amrita Shodhan, *A Question of Community: Religious Groups and Colonial Law* (Calcutta: Samya, 2001).

26. Alexander Duff, *India and India Missions: Including Sketches of the Gigantic System of Hinduism, Both in Theory and Practice*, 2nd ed. (Edinburgh: John Johnstone, 1840), 61–64.

27. Charles Taylor, *A Secular Age* (Cambridge, MA: Harvard University Press, 2007).

28. Motiwala, *Karsondas Mulji*, 56–57. Motiwala compares Mulji to Luther repeatedly, as on pp. 53, 63, 65, and 99.

29. Duff, *India and Indian Missions*, 377; Javed Majeed, *Ungoverned Imaginings: James Mill's* History of British India *and Orientalism* (Oxford: Oxford University Press, 1992), 179.

30. Motiwala, *Karsondas Mulji*, 23.

31. Karsandas Mulji, "*Pop—Yurop Khaṇḍnā Māhārājo*" ("The Popes—Maharajas of Europe"), *Nibandhmāḷā: Saṃsār Sambandhī Viṣayo* (Mumbai: Union Press, 1870), 152–56. The article was originally published on February 6, 1859.

32. *Bombay Gazette*, December 4, 1861; *Poona Observer*, March 11, 1862.

33. Karsandas Mulji, *History of the Sect of Mahárájas, or Vallabhacháryas in Western India* (London: Trübner, 1865), 45–46.

34. Haberman, "On Trial," 52.

35. I discuss these issues further in J. Barton Scott, "How to Defame a God: Public Selfhood in the Maharaj Libel Case," in "Imagining the Public in Modern South Asia," eds. Brannon Ingram, J. Barton Scott, and SherAli Tareen, special issue of *South Asia: The Journal of South Asian Studies* 38, no. 3 (2015): 387–402.

36. *Report of the Maharaj Libel Case*, 134–36.

37. Mahīpatrām Rūprām, *Uttam Kapoḷ: Karsandās Muljī Caritra: A Memoir of the Reformer Karsandas Mulji* (Ahmedabad: Ahmedabad United Printing, 1877), i–iii.

38. The translation of *Nīti-vacan* ("instruction in ethics" or "discourses on ethics") as "Moral Training" is Mulji's own from his Gujarati-English dictionary. The phrase does not appear in the first (1862) edition of the dictionary; that Mulji decided to add it to the second (1868) edition would seem to indicate that he had given the matter considered thought. See Karsandas Mulji, *A Pocket Dictionary, Gujarati and English*. 2nd ed. (Bombay: Union Press, 1868).

39. Karsandas Mulji, *Nīti-vacan*, 6th ed., ed. Keśavprasād Choṭālāl Deśāi (Ahmedabad: Jivanlal Amarshi Mehta, 1923 [1859]). *Nīti-vacan*'s sixty-five essays, which originally appeared between 1855 and 1858, were mostly published in the *Satya Prakash*, with a small number published in the *Nītibodhak*. More than half of these are translated from English. For a period response to the *Niti-Vacan*, see the reviews in the *Rast Goftar*, July 3, 1859, and July 10, 1859.

40. Mulji, *Niti-vacan*, 139.

41. Because Dodsley published his book anonymously, there was much controversy over its authorship, and other writers sought to capitalize on its popularity by publishing under the same title. In 1751, *Oeconomy of Human Life, Part the Second* was published (Donald Eddy tentatively attributes it to a Dr. John Hill) and this was subsequently appended to most later editions of Dodsley's work. Mulji's copy clearly included both parts, as the *Niti-vacan* includes translations of essays from *Part the Second* (e.g., "Revenge"). Donald D. Eddy, "Dodsley's 'Oeconomy of Human Life,' 1750–1751," *Modern Philology* 85, no .4 (1988): 460–79; Harry M. Solomon, *The Rise of Robert Dodsley: Creating the New Age of Print* (Carbondale: Southern Illinois University, 1996); John Bray, "The Oeconomy of Human Life: An 'Ancient Bramin' in Eighteenth-Century Tibet," *Journal of the Royal Asiatic Society of Great Britain and Ireland*, series 3, vol. 19, no. 4 (2009): 439–58.

42. Mulji was probably the first writer to translate Dodsley into a South Asian language, but he was not to be the last. In addition to English-language reprints of Dodsley in Calcutta (1877), Bombay (1889), and Banaras (1922), there have also been twentieth-century translations into both Panjabi and Telugu. See *The Economy of Human Life, Translated from an Indian Manuscript, Written by an Ancient Bramin: A New Indian Edition* (Calcutta: Jay Gopal Goshal, 1877) and Bray, "The Oeconomy of Human Life."

43. Eddy, "Dodsley's 'Oeconomy of Human Life,'" 460.

44. Robert Dodsley, *The Oeconomy of Human Life, Complete in Two Parts, Translated from an Indian Manuscript Written by an Ancient Bramin in a Letter from an English Gentleman Residing at China to the Earl of* ************** (Edinburgh: W. Darling, 1785), 29.

45. Ibid., 32–33.

46. Max Weber, *The Protestant Ethic and the Spirit of Capitalism*, trans. Talcott Parsons (New York: Routledge, 2001), 14–20.

47. Dodsley, *The Oeconomy of Human Life*, 33.

48. Mulji, *Niti-vacan*, 60–63.

49. Ibid., 87–90.

50. Ibid., 76.
51. Ibid., 4.
52. Homi Bhabha, *The Location of Culture*, 2nd edition. (New York: Routledge, 2004).
53. Weber, *Protestant Ethic*, 123–25.
54. Mulji's use of the word *dharm* seems to suggest the influence of the English word *religion*. For an example of his effort to delimit the semantic range of both *dharm* and *nīti* (ethics) so as to exclude subjects such as science (*vidyā*), history, and "worldly matters," which other Gujarati speakers of the time apparently felt comfortable including within the domain of the dharmic, see his criticism of the newly founded Ahmedabad newspaper, the *Dharm Prakāś* in the essay "The Dharma Prakash or Light of Religion" in *Nibandhmāla*, 220–23.
55. Later readers, on the other hand, seem to have been rather more confused by the preface. The 1887 Calcutta reprint takes the frame story as factual, observing that the book "ought to be eagerly welcomed in this the country of its origin." See *The Economy of Human Life*. For further discussion of the Oriental tale in the eighteenth century, see Srinivas Aravamudan, *Enlightenment Orientalism: Resisting the Rise of the Novel* (Chicago: University of Chicago Press, 2012).
56. Jogendra Nath Bhattacharya, *Hindu Castes and Sects: An Exposition on the Origin of the Hindu Caste System and the Bearings of the Sects Toward Each Other and Toward Other Religious Systems* (Calcutta: Thacker, Spink, and Co., 1896), 497.
57. *Report of the Maharaj Libel Case*, 125. See H. H. Wilson, *Sketch of the Religious Sects of the Hindus* (Calcutta: Bishop's College Press, 1846), 77. This is also quoted by Mulji, *History of the Sect of Maharajas*, 45.
58. Bartle Frere, "The Banians—The Traders of the Indian Seas," *MacMillan's Magazine* 32, no. 6 (October 1875): 552–62.
59. Max Weber, *The Religion of India: The Sociology of Hinduism and Buddhism*, trans. H. H. Gerth and D. Martindale (New York: Free Press, 1958), 314–15; Jürgen Lütt, "Max Weber and the Vallabhacharis," *International Sociology* 2, no. 3 (1987): 277–87.
60. Michel Foucault, *Security, Territory, Population: Lectures at the Collège de France, 1977–1978*, trans. Graham Burchell (New York: Picador, 2007).
61. Sir George Birdwood, ed, *The Stree Bodh and Social Progress in India: A Jubilee Memorial* (Bombay: The Stree Bodh Office, 1908). For a representative discussion of the politics of women's reform literature, see, for example, Barbara Daly Metcalf, ed., *Perfecting Women: Maulana Ashraf 'Ali Thanawi's* Bihishti Zewar (Berkeley: University of California Press, 1990); and Faisal Devji, "Gender and the Politics of Space: The Movement of Women's Reform in Muslim India, 1857–1900," in *South Asia: The Journal of South Asian Studies* 14, no. 1 (1991): 141–53.
62. Karsandas Mulji, *Saṃsār Sukh*, 3rd ed. (Mumbai: Rising Star Printing Press, 1887). As explained in the preface to the third edition, the book includes 47

essays, 39 of which are original, and 11 translated from English. The first edition having run out, a second edition was published in 1869 and then a third in 1887, with a preface written by Mulji's son Mangaldas Karsandas Mulji.

63. Ibid., 3–4.
64. Dodsley, *The Oeconomy of Human Life*, 61–62.
65. Mulji, *Saṃsār Sukh*, 103–4.
66. Mulji, *Niti-vacan*, 63–65.
67. Ibid., 64.
68. Quoted in Gail Minault, *Secluded Scholars: Women's Education and Muslim Social Reform in Colonial India* (Delhi: Oxford University Press, 1998), v.
69. Tanika Sarkar, "Talking about Scandals: Religion, Law and Love in Late Nineteenth-Century Bengal," *Hindu Wife, Hindu Nation: Community, Religion, and Cultural Nationalism* (Bloomington: Indiana University Press, 2001), 53–94; Geraldine Forbes, "In Search of Elokeshi: Unraveling the Tarakeswar Murder Case of 1873," unpublished manuscript.
70. Mulji, *Nibandhmāḷā*. Although the title page of the *Nibandhmāḷā* describes it as the first volume, the second volume seems never to have been realized.
71. Motivala, *Karsondas Mulji*, ix–x, 23.
72. Mulji, "The Brahmans of the Period" (*"Hamaṇānā Brāhmaṇo"*), in *Nibandhmāḷā*, 52–54. The essays in the *Nibandhmala* have both English and Gujarati titles. Whether or not the English title is a literal or entirely accurate translation of the Gujarati, I give it here with the Gujarati title in parentheses.
73. Ibid, 52–53.
74. Mulji, "Our Priests and Their Duties" (*"Śāstrabāvā ane Dasturo"*), in *Nibandhmāḷā*, 55–57 (n.d.).
75. *Report of the Maharaj Libel Case*, 2.
76. Mulji, "Immorality under the Cloak of Divinity" (*"Kṛṣṇ Avatar ane Kṛṣṇ Līlā"*), *Nibandhmāḷā*, 93–95 (July 4, 1858).
77. Mulji, "The Degraded Position of the Brahmans" (*"Paḍti Diśāmāṃ Paḍelā Brāhmaṇo"*), *Nibandhmāḷā*, 71–74 (March 14, 1858).
78. Mulji, "The Sons of Vallabha" (*"Valabhkuḷnā Bāḷako"*), *Nibandhmāḷā*, 100–103 (August 29, 1858).
79. Mulji, "The Degraded Position of the Brahmans," 72–73.
80. Mulji, "An Institution for the Blind" (*"Āndhaḷāonī Hālat Sudhārvā Viṣe"*), *Nibandhmāḷā*, 91–93 (June 27, 1858).
81. Mulji, "Our Priests and Their Duties," 55.
82. Mulji, "The Degraded Position of the Brahmans," 72–73.
83. Yadunāth Mahārāj Suratvāla, *Svadharm Vardhak ane Saṃśay Chedak*, 2nd ed. (Ahmedabad, India: Gujarat Printing Press, 1911), 9–20.
84. Richard Barz, *The Bhakti Sect of Vallabhacarya* (Faridabad, India: Thomson Press, 1976), 81–85.
85. *Report of the Maharaj Libel Case*, 126.
86. Ibid., 92.
87. Yadunath, *Svadharm Vardhak*, 18–19.

88. Ibid., 50.
89. Ibid., 13–14.
90. Barz, *Bhakti Sect*, 9–15, 31–33.
91. Yadunath, *Svadharm Vardhak*, 53.
92. Ibid., 62.
93. Ibid.
94. Ibid., 45.
95. John S. Hawley and Mark Juergensmeyer, *Songs of the Saints of India* (New York: Oxford, 1988), 4.
96. Barz, *Bhakti Sect*, 33.
97. Yadunath, *Svadharm Vardhak*, 92.
98. *Report of the Maharaj Libel Case*, 47–50. This establishes a rather complicated play of devotional identity and desire not yet fully explored by the existing scholarship. It could be argued that if the Maharaj stands in for Krishna, then the ritual gift of woman-as-property triangulates the relationship between Maharaj and devotee. This gift thus serves as a means of disavowing the very desire that it works to articulate—asserting the primacy of everyday gender norms over and against bhakti's playful inversion of those norms.
99. Yadunath, *Svadharm Vardhak*, 30.
100. Ibid., 24–28.
101. Leela Gandhi, *Affective Communities: Anticolonial Thought, Fin-de-siècle Radicalism, and the Politics of Friendship* (Durham, NC: Duke University Press, 2006), 131.

CHAPTER FIVE

1. Maharṣi Dayānand Sarasvati, *Satyārth Prakāś* (Delhi: Arya Pariwar Yojna, 2007), 232. All translations from the *Satyarth Prakash* are mine unless otherwise specified.
2. For further discussion of biographical and hagiographical writings about Dayanand, see J. Barton Scott, "Unsaintly Virtue: Swami Dayananda Saraswati and Modern Hindu Hagiography," *Journal of Hindu Studies* 7, no. 3 (2014): 371–91.
3. Henry S. Olcott, "An Address to the Arya Samaj of Meerut, Delivered on 5 May 1879" (Roorkee, India: Thomason Civil Engineering College Press, 1879), 3.
4. Henry S. Olcott, "Brahmo Samaj," *Theosophist*, March 1888, 74.
5. *Indian Evangelical Review*, January 1892, quoted in J. N. Farquhar, *Modern Religious Movements in India* (New York: Macmillan Company, 1915), 111–13.
6. For additional discussion of how Arya Samajis finessed the political semantics of the British state, see C. S. Adcock, *The Limits of Tolerance: Indian Secularism and the Politics of Religious Freedom* (Oxford: Oxford University Press, 2014), as well as "Religious Freedom and Political Culture: The Arya Samaj in Colonial North India" (PhD diss., University of Chicago, 2007).

7. Durga Prasad, ed., *An English Translation of the Satyarth Prakash, Literally Exposé of Right Sense (of Vedic Religion) of Maharishi Dayanand Saraswati, 'The Luther of India,' Being a Guide to Vedic Hermeneutics* (Lahore: Virjanand Press, 1908).

8. For a review of pertinent literature, see Noel Salmond, *Hindu Iconoclasts: Rammohun Roy, Dayananda Sarasvati, and Nineteenth-Century Polemics against Idolatry* (Waterloo, ON: Wilfred Laurier University Press, 2004).

9. For an example of this argument, see Richard King, *Orientalism and Religion: Postcolonial Theory, India, and the "Mystic East"* (London: Routledge, 1999), 144–45.

10. Gokal Chand, *The Luther of India* (Lahore, 1912), 29. The "Luther at the least" comment is part of a preface to the second edition of the pamphlet and is not included in the 1912 original edition that I consulted. *The Luther of India*, 2nd ed. (Lahore: Ishwar Chandra Arya Tract Society, 1913), ii; cited in Timothy S. Dobe, "Dayānanda Sarasvatī as Irascible Ṛṣi: The Personal and Performed Authority of a Text," *Journal of Hindu Studies* 4, no. 1 (2011): 79–100, at p. 92.

11. Homi Bhabha, *The Location of Culture* (London: Routledge, 1994).

12. Timothy S. Dobe, "Dayānanda Sarasvatī as Irascible Ṛṣi."

13. Jordens, *Dayānanda Sarasvatī*, 75–79.

14. The *Satyarth Prakash* appeared in two editions in Dayanand's lifetime. The shorter first edition of 1875 contained a handful of publishers' errors, and was written in an especially awkward Hindi—Dayanand, who was just learning the language, had to write much of the book in a hurry. The second edition of 1883 not only cleaned up the formal problems of the first edition. It also vastly expanded the number of references from canonical Hindu texts, and added the two controversial final chapters criticizing the Bible and the Qur'an. There has been a fair amount of controversy within the Arya Samaj about which edition should be understood as more authoritative, and even as to whether Dayanand actually authored the final two chapters of the 1883 edition. J. T. F. Jordens, after painstaking comparative textual study, concludes that both editions are authentic and any differences between the two indicate shifts in Dayanand's thinking in the last eight years of his life. See Jordens, *Dayānanda Sarasvatī*, 99–126. For a discussion of the controversy around the fourteenth chapter in late colonial India, see J. Barton Scott, "Aryas Unbound: Print Hinduism and the Cultural Regulation of Religious Offense," *Comparative Studies of South Asia, Africa, and the Middle East* 35, no. 2 (August 2015): 294–309.

15. Dayanand, *Satyarth Prakash*, 218–19.

16. Ibid., 316–21.

17. "*Anuvādak kī Bhūmikā*," in Devendranāth Mukhopādhyāy, *Dayānandcarit*, trans. Śrī Bābū Ghāsīrāmjī (Meerut: R. S. Dublis, 1912), xi.

18. I borrow the distinction between cultural diversity and cultural difference from Bhabha, *Location of Culture*, 49–51.

19. There are good reasons to push this date back further to 1869, when Dayanand met with Mulji's friends in Banaras, or even 1862, when he may have caught wind of the Maharaj Libel Case while living in Mathura.

20. Durga Prasad, trans. *A Triumph of Truth: Being an English Translation of Satya Dharm Vichar, or a Discussion upon True Religion among Maharshi Swami Dayanand Saraswati, Rev. G. T. Scot, Moulvie Mahomed Kasam, & other Christian and Mahomedan Priests at Chandapur, with the Autobiography & Travels of Our Swami* (Lahore: Virajanand Press, 1889), 79.

21. Svāmī Dayānanda Sarasvati, *Satyārth Prakāś* (Banaras, 1875).

22. Yogi Aurvind Ghosh, *Dayananda: The Man and His Work* (Delhi: International Aryan League, n.d.), 6–7. First published in the *Vedic Magazine*, Lahore, April 1915.

23. See, for example, Kenneth W. Jones, ed., *Religious Controversy in British India: Dialogues in South Asian Languages* (Albany, NY: SUNY Press, 1992).

24. There are various ways the *Satyarth Prakash* seems to strain against its own textuality. One notable example of this is the story of the "nose-cutters" featured in chapter 11. This story had a life in the world of oral tale both before and, expedited by the printed text, after the publication of the *Satyarth Prakash* (in which it serves as an illustration of the concept of lila, discussed below). For an earlier instance of the tale, see the journal of William Bowley in the *Missionary Register* (London: L. B. Seeley, 1819), 143. For its history after the *Satyarth Prakash*, see Kirin Narayan, *Storytellers, Saints, and Scoundrels: Folk Narrative in Hindu Religious Teaching* (Philadelphia: University of Pennsylvania Press, 1989), 142–43.

25. Dayanand, *Satyarth Prakash*, 231–32.

26. Christophe Jaffrelot's *Hindu Nationalism* reader positions the *Satyarth Prakash* as the inaugural text of Hindutva: Christophe Jaffrelot, *Hindu Nationalism: A Reader* (Princeton, NJ: Princeton University Press, 2007). Also see his *Hindu Nationalist Movement in India* (New York: Columbia University Press, 1996).

27. Dayanand, *Satyarth Prakash*, 227–29.

28. For the intersection of Dayanand's "Aryanism" with other invocations of this racialized discourse, see Romila Thapar, "The Theory of Aryan Race and India: History and Politics," *Social Scientist* 24, nos. 1–3 (November 1996): 3–29; and Dorothy Matilda Figueira, *Aryans, Jews, Brahmins: Theorizing Authority through Myths of Identity* (Albany: SUNY Press, 2002).

29. Gyan Prakash, *Another Reason: Science and the Imagination of Modern India* (Princeton, NJ: Princeton University Press, 1999).

30. My discussion of lila is based on the essays in William S. Sax, ed., *The Gods at Play: Līlā in South Asia* (New York: Oxford University Press, 1995), especially those by Norvin Hein and Robert Goodwin.

31. See J. T. F. Jordens, "Dayananda Sarasvati and Vedanta," in *Dayananda Sarasvati: Essays on His Life and Ideas*, 53–63.

32. Dayanand, *Satyarth Prakash*, 239.

33. Ibid., 275.

34. Robert E. Goodwin, "The Play World of Sanskrit Poetry," in Sax, ed., *The Gods at Play*, 54.

35. Tarachand Deumal Gajra, *The Life of Swami Dayanand Saraswati* (Lahore: Punjab Printing Works, 1915), i–ii. Brahmo Samajis were apparently making this basic argument much earlier. See David Kopf, *The Brahmo Samaj and the Shaping of the Modern Indian Mind* (Princeton, NJ: Princeton University Press, 1979), 203.

36. Adcock, "Religious Freedom," 288–89. Much of the following discussion derives from Adcock's work on the political valence of brahmacharya in Arya Samaj discourse of the early twentieth century, and I would like to acknowledge my gratitude for and indebtedness to that work here.

37. See, for example, Romila Thapar, "Renunciation: The Making of a Counter-Culture?," in *Ancient Indian Social History: Some Interpretations* (New Delhi: Orient Longman, 1984), 56–93; Patrick Olivelle, *Saṃyāsa Upaniṣads: Hindu Scriptures on Asceticism and Renunciation* (New York: Oxford University Press, 1992).

38. Satyavrata Siddhantalankar, *Samskara-candrika: Samskara-vidhi ki vaijñanika vyakhya: The Science of Making a Better Man* (New Delhi: Vijayakrishna Lakhanpala, 1977). As the preface to this text explains, Dayanand's goal was "building a new mankind" (*nava-mānav kā nirmāṇ*) (i).

39. Gokal Chand, *Luther of India*, 27.

40. Adcock, "Religious Freedom," 275–77; cf. Scott, "Unsaintly Virtue."

41. Joseph Alter, "Celibacy, Sexuality, and the Transformation of Gender into Nationalism in North India," *Journal of Asian Studies* 53, no. 1 (1994): 45–66.

42. Dayanand, *Satyarth Prakash*, 111.

43. Ibid.

44. Wendy Doniger, *The Hindus: An Alternative History* (New York: Penguin, 2009), 284.

45. Jordens, "Dayananda Sarasvati and Vedanta," 60–61.

46. For brahmacharya and the body of the polemicist, see Adcock, "Religious Freedom."

47. Dayanand, *Satyarth Prakash*, 90. Similar rhetoric can be found in classical texts like the *Brahma Purana*. I am interested in the cultural work that these classical allusions perform in their modern contexts, rather than in the simple persistence of classical tradition per se. For a similar methodology, see Simona Sawhney, *The Modernity of Sanskrit* (Minneapolis: University of Minnesotra Press, 2008). For the *Brahma Purana*, see Wendy Doniger O'Flaherty, "Karma and Rebirth in the Vedas and Puranas," in *Karma and Rebirth in Classical Indian Traditions*, ed. Wendy Doniger O'Flaherty (Berkeley: University of California Press, 1980), 15–16.

48. See Swami Dayanand Saraswati, *The Light of Truth*, trans. Chiranjiva Bharadwaja, third ed. (Delhi: D. A. V. College Managing Committee, 2011).

49. See Giorgio Agamben, *Homo Sacer: Sovereign Power and Bare Life*, trans. Daniel Heller-Roazen (Stanford, CA: Stanford University Press, 1998). Part of what

I mean to suggest is that the *Satyarth Prakash* lends itself to a study of what could be called "comparative biopolitics." That is, its concern with regulating the reproductive body of the nation through mass virtue clearly participates in biopolitical trends of its era, but the text articulates its biopolitics as part of a genealogy that is more Indic than (if our reference is Agamben) Aristotelian.

50. Dayanand, *Satyarth Prakash*, 111; cf. 103.
51. Ibid., 111.
52. Ibid., 110.
53. Ibid., 40.
54. Ibid., 110.
55. Ibid., 323.
56. Ibid., 111.
57. Ibid., 67.
58. Ibid., 31.
59. Ibid., 35–36.
60. Ibid., 34–35.
61. Ibid., 36.
62. Kenneth W. Jones, *Arya Dharm: Hindu Consciousness in 19th-Century Punjab* (Berkeley: University of California Press, 1976), 67–93, 219–23. Cf. Vickie Langohr, "Colonial Education Systems and the Spread of Local Religious Movements: The Cases of British Egypt and Punjab," *Comparative Studies in Society and History* 47, no. 1 (January 2005): 161–89.
63. Alongside their better-publicized disagreement over English-language education, these two institutions also disagreed over the centrality of brahmacharya to the curriculum. The Gurukul planned to promote "physical improvement" by teaching "*brahmacharya* (celibacy), active habits, and well regulated daily life"; "religious and ethical improvement" by teaching the Vedas; and "social or Samajic improvement" by teaching "altruistic notions of *Paropkara* (charity or benevolence) and self-abnegation, and the regulation of conduct in life accordingly." *Tribune*, January 1900; quoted in Jones, *Arya Dharm*, 220–21.
64. Dayanand, *Satyarth Prakash*, 37–38. The text seems conflicted over the precise purpose of female education. On the one hand, it extols ancient India, where Kshatriya women fought alongside their men. With this ideal in mind, it claims that women of the different *varna*s should learn the same skills as their menfolk. On the other hand, it details the various ways in which formal education will help women run the home more effectively. So, training in medical science allows women to keep their families free from disease; training in art allows them to better decorate their bodies and houses; and training in math allows them to keep track of domestic accounts (ibid., 66–67). For further discussion of women in the Arya Samaj, see Anshu Malhotra, "The Moral Woman and the Urban Punjabi Society of the Late Nineteenth Century," *Social Scientist* 20, nos. 5–6 (May–June 1992): 34–63;

and Anshu Malhotra, "Every Woman is a Mother in Embryo: Lala Lajpat Rai and Indian Womanhood," *Social Scientist* 22, nos. 1–2 (January–February 1994): 40–63.

65. Dayanand, *Satyarth Prakash*, 77.
66. Ibid, 74.
67. Ibid., 31.
68. Ibid., 271.
69. Ibid., 272.
70. The use of the shepherd-flock metaphor here is striking. According to Foucault, this metaphor was of crucial importance to the development of the Christian pastorate and thus also to the emergence of governmentality: just as the shepherd would risk his entire flock to save a single lamb, governmentality is a mode of power that attends simultaneously to "all and each" (*omnes et singulatim*). Foucault describes the metaphor as distinctive, if not unique, to Christianity. One wonders: did Dayanand absorb the language of the shepherd from Christian missionaries? Does this figure of speech have a longer history in Indic thought? How might a fuller history or genealogy of this metaphor shape how we conceptualize "Hindu governmentality"? See Michel Foucault, *Security, Territory, Population: Lectures at the Collège de France, 1977–1978* (New York: Palgrave Macmillan, 2007).
71. Dayanand, *Satyarth Prakash*, 43–44.
72. Ibid., 103.
73. Swami Dayanand Saraswati, *The Sanskar Vidhi: The Procedure of Sacraments*, trans. Acharya Vaidyanath Shastri (New Delhi: Sarvadeshik Arya Pratinidhi Sabha, 1976), 54.
74. Dayanand, *Satyarth Prakash*, 109–10.
75. Ibid., 215–17.
76. Ibid., 110.
77. Ibid., 112.
78. See, for example, Nicholas Dirks, *Castes of Mind: Colonialism and the Making of Modern India* (Princeton, NJ: Princeton University Press, 2001). My use of the word bureaucracy in the above discussion is broadly Weberian, although in a manner clearly inflected with Foucault: bureaucratic rationality works to eliminate irregularities in social systems in a manner that correlates with, but without being reducible to, the needs of the modern state and other rationalizing institutions (e.g., the corporation). Caste was not invented during the colonial period; but it may have been only during the modern period that it was regularized or bureaucratized in this way.
79. Dayanand, *Satyarth Prakash*, 110.
80. Ibid., 231.
81. Ibid., 74–75.
82. Ibid., 74.
83. Ibid., 218–19.
84. Ibid., 223.

85. Ibid., 30.
86. Indian Evangelical Review, January 1892, ibid.
87. Gokal Chand, *Luther of India*, 1912.
88. Paṇḍyā Mohanlāl Viṣṇulāl, *Svāmī jī Śrī 108 Śrī Dayānand jī Sarasvatī kā Gurūtva vā Ācāryatva, arthāt Śrī Svāmi jī Āryasamājoṃ ke Gurū vā Ācārya Haiṃ vā Nahīṃ?* (Meerut: Swamiyantralaya, 1901); cf. Scott, "Unsaintly Virtue."
89. Dayanand, *Satyarth Prakash*, 136, 145.

CHAPTER SIX

1. Henry S. Olcott, *Old Diary Leaves*, vol. 3 (Chennai [Adyar]: Theosophical Publishing House, 2002), 37–39; *First Report of the Committee of the Society for Psychical Research, Appointed to Investigate the Evidence for Marvellous Phenomena Offered by Certain Members of the Theosophical Society* (London: National Press Agency, 1884), 50–51. A facsimile of the letter is included in Blavatsky, *Collected Writings*, 2nd ed., vol. 6, ed. Boris de Zirkoff (Wheaton, IL: Theosophical Publishing House, 1975), 25–28.
2. Henry Steel Olcott, "An Address to the Arya Samaj of Meerut" (Roorkee, India: Thomason Civil Engineering College Press, 1879), 1. The event is described in Olcott, *Old Diary Leaves*, vol. 2, pp. 80–81.
3. Gauri Viswanathan, *Outside the Fold: Conversion, Modernity, Belief* (Princeton, NJ: Princeton University Press, 1999), 177–208.
4. "Statements and Conclusions of the Committee," *Proceedings of the Society for Psychical Research* 3 (1885): 207.
5. This wording of the three objects dates to an 1896 revision of the Society's constitution. See Lilian Edgar, *The Elements of Theosophy* (London: Theosophical Publishing Society, 1903), 16. Blavatsky had phrased the three objects somewhat differently: "(1) To form the nucleus of a Universal Brotherhood of Humanity without distinction of race, colour, or creed. (2) To promote the study of Aryan and other Scriptures, of the World's religion and sciences, and to vindicate the importance of old Asiatic literature, namely, of the Brahmanical, Buddhist, and Zoroastrian philosophies. (3) To investigate the hidden mysteries of Nature under every aspect possible, and the psychic and spiritual powers latent in man especially." H. P. Blavatsky, *The Key to Theosophy: Being a Clear Exposition, in the Form of Question and Answer, of the Ethics, Science, and Philosophy, for the Study of Which the Theosophical Society Has Been Founded* (London: Theosophical Publishing Company, 1889), 39.
6. Gauri Viswanathan, "The Ordinary Business of Occultism," *Critical Inquiry* 27, no. 1 (2000): 1–20.
7. Olcott, *Old Diary Leaves*, vol. 1, pp. 19, 75–76.
8. Bruce F. Campbell, *Ancient Wisdom Revived: A History of the Theosophical Movement* (Berkeley: University of California Press, 1980), 56.
9. See especially Joy Dixon, *Theosophy and Feminism in England* (Baltimore: Johns Hopkins University Press, 2001); and Alex Owen, *The Place of Enchant-*

ment: British Occultism and the Culture of the Modern (Chicago: University of Chicago Press, 2004).

10. Richard King, *Orientalism and Religion: Postcolonial Theory, India, and the "Mystic East"* (London: Routledge, 1999).

11. Campbell, *Ancient Wisdom Revived*, 56; Peter Washington, *Madame Blavatsky's Baboon: A History of the Mystics, Mediums, and Misfits Who Brought Spiritualism to America* (New York: Schocken, 1993), 33–40.

12. J. N. Farquhar, *Modern Religious Movements in India* (New Delhi: Munshram Manoharlal, 1977 [1914]), 208–90; Kenneth W. Jones, *Socio-Religious Reform Movements in British India*, New Cambridge History of India 3, no. 1 (Cambridge: Cambridge University Press, 1989), 167–79.

13. This, for example, is why Blavatsky claimed she could never convert to Buddhism. "It is true that I regard the philosophy of Gautama Buddha as the most sublime system; the purest, and above all, the most *logical* of all. But the system has been distorted during the centuries by the ambition and fanaticism of the priests, and has become a popular religion; the forms and the *exoteric* or popular cult proceeding from that system too closely resemble those of the Roman church which has slavishly plagiarized from it, for me ever to be converted to it." H. P Blavatsky, "The Real Madame H. P. Blavatsky," in *Collected Writings*, vol. 1, 3rd ed., ed. Boris de Zirkoff (Wheaton, IL: Theosophical Publishing House, 1988), 402.

14. J. Barton Scott, "Miracle Publics: Theosophy, Christianity, and the Coulomb Affair," *History of Religions* 49, no. 2 (2009): 172–96.

15. H. S. Olcott, *Old Diary Leaves: The True Story of the Theosophical Society* (New York: G. P. Putnam's Sons, 1895), 462.

16. Viswanathan, "Ordinary Business."

17. Helen Sword, *Ghostwriting Modernism* (Ithaca, NY: Cornell University Press, 2002); Owen, *The Place of Enchantment*; Corinna Treitel, *A Science for the Soul: Occultism and the Genesis of the German Modern* (Baltimore: Johns Hopkins University Press, 2004).

18. Treitel, *A Science for the Soul*, 23.

19. Sarah Willburn, *Possessed Victorians: Extra Spheres in Nineteenth-Century Mystical Writings* (Aldershot, UK: Ashgate, 2006).

20. Pamela Thurschwell, *Literature, Technology, and Magical Thinking, 1880–1920* (Cambridge: Cambridge University Press, 2001), 2; Marlene Tromp, *Altered States: Sex, Nation, Drugs, and Self-Transformation in Victorian Spiritualism* (Albany: State University of New York Press, 2006).

21. Sword, *Ghostwriting Modernism*; Owen, *The Darkened Room*; Anne Braude, *Radical Spirits: Spiritualism and Women's Rights in Nineteenth Century America* (Bloomington: Indiana University Press, 2001); Molly McGarry, *Ghosts of Futures Past: Spiritualism and the Cultural Politics of Nineteenth Century America* (Berkeley: University of California Press, 2008).

22. Tromp, *Altered States*, 75–96; McGarry, *Ghosts of Futures Past*, 66–93.

23. H. P. Blavatsky, *Isis Unveiled: A Master-Key to the Mysteries of Ancient and*

Modern Science and Theology, vol. 2, ed. Boris de Zirkoff (Chennai [Adyar]: Theosophical Publishing House, 1972 [London: J. W. Bouton, 1877]), 588.

24. Ibid., 62.
25. Ibid., 592.
26. Alison Winter, *Mesmerized: Powers of Mind in Victorian Britain* (Chicago: University of Chicago Press, 1998).
27. Ibid., 187–212.
28. H. P. Blavatsky, "Are Chelas 'Mediums'?, *Theosophist* 5, no. 9 (June 1884): 210–11; in *Collected Writings*, vol. 6, pp. 223–27.
29. Alfred Percy Sinnett, *The Occult World* (London: Trübner & Co., 1881), 24–25.
30. Dixon, *Divine Feminine*, 26–29.
31. Viswanathan, "Ordinary Business," 8–9, 15.
32. Sinnett, *Occult World*, 15, 21.
33. *First Report of the Committee of the Society for Psychical Research*, 44, 36, 42.
34. Sinnett, *Occult World*, 19.
35. Blavatsky, *Isis Unveiled*, vol. 1, p. 146.
36. The notion of the "animal Soul" surely begs further interpretation as standing at the crossroads of two intellectual worlds that are related to theosophy: psychoanalysis and animal rights. The "animal Soul" is part id, part vivisected creature. See, for example, Gauri Viswanathan, "'Have Animals Souls': Theosophy and the Suffering Body," *PMLA* 126, no. 2 (2011): 440–47.
37. Josephine Ransom, *A Short History of the Theosophical Society* (Chennai [Adyar]: Theosophical Publishing House, 1938).
38. Washington, *Madame Blavatsky's Baboon*, 85.
39. H. P. Blavatsky, "What of Phenomena?." *Lucifer* 1, no. 6 (February 1888): 504–6; in Blavatsky, *Collected Writings*, vol. 9, pp. 46–50.
40. Dixon, *Divine Feminine*, 41–66.
41. Randall Styers, *Making Magic: Religion, Magic, and Science in the Modern World* (Oxford: Oxford University Press, 2004).
42. Jeremy Stolow, "Technology," in David Morgan, ed., *Key Words in Religion, Media, and Culture* (New York: Routledge, 2008), 189.
43. Franz Hartmann, *Magic, White and Black: The Science of Finite and Infinite Life, Containing Practical Hints for Students of Occultism*, 3rd ed. (London: George Redway, 1888), 20, 10.
44. Arther Lillie, *Madame Blavatsky and Her "Theosophy"* (London: Swan Sonnenschein, 1890), 119.
45. H. P. Blavatsky, "Practical Occultism: Important to Students," *Lucifer* 2, no. 8 (April 1888): 150–54; in Blavatsky, *Collected Writings*, vol. 9, pp. 155–62.
46. H. P. Blavatsky, "Occultism Versus the Occult Arts," *Lucifer* 2, no. 9 (May 1888): 173–81; in *Collected Writings*, vol. 9, pp. 249–61.
47. H. P. Blavatsky, *The Voice of Silence: Being Chosen Fragments from the 'Book of Golden Precepts,' for the Daily Use of Lanoos (Disciples)* (London: Theosophical Publishing Society, 1889), x.
48. Ibid., 5.

49. William James, *Varieties of Religious Experience* (New York: Modern Library, 1929), 412

50. H. P. Blavatsky, *Gems from the East: A Birthday Book of Precepts and Axioms* (London: Theosophical Publishing Society, 1890).

51. Ibid., v.

52. Ibid., 2.

53. First published anonymously, the text later came to be associated with Blavatsky's name, although it is not mentioned in the *Collected Writings*. Nonetheless, it does participate in a genre that she and possibly other theosophists were exploring at this time. One might likewise question whether *Gems from the East*, although it does have Blavatsky's name on it, could have been compiled by someone else under her direction. Blavatsky-as-author is, in any case, a fraught topic, caught up with her interest in automatic writing and amanuensis, as well as her apparent penchant for plagiarism. My point here is simply that the genre of the theosophical conduct manual emerges in some association with the Blavatsky author-function after 1885.

54. *Some Practical Suggestions for Daily Life, Some Hints on the Theosophical Training of Children* (London: Theosophical Publishing Society, 1890), 3; in *Theosophical Siftings*, vol. 3 (1890–91) (London: Theosophical Publishing House, 1891).

55. Ibid., 15.

56. H. P. Blavatsky, "Chelas," *Theosophist* 6, no. 1 (October 1884): 1; in *Collected Writings*, vol. 6, pp. 285–87.

57. Michel Foucault, *Hermeneutics of the Subject: Lectures at the Collège de France, 1981–1982* (New York: Palgrave Macmillan, 2005).

58. For a more comprehensive discussion of the place of the "fakir" in colonial discourse, see Katherine Pratt Ewing, *Arguing Sainthood: Modernity, Psychoanalysis, Islam* (Durham, NC: Duke University Press, 1997), 41–64.

59. H. P. Blavatsky, "The Theosophical Mahatmas," *Path* 1, no. 9 (December 1886): 257–63; in *Collected Writings*, vol. 7, pp. 241–49.

60. Henry S. Olcott, "Asceticism," *Theosophist* 8, no. 5 (February 1892): 257–61.

61. Ibid., 258

62. Ibid., 292; cf. Annie Besant, *The Story of the Great War*, 2nd ed. (Madras: Theosophical Publishing House, 1919), 99.

63. Blavatsky, "The Theosophical Mahatmas," 261.

64. Srinivas Aravamuan, *Guru English: South Asian Religion in a Cosmopolitan Language* (Princeton, NJ: Princeton University Press, 2006), 105–41.

65. Patience Sinnett, *The Purpose of Theosophy* (Bombay: Tookram Tatya, 1887), 43.

66. *The Collapse of Koot Hoomi: An Incident in the Early History of Theosophy in India* (London: Christian Literature Society, 1904).

67. Sinnett, *Occult World*, 26–27.

68. Eric J. Sharpe, *The Universal Gītā: Western Images of the* Bhagavad Gītā: *A Bicentenary Survey* (La Salle, IL: Open Court, 1985).

69. Mishka Sinha, "Corrigibility, Allegory, Universality: A History of the Gita's Transnational Reception, 1785–1945," *Modern Intellectual History* 7, no. 2

(2010): 297–317; Eric J. Sharpe, "Early Theosophists and the Interpretation of the *Bhagavad Gita*," *Theosophy in Australia* (September 1979): 50–57; Gerald James Larsen, "The *Bhagavad-Gītā* as Cross-Cultural Process: Toward an Analysis of the Social Locations of a Religious Text," *Journal of the American Academy of Religion* 43, no. 4 (December 1975): 651–69; Ronald Neufeldt, "A Lesson in Allegory: Theosophical Interpretations of the Bhagavadgita," in *Modern Interpreters of the* Bhagavadgita, ed., Robert N. Minor (Albany: SUNY Press, 1986), 11–33.

70. Sinha, "Corrigibility, Allegory, Universality," 308.
71. Sharpe, *Universal Gita*, 80.
72. Annie Besant, *Hints on the Study of the Bhagavad Gita* (Benares: Theosophical Publishing Society, 1906), 1.
73. Sharpe, "Early Theosophists," 57.
74. Blavatsky, *Isis Unveiled*, vol. 2, pp. 562–63.
75. Krishna, she argues, can and should be spelled "Christna"—this figure drawing even closer to his Christian counterpart in the phrase *"Jai Śrī Kṛṣṇa,"* which Blavatsky renders as "Jas-i Christna! Jasas-wi Christna!" See H. P. Blavatsky, "Buddhism in America," *New York Sun*, May 13, 1877; in *Collected Writings*, vol. 1, pp. 249–52.
76. H. P. Blavatsky, "Footnote to *Bhagavad-Gita*," *Theosophist* 3, no. 9 (June 1882): 230; in *Collected Writings*, vol. 4, p. 124.
77. H. P. Blavatsky, "Our Fifth Year," *Theosophist* 4, no. 11 (August 1883), 265; in *Collected Writings*, vol. 5, pp. 67–68.
78. H. P. Blavatsky, "The *Bhagavad-Gita* and *Esoteric Buddhism*," *Theosophist* 5, no. 5 (February 1884): 122; in Blavatsky, *Collected Writings*, vol. 6, pp. 146–48.
79. Another dimension of Blavatsky's early comments on the *Gita* is her recurrent denial of the authority that European philologists like Monier Monier-Williams claimed over the text. Blavatsky sided instead with its Brahmanical interpreters. See, for example, H. P. Blavatsky, "Footnotes to *The Philosophy of Spirit*," *Theosophist* 3, no. 12 (September 1882): 298–303; in *Collected Writings*, vol. 4, pp. 191–93.
80. A native Telugu speaker, Subba Row was educated at Madras Presidency College and worked as a pleader for the High Courts of Baroda and, after 1880, Madras. First coming into contact with the theosophists in 1881, he was responsible for inviting them to create their Adyar headquarters in 1882—avowing in a letter to Blavatsky that "the little of occultism that still remains in India is centered in this Madras Presidency," including a few "solitary hermits" of the same spiritual status as the Himayalan Adepts. He remained a central figure in the Society until the controversies about Blavatsky led him to part ways with theosophy in 1888. Many of his writings were collected in 1895 in the volume *Esoteric Writings of Subba Row*, an enlarged second edition of which appeared in 1931. See T. Subba Row to H. P. Blavatsky, 3 February 1882, in *The Letters of H. P. Blavatsky to A. P. Sinnett and Other Miscellaneous Letters*, ed. A. T. Barker (Pasadena, CA: Theosophical

University Press, 1973), 316-18; H. S. Olcott, "A Sketch of the Life of the Late T. Subba Row," reprinted in T. Subba Row, *Esoteric Writings*, 2nd ed. (Chennai [Adyar]: Theosophical Publishing House, 2002 [1951, 1895]), ix-xiv; Olcott, *Old Diary Leaves*, vol. 4, p. 243; and Nallan Chakravartulu Ramanuja Charya, *A Lonely Disciple: Monograph on T. Subba Row, 1856-1890* (Chennai [Adyar]: Theosophical Publishing House, 1993).

81. T. Subba Row, *Discourses on the Bhagavat Gita: To Help Students in Studying Its Philosophy* (Bombay: Tookaram Tatya, 1888). The major reprints of the series are as follows: T. Subba Row, *Philosophy of the Bhagavad-Gita: Four Lectures Delivered at the Eleventh Annual Convention of the Theosophical Society Held at Adyar on December 27, 28, 29, and 30, 1886* (Chennai [Adyar]: Theosophical Office, 1912); T. Subba Row, *Notes on the Bhagavad Gita: To Help Students in Studying Its Philosophy* (Pasadena, CA: Theosophical University Press, 1934). The 1934 edition reprints the original text of from the *Theosophist*, restoring some omissions from the 1888 Tookaram Tatya edition.

82. Subba Row, *Discourses on the Bhagavat Gita*, i.

83. T. Subba Row, "The Idyll of the White Lotus," in *Esoteric Writings* (Chennai [Adyar]: Theosophical Publishing House, 1951), 259-78.

84. Subba Row, *Discourses on the Bhagavat Gita*, ii-iii.

85. John Stuart Mill, *Autobiography* (New York: Columbia University Press, 1944), 93-104.

86. Subba Row, *Discourses on the Bhagavat Gita*, 16.

87. Javed Majeed, *Autobiography, Travel, and Postnational Identity: Gandhi, Nehru, and Iqbal* (New York: Palgrave Macmillian, 2007), 241.

88. "Theosophy and the Churches: Lucifer to the Archbishop of Canterbury, Reprinted from the Christmas Number of *Lucifer*" (London: George Redway, 1888), 8-9.

89. A. B., "Practical Instructions for Students of Occultism: Forbidden Fruit," *Theosophist* 5, no. 12 (September 1884): 291-92.

90. Sinnett, *Purpose of Theosophy*, 10-18.

91. Newton Crosland, *Apparitions: A New Theory* (London: Effingham Wilson, 1856), 16.

92. Sinnett, *Purpose of Theosophy*, 10-18.

93. H. P. Blavatsky, "What Is Truth?," *Lucifer* 1, no. 6 (February 1888): 425-33; in *Collected Writings*, vol. 9, pp. 30-42.

94. Blavatsky, "Occultism Versus the Occult Arts," 253.

95. H. P. Blavatsky, "Is Theosophy a Religion?," *Lucifer* 3, no. 15 (November 1888): 177-87; in Blavatsky, *Collected Writings*, vol. 10, pp. 159-77.

96. Ibid., 159-60.

97. Ibid., 163.

98. Wilfred Cantwell Smith, *The Meaning and End of Religion: A New Approach to the Religious Traditions of Mankind* (New York: Macmillan, 1963), 19-50.

99. Blavatsky, "Is Theosophy a Religion?," 161, 163.

100. F. Max Müller, *Natural Religion: The Gifford Lectures Delivered Before the University of Glasgow in 1888* (London: Longmans, Green, and Co., 1889), 27–50.
101. Ibid., 33.
102. Blavatsky, "Is Theosophy a Religion?," 163.
103. Ibid., 164–65.
104. Ibid., 169, 165–66.
105. Annie Besant, *Why I Became a Theosophist* (London: Freethought Publishing Company, 1889), 4–6.
106. Edward W. Said, *The World, the Text, and the Critic* (Cambridge, MA: Harvard University Press, 1983), 290.
107. Gauri Viswanathan, "Secularism in the Framework of Heterodoxy," *PMLA* 123, no. 2 (2008): 466–76.
108. Rev. Charles Maurice Davies, *Heterodox London: Or, Phases of Free Thought in the Metropolis*, 2 vols. (London: Tinsley Brothers, 1874),1.
109. Said, *The World, the Text, and the Critic*, 290.
110. Blavatsky, "Practical Occultism," 157–60.
111. Blavatsky, "Occultism Versus the Occult Arts," 252, 254.
112. Ibid., 257.
113. Ibid., 258.
114. Henry Steel Olcott, *Old Diary Leaves*, vol. 2, pp. 80–81.
115. Giorgio Agamben, *The Kingdom and the Glory: For a Theological Genealogy of Economy and Government* (Stanford, CA: Stanford University Press, 2011).
116. Leela Gandhi, *Affective Communities: Anticolonial Thought, Fin-de-Siècle Radicalism, and the Politics of Friendship* (Durham, NC: Duke University Press, 2006), 177–90.
117. Blavatsky, "Is Theosophy a Religion?," 24.
118. Blavatsky, *Isis Unveiled*, vol. 1, p. 180.

CONCLUSION

1. M. K. Gandhi, *Autobiography: The Story of My Experiments with Truth*, trans. Mahadev Desai (New York: Dover, 1983), 59–60.
2. Ibid.
3. See, for example, Geoffrey Carnall, *Gandhi's Interpreter: A Life of Horace Alexander* (Edinburgh: Edinburgh University Press, 2010).
4. Leela Gandhi, *Affective Communities: Anticolonial Thought, Fin-de-Siècle Radicalism, and the Politics of Friendship* (Durham, NC: Duke University Press, 2006).
5. Shruti Kapila, "Self, Spencer and *Swaraj*: Nationalist Thought and Critiques of Liberalism, 1890–1920," *Modern Intellectual History* 4, no. 1 (2007): 109–27.
6. Ibid., 120.
7. Tridip Suhrud, "*Hind Swaraj*: Translating Sovereignty," in Antoinette Burton and Isabel Hofmeyr, eds., *Ten Books that Shaped the British Empire: Creating an Imperial Commons* (Durham, NC: Duke University Press, 2014), 153.

8. Joseph Alter, *Gandhi's Body: Sex, Diet, and the Politics of Nationalism* (Philadelphia: University of Pennsylvania Press, 2000).

9. Michel Foucault, "On the Genealogy of Ethics," in *Ethics: Subjectivity and Truth*, ed. Paul Rabinow (New York: New Press, 1997), 272.

10. See Isabel Hofmeyr, *Gandhi's Printing Press: Experiments in Slow Reading* (Cambridge, MA: Harvard University Press, 2013).

11. M. K. Gandhi, *Hind Swaraj and Other Writings*, ed. Anthony J. Parel, Centenary Edition (Cambridge: Cambridge University Press, 2009), 27, 36, 71, 116. I have also consulted the trilingual centennial edition of M. K. Gandhi, *Hind Swaraj* (Ahmedabad: Navajivan Trust, 2009). Page numbers all refer to Parel.

12. Ibid., 41.

13. I realize that the word *pakhandi* (imposture) does not translate directly to *priestcraft*. It clearly circulated alongside "priestcraft," however, in the nineteenth century—featuring, for example, in the title of an anticlerical Sanskrit play that Karsandas Mulji translated into Gujarati, and also probably in the title of Dayananda Saraswati's speech denouncing the "humbuggery" of the theosophists.

14. Gandhi, *Hind Swaraj*, 41–42.

15. Ibid., 54.

16. Nicholas Dirks, *The Scandal of Empire: India and the Creation of Imperial Britain* (Cambridge, MA: Belknap Press of Harvard University Press, 2008).

17. Gandhi, *Hind Swaraj*, 65.

18. Ibid., ff. 125.

19. Suhrud, "*Hind Swaraj*: Translating Sovereignty," 158.

20. Ibid.

21. Gandhi, *Hind Swaraj*, 67.

22. Leela Gandhi, *The Common Cause: Postcolonial Ethics and the Practice of Democracy, 1900–1955* (Chicago: University of Chicago Press, 2014), 1–2.

23. Kapila, "Self, Spencer and *Swaraj*," 116.

24. Gandhi, *Autobiography*, 453–54. For further discussion of this passage, see J. Barton Scott, "Unsaintly Virtue: Swami Dayananda Saraswati and Modern Hindu Hagiography," *Journal of Hindu Studies* 7, no. 3 (2014): 371–91.

25. Ibid.

26. Michel Foucault, *The Hermeneutics of the Subject: Lectures at the Collège de France, 1981–1982*, trans. Graham Burchell (New York: Palgrave Macmillan, 2005), 8–17.

27. Akeel Bilgrami, "Gandhi's Religion and Its Relation to His Politics," in *The Cambridge Companion to Gandhi*, eds. Judith M. Brown and Anthony Parel (Cambridge: Cambridge University Press, 2011), 99–101.

28. Max Weber, *The Protestant Ethic and the Spirit of Capitalism*, trans. Talcott Parsons (New York: Routledge, 2001), 145.

29. Ritu Birla and Faisal Devji, "Guest Editors' Letter: Itineraries of Self-Rule," in "Our Gandhi, Our Times," special issue of *Public Culture* 23, no. 2 (2011): 265–68, 266.

30. Gandhi, *Autobiography*, 232.
31. Ibid., 233.
32. Simona Sawhney, *The Modernity of Sanskrit* (Minneapolis: University of Minnesota Press, 2009), 90.
33. M. K. Gandhi, "Anasaktiyoga," in Mahadev Desai, *The Gospel of Selfless Action, or, The Gita According to Gandhi* (Ahmedabad: Navajivan Publishing House, 1956 [1946]), 127.
34. Quoted in Akeel Bilgrami, "Gandhi's Religion and Its Relation to His Politics," 94.
35. Gandhi, "Anasaktiyoga," 128.
36. Ibid., 131.
37. Ibid., 129.
38. Weber, *Protestant Ethic*, 45.
39. Ibid., 90.
40. Edwin Arnold, trans., *The Song Celestial or Bhagavad-Gîtâ*, 3rd ed. (London: Trübner & Co., 1886), 26, 18.
41. M. K. Gandhi, *From Yeravada Mandir: Ashram Observances*, trans. Valji Govindji Desai, (Ahmedabad: Navajivan Publishing House, 1957 [1932]), 57–58.
42. Gandhi, "Anasaktiyoga," 132.
43. Arnold, *Song Celestial*, 20–21.
44. Gandhi, *Hind Swaraj*, 10. My thoughts on reading, print culture, and the disavowal of writerly authority in colonial India have been substantially shaped by J. Daniel Elam, "The Republic of Anticolonial Letters: Reading Anticolonialism between South Asia and North America" (PhD diss., Northwestern University, 2015).
45. See Sawhney, *The Modernity of Sanskrit*. Gandhi, of course, was not the only person to have tried to recuperate the *Gita* at this moment. For discussion of the broader intellectual context, see the essays in Shruti Kapila and Faisal Devji, eds. *Political Thought in Action: The Bhagavad Gita and Modern India* (Cambridge: Cambridge University Press, 2013), as well as Richard Davis, *The Bhagavad Gita: A Biography* (Princeton, NJ: Princeton University Press, 2014).
46. Peter Sloterdijk, *You Must Change Your Life: On Anthropotechnics*, trans. Wieland Hoban (Cambridge: Polity Press, 2013), 3.
47. Kapila, "Self, Spencer and *Swaraj*," 112, 120.
48. Michael C. Behrent "Liberalism without Humanism: Michel Foucault and the Free Market Creed, 1976–1979," *Modern Intellectual History* 6, no. 3 (2009): 539–68.

Index